THE AIRLINE PASSENGER'S GUERRILLA HANDBOOK

Strategies & Tactics for Beating the Air Travel System

George Albert Brown

The Blakes Publishing Group, Washington, DC

Published by:
The Blakes Publishing Group
320 Metropolitan Square
655 Fifteenth Street, N.W.
Washington, D.C. 20005

Distributed by:
Fisher Books
4239 W. Ina Road, Suite 101
Tucson, AZ 85741
(602) 744-6110

ISBN 0-924022-04-3

Library of Congress Catalog Card Number 89-60376

Cover design and illustrations by Ross Patterson
Interior design by David H. Morgan

Printed in the United States of America
10 9 8 7 6

CONTENTS

2 Choosing Your Flight—Comfort, Convenience and Safety   29

3 Choosing Your Flight—The Cheapest Air Fare   57

4 How to Pack for the Flight   101

5 When and How to Get to the Airport 127

6 How to Wait in the Airport   157

7 How to Get onto the Plane 189

8 The Basics of Cabin Life   229

9 Things to Do on the Plane   255

10 How to End Your Flight   279

11 How to Get through and Away from the Airport   313

12 How to Deal with Special Problems of Air Travel   337

PREFACE

Air Travel in the US

According to a Gallup poll commissioned by the Air Transport Association of America, 72 percent of American adults have flown sometime during their lifetime. Each year over 52 million Americans, 30 percent of the adult population, travel by air, making over 455 million flights. That's an average of about 1.25 million passenger flights per day. Of these passengers, 87 percent are flying to a domestic destination; 13 percent, to a foreign destination. Forty-eight percent are business travelers; 52 percent, pleasure travelers. Roughly 96 percent fly economy, three percent, business class and one percent, first class.

The percentage of airline passengers who enjoy the experience is apparently too small to report.

Why You Should Read this Book

Being an airline passenger is the opposite of sex: even when it's good it's bad.

Not because the airlines are uncaring.

Well, not solely because of that.

The people who run the airports are uncaring as well.

In fact, everyone connected with air travel, from start to finish—the people who reserve your flight, sell you your ticket, take you to the airport, design your terminal, check you in, transport your luggage, serve you at the airport shops, call your flight, screen you at security, board you at the gate, configure your aircraft's seating, cater your food, serve you inflight, control your air traffic, clear you at passport control, unload your baggage, clear you through customs, provide you a rental car, drive your taxi...

Drive your taxi. What New Yorker hasn't had a foreign visitor show up at the apartment, eyes wide in terror: "I just paid $255 for a cab from the airport! ... When I came out of the Pan Am terminal, all I did was ask the driver to take me to your address as quickly as possible. .... We've been on the road for over three and a half hours. ... I think I must've seen every bridge, tunnel and automobile ferry within a 30-mile radius of Manhattan."

Yes, dear reader, it's not just the airlines.

From the moment you step out of your door to the moment you arrive at your destination it's a constant battle. You've got to be on full alert every inch of the way—as though each encounter bears the printed label:

> *Warning: The Surgeon General has determined that this experience may be hazardous to your mental health.*

To survive takes more than mere alertness. You've got to be tough. You've got to be clever. And, above all, you've got to learn to treat the airlines and their running dogs as they treat you: as something to be manipulated solely for the benefit of the manipulator.

During my many years as a business traveler, I've managed to accumulate a treasure store of guerrilla strategies and tactics to help me do just that. Some of these are merely the result of experience, such as how to find the cheapest airfare; how to get on a flight when you've been forced to stand by; how to get an empty seat next to you; the secret sleeping compartment on a 747; the miracle drug which wipes out jet lag; or how to beat the long lines at foreign passport control.

Others of the strategies and tactics I've managed to accumulate, however, are the result of my peculiar background. Trained as a lawyer, I co-founded an international, tax-oriented finance business based in a large part on uncovering loopholes in the law. By applying to air travel the approaches and techniques learned in my business, I've been able to uncover similar loopholes in the airlines' own rules. Loopholes which, for example, allow you to carry on or check more baggage than the airline's restrictions would appear to allow. Loopholes which allow you not only to fly at the cheapest possible fare but also to receive a substantial cash payment back from the airline. Loopholes which allow you to accumulate for free more frequent flyer mileage than the rules at first glance would appear to allow you. Loopholes which allow you to get a refund on a nonrefundable ticket. Loopholes which allow you to avoid the airlines' limitations of liability. And so on.

When I retired from the finance business a few years ago, I decided it was time to share my various strategies and tactics with others. *The Airline Passenger's Guerrilla Handbook* is the result.

If you are someone who is genuinely interested in how to beat the air travel system, you should find the following several hundred pages not only entertaining but instructive, and the next time you travel by air, you'll hopefully be able to do it more cheaply, more comfortably, more conveniently, more safely and, above all, with more control than you ever thought possible.

ACKNOWLEDGMENTS

I would like to thank the innumerable people who made this book possible. For special thanks I'd like to single out Chris Witkowski of the Aviation Consumer Action Project, Norm Strickman of the DOT's Consumer Affairs Division, Geoffrey Lipman and Philip Chrystal of the International Foundation of Airline Passengers Associations, Dick Livingston of the International Airline Passengers Association, Dave Jeffrey of the Airline Passengers of America, Marion Mistrik of the Air Transport Association of America, Bob Ashby, Pat Beardsley and Rich Nehl of the FAA, Linda Honts and Richard Russo of Traveltron, Mary Miller and Martin Beyer of AVMARK, Inc., Roger Osterbery of the International Air Transport Association, Sefik Yuksel of the Association of European Airlines, Chris Lyle and Dr. Michel Pourcelet of the International Civil Aviation Organization, Julius Maldutis of Salomon Brothers, Tom Cole of Boeing, Lee Howard of Airline Economics, Dr. Josephine Arendt of the University of Surrey, and all the other employees of governments, airlines, airports, citizens' organizations, universities and private companies which have provided me with information and advice on air travel, even when, as was occasionally the case, they didn't agree with my views.

In addition, I'd like to thank Barbara Hendra, David Morgan, Ross Patterson, Charlie Webster, Paul Glassman, Marc Esterman, Brian Heywood, Nancy Brown, Richard Freedman, Leofranc Holford-Strevens, Carolyn Harvey (the sexiest woman I know) and all the others who helped me in the editing and composition of this book.

This book may bear the name of a single author but its ideas, information and form are the result of a group effort.

WARNING — DISCLAIMER

This book is designed to provide information in regard to the subject matter covered. It is sold with the understanding that the publisher and author are not engaged in rendering legal, medical or other professional services. If legal, medical or other professional assistance is required, the services of a competent professional should be sought.

It is not the purpose of this handbook to reprint all the information that is otherwise available to the author and/or publisher but to complement, amplify and supplement other sources the reader may have.

An effort has been made to make this handbook complete and accurate. However, **there may be mistakes** both typographical and in content. Furthermore, this handbook contains information only up to the date when the research was done. Therefore, this text should be used only as a general guide and not as the ultimate source of information.

In addition, this book refers to many entities as sources of information, products and services. Neither the author nor the publisher have personally confirmed the honesty, creditworthiness or suitability of every entity mentioned. Those who decide to deal with any of these entities as the result of this book should confirm those matters separately themselves.

The purpose of this handbook is to educate and entertain. The author and the publisher shall have neither liability nor responsibility to any person or entity with respect to any loss or damage caused or alleged to be caused directly or indirectly by the information or advice contained in this book.

WARNING — DISCLAIMER

CHAPTER ONE

CHOOSING YOUR FLIGHT—
THE FASTEST WAY THERE

A Choice of which Even
Hobson Would Have Despaired

Box 1-1.	Major US Airlines' Percentage of Passengers Enplaned

Airline	Passenger Share
American	14.36%
USAir[1]	13.84%
Delta	13.40%
United	12.58%
Continental[2]	8.41%
Northwest	7.99%
Eastern[2]	7.96%
TWA	5.61%
Southwest	3.76%
Pan Am	3.74%
America West	2.83%
Alaska[3]	1.38%
Hawaiian	1.23%
Braniff[4]	1.23%
Midway	0.95%
Aloha	0.77%

1. Includes passengers of PSA and Piedmont, which were acquired by USAir.
2. Both owned by Texas Air Corp. Eastern is in bankruptcy and in danger of being liquidated.
3. Includes passengers of Horizon Air which was acquired by Alaska.
4. Includes passengers of Florida Express which was acquired by Braniff. Braniff is in bankruptcy and in danger of being liquidated.
(Source: *Air Transport Association Annual Report.*)

Looking at the statistics above in Box 1-1, it's clear that the airline passenger generally has a lot of choice, right?

Wrong.

In the first place, the national figures disguise the fact that the airlines tend to be concentrated in certain parts of the country and at certain airports. Thus, while TWA may have 5.61 percent of the nationwide market, it has over 80 percent of the flights out of St. Louis. Northwest, 7.99 percent of the national market, but over 80 percent of the flights out of Minneapolis. USAir, 13.84 percent of the national market, but over 80 percent of the flights out of Pittsburgh. And so on.

A study by Salomon Brothers concluded that if the Justice Department's antitrust rules were applied on an airport rather than a nationwide basis, 40 of the 50 largest airports would violate those rules and none of the mergers involving major airlines in the last few years would have been approved. (One of the reasons the Justice Department's antitrust rules were not applied at the airport level was that until January 1, 1989, approval power over mergers lay with the Department of Transportation, which was interested primarily in promoting the hub and spoke concept (see below at page 23), which tends to concentrate certain airlines at certain airports. Since then the power has reverted to the Justice Department, which is taking a tougher line.)

Even where there are no concentrations at airports, however, what the airline passenger is offered is usually less of a choice than an echo. The more competitive the route, the more likely the competing airlines are to depart at the same times, charge the same fare, fly the same aircraft and offer the same services—in effect, denying the passenger any real alternatives.

Occasionally, of course, significant differences do occur between flights; however, even here the average passenger often still lacks an effective choice because by the time he or she discovers the more attractive flight, it's fully booked.

Nonetheless, for those few times when you do have a choice, you should know how to go about exercising it.

So, please, read on.

The First Thing to do Before Choosing a Flight

When choosing which flight to take, different people find different things most important, such as schedule, service or price. I, for example, tend to give great weight to the likelihood of the plane's continued presence in the air during the flight.

The way I look at it, a precise on-time departure, royal inflight service and a rock-bottom price are not sufficient compensation for being burned alive on the arrival runway.

Before you set out to choose your flight, therefore, you should first decide what your own priorities are. To do that, you first have to understand all the major criteria involved in choosing a flight. Chapter Two will cover the criteria which can loosely be grouped under convenience, comfort and safety. Chapter Three will cover what is the most important for many pleasure travelers: the lowest fare. The balance of this Chapter One will cover what is often most important to the business traveler—getting there as quickly as possible.

How to Find the Fastest Flight

While most people choose their flight based on the time of departure, they often overlook the time of arrival. There is a tendency to assume that because two planes leave at approximately the same time for the same destination, they will arrive at approximately the same time.

Unfortunately, this assumption is not necessarily correct. One flight might use a jet, while the other uses a propeller plane. One flight might make no stops, while another makes many stops or requires connections to ongoing flights.

To choose the fastest flight, then, you should always compare flights on the time of arrival as well as the time of departure.

Sometimes, of course, you don't have the time or the information to make the comparisons. You've got to rely on your travel agent or the airline to produce a flight. In that case, following are some "red flags" that may encourage you to ask further questions.

Watch out for "Direct" Flights

The Concise Oxford Dictionary defines "direct" as:

> *straight, not crooked(ly) or oblique(ly) or round about; ... without intermediaries.*

The airlines define "direct" as:

> *We may go all over hell and back, stopping four-hundred and eighty-three times in between, but you won't ever have to change planes.*

What you and I think of as "direct", the airlines call "nonstop".

I learned this distinction in my early days of traveling. Arriving in Denver trying to make a connection to Houston, I noticed there was a slightly earlier flight labeled "direct". I took it. I don't think there was a single small town in Texas my flight didn't touch. Take off and land. Take off and land. Take off and land. I began to suspect someone had turned the pilot into a frog. (From their appearance, any one of the three stewardesses could've done it.) It wasn't until two o'clock the following morning that I finally crawled off the plane at Houston International. I could feel my insides going slowly up and down for the next three days.

So if you are told you have a direct flight, ask first if there is a comparable nonstop, and then if there isn't, ask how many stops you will make. If it's more than one, ask to compare it with other direct flights and even connecting flights for time of arrival.

Especially Avoid "Direct" International Flights

On international direct flights major delays can occur if your destination is not the first stop in the other country. For instance, if you take a flight from London to San Francisco with an intermediary stop in Seattle and the airline takes on any US passengers in Seattle, all of the London-San Francisco passengers have to get off the plane and clear US passport control and customs there. As part of this process, all the checked baggage has to be removed from the plane, claimed by the passengers, taken through customs and then rechecked onto the plane to be taken off and reclaimed again in San Francisco.

Who says the Federal government no longer provides makework jobs for the unemployed?

Even a single stop in a foreign country can create problems. Once, on a trip to Guadeloupe, my plane landed in Haiti. Although only two or three passengers were to get off and our plane wasn't flying on to another airport in Haiti, the authorities, in what our pilot told us was standard procedure, made everyone disembark and wait for an hour while a swarm of Haitian secret police searched our aircraft.

What they were searching for, God only knows. From the condition of their shirts, I suspect it must've been underarm antiperspirant.

Certainly they couldn't have been looking for anything of relevance to the security of Haiti; the plane was just passing through and this was its only stop in the country.

In any case, I learned my lesson. On foreign flights, always try to get the nonstop flight to your destination.

Look Out for Flight Number "Fraud"

Even worse than the misleading use of the word "direct", is the misleading use of a single flight number to cover what is known as a "change of gauge". For instance, I once took a flight on a major airline advertised as flight 754 from San Francisco to London. In fact, the "flight" was a flight in one aircraft from San Francisco to Boston where the passengers got off and caught another aircraft from Boston to London (hence the "change of gauge"). Though both legs had the flight number 754, the flight was really two connecting flights; it wasn't even a "direct" flight, since the passengers had to change planes in Boston.

I put the word "fraud" above in quotations because I don't know for a fact that this major airline used the same flight number for two flights in order to mislead San Franciscan ticket purchasers into wrongly assuming the flight was the normal nine-and-a-half-hour flight to London rather than a substantially less desirable thirteen-hour set of connecting flights. All I can say is that the connecting flight from Boston to London turned out to bear not only the number 754 but several other flight numbers as well—each one representing a different hidden connection from a US city to Boston.

I've encountered this practice several times since. Once I had to change not only planes while connecting but terminals as well. Somewhat of a slow learner, I now always check the arrival time of my flights against other flights and, if there's a difference, ask the travel agent whether the flight has a "change of gauge".

Three Reasons to Choose
the On-line Connection

If all else is equal between two connecting flights, you should choose the one which does not involve a change of airlines, *i.e.*, the "on-line" rather than "interline" connection. Why?

1.   The gates for the connecting flights are likely to be closer together. A different airline often means a different concourse, if not a different terminal.

2.   The ongoing flight is more likely to be held up if your incoming flight is late. An airline is more concerned about upsetting its own passengers than another airline's passengers.

3.   If you check your baggage, it is less likely to get lost during the connection. Rather than two different baggage systems, you are dealing with just one. In addition, some people think baggage handlers feel more responsibility for their own airline's on-line baggage. (Personally, I find it difficult to accept that baggage handlers could feel responsibility for anything, let alone on-line baggage. I mean, let's face it. These guys are not chosen for their powers of discrimination. As long as they can throw a bag fifty feet with one arm, they're hired.)

The Major Computerized Reservations Systems

The United States' approximately 30,000 travel agents sell about two-thirds of all US air tickets, the remaining third being sold by the airlines. Almost all of the travel agents' tickets are sold through the following five computerized reservation systems, owned primarily by seven major airlines (if you count Texas Air as representing both Eastern and Continental).

Box 1-2.	Major Airline Domestic CRSs		
SYSTEM	**AIRLINE**	**% AGENTS USING**[1]	**%BOOKINGS**
Sabre	American	34.0	39.2
Apollo	United	24.5	29.5
System One	Texas Air	18.0	11.3
PARS	TWA/Northwest[2]	14.5	14.6
DATAS II	Delta[2]	9.0	5.4

1. Ninety-four percent of US travel agencies use only one CRS.
2. Delta has entered into an agreement with TWA and Northwest to combine their two systems into one.
(Source: DOT.)

How the Travel Agents are Locked into Particular CRSs

Travel agents are usually locked into a particular service by three legal devices:

1. Liquidated damages clauses. The airlines impose substantial penalties for a travel agent terminating its CRS contract. The Airline Passenger Protection Act proposed in 1987 was supposed to limit these penalties to the remaining rentals plus the cost of removal; but, once the media turned their attention to other things, the bill was quietly shelved. The DOT, following the lead of the Department of Justice, has decided that there is no need now for regulation of these clauses.

2.   Continual extensions of the term. A 1984 Civil Aeronautics Board regulation of CRS contracts set a five-year limit on the term of such contracts; but the airlines got around this by requiring a five-year extension every time the agent got new equipment or additional services. After the proposed Airline Passenger Protection Act of 1987 came out with a provision closing this loophole, the DOT got the CRS vendors to agree voluntarily that such rollover clauses would be omitted from new subscription contracts (but not the old ones).

3.   Minimum transaction requirements. The agent is required to use the airline's equipment for a minimum number of transactions. The DOT has not felt it necessary to act against this requirement.

In addition, there are all the normal market factors tying an agent into a particular CRS, such as the costs and disruption involved in switching to another system, or such as a given airline's larger presence at a local airport, which allows the airline to offer the travel agents more inducements (free travel on the vendor airline, seat upgrades, frequent-flyer bonuses, cooperative advertising and greater commissions). If an airline has a near monopoly of a local flight market, you can be sure its CRS is likely to have a near monopoly of the local CRS market as well.

International Interlocking of CRSs

Despite Box 1-2 above, the ownership of the five major US CRS systems is now much more complex. Foreign airline systems have been buying into the US systems and visa versa. Some of the US systems have been buying into each other. And at least one US airline, USAir, has joined up with foreigners to buy into a US system, Apollo.

Worldwide it appears that there will soon be four major CRS groupings, based around the four largest US systems. (See Box 1-3 below.) Most experts assume that the Air Canada/Canada Airlines' system, Gemini, will have to join up with one of the four major international groupings.

Generally, most of the foreign systems are using the software of one of the four major US systems but making it much more biased towards the foreign airline owners. A recently proposed European Civil Aviation Conference Code may not only make the European systems less biased, but also may prohibit many dubious US practices such as code sharing (see below at page 10), flight number "fraud" and special use of the CRS data by the owner airline.

Box 1-3.	Worldwide CRS Groupings	
US System	linked with	**Foreign System**
Apollo/Covia United USAir	⟺	*Galileo[1]* British A'ys Sabena Alitalia TAP Swissair Aer Lingus Olympic Austrian KLM
System One Eastern Continental	⟺	*Amadeus[1]* Lufthansa JAT Iberia Finnair Air France Braathens Air Inter Icelandair SAS Adria
PARS / DATAS II Northwest TWA Delta	⟺	*Abacus* SIA China Airl's Thai Airways[2] Malaysia A S Cathay Pacif. Philippine
Sabre American	⟺	*Fantasia* All Nippon Japan Airlines Qantas

1. Galileo and Amadeus are cooperating on some matters.
2. The participation of Thai Airways in Abacus is currently uncertain.
(Source: *Airline Business.*)

Don't Depend on the CRS to Find You the Fastest Flight

Thanks to CAB rules which went into effect in 1984, computerized reservation systems in the US can no longer discriminate directly or indirectly in favor of the airline sponsoring the system (although in most of the rest of the world they still can and do).

When you're looking for a flight at a given time, each US system will search out a number of flights and rank them in order of convenience. However, the flights chosen and the ranking of those flights will not always be the same, and the fastest flight will not always come out first. Some of the reasons:

1. Bracketing. Each system has a different way of bracketing the flights to be displayed when a given departure time is requested. For instance, one CRS lists all flights two hours before and three hours after the requested departure time (and then ranks them according to its measures of convenience), while another takes the highest scoring twenty flights on its measures of convenience no matter how far forward or far back those flights may be.

2. Measures of convenience. Each system has a different way of measuring convenience. For instance, some do it by ranking all nonstops over one-stops over on-line connections over two-stops over interline connections and so on; others have elaborate point systems for each stop, each on-line connection, each interline connection, each inter-airport connection, and so forth.

Often the difference in rankings is significant, resulting in a longer flight having a higher ranking that a shorter flight. For instance, a direct flight with three stops could take longer than a single connecting flight, but the system could arbitrarily rank all nonconnecting flights higher than connecting flights. Or an interline connection could easily take less than an on-line connection but the system (as many do) could arbitrarily list the on-line connection higher.

In the flight number "fraud" situation discussed above at page 6, the airline's CRS apparently treats its single-flight-number "change of gauge" flights as "direct" rather than "connecting" flights, immediately ranking those flights ahead of all other connecting flights on the CRS screen.

3. Code sharing. Certain trunk airlines agree to share their computer code designation with a feeder or foreign airline. The result is that what is really an interline connection gets bumped up to an on-line connection in the CRS ranking—even if it has a significantly greater connecting time than the interline flights.

4. Marketing agreements. At least one program ranks all interline connections between airlines who conduct joint marketing together (such as a major and a feeder) higher than connections between those without, regardless of the fact the former connections might take much longer. (Needless to say, the airline which uses this ranking factor has several important interline marketing agreements.)

5. Departure time. Some programs add to the flight time the time between the passenger's initially requested departure time and the scheduled departure time of the flight. If a passenger asks for a scheduled departure time which falls on the hour (as most passengers do), those flights which are scheduled before or after the hour are treated as taking longer, even though they in fact may be shorter. (This is why the airlines try to schedule their flights to leave on the hour, producing a delay-causing bunching of flights.)

6. Nonuse of elapsed time. A final problem occurs because under DOT pressure the CRS operators have all agreed not to use differences in scheduled elapsed flight times to rank nonstop flights. In other words, the fact that one nonstop flight is faster than another cannot be used to move that flight to a higher and hence more desirable position on the screen.

The DOT's concern was that allowing differences in scheduled elapsed time to be used to rank flights would encourage the airlines to use unrealistically short estimates of elapsed time. For some reason the DOT thought the best solution to this potential problem was to throw the baby out with the bath water. Now, those airlines who fly their routes faster (because they're willing to use more fuel or buy a faster and probably more expensive airplane) won't be able to get their flights ranked higher in the various CRSs, making it more difficult for your travel agent to find the fastest flight on the screen.

To add to the confusion, the elapsed-time restriction does not apply to direct and connecting flights. Thus, although each leg of such flights is a nonstop flight which cannot be ranked by elapsed time, the overall direct or connecting flights *can* be ranked by elapsed time. The result is that if an airline is willing to keep separate books, a direct or connecting flight may have a higher ranking than the sum of its parts.

All the above problems, of course, wouldn't be serious if travel agents looked beyond the ranking on the screen to see which flights were actually faster. Unfortunately, though, they don't. Fifty percent of agent bookings come from the first line; seventy percent from the first page.

One reason the agents don't look further is laziness. Another is a lack of real understanding how their computer system works. If you ask, the average travel agent will tell you that their CRS ranks all flights according to how quickly the various flights get you to your destination—which as the discussion above shows, it doesn't.

So if you are primarily interested in getting to your destination in the least amount of time, be sure to ask the travel agent to check all the listed flights by hand on that basis—particularly if his or her first pass has produced a nonstop propeller-driven flight, a multistop direct flight or an on-line or code-sharing connecting flight.

How the Frequent Flyer can Put Power in His or Her Pocket

Knowledge is power. The airlines and travel agents know this. They know if they can keep you ignorant about the alternatives available to you, they can route you in a way that produces the largest profit or most convenient operation for them and you won't know enough to be able to do anything about it.

If you are a frequent flyer, your defense is to have a pocket flight guide, a monthly publication which lists all the scheduled nonstop and direct and some connecting flights, times of departure and arrival, the type of plane, what type of meal service is available and the required connecting times at the airport between various airlines. For ease of use, the guide usually groups the flights according to destination and then within that group breaks them down into subgroups based on the point of departure. The flights in the subgroups are listed chronologically. Where connecting flights are not listed, you can put together your own connecting flights by combining various direct flights.

Box 1-4.	North American Monthly Pocket Flight Guides		
Guide	**Phone**	**Cost/Yr**	**Other Editions**
OAG Pocket Flight Guide[1]	(800)323-3537 (800)942-1888 IL	$59	Europe/Mid-East; Latin Am/Carrib; Pacific.
American Express Sky Guide	(800)327-2177	$35	Europe/Mid-East.
Executive Flight Planner	(617)262-5000	$69	None.[2]

1.The discussion in the text above was based on this, the oldest and most popular flight guide.
2. *Executive Flight Planner*, different from the others, also includes North American gateway-city flights to 49 major foreign destinations.

A pocket flight guide gives you greater control in finding the quickest flight. For example, many airlines require at least an hour to transfer luggage from one connecting flight to another; thus, they refuse to let you know about any connecting flight that occurs during that period, even if you have only carry-on luggage. With a pocket flight guide you can find out about the earlier flight and book it yourself separately ahead of time.

More importantly, the guide allows you to get somewhere quicker during the trip in the light of unforeseen circumstances. If your business meeting or arriving flight is earlier or later than originally scheduled, the guide will tell you immediately what your options are so you can change your departing flight to get there faster. The guide even gives the airline reservation phone numbers in all the major cities.

Understanding the CRS On-time Performance Rating

The Department Of Transportation now requires monthly flight delay statistics from every airline which handles more than one percent of domestic passengers nationwide on its domestic flights (currently 12 airlines, accounting for roughly 90 percent of domestic passengers). The airline is to report the percentage on-time performance for each numbered flight involving a US airport which handles more than one percent of domestic passengers nationwide (currently 27 airports, accounting for over two-thirds of US enplanements)—excluding Alaska and Hawaii.

The on-time percentage given to the DOT is then rounded down to the nearest ten, divided by ten and inserted as a single digit next to the flight data in the various CRSs. For instance, a flight with a monthly 89 percent on-time record would show up in the CRS as an "8" on-time record.

Unfortunately there is no requirement that either the airline or the travel agent volunteer this information to you. You have to ask for it, and even then the travel agents, at least, don't have to give it to you.

Even worse, the DOT prevents any computerized reservation system from using the on-time data to rank the flights on the screen. The DOT says it is concerned that if the CRS ranking reflected *real* travel times rather than *imaginary* ones, the airlines might be tempted to cut corners on safety in order to gain a higher ranking.

Question: Why doesn't the DOT have similar safety concerns about the single-digit delay-data coding in the CRS?

Answer: The DOT knows that, unlike using the on-time data for ranking flights, merely putting such data in the form of a tag-on single-digit code next to each flight is unlikely to have much effect in steering passengers towards the quickest flight.

How to Avoid the Pitfalls of the CRS On-time Rating

If you want to use the CRS on-time information, you should be aware of the following problems:

1.   Delays are defined as arrivals which are delayed more than 15 minutes. So flights which are consistently delayed under 15 minutes will not appear. Likewise, there is no distinction between flights delayed 16 minutes and those delayed 16 hours. These two problems could have been avoided had the DOT required the CRS vendors to display the *average* minutes delay for a given flight. It wouldn't have been much too difficult for the airlines since they already compile and submit the average minutes delay per flight each month to the DOT. To put such average minutes delay in the CRS, however, would have given air passengers more information in a more understandable form than the DOT and the airlines apparently thought advisable.

2.   The data excludes delays and cancellations caused by mechanical problems. Although aircraft maintenance is something in the control of the airline (certainly more in control than weather or air traffic control delays which are included), the DOT has excluded mechanical delays and cancellations so as not to give the airlines an incentive to cut corners on safety to improve their on-time performance. In other words, if an airline's maintenance is so terrible that it's always delaying flights to add more chewing gum and baling wire to keep its planes together, the DOT wants to make sure that that airline appears in the CRS as having an excellent on-time rating.

3.   The data could be more than three months out of date and thus will not be a good predictor of delays caused by seasonal variations, such as peak travel and/or weather. The DOT rules require a month's average data to be in the CRS by twenty days after the end of the month. That means that on the 19th of the month, the data displayed could be for the month ending a month and 19 days earlier. If you add to this (i) that the data itself is an average of that earlier month and (ii) that you are likely to choose your flight in advance of the date you want to fly, you could be relying on statistics from flights occurring more than three months before your flight. That is, you might be trying to get an idea what the flight delay situation would be out of Minneapolis in June based on flights occurring there during the month of February.

The delayed flight data would still give you some indication of the relative delay record of different airlines flying the same route out of

Minneapolis; however, to try to predict the delay record in June, you'd have to abandon the CRS and have your travel agent go into the historical records. In that case, however, your data would be even more out of date.

4.   There is no delay data on airlines with less than one percent of domestic passengers nationwide. For that reason, delay data is not available on most of the commuter lines, even if through code-sharing, they appear on the CRS screen as a major airline.

5.   There is no delay data on international flights. Since the data are on arrivals at domestic airports (within the control of the DOT), data on outgoing flights are by definition excluded. Data on incoming international flights are excluded for two basic reasons (according to the discussion in the DOT ruling which set up the on-time data system):

(a)   Greater delays in international travel. Since the exigencies of foreign airports and international travel are more likely to create delays, the overall on-time record of international US airlines would be prejudiced as against domestic US airlines. In other words, in order to protect the name of the international airlines, the public should be kept in ignorance of the greater delays in international travel.

(b)   Discrimination against US international carriers. Since foreign airports tend to discriminate against non-national airlines, the on-time record of foreign airlines flying into the US would tend to be better than those of US airlines. In other words, in order to protect the business of U.S. international airlines, the American public should be kept in ignorance of the fact that the foreign airlines have faster flights.

Do you get the feeling the DOT is representing the airlines more than it's representing the airline passengers in this matter?

6.   Since everything is rounded down to the lowest ten percent, performances which are only one percent apart, *e.g.*, 89 and 90 percent, will appear ten percentage points apart in the CRS. Likewise, those which are 11 percentage points apart, will appear more than 20.

The more detailed percentages are available for inspection at the Reports Reference Room (Room 4201) of the Office of Aviation Information Management at DOT's headquarters in Washington, DC, or if you're willing to purchase the printout and/or computer tapes, from the Transportation Systems Center in Cambridge, Massachusetts—neither of which the average passenger in Peoria is likely to take advantage of.

If you call the DOT and ask them to look up the detailed flight-delay statistics for your flight, they won't do it. If you're lucky enough to have a flight that arrives late 80 percent or more of the time, the DOT will give the exact percentage in a monthly report (see next section) available upon request. However, once a flight has an on-time record of 20 percent or less, there aren't that many passengers who are interested in the precise details.

7.   The data does not give the on-time record of connecting flights. To determine those, you have to look at the on-time record of each leg. You have to look at the first leg in order to see if you are likely to make your connection; the second leg, in order to see how late you are likely to be at the end.

8.   The data measures the on-time record of a direct flight by the on-time record of the last leg. This is only a problem if you are planning to not use the last leg, as occurs, for instance, in a money saving technique known as the "hidden-city discount". (See below at page 60 for the details.) In that case, be sure to check the record to the intermediate hidden city.

How to Get Free Information on the Airline Baddies

The DOT puts out a free monthly *Air Travel Consumer Report*, which collates a lot of the flight-delay information in a digestible form. It shows each airline's overall on-time record, its on-time record at each airport and its ranking according to the percentage of its flights arriving late 70 percent or more of the time. There is also a listing and ranking of each specific flight arriving late 80 percent of the time or more and a listing of each airport's departing and arriving on-time record according to time of day.

The DOT on-time data in the report, of course, has many of the same problems mentioned above with the CRS on-time information. However, the different collations make it easier to see patterns in the data. In addition, the monthly report also gives some non-delay consumer information on each airline, such as the rates of mishandled baggage, bumpings and consumer complaints—the latter broken down according to what the complaint was about.

You can obtain a single copy of the monthly report for free by writing to the Office of Consumer Affairs, U.S. Department of Transportation, 400 7th Street, S.W., Room 10405, Washington, DC 20590. Unfortunately, the DOT refuses to establish a mailing list, so you have to write separately for each month's copy. However, there are indications that an independent contractor may begin distributing the reports soon for a price of around $25 per year. Check with the DOT if you are interested.

If you do not travel enough to go through the hassle of reading the report each month, you should at least require your travel agent to obtain the report and use it when making your reservations.

Box 1-5.	US Airlines' On-time Performance

DOMESTIC FLIGHTS	
Airline	**Percent Arrivals On Time**
America West	93.9
Southwest	91.5
Delta	86.1
Alaska	86.0
American	85.9
Continental	83.0
United	80.9
Northwest	79.2
Eastern	77.1
TWA	76.6
USAir	74.4
Pan American	68.8

A flight is on time if it arrives less than 15 minutes after its scheduled arrival time, excluding any delays due to mechanical reasons.
(Source: DOT.)

How to Make use of Overall Airline On-time Ratings

Occasionally you will see published in the newspaper overall on-time ranking charts like the one above. Before you waste any time studying such statistics, you should know that these overall figures are virtually meaningless. (I'm sorry if you already wasted time studying the above chart. I should have told you earlier.)

The reason they are virtually meaningless is that you have no certain way of knowing whether the differences in the on-time performance occur because of operating deficiencies at each airline or merely because each airline has a different pattern of routes from the others. For instance, those airlines which fly congested routes at congested airports on multistop flights which are more likely to encounter extremes of weather will have a worse on-time record than those which fly uncongested routes at uncongested airports on long haul flights which are more likely to encounter moderate weather.

When you are making a choice of airline, you are usually making a choice on one specific route. The fact that a given airline's overall statistics might be better because it flies better routes overall is fairly irrelevant to whether you choose it on the route under consideration.

So when you see such overall statistics, just ignore them. They might sell newspapers but they don't really help the air passenger choose his flight.

Whatever Happened to the Airline Passenger Protection Act?

In 1987, in response to media attention on air travel problems, Congress proposed the Airline Passenger Protection Act, which would have helped passengers avoid delays. Among other things it would have:

(a) required the airlines to report in CRSs the actual average elapsed time of each scheduled flight;

(b) required on-time reporting not just in the percentage of flights later than 15 minutes but also in the average number of minutes each flight was late;

(c) required reports of missed connections at hub airports due to the delay;

(d) required reports breaking down delayed flights by cause, *i.e.*, airline mechanical problems, airline non-mechanical problems and non-airline problems, such as air traffic control or weather;

(e) required for each flight a reporting of the time elapsed between leaving the gate and leaving the ground;

(f) required airlines and travel agents to have available at their ticketing offices monthly reports of the above statistics compiled by the DOT;

(g) required the computerized reservation systems to provide the reported information in a manner and location most useful to passengers;

(h) required the airlines to provide a 24-hour tollfree hot-line, which among other things, could be used to find out about delays, and to advertise the tollfree number on ticket jackets and in prominently displayed airport signs;

(i) required the DOT to establish a telephone number which anyone could call to get the reported information;

(j) forced the DOT to enforce scheduling criteria which would cause the airports to operate within their capacity at all times; and

(k) required the airlines to notify passengers of delayed flights, the approximate length of delay and the reasons for the delay and force the airlines to refund fares if passengers were not so notified.

The proposed legislation also covered many other matters such as cancellations (passengers would get the same compensation as bumping), delayed baggage (compensation equal to a free one-way flight if the delay was over two hours, a round-trip flight, if over 24 hours), required reporting of flights where bumping exceeded one percent, proper notification of restrictions in fare advertisements and on tickets, time limits within which airlines had to process refunds (less than 30 days), gave passengers the right to cancel nonrefundable tickets (within two days of purchase) and specified complaint procedures and substantial penalties for violations.

Wonderful, wasn't it.

To head off this legislation, the DOT (i) started its monthly *Air Travel Consumer Report* (discussed above) which includes a lot less information and is available only from the Washington office on request, (ii) promulgated regulations which required the airlines to put the one-digit flight-delay code in the CRSs (the inadequacies of which code were discussed above), and (iii) asked the nation's largest carriers to sign consent decrees promising to stop unrealistic scheduling at four airports ("unrealistic" being defined as having 50 percent to 75 percent of their flights more than 30-minutes late) and to notify ticket buyers of delays.

Sure enough, shortly thereafter the media's attention turned elsewhere and Bozo the Congress forgot about the proposed Airline Passenger Protection Act. Aided by industry lobbyists, the House and Senate Conference Committee never bothered to work out their differences and the Act died with the Congress at the end of 1988.

How to Make Time of Arrival Lengthen Your Working Day

Most people are aware that flying westward, all or a part of your flight time can be offset by the gain in hours from crossing time zones. For instance, an eleven-hour flight from Paris to San Francisco will, with the nine-hour time difference, mean you arrive only two hours later on the clock. From New York to San Franciso, almost three hours later on the clock. Thus, if you leave in the early morning, you can arrive in plenty of time for lunch.

Likewise most people know that if you fly Concorde westward across the Atlantic, you will arrive in clock time before you leave. What less people are aware of, however, is that you can get the same effect taking a short flight from Grand Rapids, Michigan, to Chicago, Illinois, or Atlanta, Georgia, to Montgomery, Alabama—short westward flights that cross over the division between two time zones.

So if you're a business traveler putting in two or more stops a day in neighboring time zones, you should plan your meetings to start in the east and move west during the day. When the day is over, fly east to spend the night in the city in which you will have your following morning's meeting. You'll generate an extra hour of meeting time each day.

Choosing a Flight Based on the Places of Departure and Arrival

In choosing a flight, most people consider it fairly important that the plane leave from the place where they are (or will be) and end up in the place to which they intend to fly. However, within that reasonable constraint there is often a lot of choice.

Many metropolitan areas have a choice of two airports. Some, such as London, New York (including Newark International) and Washington, DC (including Baltimore-Washington International) have three. Chicago (including Midway, Meigs Field and PAL-Waukee) has four. Los Angeles (including Long Beach, Burbank, Ontario and Van Nuys) has five.

Likewise, most major airports have more than one terminal. Los Angeles International, for example, has eight terminals plus seven satellites. Even within a given terminal, there will be many concourses and, within each concourse, of course, many gates.

Even where there are not multiple airports, terminals, concourses or gates at a given location, when making cross-country connections, you often have a wide choice of airports (and hence of terminals, concourses and gates) through which you can connect. For instance, going from

Charlotte to Los Angeles, you could connect through Atlanta, Dallas, Chicago, Pittsburgh or St. Louis—any one of which might have a better setup as far as terminals, concourse or gates for your particular situation.

The Most Important Speed Factor in Choosing an Airport, Terminal, Concourse or Gate: How Close is it to your Starting and Ending Points?

Following are some examples:

1. Airports. Some airports, such as Dallas' Love Field, Chicago's Midway Field, Detroit City and Washington's National Airport are near downtown; others, such as Dallas-Fort Worth International, Chicago's O'Hare International, Detroit Metro and Washington's Dulles, are 20 or 30 miles out of town. If you're going to the center of town, you'll want to fly to the closer airport.

2. Terminals. Driving into JFK from Manhattan at a crowded time (when it can often take 45 minutes to make a circuit of terminals), you should be flying to London on Delta or Pan Am, which are close to the entrance to the airport rather than on TWA or British Airways, which are much further on. Taking the helicopter into JFK, you should be flying to London on TWA, since that is the terminal at which the helicopter lands. Flying in on a connecting flight from USAir, you should be flying to London on British Airways since they share the same terminal. Dropping off a rental car or parking a car in the long-term lot, you should be flying to London on Delta or Pan Am, since they have the terminals closest to the rental car return and the long-term parking lot.

3. Concourses. Unless you're in training for the four-minute mile, you want your connecting flights to be not only in the same terminal but in the same concourse. O.J. Simpson may be able to make millions running through an airport, but all you'll end up with is shin splints, "luggage shoulder" and a full set of clothes soaked in sweat.

4. Gates. Older terminals such as O'Hare, Minneapolis, Denver and St. Louis tend to have very long concourses. To avoid a long walk, you'll want your flight to leave from a gate nearest the terminal lobby. In most airports that means avoiding the small airlines and flying the majors who have the political muscle to get the close-in gates.

The Second Most Important Speed Factor in Choosing an Airport, Terminal, Concourse or Gate: Is it Congested?

If an airport is congested, it is handling more passengers and flights than it was built for and this means there will be long delays—on the roads coming into the airport, in the parking lots, at the check-in desks, in the waiting areas, in the restaurants and shops, on flight arrivals and departures, at baggage claim and at customs and immigration. The same thing holds true for congested terminals, concourses and gates.

According to the FAA, eighteen major airports now operate at significant overcapacity (20,000 hours or more of delay a year). If there are no increases in capacity nationwide, it's estimated that at least ten new airports will be needed by the year 2000; yet only one new airport (a replacement at Denver) is on the drawing boards. As it takes eight to twelve years to build a new airport, the congestion is likely to increase substantially in the coming years.

Unfortunately, apart from talking to people with personal experience of various airports, terminals, concourses and gates, it's difficult for the novice to know directly which are congested. There are, however, two major indirect ways of determining congestion.

1.   **Look at the on-time records.** The DOT monthly *Air Travel Consumer Report*, mentioned above, gives each airport's arrival and departure delays broken down according to time of day. Your travel agent should have it.

If your agent doesn't have the DOT monthly *Air Travel Consumer Report*, ask him or her to give you from the CRS the average delayed-flight code for a variety of flights arriving at and departing from your alternative airports. You can be sure that next time you call, your agent will have the DOT *Report*.

In the same way that the *airport* on-time records should give you an idea which airports are congested, the *airline* on-time records discussed before should give you an idea which airlines are congested. In which case you should avoid the terminals, concourses and/or gates used by those airlines. (See discussion at 190 below on how to determine the airport location of an airline.)

Box 1-6.	US Airports' On-time Record	
Airport	**Arrivals**	**Departures**
SLC Salt Lake	92.3	93.9
PHX Phoenix	91.6	91.9
LAS Las Vegas	90.9	93.7
DFW Dallas	89.3	90.1
IAH Houston	88.5	87.2
SAN San Diego	88.0	90.4
LAX Los Angeles	87.5	89.3
DEN Denver	85.7	85.6
SFO San Fran	84.9	87.4
ATL Atlanta	83.8	86.4
SEA Seattle	82.1	87.2
MEM Memphis	82.0	88.0
TPA Tampa	81.2	84.7
MCO Orlando	80.5	86.1
MSP Minneapolis	80.3	83.6
STL St Louis	78.8	84.9
ORD Chicago O'H	78.0	84.4
MIA Miami	75.5	80.4
DCA Wash. Nat'l	73.6	85.3
CLT Charlotte	73.1	72.3
BOS Boston	71.7	80.5
PIT Pittsburgh	71.5	74.6
PHL Philadelphia	67.7	78.3
LGA La Guardia	67.4	81.6
EWR Newark	66.6	73.4
JFK New York	62.2	66.0

Percentage of flights delayed 15 minutes or more. Mechanical delays and cancellations excluded.

The moral of this chart: Fly in Texas and the West. Whatever you do, don't fly in the Northeast.

(Source: DOT.)

2. Avoid hub airports and airlines. Over the last decade, as an economy measure, major US airlines have converted to the hub and spoke method of flight scheduling. The airline selects a few hub airports with radiating flights out to other cities. Whereas before, a passenger in a city at the end of one spoke could fly nonstop to a city at the end of another spoke, now he has to connect through the hub (in the process increasing his travel time considerably). The sheer volume of passengers passing through the larger of these hubs insures, if not necessarily flight delays, at least passenger congestion in the airport itself—particularly in the parts of the airport used by the hub airline.

For that reason you should try to avoid the hub airports, particularly the larger ones, and the terminals, concourses and gates used by airlines who use the airport as a hub.

Box 1-7. Airline Hub Airports' Traffic

Airport	Airline	Enplaned Passengers
Chicago O'Hare	American, United	26,121,921
Atlanta	Delta, Eastern	22,649,433
Dallas-Ft. Worth	American, Delta	19,904,665
Los Angeles	Delta, USAir	18,969,780
Denver	United, Continental	15,593,583
San Francisco	United, USAir	13,116,774
Newark	Continental	11,288,941
Boston	Northwest	10,255,305
New York JFK	TWA, Pan Am, Eastern	10,140,009
St. Louis	TWA	9,727,239
Miami	Eastern, Pan Am	9,342,215
Detroit	Northwest	9,254,473
Phoenix	America West	8,784,880
Minneapolis	Northwest	8,310,150
Pittsburgh	USAir	8,156,015
Houston Int'l	Continental	6,928,902
Seattle	Alaska, United, Northwest	6,825,552
Philadelphia	USAir	6,602,687
Charlotte	USAir, Eastern	6,021,104
Memphis	Northwest	5,023,047
Washington Dulles	Continental, United, Pan Am	4,916,890
Salt Lake City	Delta	4,728,595
Kansas City	Eastern, Braniff	4,481,372
Baltimore	USAir	4,009,780
Houston Hobby	Southwest	3,929,891
Cincinnati	Delta	3,264,622
San Juan, PR	American	2,994,513
Nashville	American	2,987,233
San Jose	American	2,807,161
Dallas Love	Southwest	2,435,525
Raleigh-Durham	American	2,316,211
Dayton	USAir	2,166,547
Orange County	American	2,119,664
Syracuse	USAir	1,499,559
Long Beach	Alaska	605,021

*Piedmont data has been included under USAir due to acquisition.
(Source: FAA.)

Remember Congestion also Depends on the Time of Day

Like everything else, airports and airlines are more congested at rush hours than not. Friday evenings, Sunday evenings and Monday mornings are usually most crowded at US airports. The evenings beginning and ending holidays are also bad. During the week, late afternoon and evenings are the worst with late mornings next worst; early mornings are generally best. Note, however, in Europe very early mornings in the transatlantic flight terminals are worst, since that is when most of the overnight flights arrive.

Box 1-8.	Percentage of US Flights Arriving on Time	
Scheduled Arrival Time		**Percent on Time**
6:00-6:59 A.M.		86.5
7:00-7:59 A.M.		91.1
8:00-8:59 A.M.		87.7
9:00-9:59 A.M.		86.5
10:00-10:59 A.M.		87.3
11:00-11:59 A.M.		85.3
12:00-12:59 P.M.		84.0
1:00-1:59 P.M.		85.1
2:00-2:59 P.M.		85.1
3:00-3:59 P.M.		81.2
4:00-4:59 P.M.		77.5
5:00-5:59 P.M.		75.7
6:00-6:59 P.M.		73.4
7:00-7:59 P.M.		72.4
8:00-8:59 P.M.		73.1
9:00-9:59 P.M.		71.6
10:00-10:59 P.M.		74.8
11:00-5:59 A.M.		79.5

On-time is defined as arriving within 15 minutes of scheduled time. Mechanical delays are excluded.

(Source: DOT *Air Travel Consumer Report*.)

The DOT's *Air Travel Consumer Report* (see page 16 above) provides the time-of-day breakdown of departure and arrival delays for *each* of the major airports reporting. If your travel agency has a copy of this report, it should be able to give you a good idea of the most congested times of day at the airports you are considering.

If not, don't hesitate to ask your travel agency to try to approximate the results by collating all the on-time codes in the CRS for all the airlines at the airport according to time of day. It won't take long for your agency to get the idea and order the *Air Travel Consumer Report*.

The Third Most Important Speed Factor in Choosing an Airport, Terminal, Concourse or Gate: Speed of Throughput

Speed of throughput is much broader than flight delay and congestion. It covers the adequacy of a wide range of facilities, including: The availability of a rapid mass transit system both to the airport and within the airport. The frequency of shuttle buses from the parking lots. The location of rental car lots at the terminal. The availability of curbside check-in. Adequate trolleys and porters. Separate check-in lines for passengers with only carry-on. The use of X-ray rather than hand-search security checks. Use of skyways rather than mobile lounges or stairs. If you are disabled, special services to speed you on your way. Separate customs lines for passengers not declaring items. Adequate passport control staff. (In the past passport control at San Francisco has been so slow that some experienced international passengers claim to have found it faster to fly from Europe to Dallas, clear passport control there and then connect to San Francisco on a domestic flight.)

In addition, there are a variety of facilities, which while not directly contributing to the speed of throughput, do help to increase your general efficiency while in the airport, such as business centers (conference rooms, secretarial services, faxes, computer modems, *etc.*), advanced pay phones, quick medical assistance, children's nurseries (for parking the kids while you deal with the tickets and luggage), good restaurants for entertaining, pleasant waiting areas for working, extensive duty-free shops for getting gifts quickly, chapels for reflection, and exercise rooms, video game parlors and bathing and sleeping areas for relaxing.

Box 1-9	Top Ten Airports in the World

Frequent Travelers[1] Preferring Worldwide	
Airport	**Percent**
Amsterdam	12
Singapore	9
Tampa	9
Atlanta	7
Frankfurt	6
Zurich	6
London Heathrow	5
Paris Chas De Gaulle	5
Dallas/Fort Worth	5
Chicago	3

1. Those making 20 or more round-trip air journeys in the past year, with a median trip frequency of 28.

(Source: International Foundation of Airline Passengers Associations.)

How to Find Out What's Where

Naturally a lot of information about airports, terminals, concourses and gates can be obtained only through experience. You should be able to find out the major things, however, from a good travel agency. If they don't know from experience, they should have a copy of the *OAG Travel Planner* (there are North American, European and Pacific Asia editions) which has a lot of information, including distance from town, ground transportation, parking costs and terminal, concourse and gate plans of the major airports.

If you are a frequent traveler, your pocket flight guide mentioned above at page 12 will give the distance from town of multiple airports serving a given city. But for more extensive information, you should subscribe to the *Airport Pocket Guide*, which gives the locations of ticket counters, each airline's gates, baggage claim, ground transportation, car rental, cocktail lounges, snack bars, restaurants, shops, duty free, airline clubs, information desks, first aid, immigration, lockers, telephones, lost and found, mail, nurseries, parking, banks, automatic teller machines, business centers and health clubs, plus a description of the inter-terminal transportation system for the 82 major US airports which handle 90 percent of US air passenger traffic. Cost: $9.95 for one copy, $37.95 per year for an updated copy each quarter. For information call American Data Services at (617)229-5853. They plan to have an international edition out soon as well.

Also, it is rumored that OAG, maker of the *Pocket Flight Guide*, will be coming out with a *Pocket Travel Planner* which may include a lot of the same information in the *Airport Pocket Guide*. Check with them at (800)323-3537 or, in Illinois, (800)942-1888.

If all else fails, call or have your agent call the airline or airport authority itself for the information you need. (See Appendix One at page 385, which lists the phone numbers and three-letter codes of the major airports.) The authority is certain to have the information; the main problem will be locating the person who knows where it's kept.

CHAPTER TWO

CHOOSING YOUR FLIGHT— COMFORT, CONVENIENCE AND SAFETY

The Importance of Choosing the Less Crowded Flight

For passengers riding in economy, by far the most important element relating to comfort is whether or not the plane is crowded.

The airlines, as a matter of economics, have designed the zone of comfort in economy class to run only from zero to two-thirds full. They have to attract at least that many passengers to break even.

Beyond that point the passengers are all gravy—and treated accordingly.

For instance, the armrests in economy are only wide enough for a single elbow. This is no problem as long as the flight is not more than two-thirds full because there will be an empty seat in between. Once the two-thirds is exceeded, someone will either lose an armrest or spend the flight elbow-fencing with his neighbor.

I recall one flight I spent going at it with one little old lady from Dubuque. What an elbow that woman had! Looking back on it now, I'm amazed I made it through the flight without being seriously injured.

Another time, stuck in a middle seat, I decided as an experiment to see if I could position my body so that it wouldn't touch the persons on either side—in this case two lepers from Equatorial Guinea. After trying out various contortions, I eventually succeeded in achieving the right position and held it for the duration of the flight—proving to myself that it could be done. I was, however, in considerable pain for the balance of the week.

War stories aside, it's not just the number of economy-class armrests which will be insufficient if the plane is more than two-thirds full. There's also the number of overhead luggage bins, of toilets, of flight attendants, of drink and food trolleys, of aisles, of doorways, you name it. So even if you don't have elbows, if you book a plane which is crowded, you're certain to have problems.

How to Choose the Less Crowded Flight

Recently with deregulation, the lowering of prices and the airlines' active solicitation of those who in the past have been restricted by a sort of *cordon sanitaire* to traveling by bus, the crowding on airplanes has gotten even worse. There still is, however, a wide variation in the suffocation index of various flights.

To help you find the less crowded flight:

1.   Avoid flights to and from hub airports. Why? Because the sole purpose of the hub and spoke system is to increase the airline's load (read "sardine") factor by bringing passengers together from all over. (See above at page 24 for a list of hub airports.)

2. Avoid airlines which habitually overbook their flights. Even if you don't get bumped, your plane is more likely to be crowded.

Box 2-1.	US Airlines' Bumping Records Per 10,000 Boardings		
Airline	**Involuntary**	**Voluntary**	**Total**
United	4.68	28.54	33.22
Eastern	3.70	24.24	27.94
Braniff	3.74	23.10	26.84
Continental	6.82	18.50	25.32
America West	12.05	12.09	24.14
Southwest	6.18	15.61	21.79
Northwest	5.24	16.22	21.51
Pan Am	17.20	2.39	19.59
USAir	3.89	15.67	19.56
TWA	6.69	12.15	18.84
American	.06	18.24	18.31
Alaska	1.24	10.93	12.17
Midway	1.36	10.62	11.98
Delta	1.06	4.58	5.64

Passengers who are voluntarily denied boarding are those who voluntarily give up a seat in return for compensation. As an indication of crowdedness, the ranking of total denied boarding is more important than that just of involuntary denied boardings. Many airlines fly routes where passengers are less likely to give up their seat voluntarily, such as those to international destinations.

3. Fly the less popular flights. See the discussion below beginning at page 61 on how to find the less popular flights. Beware, though, it is on the less-popular flights that group tours are most often booked. Your less popular flight could be virtually empty; or it could just as easily be packed to the chest with drunken cowboys riding the plane like a steer.

4. Ask the airline reservations clerk. This method can be particularly helpful in avoiding tours since tours are usually booked far in advance. Unfortunately, effective results depend on a standard of veracity in the reservations clerk not actively encouraged by the average airline, which, as you might imagine, is primarily interested in cramming as many sardines as possible into the can.

5. Book alternative flights and just before departure check at the desk to see which plane appears least crowded. Be warned, however, that even this technique works only some of the time. Either the alternative flight will also be crowded, or it will have plenty of space and hence be sufficiently uneconomic that it will be canceled by the airline on "mechanical" grounds. Such a cancellation not only deprives you of an uncrowded alternative but also results in your flight immediately becoming packed with all the canceled flight's passengers transferring over.

A Note on Passenger Ethics

Some readers may question the morality of a passenger booking flights to the same place on several different airlines, knowing that he or she will end up taking only one.

I agree that in an ideal world multiple bookings should not occur. However, in an ideal world the airlines wouldn't routinely overbook their flights and then callously bump the excess passengers.

"But the airlines overbook," a chance seatmate once said in answer to my argument, "precisely because passengers make multiple bookings. If passengers made only one booking and stuck to it, then the airlines wouldn't have to overbook to make allowance for no-shows."

"Don't be specious," I replied, unable to find a flaw in his logic.

One of the worst things that can happen to you is to have somebody intelligent around when you're trying to rationalize your behavior.

Actually, some time later I did come across a study by the International Chamber of Commerce's Committee on Air Transport which indicated that over 50 percent of no-shows were caused by airline or travel agent error, *e.g.*, incorrect name, date, time or destination on the ticket, interline computer miscommunications or failure to notify the passenger of flight changes.

Unfortunately I'd neglected earlier to get Mr. Smarty Pants' address, so I was unable to straighten him out.

Why You Should Choose the Flight With the Best Conditions of Carriage

Would you sign a contract without reading it? No. Well, you probably do every time to buy an airline ticket. If you read the back of the ticket, you'll notice it says that the ticket plus the airline's "conditions of carriage" (or "terms of transportation") form a contract between you and the airline.

The conditions of carriage contain all the rules and policies of the airline towards its passengers: the detailed baggage allowances, restrictions on types of baggage, various check-in deadlines, acceptance standards for different types of passengers (including the disabled and the underage), refund rights, ticket validity and claims procedures.

The terms vary from airline to airline and by reading them carefully you can quite quickly separate the airlines which are merely indifferent to the rights of the passenger, from those which are positively oppressive. In the conditions you can discover which airlines deny you a right to amenities in case of diversion of the flight, which airlines won't give any refund at all for a lost ticket, which airlines charge exorbitant amounts for excess baggage, which airlines discriminate against the handicapped, *etc.*

As you might imagine, the airlines are not particularly interested in you reading their conditions of carriage before you buy your ticket. None of them will volunteer a copy. Even if you request one at the time you buy your ticket, most will not give you a copy then and there. In a survey I conducted of eight airline ticket offices in downtown Washington, DC, only two provided me with a copy. The rest either didn't know what I was talking about, referred me to the home office or hauled out a fifty-page loose-leaf manual which they said I could look at briefly. One clerk told me that a passenger was allowed to see the conditions of carriage only after the passenger had a problem so that the airline could show the passenger how he had violated the conditions. I finally was able to obtain copies by writing each of the airlines (some of them more than once).

Where to Write for Conditions of Carriage

To receive information, on conditions of carriage for a particular airline, write to:

> **Aloha Airlines, Inc.,** Customer Relations, P.O. Box 30028, Honolulu, HI 96820.

> **Alaska Airlines,** Consumer Affairs, P.O. Box 68900, Seattle, WA 98168.

> **America West Airlines,** Consumer Affairs, 222 South Mill Avenue, Tempe, Arizona 85281.

> **American Airlines, Inc.,** Executive Office, P.O. Box 619616, Dallas-Fort Worth Airport, TX 75261-9616.

> **Braniff Inc.,** Customer Relations, 7701 Lemmon Avenue, P.O. Box 7035, Dallas, TX 75209.

Continental Airlines, Customer Relations, P.O. Box 4607, Houston, TX 7210-4607.

Delta Air Lines, Inc., Law Department, Hartsfield Atlanta International Airport, Atlanta, GA 30320.

Eastern Air Lines, Inc., Consumer Affairs, Building 11, Room 1433 (MIALS), Miami International Airport, Miami, FL 333148.

Hawaiian Airlines, Consumer Affairs, Honolulu International Airport, P.O. Box 30008, Honolulu, HI 96820-0008.

Midway Airlines, Consumer Affairs, 5959 South Cicero Avenue, Chicago, IL 60638.

Northwest Airlines, Inc., Customer Relations, Minneapolis/St. Paul International Airport, St. Paul, MN 55111.

Pan American World Airways, Inc., Consumer Affairs Department, 200 Park Avenue, New York, NY 10166.

Southwest Airlines Co., Customer Relations, P.O. Box 37611, Love Field, Dallas, TX 75235-1625.

Trans World Airlines, Inc., Customer Relations, 605 Third Avenue, New York, NY 10158.

United Airlines, Customer Relations, P.O. Box 66100, Chicago, IL 60666.

USAir, Consumer Relations, Washington National Airport, Washington, DC 20001.

Be sure to ask for the *full* copy of the conditions. Otherwise they will try to give you just a three page summary of the limitations of liability sections. If the airline refuses to give you a full copy, complain to the DOT Office of Consumer Affairs at (202)366-2220.

Where Your Travel Agent can Obtain Copies of Conditions of Carriage

Much of the policy information in the conditions of carriage is available in your travel agent's CRS. However, a good travel agent should have an updated copy of the actual conditions of carriage, which represents the actual legally enforceable document. Fortunately, all the conditions of carriage can be purchased from an airline-controlled, nonprofit clearing house, the

Airline Tariff Publishing Company at (703)471-7510. The price is $55 for one set or $250 per year for a subscription which is updated every two weeks.

If your travel agent doesn't subscribe, ask why.

How Some Conditions of Carriage are More Valuable than Others

Most airlines' conditions of carriage are detailed affairs based on the old Civil Aeronautics Board rules. Each subject is dealt with under a standardized rule number. For instance, Rule 35 deals with the grounds on which the airline can refuse to transport you. Rule 270 deals with your refund rights if your flight is terminated involuntarily. Rule 240 deals with your rights to alternative flights if the the airline fails to operate on schedule. And so on.

Recently, however, some airlines, such as American, Braniff and USAir, have edited their conditions of carriage down to a few pages of general rules. While easier to read, these conditions of carriage provide much less detail, giving the airline much more discretion in dealing with its passengers. To find out his or her detailed rights, the passenger now has to go beyond the conditions of carriage to try to find the airline's internal rules, if such rules exist at all, and then argue that those rules should be treated as part of the conditions of carriage.

In my opinion, the DOT, which requires the conditions of carriage to be published, should also require that they contain sufficient detail to inform the passenger of all of his rights—including any internal airline rules which formerly would have been part of the conditions of carriage. Unfortunately, as a mere passenger, my opinion doesn't carry a lot of weight at the DOT.

The Hidden Advantage of Choosing the Flight with Preassigned Seating

If you make a reservation through the airline directly or through qualifying travel agencies, you can often reserve a seat even before purchasing your ticket. (See Box 2-2 at page 38 below for the various airline time limits.) Qualifying travel agencies are those which subscribe to a computerized reservations system (CRS) which allows the travel agency direct access to a participating airline's internal reservations system. A participating airline can be any airline, not just the sponsor of the CRS. For instance, American Airlines, which sponsors its own public CRS, Sabre, also is a participating airline in the United, TWA-Northwest, Texas Air and Delta public CRSs as far as allowing travel agencies subscribing to such systems to access directly American's own internal reservation system. The obvious advantage of choosing a flight on which you can be assigned a seat at the time of ticket purchase is that as long as you show up at the airport by the requisite deadline, you don't have to show up early at the airport to get the seat you want.

The hidden advantage is that you decrease substantially your chances of being bumped. Again, as long as you show up by the requisite deadline, you will have priority over those passengers without preassigned seating. They will be bumped before you.

How to Make the Preassigned Seating Paradox Work for You

The fact people with preassigned seats will probably have asked for good seats has had two paradoxical effects on those who select their seats at the airport. First, no matter how early someone arrives at the airport to select a seat, there will be fewer "good" seats available to select from. Second, to the extent there are no-shows among those with preassigned seating, there will tend to be more "good" seats available at the last minute.

If the flight is overbooked, these last-minute "good" seats will be going to the standbys. In this case, if you have been assigned a bad seat and want a better one, ask the staff if you can be wait-listed for a better seat ahead of the standbys.

If the flight is underbooked, then the preassigned seating will probably not be reassigned (in case the passenger with the preassigned seat shows up at the last minute) and the standbys will be given other, worse seating. In this case, if you have been assigned a bad seat, want a better one and have been unable to get one through wait-listing, you can board the plane, wait until the doors are closed and then take the first empty good seat you see—it undoubtedly belonged to a no-show with preassigned seating.

Why You Should Ask for the Flight Which Offers Preissued Boarding Passes

A boarding pass issued at the time you purchase your ticket has all the advantages of a preassigned seat plus, if you use only carry-on luggage or check your baggage at curbside, you can proceed directly to the plane, bypassing the check-in lines in the main terminal and at the gate podium. (If you have luggage to check but there is no curbside service, some of the airlines offer special baggage check-in desks for those with preissued boarding passes.)

On some international flights, you can get through passport control on the strength of a preissued boarding pass; but before proceeding to the gate you must have your boarding pass verified at the airline's transfer desk. Although not as quick as going directly to the gate, the preissued boarding pass is still an advantage because the lines are usually shorter at the transfer desk and it takes the staff less time to verify preissued boarding passes than to issue new ones.

A preissued boarding pass does not effect your ability to change flights at the last minute. Since you still retain your ticket, you merely discard the boarding pass and transfer the ticket as you would normally.

Even if you can obtain a preissued boarding pass, you can still be bumped from a flight if you don't show up before the requisite closing time. (See discussion of gate appearance deadlines at page 128.) So be sure your travel agent checks the airline's conditions of carriage for its closing rules.

The Three Major Reasons You Might Not be Able to Obtain a Preissued Boarding Pass

1. Time and other limits. Most of the airlines have a period before which they will not issue a boarding pass. (See Box 2-2 below.) A few of the smaller airlines do not allow the preissuance of boarding passes at all. Some have different limits for passes issued by travel agents and those issued by the airline itself. One airline allows you to obtain a preissued boarding pass only if you don't check your bags.

2. Heavy booking. Once more than a certain percentage of the passengers obtain preissued boarding passes, *e.g.*, 60 percent, many airlines refuse to issue any more. If you can't get a preissued boarding pass from an airline, ask why. If it's because of heavy booking, try to get another flight or, at the least, be sure to arrive at the airport early to avoid being bumped.

3. Travel agent inadequacies. As with preassigned seating, a travel agency is allowed to preissue a boarding pass only if it is using a CRS which allows the agency to directly access the internal reservations system of a given airline. If your travel agency can't preissue a boarding pass for this reason, then consider getting an agent who can, or go to the airline ticket office yourself and get a boarding pass issued there.

Box 2-2.	Maximum Days Before Departure Seat Will be Reserved and Boarding Pass Issued			
Airline	**Seat**		**Pass**	
Alaska	45		0	
Aloha	0		0	
America West	0		0	
American	330		30	
Braniff	365		4	
Continental	34		21	
Delta	31	(TrvlAgt)	31	(TrvlAgt)
	60	(Airline)	60	(Airline)
Eastern	33		33	
Hawaii	30		30	(If no luggage)
Midway	30		30	(TrvlAgt only)
Northwest	60		60	
Pan Am	350		30	(Full fare only)
Southwest	0		0	
TWA	30		30	
United	331		30	
USAir	21		21	

The Advantages of Choosing a Flight on a Very Small Plane

Flights on very small planes have some advantages. In the first place, they are usually connected with very small airlines. In very small airlines each employee tends to have a more direct interest in the success of the airline and to play a multiplicity of roles unafflicted by the bureaucratic mentality of the large airlines. In addition, since the airline's total number of passengers is so much smaller, each individual passenger represents a larger percentage of overall revenues and is correspondingly more important. The result is small airlines will bend the rules in your favor more often than large airlines.

For instance, if you know you're going to be five minutes late for check-in, you can often get the airline to delay the flight. Likewise, if everyone who booked the flight has arrived, you can sometimes get the airline to leave before the scheduled departure time. And when you land, you're often able to collect your checked luggage right at the plane rather than having to go to baggage claim to wait for it. (Some do this as a matter of course; others, only on request.)

The small planes are also easier for a passenger to control. For example, once when traveling with two business associates and trying to catch a Freedom Airlines flight on a small plane out of Midland, Michigan, I got stuck behind a long line at the security X-ray machines at the entrance to the concourse. Leaving my bags with my friends to put through X-ray, I dashed through the metal detector, down the concourse, through the closing flight gate, waving my ticket, and out to the plane, which, with its propeller whirring, was just about to pull up the fold-down stairs into the passenger doorway.

I immediately sat down on the stairs and began tying my shoelaces.

A minute and a half later my friends finally arrived at the plane to find me still fumbling with my shoelaces as I simultaneously tried to communicate with an angry pilot, copilot, stewardess and wheel-block man through my own amiable imitation of the American Sign Language For The Deaf.

I don't think I would have gotten away with it if the plane had been a 747.

The Disadvantages of Choosing a Flight on a Very Small Plane

On the whole, the disadvantages of very small planes outweigh the advantages.

1. Small planes are slow. You may get them to leave ten minutes ahead of schedule, but they'll still take a half-hour longer to get there than a big plane.

2. They're cramped. The reason you've got to spend your time on landing trying to get your checked luggage directly off the plane is that your carry-on had to be checked into the luggage compartment because it wouldn't fit under the seat.

If a rule similar to the one requiring items to fit *under* the seat was applied to the passengers *on top* of it, most of the passengers would have to be checked into the luggage compartment as well.

Who are the seats in these small planes designed for anyway? Limbless amputees with a single buttock? The only time your knees aren't in your chest is when the seat in front of you is empty so you can fold it forward, out of the way.

And then there's the lack of headroom. Mississippi Valley Airlines, which I flew once into Carbondale, Illinois, required their stewardesses on that flight to be under four and a half feet so they could walk up and down the aisle without stooping. "What about the passengers?" I remember wondering at the time.

Maybe Mississippi Valley Airways was trying to carve out a niche for itself among the Southern Illinois hunchback community.

3. Very small planes are often unpressurized. This is not much of a problem when you're in the air; the planes usually don't go high enough to cause oxygen starvation. The problem is the pressure in your ears when you land.

On one trip, when I had a cold and hence difficulty readjusting to the pressure, I ended up with ear cavities filled with blood. Apart from making everything sound as though I was sitting at the bottom of a swimming pool, it created certain aesthetic difficulties when I leaned forward to shake hands with a client waiting for me at the airport and blood ran out of my ears.

When I flew Mississippi Valley Airways, they tried their own high-tech solution to the problem of pressure changes: each of the passengers was given a stick of gum to chew.

I don't know if you've ever been in a rapidly descending plane full of people intently chewing gum with their mouths open. The way they pause every few moments to ritualistically swallow their saliva and move their open lips like a fish—I can tell you it is not a reassuring experience.

4. Very small planes are generally noisy—sometimes to the point of damaging your hearing. Once on a small plane from Nuremberg to Stuttgart I felt like I was sitting up front at an *avant-garde* rock concert in which all melody, rhythm and harmony had been removed, leaving nothing but a droning white noise shredding my eardrums. I walked around for days afterwards, turning suddenly and randomly in different directions saying "What? Huh? Come again?"

Needless to say, my business deal in Stuttgart fell through.

The noisiness of small planes is partly because they're of lighter construction and partly because they use propellers, which create much more vibration. If you get stuck on a small plane, sit as far away as possible from the propellers (preferably at the back since that is also usually where the exit door is) and, if you are not particularly concerned what people think of you, stick your fingers in your ears.

In fact, if you are not particularly concerned what people think of you, sticking your fingers in your ears is probably a good course of action in almost every difficult situation you find yourself in.

5. Small planes definitely make you feel less safe than large planes—whether or not very small planes are less safe (the statistics are debatable). Whenever I ride one, I find I spend most of my time peering out the window trying to locate emergency landing strips on the ground.

One of the reasons small planes make you feel less safe is the way they look—flimsy, tinny, held together with baling wire. And the shape of some of them. Have you every flown in a Shorts 330? You know, the one that looks like a pregnant cube? I mean, what in God's name were the designers at Shorts thinking of? Hadn't anyone there heard about wind resistance?

Another reason small planes make you feel less safe is their greater sensitivity to turbulence. Say you have a cup filled with soda resting on your tray table. Hit an air pocket in a 747 and you'll notice a ripple on the surface of the soda. Hit the same air pocket in a Beechcraft 1500 and you'll be looking at your cup at eye level. Where the soda will be depends on the quickness of your reflexes and the height of the cabin ceiling.

Yet another reason small planes make you feel less safe is the shoestring character of their owner airlines. They're so short of staff that on many of them the guy who pilots the plane is the same guy who loads your luggage. Personally, I don't mind if my pilot acts as the baggage handler. What worries me is how to tell the difference between that and the baggage handler acting as my pilot.

Many small airlines are on the verge of insolvency. I recall once taking a small plane from Springfield, Missouri, to St. Louis. There was nobody on the plane but the pilot and me. It was night. We were flying through a thunderstorm. The pilot came on the public address system. He was the owner of the airline. Things were tough. He'd mortgaged everything yet he still didn't have enough money to keep his plane airworthy. Just before we'd taken off, he'd been forced to declare bankruptcy. This was to be the airline's very last flight. Life didn't seem worth living.

Fortunately, I was able to tell the man I had an investor in St. Louis who wanted to put $25 million into a small airline.

I wasn't taking any chances on the guy committing seppuku before we reached Lambert International.

Sometimes I wonder what he did the next day when I failed to call him.

Choosing a Flight Based on the Most Comfortable Seating

Apart from very small planes, the size of an aircraft, in my experience, is no predictor of comfortable seating. The 747 jumbo may be bigger than the DC-8 but that just means it has more room to pack people in. This is because a given aircraft's seating comfort is determined not by the manufacturer but by the airline, which chooses the seating configuration.

There are three major factors which determine seating comfort:

(a) Seat width. Normally the width will be somewhere between 20.5 inches and 18.5 inches. The wider the better, of course.

(b) Number of seats per row. The most comfortable are seven across (2/3/2) used in 767s and nine across (2/5/2) used in DC-10s and L-1011s, five across (2-5) used in DC-8s, MD-80s and DC-9s and five across (3-2) used in BA-146s. The worst are ten across used in 747s, DC-10s and L-1011s and six across used in DC-8s, 727s and 737s.

(c) Seat pitch. Seat pitch means how far apart the rows are. For most domestic flights the front to rear seat space of economy class is 31 to 32 inches, and for most international ones, 32 to 34 inches. Because of special considerations such as emergency exits and convertibility to cargo space, not all seats within a given plane are likely to have the same pitch.

Box 2-3. Most Comfortable Domestic Planes
According To *Consumer Reports Travel Letter*

Airline	Plane	Comfort Score %
American	BA-146	85
US Air	BA-146	85
TWA	L-1011	83
United	767	83
American	737-200	81

Note: The comfort ranking above depends on the configuration given to it by the airline. Another airline may have the same plane but configure it differently. For instance, while TWA's L-1011s are among the most comfortable, Hawaiian's L-1011s are among the least comfortable, with a score of only 67%.
(Source: *Consumer Reports Travel Letter*.)

Your travel agent or the airline should be able to tell you the relative width, configuration and pitch of the seating on any potential flights you are considering. If you are a frequent traveler, you can subscribe to the pocket-sized, quarterly *Airline Seating Guide*, which gives the configuration of each airline's aircraft. (It doesn't give you the pitch but it does give you the number of rows from which you can estimate the relative difference in pitch.) There are U.S. and international editions. Cost: $39.95 and $44.95 per year respectively. To order one contact Carlson Publishing at (213)493-4877. (For what else the *Airline Seating Guide* contains, see page 232 below.)

On the whole, however, the differences are minor. No matter what flight you take, unless you fly first class or business, you're not going to have enough room in your seat to get comfortable.

Which are the Safest Flights?

Apart from differences in weather (which won't exist if you are choosing between two flights on the same route at the same time), the choice of the safest flight breaks down into three major questions:

1. Which are the safest airlines? Certain airlines are much less safe than others—those of most Communist and basket-case countries, for instance. Undercapitalized commuter airlines are also risky (see below). Of the major airlines certain ones are, rightly or wrongly, perceived as safer than others.

Box 2-4.	Most Safety Conscious Airlines

Percent of Recent Users Nominating	
Airline	**%Users**
El Al	47
Swissair	34
Lufthansa	32
Qantas	26
Delta	23
South African Airways	16
Singapore	16
American	15
SAS	15
KLM	14
United	13
British Airways	13
JAL	12
Saudia	11
Air Canada	10
Air New Zealand	10
Alaska	10
All Nippon	9
Cathay Pacific	8
Varig	8
Northwest	7
TWA	6
Pan Am	6
Air France	6
Canadian Pacific	6
Finnair	6
Kuwait	6

(Source: International Foundation Of Airline Passengers Associations.)

2.   Which are the safest airports? A study by the *Wall Street Journal* in 1987 of near-collision rates at various airports concluded that, contrary to what you might think, the rates were significantly higher at the smaller airports than at the large congested airports. For instance, the rate of near collisions was over eight times higher at Chicago Midway than Chicago O'Hare; over five times higher at San Jose than San Francisco International; five times higher at Los Angeles Ontario than Los Angeles International; and infinitely higher at Houston Hobby than Houston International. (In fact, Hobby's rate was about average for the small airports studied; it's just that Houston International had no near misses during the period studied.)

The *Wall Street Journal* felt the difference in near collision rates was probably attributable to the smaller airports' less extensive air traffic control, less experienced pilots and greater number of helicopters.

3.   Which are the safest aircraft? The safety record of various aircraft is debatable. Some studies have shown that you are three times more likely to be involved in an accident in a small commuter aircraft. But a second look at the statistics has indicated that the higher rate of accidents is attributable not to the type of aircraft but to whether the aircraft was being flown by an undercapitalized commuter airline. The small aircraft of a well-capitalized commuter airline were as safe as the larger aircraft of a major airline.

Newer aircraft of whatever type are more likely to have advanced safety devices and less likely to be suffering metal fatigue. These apparent advantages, however, may be offset by the fact the newer aircraft usually have more glitches which have to be worked out. For instance, in 1980, a ten-year survey of accidents determined that, once again contrary to what you might think, turboprops were safer than turbojets; and short and medium haul twin and tri-jets were safer than wide-bodies and first generation long-haul aircraft. If that survey was done today, when entirely new narrow-body and turboprop aircraft are being introduced, the statistics might be reversed.

The intuitive feel of most experts is that you are more likely to survive a crash in a wide-body since it has more space between its underside and the passenger compartment. Also, very few wide-body aircraft have ever been hijacked—probably due to the difficulty of maintaining control with two aisles.

(For additional information on airline safety see pages 338-342 and pages 345-348.)

The Value of the Above Safety Information

Before you decide to fly nothing but El Al 747s to and from Houston International, however, you should get all the above safety information in perspective. The overall risk of dying in an air crash on any kind of commercial flight is less than one in a million. (See *So Should You Be Afraid Of Flying?* at page 342.) The fact that you might be three times more likely to die on one flight than another, doesn't sound quite as serious when you express it as the difference between 0.5 per million and 1.5 per million.

During years of my flying in all conceivable situations, not once did any flight I avoided for safety reasons actually crash. Choosing the "safer" plane undoubtedly comforted me (in much the same way that turning away from a path crossed by a black cat might comfort the superstitious); but there is no doubt I would have been much better off forgetting about safety and choosing my flight on something more important—say, the inflight movie.

Choosing Your Flight Based on the Inflight Movie

Actually, despite the foregoing, this is not a worthwhile basis on which to choose a flight. Choosing a flight on what newspapers and magazines are provided in the rack at the rear of the plane would be more productive. There are three reasons for this.

1. Same film. So many competing flights show the same film that I've considered asking the government to institute some kind of antitrust investigation. But then what would my treble-damages award be? Having to watch three boring and tasteless movies instead of one?

2. Other section. On flights on which there is a movie you haven't seen, it will invariably be shown only in the sections of the plane where you're not sitting. In your section they'll show only movies you've seen.

3. Obstacles. You can try to move to another other section but, pursuant to some unwritten code of airline practice, that other section is the one in which the projector has been designed to break down or the earphones are plastic novelty devices meant to periodically pop out of their armrest plugholes or, and this is the worst, the film has been treated with subliminal messages which cause the mother who always sits at the bulkhead under the screen to jump up during the most interesting parts and start burping her baby in the light.

It's not worth the price of admission.

Box 2-5	Airlines Rated Favorite By Their Own Users

North American Users Only

Airline	Percent
Singapore Airlines	45
Swissair	42
KLM	22
SAS	21
Qantas	21
El Al	20
Cathay Pacific	18
Lufthansa	18
Thai	18
Air New Zealand	17
Varig	15
Delta	15
American Airlines	15
British Airways	14
Japan Air Lines	12
United Airlines	11
TWA	10
CP Air	9
Pan American	9
Finnair	9
South African	9
Air Canada	7
Air France	7
Alaska Airlines	7
All Nippon	6
Aer Lingus	5
Alitalia	5
Korean	5
Northwest	5

(Source: International Foundation Of Airline Passengers Associations.)

Choosing Your Flight Based on Standards of Airline Service

While some airlines are reputedly less brutal than others, any differences are in fact quite insignificant. All airlines follow the same basic service routine, *i.e.*, trying to have as little contact as possible with the passengers. Of course, some airlines' staff smile a little more; some have a little better food; some, a little quicker service; some (such as Thai International,

Singapore Airlines and Cathay Pacific, which do not belong to IATA (see below at pages 75-76) provide free liquor and/or small travel packs in economy class (which used to be prohibited under IATA rules). And, of course, there are the extremely bad airlines you should avoid. Several of the Communist bloc carriers, for example. You could put their flight attendants in the gorilla cage at the zoo and no one would know the difference—except perhaps that the gorillas would be less hairy.

Unfortunately, there are no recent studies which rank the various airlines according only to their standards of service. However, you can get some idea by looking at the airline rankings in Box 2-5 above, *Airlines Rated Favorite By Their Own Users*.

Also, for the US airlines, you can get some idea of service by looking at the monthly complaint statistics published in the DOT's *Air Travel Consumer Report* mentioned above at page 16. Airlines which have a large number of complaints are probably less likely to provide a high standard of airline service.

Box 2-6	Consumer Complaints Against US Airlines

Per 100,000 Passengers	
Airline	**Complaints**
Pan Am	17.14
Hawaiian Airlines	13.18
TWA	10.75
Continental	9.94
Eastern	8.72
Northwest	6.20
Braniff	5.41
Midway	3.61
USAir	3.48
United	3.23
Aloha	2.71
American	2.67
America West	2.16
Delta	1.22
Southwest	0.81
Alaska	0.62

(Source: DOT *Air Travel Monthly Consumer Complaint Report.*)

When to Choose a Flight Based on the Frequent Flyer Program

Many airlines today, particularly in the United States, have frequent flyer programs under which passengers can accumulate points for flying on the airline and then redeem them in the form of free travel-class upgrades, free tickets to selected destinations or free hotel and/or car rentals.

The programs were designed primarily for the business traveler. (One recent survey indicated two-thirds of such travelers are in at least one such program.) Not only is the nonbusiness traveler unlikely to travel sufficient miles during the year to obtain a worthwhile award but the programs usually make most economic sense when the person receiving the award is different from the person paying for the ticket which generates the award—as is the case with most business travelers.

The ticket upgrades, although theoretically giving you something of value, don't really "save" you money if you would normally fly economy class anyway. Even worse, several airlines have allowed the upgrade to be used only if you have paid the full lower-class fare. Since you can usually buy a lower-class ticket for 40 percent of the full lower-class fare, using the "free" upgrade actually costs you money.

The free flights obviously save you the cost of a flight but often you could have saved much more on the flights you used to accumulate your points by shopping around among the various airlines for the cheapest fare—especially if you were a business traveler who, due to the short notice of your trips, probably paid full fare on each of your flights with the frequent-flyer program airline.

The frequent flyer program is, therefore, primarily a method of bribing a business traveler so he will arrange for his company to purchase a flight on the airline. It's no different from any other potential supplier to a company agreeing to pay money to the company's employee as a reward for the employee arranging for the company to award a contract to the supplier—except that in this case everyone in the company who flies is on the take—including the company president.

Frequent-flyer employees, in order to increase their accumulation of frequent flyer mileage, continually (i) choose the same airline even though it may be more expensive on a given route, (ii) take a later flight which allows less time for business to be done at the destination, (iii) add miles to their schedule to connect with their airline (such as taking the shuttle to New York from Washington to catch Pan Am to San Francisco rather than take American Airlines direct from Washington to San Francisco), and (iv) push for the more costly business- or first-class ticket which will result in a bonus mileage award. The abuses are manifold.

If you're an unethical business traveler whose company has inadequate travel-expense controls (see last paragraph of Traveltron discussion below at page 72), you'd be a fool not to engage in them all.

Additional Ways You Can Cheat Your Employer Through the Frequent Flyer Programs

Not content with corrupting employees in the choice of airline flights, the airlines have expanded the programs to hotels, rental car companies, credit cards, long-distance telephone companies, travel agencies, airport buses and, in England under one program, almost any type of retail store—the use of which can generate frequent flyer points for the airline.

Again, if you're an unethical employee whose company has inadequate travel controls, all you have to do is apply the lessons learned above to these other areas of travel expense. When choosing which hotel, rental car company, travel agency or airport bus to use, forget about convenience, time or expense, and go for the one which will lead to the quickest accumulation of usable points.

How You Can Cheat the Government as Well

If the ticket was not purchased for business purposes, the frequent flyer award should not be taxable. However, if it was purchased for business purposes, then logically the frequent flyer awards should be taxable:

(a) **as a rebate**, if the receiver of the award deducted the cost of the ticket as a business expense;

(b) **as indirect compensation**, if the award is received by an employee on a ticket purchased by his or her employer with the consent of the employer; or

(c) **as a bribe**, if the award is received by an employee on a ticket purchased by his or her employer at the suggestion of the employee.

Despite this clear reasoning, virtually nobody reports frequent flyer awards as income. Nor, as of this date, has the IRS tried to get the easily available award information from the airlines.

So, for at least a while, you should be able to cheat the government with impunity.

Three Ways to Get Those Few
Extra Bonus Frequent Flyer Miles

Say you are close to a given award level for a holiday you want to take soon. Following are three possible ways get that extra mileage:

1.   Be a pusher. Go to the nearest airline ticket office, take away a handful of the applications for the frequent flyer program, fill out all the names of your friends who aren't regular flyers, fill in your name and frequent flyer number at the bottom in the space marked "recommended by," mail in the application postage-free and wait to collect a substantial bonus mileage bounty from the airline for your services as a frequent-flyer pusher.

2.   Break your flight into short legs below the minimum mileage award. Many airlines have a minimum mileage award. So, for example, if you fly only 250 miles, you'll still get a credit for a minimum 500. Sometimes it costs you no greater fare (and in fact may save you fare) to split your trip into two or more flights. (See discussion of the split-ticket trick below at page 60.) In this case, to the extent each leg is less than the minimum mileage award, you will be accumulating bonus mileage for free.

3.   Fly more miles than necessary at no additional cost. Sometimes, because of differences in competition between two points, it is cheaper to fly round-trip from point A to point C going through point B than it is to fly round-trip from point A to point B. (For details, see the discussion of the hidden-city discount at page 60 below.) In this situation, although you intend to fly only round-trip from A to B, you can buy a round-trip ticket from A to C through B but when you get to C turn around and come back to B. After doing your business, you return home on the B-to-A ticket. The result: You not only accumulate the mileage for a round-trip from A to B but also, at no more cost, accumulate additional mileage equal to a round-trip between B and C.

Some aficionados of the increased mileage technique have been known to book discount round-trips or triangle fares on several different routes, separate the various legs and recombine them all into a massive roundabout circle which gets them from point A to point B at approximately the same cost but several times the mileage of a direct flight from A to B.

Needless to say, these people tend to have somewhat obsessive personalities.

Where to Get Information on Frequent Flyer Programs

The frequent flyer programs change so often that anything detailed put into this book would quickly be out of date. There are two major ways to get up-to-date information:

1. Contact the airlines themselves.

Box 2-7.	Major Airline Frequent Flyer Programs	
Air Canada Aeroplan (800)361-8253	Braniff Get-It-All Frequent Flyer (800)346-8108	Pan Am World Pass (800)348-8000 (617)273-4233
Alaska Gold Coast Travel (800)942-9911 (800)654-5669 WA	Continental/Eastern One Pass (800)525-0280	TWA Frequent Flyer (800)325-4815
America West Fly Fund (800)247-5691	Delta Frequent Flyer (800)323-2323	United Mileage Plus (800)421-4655
American AAdvantage (800)433-7300	Northwest World Perks (800)435-9696	USAir Frequent Traveler (800)USAIR-FT

In addition to the above, many commuter and foreign airlines either have programs of their own or programs run in conjunction with the majors above.

2. Subscribe to a frequent flyer periodical. Despite what I said above about the frequent flyer programs generally making little economic sense to the nonbusiness traveler, if you stick to special promotions involving multiple mileage, you sometimes can make it work. Two monthly publications which do nothing but report new special frequent flyer promotions are:

(a) **Business Flyer.** Cost: $45 per year. For information call 800-343-0664, Ext.935, or in Massachusetts, (800)322-1238.

(b) Frequent. Cost: $28 per year. For information call (719)597-8889. This publication also has a program for overseas residents who need a US address to enroll in a program. Frequent will provide a US address, enroll overseas residents in the programs and keep track of their mileage.

How to Keep Your Frequent Flyer Points Organized

Once you've got the information, you might consider purchasing a computer program to assist you in keeping track of your mileage and airline frequent flyer program changes. If interested, call the OMT Group at (408)732-8565 and ask about Freequent Flyer. Cost: around $50.

Your Rights if Your Frequent Flyer Program is Changed

The frequent flyer programs are becoming so popular that the free-flight awards are beginning to cut into the airlines' profits. According to one recent estimate, up to 33 percent of the seats on popular vacation routes are being taken up by free frequent-flyer tickets. At the same time, since many frequent flyers are now joining several programs at once, the "brand loyalty" effect of the programs is diminishing.

The airlines are responding to these problems by trying to renege on the deal—requiring more points for an award, imposing shorter usage deadlines, designating more blacked-out days and routes, limiting seat availability and instituting more difficult claiming procedures. (Recent statistics show that now much less than half of accumulated frequent flyer points are being claimed.) It's only a matter of time before the airlines get together and try to squelch the programs altogether.

Don't expect your frequent flyer program to protect you. After all, the airline drafted the contract and undoubtedly put language in allowing it to make changes.

As the Federal government does not get involved in regulating this area, your main hope is that the way the change is made violates your state law on unfair and deceptive business practices.

The National Association of Attorneys General (NAAG), which represents the attorneys general of 43 states, recently established a set of guidelines to be used by its members in enforcing their various state unfair and deceptive business practice statutes. According to these guidelines, a frequent flyer program, in the absence of clear and conspicuous disclosure of the right to do so, must:

(1) Give not less than one year's notice to vested members of any adverse changes in the program, including termination. In other words, a member with vested points must have at least a year after notice to accumulate and redeem points under the pre-change program.

(2) Not impose any capacity controls on the use of vested points, such as blackouts or limited frequent flyer seats per plane, which would prevent the passenger from obtaining a seat:

(a) within 15 days before or after the date originally requested, or

(b) if all the flights during this period are fully booked at the time the request is made, then by the closest available date outside the period when the plane is not fully booked.

(3) Not have any limitations on the type or class of fare with which an upgrade certificate, discount flight coupon or free companion coupon may be used.

(4) Not have any restrictions on the use, extension or re-issuance of certificates.

(5) Refuse to honor award certificates within a year of their issue.

(6) Take longer than 14 days to process redemptions.

(7) Delete members from its mailing list for notices and statements.

All this sounds great. The catch is that as pointed out above, even if your local attorney general follows the guidelines, the airlines don't have to conform to any of the recommended procedures as long as they give you clear and conspicuous notice before you start that they reserve the right to do less than is required by the recommendations.

According to the NAAG, adequate notice would not be given by something such as:

> *Program rules, regulations and mileage levels are subject to change without notice.*

The airline would have to go on with something more specific such as:

> *This means the airline may raise mileage levels, add an unlim-*
> *ited number of blackout days or limit the number of seats*
> *available to any or all destinations without notice. Program*
> *members may not be able to use awards to certain destina-*
> *tions, or may not be able to obtain certain types of awards*
> *such as cruises.*

Check your frequent flyer program and see if the airline has had the temerity to put notice language like this into its description. Most airlines haven't. Instead, they've tried to incorporate all or part of the NAAG recommendations into their operating rules.

To the extent you have a dispute and your program neither incorporates the NAAG recommendations nor gives clear and conspicuous notice of the program's rights to do less than is required by the recommendations, contact the consumer protection bureau of your state's attorney general's office and report the airline for unfair and deceptive business practices. It could tip the scale in your favor.

Postscript: A Cautionary Tale

You remember back at the start of deregulation all those independent regional and commuter carriers? Many of them were offering cheaper and more convenient services than the larger airlines; yet most of them have since either disappeared or, at the least, lost what independence they had. Why?

Because in the airline business, might makes right.

Some of the things which happened:

1.   Frequent flyer programs. That's right, frequent flyer programs. The smaller airlines didn't have the long routes which (i) allowed members to generate a lot of points and (ii) provided attractive destinations for using awards. The result was that even though the smaller airlines offered lower prices and more convenient services, they lost to the majors those business flyers who were more interested in accumulating frequent flyer points than saving their employer's time and money.

Some small airlines managed to connect their frequent flyer program to a major airline's program—which helped to stem the loss of frequent flyers. However, different from before where awards usually didn't cost the small airlines anything because the passenger was taking up an otherwise empty seat, now they had to pay the major airline for each award made—even though, for the same reasons, the award probably didn't cost the major airline anything either.

2. Yield management pricing. Where a smaller airline was offering all of its seats at low overall fares, the majors countered by offering just enough low-cost fares to keep the smaller airline from getting enough passengers per plane to break even.

3. Airport monopoly. Being larger and more established at the various airports around the country, the majors were able to make it difficult for newer or expanding regionals to obtain gates and departure/arrival slots at crowded airports. The majors often owned the gates and slots and either refused to sell them or leased the gates to the new airlines at high rates. In situations where the new gates or slots were auctioned off, the smaller airlines didn't have the financial muscle to win the bid. (Many of the small airlines which have so far survived, by the way, have done so by being able to dominate airports underserved by the majors, such as Southwest at Dallas' Love Field, Midway at Chicago's Midway, America West at Phoenix' Sky Harbor, Braniff at Kansas City in Missouri, Alaska at the Alaskan airports and at Long Beach, and Hawaiian and Aloha at the Hawaiian airports.)

4. Travel agent "bribery". Most bookings are made through travel agencies. Because of their volume, the majors were able to offer travel agents bonus commissions for reaching a certain level of sales. (Those airlines with a popular CRS program had ready data on which travel agents were booking the most flights.) Smaller airlines couldn't. The result was that many travel agencies effectively became mere dealerships for certain major airlines, pushing all their clients towards the flights which would generate the bonus commissions. (See discussion below at the top of page 74.)

5. Computerized reservation systems. As discussed above, until the computerized reservation systems were regulated in 1984, they tended to discriminate in favor of the major airline sponsoring the system. Smaller airlines either couldn't get listed on the systems or, if they could, found themselves relegated to page three. Even after 1984, though, the systems arguably gave their airline sponsors leverage over the travel agents.

Some smaller airlines were able to survive by striking "code sharing" deals with the majors (discussed above at page 10), where the small airline's flights shared the same airline computer designation code as the major. The smaller airline, though, had to (i) pay for this service and (ii) give up a lot of control of its scheduling and other matters to the major—

often going so far as to change its name on everything except its gates and planes to a standard nationwide "feeder" name incorporating the name of the major.

The result: A recent *Wall Street Journal* article indicated that the eight largest airlines now have control of 48 of 50 regionals through either ownership or code sharing.

So next time your hear one of those independent regional airline names from the past, you'll know what happened. Despite their generally lower prices and more convenient flights, they succumbed in the end to the muscle of oligopoly.

Makes you proud to be an American, doesn't it.

CHAPTER THREE

CHOOSING YOUR FLIGHT— THE CHEAPEST AIR FARE

The Four Major Sources of Differentials in Airfares

Many airfares are identical. As the industry gradually has become more oligopolistic since the first burst of deregulation, the setting of fares has moved further away from a free market and closer towards arbitrarily identical fares. Rather than getting together in a hotel room (which would be illegal), major airlines now float new nonmarket fares on their computerized reservation systems and see whether their fellow oligopolists go along. Thus, for instance, last year there was a move towards setting fares purely on the basis of mileage covered, regardless of market differences on various routes.

Despite the move away from the competitive market, differentials in fares still exist. Generally, apart from the obvious differences in the class of travel (first class, business class or economy), there are four basic sources of differentials in airfares:

1. Differentials in an airline's costs. Once an airline has committed to flying a given flight, it costs the airline very little more to fly an additional passenger than it does to fly an empty seat. The marginal food, service and fuel costs are minimal. The real difference in airline costs, then, arises not in the marginal cost of additional seats but in the average cost per seat (both filled and unfilled) between various airlines. For instance, the average cost per "available" seat mile for the four largest nondiscount airlines is roughly eight and a half cents; for the discount airlines, around six cents.

2. Differentials in competition. The more competition on a given route, the lower the price. For instance, according to *Consumer Reports*, last year TWA was charging $200 for a one-way coach fare from St. Louis to Indianapolis where it had no competition, but only $59 for slightly less distance from St. Louis to Chicago where it was competing with Southwest Airlines. Despite the move towards nonmarket per-mile fares, it would be difficult for TWA to do away with this difference if Southwest refused to go along.

3. Differentials in passenger demand. The higher the passenger demand, the higher the fare. The lower the demand, the lower the fare.

4. Differentials in what different types of passengers are willing to pay for a flight. Airlines try to charge a high fare to those whose decision to fly the airline is *not* governed by price, and a low fare to those whose decision *is* governed by price. The first category is made up mostly of business travelers—in part because their time is money so they can't afford to take a cheaper but less convenient flight, and, in part, probably the major part, because with business travelers (i) the person making the decision to take a particular flight, *i.e.*, the businessman or business-woman, is different from (ii) the person paying the bills, *i.e.*, his or her employer.

The airlines, of course, can't charge business travelers a higher fare purely because they're business travelers. That would be an administrative as well as public-relations disaster. Instead, the airlines have come up with restrictions on their cheap tickets which business travelers are likely to fail, such as having to book 21 days in advance, having to stay at least seven days or over a weekend and not canceling at the last minute. And the airlines purposely limit the number of the low-price promotional fares so they will be gone long before the average business traveler knows he or she will have to fly. (Ironically the business travelers aid the airlines in designing these restrictions by providing detailed information on their flight patterns through the frequent flyer programs.)

Arguably the advance booking and nonrefundable restrictions benefit the airline by providing some certainty. The real benefit, though, is that they allow the airline to charge its business travelers a higher fare. The proof? Since not all price-conscious, nonbusiness travelers can meet the restrictions, the airline effectively waives the restrictions through large discounts for the largest groups of such nonbusiness travelers, *i.e.*, children, students, senior citizens, soldiers and, to a lesser extent, the clergy.

How to Use the Four Major Sources of Differentials to Lower Your Airfares

1. Fly the airline with the lowest costs. In the US, these are primarily the discount, usually nonunionized airlines, such as America West, Braniff, Continental, Midway, Presidential, Southwest and Virgin Atlantic. (See Appendix Two at page 389 for their tollfree phone numbers.) You should do this as soon as possible, though. The discount airlines are rapidly disappearing. (See discussion beginning above at page 54 as to why.)

2. Fly the more competitive route. Try to reroute your ticket so it includes those routes on which the greatest number of airlines or the discount airlines are competing. For instance:

(a) **If your destination city or airport is dominated by a single airline which is keeping the fares high, fly to another more**

competitive city or airport within easy ground transportation of your true destination.

(b) Instead of flying nonstop on a noncompetitive route, break it into two competitive flights. For instance, let's say you want to fly from A to C but there is only one airline flying that route and it keeps the fares high. The routes from A to B and from B to C, however, are so competitive, that the total of the two fares on those routes are less than the fare from A to C. So instead of buying a ticket from A to C, you buy a ticket from A to B and another one from B to C. This is known in the trade as the "**split-ticket trick**".

Note, if you're flying round-trip, buy a round-trip ticket from A to B and another from B to C. If you ask for the single round-trip from A through B to C, the airline will charge you the higher A-to-C rate.

(c) Instead of booking your flight to the noncompetitive city, book a direct or connecting flight to a competitive city which goes through the noncompetitive city and then get off the plane in the noncompetitive city. This is the **hidden-city discount** referred to a few times above. Let's look at an example:

(1) You want to fly from A to B, but B is a hub dominated by a single airline which is keeping fares high from A to B.

(2) The hub airline has a flight from A through B to C.

(3) There is a discount airline which flies nonstop from A to C.

(4) The hub airline, in order to remain competitive with the discount airline, lowers the price of its A-through-B-to-C flight below what its own A-to-B fare would cost.

So what do you do? You buy a ticket from the hub airline for the A-through-B-to-C journey but get off the plane in B, discarding the B-to-C leg.

The airlines, of course, claim that this practice violates their rules. The legal significance of this violation is unclear. If it unlikely the airlines will sue you for a deficiency judgment because you failed to take the entire trip you paid for. However, at the very least, the airline will not allow you to check your bags to the intermediary hidden city. Some travelers have claimed they've been able to tip the check-in porter at curbside to use a hidden-city tag; however, you probably ought to travel only with carry-on.

In addition, if you're employing this device with a round-trip ticket, you should beware of the following two problems:

(1) Cancellation of reservations. Since you're not using the B-to-C outbound leg or the C-to-B return leg, your return reservation out from B to A may be canceled. To avoid this, you should make a separate B-to-A reservation, unrelated to the previous legs.

(2) Denied boarding. Technically the airline may have the right to stop you from using your B-to-A return ticket unless you give them proof that you have used the C-to-B return ticket. As a practical matter, however, if you present a confirmed B-to-A ticket, the airline check-in staff will probably not raise the issue.

(d) Instead of booking your flight as originating out of a non-competitive city, book the flight from a competitive city into the noncompetitive city and then out to your destination and discard the first leg. This device is the reverse of the hidden-city discount. It works most often when your local airport is a hub dominated by a single airline. In this case, assuming you live at B, you buy the A-through-B-to-C ticket, but use only the B-to-C portion. Because you're not using the A-to-B portion, though, you may encounter problems similar to those in (c) above.

3. Fly the less popular flights. Flights can be less popular for a variety of reasons.

(a) The airline is less popular. For instance, it may have a lousy image for on-time performance, safety or service. (For a ranking of the airlines on those matters see the boxes at pages 17, 44 and 46 above.) If one airline appears in the news ranked highest in the rate of customer complaints, it's likely to lower its rates to compensate for the adverse publicity. If there's a scare about the safety of a particular aircraft, such as the DC-10, the airline with primarily DC-10s is likely to lower its fares to compensate.

As third-world and Eastern European airlines are generally avoided by North Americans and Western Europeans, those airlines tend to offer lower fares. (Note, this occurs most often on routes outside the home country of such airlines, especially between New York and London. Routes to and from and within each airline's country are usually protected economically.)

An airline might also be less popular on a given route not because it has a poor image but merely because the airline or its flight is less known. This often happens when an airline is new to a given market or when an airline schedules a given flight only sporadically in order to reposition an aircraft in its system. To try to attract more customers, the airline will lower its fares substantially.

(b) The flight is inconveniently routed. Those flights which require several connections at out-of-the-way places between different airlines at opposite ends of the terminal involving waits of several hours are going to be cheaper than a nonstop flight. In the past, fares on connecting flights have been ten to 25 percent below nonstop or direct flights. Although recent oligopolistic pricing moves by the airlines have attempted to reduce this difference, it remains to be seen whether they can hold the line against the need to attract passengers to the less convenient flights.

(c) The flight is at a less popular time. Think of the times you would be less likely to fly, and those probably will be the cheapest times. Very early morning. Very late at night. Saturdays (except for international flights), midweek, or on a holiday. Christmas Day usually has the lowest load factor of the year. Thanksgiving Day runs a close second.

Generally the lowest air travel season during the year is from the first week in January to the second week in March, except to the ski and sun resorts. If you want the cheapest airfare to the ski resorts, try going in August; of course, you won't find the skiing all that attractive but then this handbook is about air travel not about skiing. The off-peak period for the sun resorts runs from September through the second week in December. The peak air travel period generally is from June through August.

(d) The destination is less popular. This isn't merely a matter of only traveling to places no sane person would want to go, like Bakersfield, California, or Fargo, North Dakota. Often you can travel to a popular place by flying to a less popular airport nearby and then taking ground transportation. For instance, to get to Los Angeles, it's often cheaper to fly to San Diego; to Washington, to fly to Richmond, Virginia; to Chicago, to Milwaukee; to San Francisco, to Oakland; to London, to Manchester; to Paris, to Luxembourg.

4.   Fit into the airline ticket restrictions. A recent survey showed that 91 percent of US air passengers paid an average 40 percent of the full fare price for their tickets. In other words, only nine percent of air passengers totally failed to meet airline restrictions for lower fare tickets.

Two conclusions can be drawn from this. One, if you pay full fare, you're probably an idiot. Two, if you're anything but an idiot, you should be able to get an average of 60 percent off full fare by meeting the airline restrictions.

There are several ways to accomplish this:

(a) Fit the restrictions directly. If you are a child, student, senior citizen, soldier (including seven days after discharge) or minister, find out what discounts are available. Book and purchase your seats the required period in a advance, stay over Saturdays and take the risk of nonrefundable tickets (which can be as low as 20 percent of the full fare).

(b) Fit the restrictions indirectly. If you can't meet the restrictions in a straightforward manner, be devious. Take as an example the **imaginary-Saturday-night-stay-over**, based on the cheaper fare if you stay over a Saturday night:

(1) Double round-trips. Recharacterize two round-trips to the same destination (Monday out, Friday back, Monday out, Friday back) as (i) one round-trip from home (Monday out, second Friday back) and (ii) another round-trip from the destination (first Friday "out" to home, second Monday "back" to the away destination)—thus, appearing to have stayed over a Saturday night on both round-trips.

(2) One-way round-trips. Similarly, if you want to make a single round-trip during weekdays (Monday out, Friday back) but would have to stay over Saturday night to get a discount of more than half the non-Saturday-night-stay-over round-trip fare, book a round-trip from *home* going out Monday and coming back the following Thursday and a round-trip from the *destination* going "out" to home on Friday and going "back" the following Thursday, and use only the outbound ticket on each round-trip, discarding the returns.

(c) Wait for the restrictions to change. If you can't fit into the restrictions even by devious means, don't despair. If, as the flight date draws nearer, the flight is still only partially booked, the airline often will lift the restrictions (or expand the low fare allocation) for new purchases. (Since it costs them virtually nothing to fly an extra passenger, they can lower the fare to whatever it takes to entice that passenger to fly and still make money on the margin.) Try to get yourself wait-listed for these changes. If you can't, call back periodically to see if anything has opened up. The best times are the day immediately after the various deadlines for advance purchase of reserved discount tickets.

(d) Get the restrictions waived. If the restrictions aren't changed, try to get the airline to waive the restrictions. If your travel agent does enough business with the airline, the airline may do it as a favor—especially if your agent tells the airline you will fly another "more convenient" airline if they don't waive the restrictions. If your travel agent fails, go to the airport before you purchase your ticket and ask the ticket desk supervisor to do it. If they're desperate enough to fill the plane, they'll do it.

How to Protect Yourself Against Airline Deceptive Advertising Practices

Although the Airline Deregulation Act of 1978 pre-empts states from enacting or enforcing any law relating to air-travel rates, routes or services, states still have the power to prosecute an airline for unfair and deceptive advertising. Accordingly, the National Association of Attorneys General, mentioned above at page 52, last year issued recommended guidelines for proper disclosures in air-travel advertising.

The guidelines basically require the airlines to disclose clearly and conspicuously sufficient information to allow the consumer to determine (i) if he or she can meet the eligibility requirements for an advertised low fare, (ii) the likelihood of the low fare being available when the consumer contacts the airline and (iii) the financial risks to the consumer of changing travel plans after purchasing the tickets.

Needless to say, the issuance of the guidelines was strenuously opposed by both the airlines and the Department of Transportation. It was argued, among other things, that requiring adequate disclosure to consumers might discourage the airlines from competing on price. Perhaps they were afraid that once the consumer was able to compare apples with apples, he'd discover that there really wasn't any price competition between the airlines, and the airlines would have to turn to some other deceptive practice to attract passengers.

Unfortunately, the guidelines are not regulations themselves but merely recommendations to the various attorneys general on how to enforce their own general statutes on unfair and deceptive advertising. So you still can't depend on an airline following the guidelines. However, the guidelines do give an excellent list of what the airline may be neglecting to tell you in its ad:

1.   Limited time availability. For instance, the offer expires the day the ad appears. (The DOT has said it is trying to stop this practice.)

2.   Limitations on right to refund or exchange a ticket. For instance, if you change your mind about your flight, your ticket will be nonrefundable, nontransferable or nonexchangeable.

3.   Time of day or day of week restrictions. For instance, the advertised fare is valid only for flights on Tuesday, Wednesday and Thursday afternoons.

4.   Length of stay requirements. For instance, you've got to stay over a Saturday night or away seven days.

5.   Advance purchase requirements. For instance, you've got to pay for the ticket thirty-days in advance.

6.   Round-trip purchase requirements. The advertised one-way fare applies only if you purchase a round-trip ticket. This is not unlike an automobile tire dealer advertising a single-tire price which turns out to be available only if you buy a set of four tires.

7.   Variations in fares to or from two or more airports serving the same metropolitan area. For example, the low-fare price to New York is, in fact, to Newark, New Jersey.

8.   Limitations on or extra charges for breaks or changes in itinerary. For instance, if you stay two days rather than one in Milan, you'll have to pay full fare for your whole itinerary.

9.   Limited availability of seats. For instance, there are only one or two seats available at the advertised low fare, which will be filled before you're able to look up the airline's phone number. (Does "bait and switch" ring a bell? Perhaps, "used car dealers"?)

10.   Variable availability of seats. For instance, an ad appears on Monday for a flight on Thursday. You call and are told there are no more low fare seats available. You pay the higher fare on Tuesday and on the flight sit next to somebody who tells you he bought the low-fare seat on Wednesday when the airline decided to make more available.

In addition, the guidelines prohibit adding surcharges (*e.g.*, for increased fuel costs) to the published fare. The fare may be only $20 but the surcharges for departure tax, landing fees, security, meals, fuel, labor and baggage handling adds up to $280.

Finally, the guidelines limit the use of words such as "sale", "discount" or "reduced" to describe only those special, briefly available fares which provide a substantial savings over the normal Apex or similar fare paid by 90 percent of airline passengers.

So when looking at any airline advertisements, be sure to go through the list above and see if any of the points are addressed. If they're not, ask the airline's reservations clerk. If the airline fails to disclose any of these things and then tries to apply it to you, you will have a good claim for unfair and deceptive advertising practices.

Why it's Difficult to Find the Really Cheap Fare

1. The information on the really cheap fare is in the control of those who want the passenger to pay more—*i.e.*, the airlines, who are selling the tickets, and the travel agents, whose commissions are a percentage of the ticket price. The normal travel agent commission is ten percent on domestic tickets and eight percent on international ones. (See also discussion of bonus commissions beginning below at the top of page 74.)

2. There is a generally high level of travel-agent stupidity and ignorance. Although the DOT requires all travel agents to have a policy of disclosing the lowest possible airfares to their customers, one survey on flights from San Francisco to Washington, DC, found only one out of twenty agents correctly found the lowest fare. Several quoted a "lowest fare" that was over three times the actual lowest fare.

3. More often than not, the airlines don't advertise their cheapest fares. They certainly don't advertise the loophole fares, such as the hidden-city discount and the split-ticket trick. But they also don't fully advertise many of their special promotional fares, because:

(a) Many of such fares are too short-lived.

(b) People who've already bought tickets don't like seeing their seat subsequently advertised for half the fare.

(c) If (b) happens too often, people will be discouraged from buying their tickets early at what is likely to turn out to be a high fare.

4.   Most of the airline's telephone reservation personnel are monitored by computer, which requires them to complete their business with you in under an average number of seconds. You ask them if rather than going direct to Dulles, it would be cheaper to take a red-eye to Chicago, catch the special-offer breakfast flight to New York and then do an off-peak weekend shuttle fare to National Airport, and you suddenly find yourself listening to the dial tone.

It's interesting that some airlines have begun using prison inmates as telephone-reservation personnel. Can you imagine? Some guy whose big trip each day is from a ten-by-eight cell he shares with a musclebound, violent, bisexual rapist and a six-foot-six, foreheadless country-boy who likes to strangle people in their sleep, down to a three-foot cubicle in the phone center in the basement of the prison where he's required to take orders from a computer—and then you call him up trying to find the cheapest way of flying from San Diego to Tahiti.

Talk about cruel and unusual punishment.

No wonder the itinerary he gives you includes a two-and-a-half-day layover at the airfield in Guam.

Gathering Flight Information Yourself

With deregulation, there are many more fares than before. On one day in June, for example, there were 334 different fares from Dulles International Airport to Los Angeles International. In addition, air fares are now adjusted almost continually to take account of changing market conditions. There are over 200,000 (that's right, 200,000) fare changes each day in the US. The average life of a fare is around five days.

The airline fare-setters have literally become like commodity brokers (which, in effect, is what they are), sitting in front of their screens, trying to squeeze the last bit of profit out of the market by changing the allocations of low-priced fares. If there are a lot of empty seats, more low-priced fares with less restrictions are offered. If a check of the competing airline's CRS shows a flight is sold out, the first airline immediately withdraws all its own low-priced fares on its competing flights.

To get on top of this constantly changing fare information yourself, you have to do the following:

1.   Check every airline and travel agent in your area. To find all the airlines flying a certain route, call the reservations clerk for an airline you know doesn't fly that route. The reservations clerks are least busy before 8 a.m. on weekdays.

2.   **Read the major consumer air travel periodicals.**

Box 3-1.	Major Consumer Air Travel Periodicals		
Publication	**Phone**		**/Year**
Airline Passenger Services	(213)493-4877		$75
Best Fares	(800)635-3033		$68
The Business Flyer	(800)343-0664	x935	$36
	(800)322-1238	MA	
Business Traveler's Letter	(800)942-9949		$59
Business Travellers International[1]	(212)697-1700		$30
Consumer Reports Travel Letter	(800)525-0643		$37
Corporate Travel Magazine	(800)223-6767		$55[2]
Executive Travel[1]	(212)867-2080		$65
Frequent	(719)597-8889		$28
Frequent Flyer	(800)323-3537	x0652	$52[3]
First Class	(214)404-9980		$99[4]
Nationwide Intelligence Bulletin	(517)752-6123		$95[5]
Runzheimer Reports Trvl Mgt	(708)291-9011		$295
Travel Smart	(800)FARE-OFF		$37
Traveler's Advisory	(800)222-9477		$24[6]

1. Published in England. Focuses on European air travel.

2. Free to qualifying subscribers - generally corporate travel decision makers.

3. Free with *OAG Pocket Flight Guide* subscription.

4. Free with membership in the International Airline Passengers Association, a 25-year-old organization providing substantial air, car rental and hotel discounts, travel insurance, airport business centers and other travel benefits to its over 100,000 members.

5. Detailed, expanded service available for $350 per year.

6. Free with membership in Airline Passengers of America. (See page 382.)

3.   **Pursue the cheap flight advertisements** in the back of the Sunday newspaper travel section.

4.   **Subscribe to one or more computerized flight schedules** which you can access over the phone with your home computer. (See Box 3-2 below.)

5.   **Organize on a master sheet all the information you've obtained,** taking special note of the various restrictions and penalties of each.

6.   **Continually recheck all your sources** to see if there have been any changes.

7.   **Gauge the market as to when the probability of a better deal occurring is less than the deal you will lose by waiting.**

Box 3-2.	Computerized Flight Schedules	
System	**Phone**	
ABC Worldwide Hotel and Travel Guide	(617)262-5000	
EASY SABRE	(800)433-7556	x4813
OAG Electronic Edition	(800)323-3537	
	(800)942-1888	IL
TWA Travelshopper	(800)892-1011	

These services are available variously through the Source, Compuserve, Delphi, Dow Jones, MCI Mail, Exchange, General Electric Network for Information, Tymnet and Prodigy. Prodigy, which carries EASY SABRE, substitutes onscreen advertising for connect charges and thus is probably the cheapest.

If you do all this, then you can be fairly certain of saving in price up to half what it cost you in time and effort to achieve the savings.

Let's face it. Unless you've got a mind like a Cray computer, it'll be virtually impossible to make sense out of all the times, routes, restrictions and penalties and then piece them together into a coherent journey. A friend of mine spent three weeks locked in a room trying to work out the cheapest fare from Montreal to Birmingham, Alabama. He was eventually pulled from the room, screaming at the top of his lungs and slapping at flight numbers which he said were crawling up his arms.

I got a letter a few days later from his mother, saying that he was doing as well as could be expected, and promising to send me an invitation to the funeral if any of his future suicide attempts were successful. She later sold an outline of the itinerary to Dungeons & Dragons. She couldn't use it for flying because it had been out-of-date as soon as it was completed.

The Easy Way to Find the Cheapest Domestic Fare

Assuming you've got better things to do with your life than spend it finding the cheapest airfare, the easy way to do it is simply to go to a low fare specialist. A highly recommended one is Traveltron, a division of Associated Travel Services, Inc., in California. It's two main advantages are:

1. **It uses a much greater variety of computer systems, including:**

   (a) **The OAG electronic tariff system.** This is an updated-daily computerized version of the monthly tariff book most travel agents use. By using it, Traveltron's staff can be much more up-to-date not only on the daily changes in US air fares (including introductory and promotional fares) but also on the filed-for changes which are to go into effect on a future date. In the latter case, Traveltron has often been ahead of even the airlines' own reservations staff.

(b) Three major airline computer reservation systems. Most travel agents use only one; and only 0.6 percent use three or more. The three programs allow Traveltron not only to reach second tier airlines which may participate only in one public CRS but also to overcome the delays in information transmittal between systems. Two areas where this is particularly important are:

(1) Last-seat availability. Because of communication delays between systems, airlines often estimate how many booking they will receive from other systems. When the estimate turns out to have been too large, the communication delays then mean the availability of these last seats will appear first on the airline's own internal CRS. The only way around this problem is for an agent to be able to directly access an airline's internal CRS through (i) the airline's own *public* CRS (in the case of each of the sponsors of the five major CRSs), or (ii) through a major public CRS in which the airline participates in a direct access feature (see preassigned seating discussion at page 35 above).

Unfortunately, there is no way to get such direct access to all airlines by subscribing to just one CRS. Although some airlines participate in the direct access feature through all five of the public CRSs, others do not. (In addition, some, such as Southwest, probably the lowest price airline in the US, don't participate in any of the five major systems.) So by subscribing to three of the major CRSs (as well as Southwest's own internal system), Traveltron increases substantially its ability to be first in uncovering the last available seat.

(2) Low-fare availability. A similar pattern occurs when the airline reassigns (as the date of an under-booked flight gets closer) unsold regular seats to the low-fare category or creates entirely new low-fare categories. Here, even when users of various systems can get direct access to an airline's *internal* system, those who don't subscribe to the airline's *public* system may not know all the access codes necessary to find the new types of fare—either because of inexperience with the airline's access coding or because the airline provides any new access codes for new fares first to subscribers to its own public system. By using the three CRSs, Traveltron has a much better chance of getting first crack at any newly created low-fare seats.

(c) **Traveltron's own auditing program** which:

(1) Ranks all flights on each route according to lowest fare;

(2) Checks any chosen fare to see if it's the lowest available; and

(3) If all the low-fare tickets on your preferred flight are gone, (i) books you at the available fare, (ii) waitlists you for a lower fare on that flight and (iii) *thereafter, automatically and repeatedly, day and night, keeps going back into the airline's internal CRS looking for a lower fare to open up on that flight,* allowing Traveltron to snatch it up before anybody else.

Traveltron also uses the same auditing technology for other things, such as when you've been forced to settle for a middle seat. After reserving you the middle seat, the program puts you in a queue with Traveltron's other clients and thereafter repeatedly searches the airline's database, looking for an aisle seat to become available (usually due to a cancellation).

Note, recently, some of the five major CRSs have begun introducing auditing features of their own. However, they apparently will be charging for each auditing access.

2. Traveltron has a staff experienced in finding the lowest fares. In searching for the cheapest flight, Traveltron does more than rank the published fares. Through years of experience, its staff is able to ferret out bargains not readily apparent in the published fares by using various loopholes, such as the split-ticket trick, the hidden-city discount, or the imaginary-Saturday-night-stay-over.

To give Traveltron the most to work with, they ask you to (i) start early, since that's when the largest number of cheap fares are available, and (ii) be as flexible as you can about dates, times and locations of your flights. To the extent you find the lowest fare too inconvenient for the savings, Traveltron will go up their list until you find an acceptable flight. Naturally, as with everything else in air travel, the amount of effort Traveltron puts into finding the lowest fare reflects how hard the customer wants them to push.

You can reach Traveltron at 1241 East Dyer Road, Suite 110, Santa Ana, CA 92705 or phone them at (714)545-3335. (If you buy a ticket from them and send them a copy of your phone bill, they'll reimburse you.)

Their business hours are 8:00 A.M. to 6:00 P.M. Pacific time, Monday through Friday. You can pay for your ticket using your credit card number over the phone. They'll mail you back the tickets (with boarding passes, if available) or send them to you Federal Express for around $8.75 overnight or $6.75 for two-day delivery. For a higher charge they can arrange for you to pick up the prepaid tickets at the airport.

Note, for an annual charge of $35, you can also join the Traveltron Express which gives you use of an 800 number, 24-hour emergency service, preferential treatment and negotiated rates on hotels and rental cars.

Note also, if you run a business, Traveltron's monthly report of your employees' travel will show how much more each flight cost than the cheapest published fare and why the employee chose the more expensive flight, *e.g.*, fewer connections, a shorter layover or, one of the commonest reasons, to accumulate additional frequent flyer coupons on a certain airline.

Ten Questions Which will Help You Choose the Travel Agent Who will Get You the Lowest Fare

Assuming you want a travel agent closer to home than Traveltron, there are ten questions which you can ask prospective travel agents to quickly separate the wheat from the chaff.

Question 1: Is your travel agency a member of ASTA [the American Society of Travel Agents]?

Wrong Answer: Who?

Correct Answer: Yes.

Comment: ASTA members are supposed to follow certain Principles of Professional Conduct and Ethics—though, as with most professional organizations, the policing is not always as strong as the consumer would wish. ASTA also runs a mediation/arbitration service between member agencies and their customers.

Question 2: Who on your staff is a Certified Travel Counselor?

Wrong Answer: What do you mean, "certified"?

Correct Answer: The person you will be dealing with.

Comment: The Institute of Certified Travel Agents certifies agents with at least five-years' full-time experience who've completed and passed the exams for a special training course. If the person you're dealing with doesn't have this, he or she probably doesn't have the experience necessary to find the best deal for you.

Question 3: Do you have a 24-hour, tollfree emergency number?
Wrong Answer: You mean 911?
Correct Answer: Yes. Our 800-number is printed on every itinerary.
Comment: This is crucial for the air traveler who needs quick changes to his or her itinerary while traveling, especially if trying to get the cheapest fare.

Question 4: How many CRSs do you use?
Wrong Answer: Can't you see? We use three of them *(pointing at three identical screens which all tie into the same system).*
Correct Answer: We use all five major systems plus Southwest Airlines' internal system.
Comment: If the agency uses less than five CRSs, it may be missing certain last-minute availability (see Traveltron discussion above) or be unable to obtain preassigned seating and preissued boarding passes for you (see travel agent inadequacies discussion above at page 37). If no agency you're considering can give you even a partially correct answer here, the agency should, at least, as a matter of policy, check last-minute seat-availability by phone with all airlines for which it does not have direct access on its CRS.

Question 5: Do you subscribe to the OAG electronic tariff system?
Wrong Answer: You mean this big book here?
Correct Answer: Of course. We check it every morning first thing when we come into work.
Comment: See Traveltron discussion above.

Question 6: Do you have an independent auditing program which finds the lowest fare and then continually searches for a lower fare to open up?
Wrong Answer: Why would you want that?
Correct Answer: Yes.
Comment: *Ditto* above.

Question 7: Have you ever received bonus commissions from an airline?
Wrong Answer: I don't see how that's any of your business.
Correct Answer: No. We spread our business around too much.

Comment: Bonus commissions are usually paid if the agent exceeds a certain amount of business with the airline—and then are paid on *all* the agent's business with the airline, not just the excess. If the agency is receiving bonus commissions, it probably means it's booking tickets with one airline to the detriment of its customers.

Question 8: Do you use a consolidator for your international tickets?
Wrong Answer: Isn't that illegal?
Correct Answer: We use several depending on the destination.
Comment: See discussion of consolidators/bucketshops below beginning at page 79. The agency should use different groups for European, Far Eastern and Indian subcontinent and within each group compare the prices of various consolidators.

Question 9: Can you give me a current hidden-city flight?
Wrong Answer: Say what?
Correct Answer: I can show you three.
Comment: See page 60 above.

Question 10: If I had to go from Los Angeles to New York on Monday, return to Los Angeles on Friday, go back out to New York on the following Monday and return to LA on the following Friday, how would you book the flights to get the cheapest fare?
Wrong Answer: On the CRS.
Correct Answer: In order to get the cheaper Saturday-stay-over fare, I'd book first and last flight a round-trip out, and second and third flights a round-trip from the other direction.
Comment: See imaginary-Saturday-night-stay-over at page 63 above.

If you can find an agency which gives the correct answer to these ten questions, snap them up. They'll be one in a thousand.

How to Reduce Travel Agent Commissions

Buying directly from the airline will not save you a travel agent's commission. The airline charges the same price to the consumer whether or not it has to pay a commission to a travel agent.

If you are going to do all the work yourself finding the cheapest fare, then you will want to use a travel agent who will rebate you part of the standard commission. McTravel Travel Services in Chicago charges only a flat $8 for issuing a domestic ticket and $20 for an international ticket. They then rebate to you in the price the full eight to ten percent agent's commission. If the commission is eight percent, you'll be saving money on any ticket which costs over $100. (You can reach McTravel at (800)333-3335, (312)876-1116 or (312)498-9390.)

If you don't want to deal with an out-of-town agency, some bank-related and credit-card-affiliated travel agencies offer discounts on tickets purchased through them which are effectively a rebate of the commission.

Failing that, ask your own travel agency whether they will rebate part of their commission to you. If you've done all the work and all they have to do is issue the ticket, they may be willing to do it.

Two Causes of Fare Differentials Which Apply to International Flights

In addition to the four major causes of fare differentials discussed above, there are two additional ones which apply to international flights.

1. Government regulation. Pursuant to the Chicago Convention of 1944, the various national governments retain ultimate control of flights to or from their country and the fares charged. Pursuant to the Federal Aviation Act of 1958, US airlines are prohibited from charging fares less than the government-approved ones. However, the Department of Transportation basically approves any reasonable fares the airlines want to set.

The problem is if a foreign government is protecting the profits of its flag carrier, then it will not allow US carriers to charge more competitive fares on flights to or from that country. (It may also try to limit the number of US carrier flights to or from the country—although it can't go too far because the US government demands reciprocity for allowing the foreign flag carrier's flights to or from the US.)

Unless both countries on a route are prepared to let the fares be set by competition, in practice what happens is that the fares are set either (i) by a bilateral agreement between the two countries' major airlines which have been granted the routes by their government or (ii) by a multilateral agreement among many such airlines, usually through the International Air Transport Association (IATA), a trade association of over 175 of the world's airlines.

2. Exchange rate fluctuations. IATA agreements require airlines to price their international tickets in the currency of the country where the journey begins. So if one currency falls or rises against another, the effective cost of a fare in one country will be different in the other.

The US government does not allow any automatic adjustment of fares due to changes in exchange rates. Instead each airline has to file a new fare which takes the change into account. Before filing the fare, those airlines who are members of IATA usually wait for the fare to be adjusted by IATA for currency movements (once every three months). The result is that fares tend to lag the foreign-exchange market somewhat.

How to Take Advantage of the Government Regulation of International Air Fares

1. Fly the carriers which do not belong to IATA. The major ones are Aeroflot (though they have recently applied to join), Continental, Icelandic, Northwest, Thai International, Singapore and Cathay Pacific. The fact they are not members does not automatically mean their fares will be lower. Most still attend IATA meetings as observers and often follow IATA rules when it is to their advantage. On the other hand, Aeroflot's fares have been so low at times that it's been accused of "dumping" its seats on the market just to raise hard currency.

2. Utilize the limited advantages of IATA fare-fixing rules.
For instance:

(a) Standard discounts. There are standard discounts for infants, children, students, youth, airline staff, seamen, school party groups and IATA sales agents.

(b) Maximum Permitted Mileage Rule. Under this rule, you can deviate from the one-way direct route between two points by 20 percent and make stopovers at no extra cost. By increasing the fare pro-rata you can increase the Maximum Permitted Mileage up to another 25 percent. Since the rule applies only one way, any unused portion of the 20 percent allowance for the outbound trip cannot be used for the return trip, and vice versa.

In addition to achieving free out-of-the way stopovers, the Maximum Permitted Mileage Rule can be used in conjunction with "hypothetical" destinations to lower your fare. For instance, let's assume that fares are charged purely on a dollar-per-mile basis. You are taking the following trip:

Figure 3-1. Maximum Permitted Mileage Rule
Without Hypothetical Destination

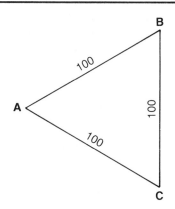

Your fare would be 280, the sum of (i) the A-to-C mileage (100), (ii) the C-to-A mileage (100) and (iii) the amount by which the A-to-B-to-C mileage exceeds 120 percent of the A-to-B mileage (80).

Now add a hypothetical destination B*.

Figure 3-2. Maximum Permitted Mileage Rule
with Hypothetical Destination

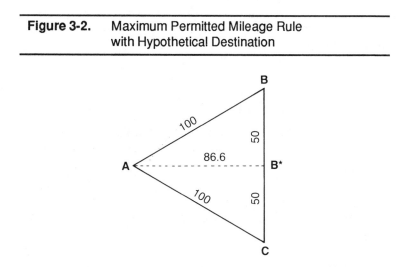

Your fare from A through B to B* would be 133.4, the sum of the A-to-B* mileage (86.6) and the amount by which the A-to-B-to-B* mileage exceeded 120 percent of the A-to-B* mileage (46.8). The fare from B* through C to A would also be 133.4, the sum of the B*-to-A mileage (86.6) and the amount by which the B*-to-C-to-A mileage exceeded 120 percent of the B*-to-A mileage (46.8). Add both halves together and you get a total cost of only 266.8.

Amazingly, under IATA rules, once you've calculated the fare on the hypothetical ultimate destination basis (*i.e.*, A to B to B* to C to A), you can then legitimately use the Maximum Permitted Mileage rule to get your tickets issued at the cheaper fare with the hypothetical ultimate destination cut out of your itinerary (*i.e.*, A to B to C to A).

The above example is only one of the many variations on this theme. So be sure to check with your travel agent on the applicability of the rule to your situation.

(c) Inclusive tour. There is an exception in the IATA rules for fares which are part of an inclusive tour. To qualify as an inclusive tour you will need to have your agent prebook your hotel and/or rent-a-car for a couple of days and sell you the flight as part of the package. Unfortunately, except to the USSR, East Germany, the Far East and Africa, the lower rates are usually still higher than the normal advance-purchase fares.

3. Buy your ticket from someone who is willing to violate the international agreements on fares. This by far is the easiest way to get a rock-bottom airfare to a popular international destination—particularly in those countries such as the US and Britain where the government does not try to enforce internationally agreed airfares.

Note: if an airline in the US sells its tickets to someone at a fare lower than the fare it has filed with the DOT, then technically the airline is in violation of the law; however, as a practical matter, the DOT has not shown much interest in pursuing such violators since all the airline has to do to make the fare legitimate is file it. The DOT has recently indicated it will prosecute violators only when the discounting is accompanied by some other form of illegal or deceptive activity, such as fraud, invidious discrimination or antitrust.

Generally, if the international airlines have tickets they can't sell at the approved fare, they sell them off quietly to certain wholesale travel agents. Usually the tickets are sold at the approved price, but, to get around the international agreements, the airlines pay an inflated commision (25 or 35 percent rather than the normal eight percent), effectively discounting the ticket. The wholesale travel agents, known as "consolidators" or "bucket shops", then turn around and sell the tickets to the public and certain travel agencies at below approved prices.

What You Should Know About Bucket Shops

Bucket-shop fares are usually significantly below even those you could obtain from a low-fare specialist (since the low-fare specialist deals primarily with legal, published fares), and don't have the requirements for advance booking, minimum and maximum stay-overs or even round-trip. Also, although it may be technically illegal for the bucket shop to sell you the discount fare ticket, it usually is not illegal for you to buy it.

The disadvantages of bucket shops are that:

(a) during peak periods the number of tickets can be limited;

(b) you often are unable to choose your airline, flight time (although you can pick the date) or specific route to your destination;

(c) the tickets are usually good only on the issuing airline and then only for the flight for which they were issued;

(d) there may be substantial penalties if you cancel or miss the flight (so you may want to arrange travel-cancellation insurance to cover yourself);

(e) flights originate only from gateway cities, primarily New York for European flights and San Francisco for Asian flights, so you have to arrange your flight to the gateway city separately;

(f) the flights may not qualify for frequent flyer points;

(g) you can't upgrade your ticket;

(h) there are often no or only nominal child discounts; and

(i) since bucket shops are unregulated, some are financially unsound and/or crooked. (To help mitigate this problem, deal only with bucket shops which take credit cards. If something goes wrong, you can refuse to pay that part of your bill when it comes due. Also, as soon as your ticket is issued, check with the airline to see that you have a reservation.)

There is a substantial bucket shop industry in London with a wider selection of destinations than the US. Many people take a US bucket-shop flight to London and then use a London bucket shop for beyond. Some London bucket shops will sell tickets over the phone on your credit-card number so you can purchase your onward ticket before you leave the US.

Bucket shops tend to be confined to the large metropolitan areas. You'll find them advertising unbelievably low fares in small classified ads at the back of the travel section of the Sunday edition of major newspapers. You can also sometimes find them by asking an airline for its "consolidator"; the third-world carriers in particular are happy to give you this information. Periodically you can also find lists of "consolidators" in *Consumer Reports Travel Letter*, mentioned above at page 68. For a listing of London bucketshops, call the Air Travel Advisory Bureau in London at 011-44-1-636-5000.

The initially quoted rates are usually lower than you will eventually be able to get but what you do get will still be low. Be sure to shop around; there is a wide variation in ticket availability and price.

Box 3-3.	Consolidators/Bucket Shops	
Company	**City**	**Phone**
Access International	New York	(800)333-7280
		(212)333-7280
Airlink Travel	New York	(212)867-7770
Bargain Air	Rolling Hills	(800)347-2345
		(213)377-2919
Destinations Unlimited	New York	(212)980-8220
Interworld Travel	Miami	(305)443-4929
Jupiter Travel	London	(01)434-0734
		(01)439-1712
McTravel	Chicago	(800)333-3335
		(312)876-1116
Maharaja Travel	New York	(800)223-6862
		(212)391-0122
STA Travel	London	(01)581-1022
Sunbeam Travels	Los Angeles	(213)483-8363
Sunline Express	San Francisco	(800)877-2111
		(415)541-7800

Note: There are many more consolidators/bucket shops than listed here. This list is only to get you started. For others, look in the sources mentioned above.

How to Take Advantage of Currency Fluctuations When Purchasing an International Flight

1. Down-currency one-way fares. As mentioned above, tickets must be purchased in the currency of the country where the journey begins. If the journey is a round-trip, the journey begins in the country where the round-trip beings. If the currency of the foreign country to which you want to go has declined substantially against the dollar, however, you could split your round-trip into a one-way flight to that country priced in dollars and a one-way flight back priced in the currency of that country. For many countries, you can buy the return one-way fare in the US before you leave in the foreign currency (or the current dollar-market-value of that currency). IATA has recently introduced new rules applying to one-way fares purchased in the US for travel between points outside the US. Under these rules, if a flight in one direction will be more expensive than the flight in the other direction, you must pay the higher fare between the two points, no matter which direction you are traveling. Fortunately, this rule probably will not be applied as the DOT has recently refused to approve it on the grounds it is discriminatory against US travel agents, (since it does not apply if you purchase the all-foreign ticket outside the US).

2. Down-currency round-trips. If you are going to make two round-trips to the country, you make the first and fourth legs a round-trip from home and the second and third legs another round-trip from the foreign country, getting at least one of your round-trips purchased in the foreign currency.

3. Imaginary origin. This is best explained through an example. Let's say you want to fly from Frankfurt to New York. Because of the decline in the Polish currency (or merely because there is less demand for air tickets in impoverished Poland), it is cheaper to buy a ticket in zloty from Warsaw to New York connecting through Frankfurt, than to buy a ticket in marks from Frankfurt to New York. So you buy the Polish ticket, discard the first leg and use only the Frankfurt-to-New York leg. Under a new IATA rule, however, this trick will now work on nonexcursion, nonconsolidator fares only if you buy the ticket in Poland. If you buy the ticket in the US, you'll have to pay the higher fare from Frankfurt to New York.

One way to avoid the new IATA rule on nonexcursion, nonconsolidator fares is to use an international travel agency with offices in Poland (or whatever cheap country you're targeting). Another is to make your trip only on a direct flight (where the plane stops in Frankfurt but you don't have to change planes) since the rule applies only to connecting flights. Another possibility: take an on-line connecting flight on a foreign airline which is willing to ignore the rule. (The airline is unlikely to be challenged—especially if it camouflages what is happening by giving both legs the same flight number (see discussion of flight number fraud below at page 6)).

Nine Not-Well-Advertised Ways that the Obsessive can Obtain Even Cheaper Fares

1. Ask the airlines whether they have flat-cost passes, set-price tickets or discount coupons. Flat-cost passes allow you to take unlimited flights for a set period. Set-price tickets give you a certain number of one-way flights for a set price, or a set price per flight for as many flights as you want. And discount coupons give you a set discount on each ticket as purchased. You'll have to press about these three programs. Often even the airline's reservation clerks don't know about them. Domestically these programs usually are limited to certain groups, such as seniors or students, or sold as part of joint promotions with travel clubs. Internationally the programs are usually open to all persons resident outside the country or countries within which the flights are to take place.

Note, US airlines offer similar programs for domestic US flights to persons resident abroad (even if those persons are US citizens). As a result, some US residents have been known to enroll in such programs while abroad, giving a foreign address, and then use the passes, tickets or coupons in the US.

2. Arrange to get yourself bumped (voluntarily or involuntarily) from an overbooked flight and receive free flight vouchers as compensation. (See *What Are Your Rights If You Are Involuntarily Bumped* at page 209.) The chances of getting bumped on any given flight in the US are slightly less than one out of 500 but with a little thought you can improve those odds greatly by choosing the airline with the worst bumping record at the most congested airport at the most congested time. (To do so, simply reverse the advice on how to avoid congested airlines, times and airports on pages 22 through 26 above, volunteering to get bumped as soon as possible.) Your odds will be increased even further, if you fly on a hot summer day when the thinner air means less passengers can be flown.

3. Purchase other people's frequent-flyer awards through a frequent-flyer broker. The savings here are not that great for economy-class tickets; but can be substantial for business- and first-class tickets. Some of the airlines allow coupons to be transferred to others; most don't. In fact, some airlines have brought lawsuits against some coupon brokers.

Even the airlines which supposedly do not allow transfer of coupons, however, often don't check to see if the person using the free ticket is the same as the person whose name is on the ticket. Some brokers will give you a refund if the ticket is not honored. Some people whose tickets have not been honored have bought a replacement ticket with their credit card and then refused to pay the bill on the grounds the coupon ticket should have been honored. Although not strictly legal, this technique did put them in a better bargaining position *vis-a-vis* the airline, which then had to decide whether it was worth the effort to contest the issue in court.

Box 3-4. Frequent-flyer Coupon Brokers		
Broker	**Phone**	
Airline Coupon Co.	(800)354-4489	
	(800)338-0099	(CA)
Coupon Bank	(800)292-9250	
	(800)331-1076	(CA)
Coupon Connection	(800)552-0700	
	(602)829-7300	(AZ)
Flyer's Edge	(312)256-8200	
Go in Class	(800)872-8587	
	(312)236-9696	
International Air		
Coupon Exchange	(800)558-0053	
	(713)781-1453	(Houston)
Travel Deluxe		
International (TDI)	(212)826-6644	

Note: Some of the companies also broker free-flight vouchers obtained from passengers who were bumped.

4. Purchase other people's bartered travel credit. Several airlines will pay suppliers or employees in whole or in part in the form of travel credit, which allows the suppliers or employees to travel free on the airline. The suppliers or employees then turn around and sell or barter these credits to other people. Discounts can range between 15 to 40 percent. Check your local newspaper or yellow pages under "Barter" or "Trade Exchanges".

Box 3-5.	Potential Sources of Bartered Air Travel Credit
Source	**Phone**
IGT (In Good Taste)	(800)444-8872
	(212)725-9600
Travel World Leisure Club	(212)244-3562
Barter Network	(203)874-8962
National Association of Trade Exchanges	(617)828-3221
International Reciprocal Trade Association	(703)931-0103

5. Volunteer as a free-lance air courier. Call the air courier services in the yellow pages or a courier broker, such as Now Voyager at (212) 431-1616. Advantage: a fare somewhat below bucket shops. (That's right, you don't fly for free). Disadvantages: limited destinations, often last flight of the day, carry-on only (the service uses your checked baggage allowance), no bumping protection and customs clearance delays. Integrated air freight and fax machines are rapidly depleting the demand for air couriers, so act quickly.

6. Use a standby broker. Many people know that during the peak travel months you can standby for flights between North America and Europe and obtain amazingly inexpensive tickets. (Elsewhere standby fares are generally no cheaper than regularly booked fares.) What people don't realize, however, is that at all times substantially discounted standby seats are available from standby brokers who receive last-minute empty seats from the airlines.

You have to be very flexible, however, since the availability for any specific date and destination is a matter of chance and the flights are only one way. (Two such brokers are Access at (212)333-7280 and Airhitch at (212)864-2000; the latter also does guaranteed return "Sunhitch" standbys to countries south of the US.)

7.   Construct a round-the-world fare. Groups of airlines sponsor combined fares in which you have unlimited travel for a specified period (usually six months, sometimes a year) as long as you keep traveling in a westerly (or easterly) direction and don't go past where you started. The savings here are particularly substantial in first or business class, but also exist in economy. Even with just a single destination in mind, it can be cheaper to get there and back by going around the world.

Unfortunately, there are not many round-the-world fares which take in Africa, South America or the Caribbean. Ask a good travel agent.

8.   Negotiate a lower fare with the airline. This is virtually impossible for an individual flyer to do other than with a very small airline. However, large companies do it all the time. According to one recent estimate, over ten percent of the fares paid by large companies are unpublished fares negotiated with the airline.

9.   Have a relative in a destination city die. Most of the major airlines have "bereavement" fares, which allow you basically to fly to a relative's funeral at the excursion fare without having to meet advance purchase and other restrictions. Normally an undertaker's certificate or newspaper clipping is required; if you can't get them until later, most airlines allow you to pay full fare and then claim a refund.

Don't Waste Your Time on Charter Flights

Admittedly charter flights can be somewhat cheaper than APEX fares but this one advantage is usually more than outweighed by the disadvantages:

  (a)   limited and inflexible schedules,

  (b)   special aircraft with cramped seating,

  (c)   crowded airplanes,

  (d)   late departures and arrivals,

  (e)   lower safety standards than required of regularly scheduled airlines,

  (f)   tour operators who are less willing to accept liability for lost or damaged luggage and tend to go bankrupt, and

  (g)   no computerized reservations system, so it is much harder to find and compare prices.

Your best but least certain charter deal will be to get a last- minute flight from a charter company which has been unable to fill its plane.

Sometimes the flights alone are offered but usually it is the whole tour; even then, the total cost can be less than the normal air fare alone. The easy way to find out about such flights is to join a "last minute travel club" for an annual fee of $35 to $50 per family or household. As a member, you then receive periodic bulletins and/or have access to a club phone hot-line. Despite the name, "last minute", tour flights usually become available several weeks ahead of the departure date.

Box 3-6.	Last-minute Travel Clubs	
Name	**Phone**	**Annual Fee**
Discount Travel Int'l	(800)253-6200	$45/family
Encore Short Notice	(800)638-8976	$35/household
	(301)459-8020	
Moment's Notice	(212)486-0503	$35/family
OAG Travel Club	(800)358-5858	$129[1]
Stand-Buys Limited	(800)255-1488	$45/family
	(312)943-5737	
Vacations To Go	(800)624-7338	$50/household
Worldwide Discount		
Travel Club	(305)534-2082	$45/family
1. Last-minute travel here is only one of many discounts provided.		

If a charter operator is not known to you, call the US Department of Transportation Office of Consumer Affairs, (202)366-2220, and see if there are any complaints on file against the operator.

What Ticket-Purchase Date You Should Give the Airline

After you have made your reservation, it is always best to tell the airline that you will purchase your ticket at the latest possible time for the fare you want. On nonrestricted tickets this can be as late as thirty to sixty minutes before flight departure, depending on the airline. If you give the airline an earlier date, on most airlines your reservation is subject to being canceled if you fail to purchase by that earlier date.

Note, a few airlines will cancel your reservations for unrestricted tickets if you have failed to purchase the ticket by a date roughly halfway between the reservation date and the departure date. However, if you make a special point of telling them you will buy it later (say at the airport before the flight), you can usually keep your reservation alive until that time.

When You Should Actually Buy Your Ticket

If you are fairly certain you are going to take a particular flight, you should purchase your ticket as soon as you make the reservation. Once you've bought your ticket, future increases in fare will not affect you— unless the airline has specifically reserved in conspicuous writing on the ticket the right to raise the fare. To be safe, before buying your ticket, check to see if there will be such a reservation on the ticket.

Note, if you make any change in your flight or in any flights which are part of the overall itinerary, then you will be subject to any increases in fare.

If your ticket is for a specific flight (*i.e.*, not an "open" ticket) and the airline subsequently lowers the fare for that flight, most airlines will give you a refund of the difference upon request. However, in order to obtain the refund, at the time of the request, you must be able to meet all the conditions of the new lower fare without regard to the fact you have already purchased a ticket at the earlier fare. For instance, if the new fare has a seven-day advance-purchase requirement, you have to make your request seven days before departure, notwithstanding the fact you bought your original ticket thirty days before departure.

For most airlines, there is no service charge for this refund.

Note: Don't depend on the airline to notify you of any reductions in fare. They won't. It's up to you to keep checking back to determine what's available. The best times to do this are immediately after the deadlines for advance purchase for various fares expire, such as 30, 21, 14, 7 and 3 days in advance.

The Best Way to Pay for Your Ticket

Not with a check. Not with cash. But with a credit card. Payment by credit card has the following advantages:

1. Phone purchase. You can purchase your ticket from the airline over the phone using your credit-card number and either pick it up at the airport or have it mailed to you. (Note, if you purchase a ticket to be picked up by another traveler at the airport, there will be a charge.)

2. Use of your money You will continue earning interest on your money until you pay your bill.

3.   Refund deadline. If you don't use a ticket you've purchased with a credit card and submit it to the airline for a refund, the airline by law must process the refund within seven days of receipt. There is no time limit set by law for refunds of tickets purchased by cash or check (although the Department of Transportation does recommend a limit of 28 to 30 days). The credit-card rule, of course, applies only if you bought the ticket from the airline. If you use a travel agent, make sure your agent pays the airline using your credit-card number.

4.   Bankruptcy protection. If the airline goes bankrupt before you can use the ticket, then within 60 days after the ticket has appeared on your bill (even if you've paid the bill), you can notify the credit-card company of this information and get a credit on your bill. Under the Fair Credit Billing Act of 1974, a creditor cannot force you to pay for a service that you did not receive.

5.   Dispute resolution. If you get in a dispute with the airline over cancellation or other such penalties, some credit-card issuers allow you to refuse to pay the amount billed. Most US bank and travel-and-entertainment cards limit your right to refuse payment to transactions made within your state or 100 miles from your home. However, as a matter of practice, many of the card issuers will waive those geographical limits for valued customers. The item and the finance charges accruing on the item usually continue to show on your statement, but the finance charge may ultimately be forgiven, sometimes even if you ultimately decide to pay the bill. Check with your credit-card company as to what their practice is.

6.   Ticket number. Your airline ticket number will be imprinted on your credit-card receipt, so if you lose your ticket, you'll be able to get a new ticket much more quickly than you would without the number.

7.   Theft protection. If your airline ticket is stolen, the thief cannot get a cash refund. All refunds on such cards must be credited to your credit-card account.

8.   Free insurance. You will get free life, accident (including rental car collision) and, with some cards, baggage and travel delay insurance. Check with your card company to see what insurance it provides.

9.   Favorable exchange rate. If you are buying the ticket abroad, you will often get a more favorable exchange rate. (See below at pages 175-176.)

10. Tax receipt. You will have a receipt of your expenditure for tax purposes. Some of the Gold cards now provide an annual breakdown of all charged expenses, broken out according to type of expenditure.

11. Rebate. If you buy the ticket on certain cards, you can get a five-percent rebate on the price of the air ticket—although you usually have to buy the ticket through an associated travel agent.

12. Check-in facilities. A few airlines allow those using certain credit cards to use the business- or first-class check-in facilities.

13. Frequent-flyer credits. Most of the major carriers now sponsor credit cards under which you can get frequent-flyer credits for amounts charged on the cards *for any purchase,* not just for a travel-related purchase. Most give you one free mile of credit towards the frequent flyer program for each dollar spent on the card. These cards usually have a higher annual fee than a normal card; but you also get several thousand in bonus miles when you sign up.

How to Charge Ticket Changes

If you decide to change flights and buy another ticket at the airport, the airline sales agent may wish to charge the new ticket on a separate credit-card form. Only go along with this if you are pressed for time. Otherwise, tell the agent to credit the old ticket towards the price of the new ticket and either bill or credit your card for the difference in price. It takes longer but you get billed only once for the flight.

Travel Agencies as Luddites

Several of the airlines have been experimenting with interactive automated ticket machines, similar to ATM cash dispensers. Using your credit card in one of these machines, you'll be able to research schedules and fares, make reservations, and purchase and receive tickets and boarding passes without the intercession of a human agent.

Unfortunately the human agent you'd be bypassing most likely would work for a travel agency. For that reason, certain travel agency organization—as always putting the interests of their customers first—have threatened to boycott any airline that relies heavily on self-ticketing machines. As a result, the airlines have failed to carry the idea beyond a very limited stage.

A similar problem has arisen with the airlines' simplified computer-ized reservations systems which can be accessed by home computers. (See above at page 69.) To avoid offending the travel agents, the airline-owned systems are designed so that the home user must select a travel agent to finally issue the ticket—insuring that a travel agency will get a commis-sion for doing virtually nothing. The OAG home computer reservations system, on the other hand, not being owned by the airlines, allows the user to have tickets direct-mailed or held at the airport by the airline, bypassing travel agencies (although, even here, American and TWA have required that any of their tickets issued through the OAG system must go through a Thomas Cook agency).

Needless to say, although in both of the above systems it is the consumer who does all the work obtaining a ticket, neither the travel agents nor the airlines have suggested that perhaps it might be fair to rebate some of the commission to the consumer. "Fairness to the consumer" is not a concept commonly used by travel agents and airlines when discuss-ing commissions.

How You can Check if the Information on Your Ticket is Correct

When you pick up your ticket, be sure to read it carefully. Besides checking the airline code and flight times and cities, check:

1.   Airport. If there is more than one airport at a city of departure or arrival, is the airport specified?

2.   Airline. Because of code-sharing, often your flight on a commuter airline or foreign airline will be marked on your ticket with the code of the major airline whose code it shares. In other words, from your ticket it will appear that you are flying on the major airline rather than the commuter—which could cause you some confusion when you get to the airport. Ideally the itinerary from your travel should tell what the real name of the airline is; sometimes, however, your agent will forget. For that reason if:

(a) your ticket has an asterisk or similar mark to the right of the airline code, or

(b) the route of your flight is one a major US airline is unlikely to fly, such as to a small town or to a foreign country, or

(c) the flight number is more than three digits, especially if it begins with something other than a "1", then ask your travel agent to check if the airline you're flying is really the major airline specified in the code. If your travel agent comes back and says the name is something like American Eagle, United Express or Continental Express, ask your agent to go back and find out the *real* name of the airline; names such as American Eagle *et al* are generalized "feeder" designations which can cover any number of small, "independent" commuters feeding the eponymous major airline. When you get to the airport, the flight gate and the plane may bear the name not of the generalized feeder designation but of the small independent commuter airline.

3. Confirmed reservation. Is the status box for *each* of your flights marked "OK"? If it isn't, then you don't have a confirmed reservation. This is exceedingly important. If you have a ticket which indicates a confirmed reservation, then, as mentioned above, under most airlines' conditions of carriage, the ticket will take precedence over whatever is or is not on the computerized reservation system.

Note, some international foreign carriers issue tickets without the "OK" because you have to reconfirm within 72 hours of flight time. Most, however, now include the "OK". Although they may request you to reconfirm within 72 hours of the flight, if you fail to do so, the "OK" on your ticket means you will still have a confirmed reservation.

4. Fare basis. What is the code marked in the fare-basis box? If you don't recognize the code from previous flights, ask the agent to decipher it for you.

5. Baggage. The "Allow" column of the "Baggage" section should contain the free baggage allowance to which you are entitled. "PC" indicates piece method. Otherwise, it should show the number of pieces and their weight. (See discussion of excess baggage rules below at page 111.)

6. Stamp. Is there an airline or travel agent stamp in the "place of issue" box in the upper right-hand corner? If not, your ticket is not valid.

7. Notices. Are there any notices of restrictions or penalties on or with the ticket? If there are, make sure you understand them completely. For domestic airlines, if there is not a conspicuous written notice of:

(a) restricted refunds;

(b) monetary penalties; or

(c) the airline's reservation of the right to increase the price after you've bought it, the airline cannot enforce those provisions.

Keeping a Record of Your Ticket Serial Number

It's important to keep a record of the serial number on the ticket. However, normally you don't have to make a special effort to note it down. If you buy your ticket using your credit card, the number will be on the receipt. If you buy your ticket from a travel agent, the printed itinerary the agent gives you will probably have the number on it or, if the agent is one of the larger travel agencies with a 24-hour emergency hot-line, they'll be able to get the number for you from their computer files.

Nonetheless, if you're one of those people who want to plan for every eventuality, you may want to make a photocopy of your ticket and pack it in your second bag. Presenting not just the number of your ticket but a copy of it as well will increase your credibility and hence speed up the lost ticket refund process considerably.

Note, in the same way, you might consider packing in your second bag a photocopy of all your important travel documents, such as your passport, inoculations record and visa. The photocopy can sometimes be as good as the original and, as with the ticket, will aid replacement if the original is lost.

How to Get an Immediate Refund if Your Tickets are Lost or Stolen

Your rights if you lose your ticket depend on the conditions of carriage of the issuing airline. The "issuing airline", the one which gives you the refund, is the one whose logo is printed on the ticket. The issuing airline is usually but not necessarily the first airline in your flight schedule.

Some airlines will not refund a lost or stolen ticket, period. Most airlines, however, will. Unfortunately, they also:

(a) charge you a $25 to $50 processing fee;

(b) take up to six months to get the refund to you;

(c) refuse to pay if anyone uses the ticket during the interim; and

(d) require you to sign an indemnity if someone subsequently uses the ticket.

Most airlines also require you to request your refund within certain time limits. For some this is as short as 30 days after departure; for others as long as a year and 30 days.

If, after losing your ticket, you still want to take the flight, your best chance to obtain a quick refund is to go to the airport on the day of your flight, present a photocopy of the ticket and loads of identification to the ticketing staff, and ask them to give you a replacement ticket on the spot. Imply that if they don't give you a replacement, you won't take the flight. Many airlines allow their ticketing staff to make such a replacement and even waive the normal fee if "hardship" can be demonstrated. Most airlines, however, will require you to sign an indemnity if the lost ticket is subsequently used by someone else.

If the ticketing staff say they can't give you a replacement ticket and require you to send your lost ticket form through their normal procedures (which may take months), you'll have to purchase the replacement ticket. Most airlines will charge you the going fare for the new ticket rather than the fare you paid for your own ticket; however, normally the amount of the ultimate refund will be the new rather than the old fare. *If the new fare is cheaper, be sure to request a refund for the lost ticket rather than the replacement ticket.*

Some passengers have been known to try another method of obtaining an instant refund. What they do is charge the replacement ticket to their credit card. Then, when they receive their credit card bill, they refuse to pay the charge for the new ticket on the grounds that the airline is refunding the cost of the new ticket. The airline may still take several months to go through its procedures, but now the passengers are in the same position as though they had obtained an immediate refund of the price of their lost ticket when they purchased their replacement ticket—assuming the credit card company is willing to waive the finance charge upon settlement. With appropriate finesse, some people have apparently been able to avoid the airline's processing fee as well.

How to Lose Your Right to a Refund on a Fully-Refundable Ticket

Most airline tickets cease to be valid after a year. Depending on the airline, at that time or sometime during the subsequent year, you lose your right to obtain a refund as well.

As a practical matter, however, no passenger ever lost any money because of a failure to get a refund. This is because the only people who ever fail to request a refund within a year or two are business travelers who aren't paying for the tickets themselves.

In fact, it's precisely because they aren't paying for the tickets themselves that businesspeople can let their unused tickets lie around scrunched up at the bottom of their desk drawers until the right to refund has expired.

If you happen to be an employer, don't despair. Even though your right to a refund expires, the more reputable airlines will still give you a refund as a matter of policy.

How to Lose the Right to a Refund on Certain Foreign Fully-Refundable Tickets

Several foreign carriers will not allow a full refund on a fully-refundable ticket if you fail to turn up for the flight. To get the full refund, you have to have canceled your reservation before the flight.

What Happens if Your Flight Coupon Becomes Separated from the Passenger Coupon

Answer: Nothing.

In airline lingo, the portion of your ticket which is torn out for the flight is the "flight coupon" and the red carbon copy backing is the "passenger coupon". Generally the airlines' conditions of carriage say they will honor a flight coupon as long as it is presented with the passenger coupon. Except for one airline, American, the US airlines' conditions of carriage do not say that the flight coupon has to be *attached* to the passenger coupon.

Why Some Partially-Used Tickets Produce Larger Refunds than Others

If your itinerary involves more than one flight and you terminate your trip before all the flight coupons are used, the amount of your refund depends on whether your termination is considered voluntary or involuntary. If it's voluntary, then generally you receive back the fare for the balance of the trip. If it's involuntary, then generally you receive back the difference between the original fare and the fare for the portion used.

In an ordered world where there were no discount fares and all fares represented merely the number of miles traveled, there wouldn't be any difference between the refunds for voluntary and involuntary terminations. However, in the real world there is often a major difference. For instance, let's take the hidden-city discount discussed above at page 60, in which due to competitive pressures, it is sometimes cheaper to fly from A through B to C than it is to fly from A to B. Let's assume you buy a ticket from A through B to C, but terminate your flight at B. If your termination is involuntary, you will get back the fare from B to C. If your termination is voluntary, you will get back nothing, because the fare from A to B is more than the fare from A through B to C.

Differences can be increased further by the way some airlines define their "deemed" fares. For instance, some airlines say the deemed fare for the used portion of the trip shall be the *full* fare, even though you, like most travelers, are traveling on a non-full-fare ticket. So if you buy an apex-fare round-trip ticket to Europe saving you 60 percent off full fare and then terminate the trip voluntarily after the outbound leg, the fare for your outbound leg will be deemed to be that for a full-fare one-way trip; since this will be more than the apex-fare round-trip, you won't receive any refund at all. On the other hand, if you terminated involuntarily, you'd be refunded the fare for a one-way trip back. (Generally this latter fare would be the lowest "comparable" fare, not, as it would be if the airlines were consistent, the full fare.)

How to Obtain the Largest Refund for a Partially-Used Ticket

Answer: Characterize your termination as involuntary rather than voluntary.

This is easier than it may sound because the airlines' conditions of carriage tend to define involuntary rather broadly. Of course, you'll have to check your particular airline's conditions of carriage to see what they say. (For those which follow the old CAB format, the involuntary termination provisions will be under Rule 260.)

For most airlines, there are two methods which could possibly work to get your termination qualified as involuntary. As an example, let's take the hidden-city A-through-B-to-C situation above, where you terminate your flight at B. In that situation your termination would qualify as involuntary if:

(a) **Your B-to-C flight is delayed or canceled or your A-to-B flight is late so you would be unable to take your B-to-C flight even if you wanted to, and the airline does not offer you a replacement flight suitable to you.** Note the language: "suitable to you". This means, for instance, if you had in fact intended to take the B-to-C flight and your missing the connecting flight has made you miss a meeting at C which was the purpose of your B-to-C trip, any replacement flight is going to be unsuitable, so your termination would still qualify as involuntary.

Note, technically, under most airline conditions of carriage, *any* delay of your B-to-C flight could trigger an involuntary refund; however, as a practical matter, the delay should probably be long enough to give you a colorable reason for not going ahead with the flight.

(b) You become unacceptable as an airline passenger. Most of the airlines have detailed rules on what makes a passenger unacceptable (see details below beginning at the bottom of page 215); if they refuse to board you on the B-to-C flight because you are unacceptable, your termination of the flight should be treated as involuntary—even if the unacceptability is somehow within your control.

Among the items listed in many airlines' conditions of carriage which would make you unacceptable: your refusing to allow you or your baggage to be searched; your refusing to produce identification if requested; your not having your passport or visa (on international flights); your having a contagious disease or a bad odor; or your being disorderly, abusive, violent, drunk, barefoot, mentally deranged, both blind and deaf or unwilling to comply with the no-smoking requirements. The fact that any of these things began only after you took the A-to-B leg of your journey should not prevent your termination from being involuntary.

Check the airline's conditions of carriage for passenger unacceptability. For those US airlines following the old CAB format, these are under Rule 35. You'll have to be prepared to quote chapter and verse because the airline will naturally want to resist allowing your voluntary act to cause your termination to fall under the definition of involuntary for purposes of a refund. Nobody likes being hoisted on their own petard.

The result: In the hidden-city discount example above, you not only travel more cheaply between A and B by buying a ticket from A through B to C and getting off at B but, if you're successful at having the termination legitimately qualify as involuntary, the airline will pay you a refund for the B-to-C trip you didn't take. In effect, the airline will be paying you a substantial amount for taking what is already the cheapest fare.

It makes you think there really may be a God out there somewhere after all.

How to Use Your Ticket for a Different Airline's Flight

1. **Full-fare tickets.** Full-fare tickets are generally transferable among major (but not necessarily the minor) airlines of the same country—though you will have to make up any difference in price. If you wish to

use a ticket from one country's airline on another country's airline, transferability depends on the existence of an agreement between the two airlines. British Airways and Air France, for instance, have such an agreement on certain routes. If there is no such agreement, then you will have to go to the issuing airline's ticket counter and get the ticket endorsed over to the other airline. Depending on the lines, this can be a time-consuming process.

2. Restricted-fare tickets. For restricted fares, transferability depends on the inter-airline agreement and the ticket contract. If the ticket is refundable, you can usually, without endorsement, use the restricted ticket on a competing domestic airline which has the same type of fare—though you will probably be on a standby basis. With endorsement there should be no problem. If the fare on the alternative flight is higher, you will probably have to make up the difference to get the endorsement or have it endorsed only up to the amount of the original fare.

3. Nonrefundable tickets. If the ticket is not totally refundable, it must be endorsed to be transferred and the airline will normally do so, if at all, only if you pay all the cancellation penalties or the airline is somehow to blame for you having to change flights.

Using Your Restricted Ticket on an Earlier Flight

Many airlines will allow you, as a matter of discretion, to use their restricted ticket to take an earlier flight to the same destination on a standby basis. Thus, for example, if there were a potential on-line connection which your travel agent would not book because it was too close to the arrival time of your incoming flight (so instead your agent booked you on a much later on-line connection), you could still try to make the earlier on-line connection on a standby basis at no extra cost and save yourself a lot of waiting at the airport.

Profiting from the Transferability of Nontransferable Tickets

Technically most airlines' conditions of carriage prohibit you transferring your ticket to another person. However, as a practical matter, on domestic flights, airlines seldom ask for identification. (On international flights, they normally have to see your passport and/or visa to be sure you'll be admitted into the destination country; if the foreign country won't admit you, the airline is usually required to bring you back whether or not you can pay.)

The lax enforcement of the nontransferability provision has made it possible for people who buy low-price advance-purchase domestic tickets to resell them after the advance purchase deadline has expired for a price somewhere between what they paid for them and the higher fares now required because the advance-purchase deadline has expired. You see these people advertising in the "Tickets" section of the Sunday newspaper all the time. Rather than pay a penalty to the airline for canceling their reservations, these people are actually making a profit by selling their cheap tickets for more than they paid for them. I wouldn't be surprised if some of them are actually speculators who never intended to take the flight anyway.

The people buying these tickets from the newspaper ads also are "profiting" from the transferability of the tickets since they are able to buy the tickets after the airline's advance-purchase deadlines have elapsed more cheaply than they could now buy a ticket from the airline. Occasionally, when the market is going their way, they are even able to pick up tickets at below the seller's cost. Of course, anyone buying such tickets always has the risk that the airlines could get sticky about enforcing the nontransferability rules.

When You can Get a Refund (or Another Flight) on a "Nonrefundable" Ticket

1.   Airline fault. Despite the fact that your ticket says it is nonrefundable (or only partly refundable), the conditions of carriage usually require the airlines to give you a full refund if your flight was canceled for whatever reason or the airline was responsible for you missing your flight.

2.   Illness or death. If you missed the flight due to an illness or death in your immediate family or, on some airlines, the illness or death of the person traveling with you, and can present written proof of this from a doctor or funeral director, most conditions of carriage allow you to use the ticket on a later flight to the same destination. A few will even allow you to cancel the trip altogether and obtain a refund of the full fare. If you don't have the proper certificate with you, many of the airlines will require you to buy a new ticket but allow you to apply for a refund when you finally obtain the necessary documents.

3.   Other legal cause. Although not required to by their conditions of carriage, some airlines will also allow you to take a later flight or even cancel and obtain a refund if you're subpoenaed or called for jury duty.

4.   Late arrival at the airport. If you arrive at the airport after your flight has departed (say, because automobile traffic was heavily congested), many of the better airlines, as a matter of discretion, will let you use your nonrefundable ticket to standby for a subsequent flight on the same airline to the same destination. You won't get a refund but you won't lose the value of your ticket.

How You can Get a Little Something Back Even if You Didn't Get Refunded Everything

In the price of a ticket, the airlines include an eight-percent Federal transportation tax. When the ticket is not used, the tax is not due. But many of the airlines have still been basing the nonrefundable portion of the ticket on the whole price of the ticket, including the tax. Several suits have been brought to force the airlines to refund the part of the penalty based on the tax portion.

One lawsuit brought against Western was settled after the airline was taken over the Delta. Delta offered passengers who had paid 25-percent and 50-percent penalties, cash refunds of $4.80 or 7,000 frequent flyer miles.

If you've had to pay a penalty recently based on the full price including tax, check with the airline and/or watch the newspapers to see if there's a settlement offer out there for you.

I know $4.80 is not a lot. But I don't want you saying *The Airline Passenger's Guerrilla Handbook* failed to save you any money at all.

C H A P T E R   F O U R

HOW TO PACK
FOR THE FLIGHT

The *Sine Qua Non* of Successful Air Travel

If you're going to have the freedom to employ the various strategies and tactics set forth in this book, then you've got to learn to travel light. Never take more than what you can carry into the plane. Otherwise you'll soon find yourself in chains, held hostage to what can only be described as "the tragedy of checked luggage".

I'm sure you know what I'm talking about. You've seen those pathetic people, more bags than hands, staggering through the airport looking for a check-in line less than two hundred yards long; or after check-in, hanging around for a five-hour-delayed flight because they're unable to retrieve their luggage from the belly of the beast to get on an alternative plane; or after the flight, waiting most of the night in baggage claim for their half-destroyed suitcase finally to be puked up by the mechanical luggage eater; or, stripped down to their shorts, fighting their way through the mobs around the revolving rubber track where their bags are running a frantic gauntlet of thieves and the nearsighted.

Or perhaps you've heard of passengers who anger their airline in some unknown way and discover, let us say, after a flight from London to Paris, that their bag has been routed by way of Waco, Texas. There, in the infamous luggage graveyard, the bag invariably either vanishes into the eleventh dimension or, if it's not particularly lucky, is spirited away by a local cargo cult to be used in a charismatic ceremony involving an unwilling donkey.

Not a pretty sight, I can tell you.

The Perfect Luggage for Traveling Light

The first step on the road to traveling light is to choose the right luggage. It's got to be something that is easy to:

(a) carry on the usual fifty-mile hike to the gate;

(b) sneak onto the plane with you; and

(c) store in the inadequate cabin space once you get there.

I've found these criteria are best met by (i) a small nylon suitcase with wheels and a leash, supplemented by (ii) a nylon garment bag that can be carried by a shoulder strap.

I say nylon because it's light. I know leather has high status. But who wants to carry half a cow with him just to impress passers by? Remember, you're going to be carrying these bags everywhere. You don't want to have something which, when empty, feels like it's already packed.

A few other thoughts:

1.   Suitcase. There are a lot of good suitcases around. The main criterion (apart from weight) is that it have at least one nylon-thin side which unzips so that if the suitcase is lying on its side under the seat, you can gain access merely by unzipping part of the top side—as opposed to having to lift the case out as you would have to do with a normal hinged case. Ideal is the three-partition case which has zippered access on either side plus a hinged central compartment for heavy items.

2.   Garment bag. Contrary to suitcases, a good garment bag is hard to find. Generally, a garment bag should have the following eight characteristics:

(a) **No frame** on either the main compartment or the pockets, except for a firm spine across the back of the fold where the shoulder strap attaches. In order to be hung easily in the coat closet or placed in the overhead rack, the garment bag's thickness and foldability should be determined primarily by its contents not by a frame. The same goes for any pockets on the outside.

(b) **No ridged or buckled pockets on the side which rubs against your spare tire** when you're carrying the folded bag by the shoulder strap.

(c) **A large, fixed shoulder-pad on the strap.** Nothing's worse that having to keep adjusting a small pad that's sliding up and down the strap.

(d) **A hook which does not have to be disconnected and is stored in a small Velcro pocket or snap lock near the end.** That way, every time you want to hang the bag in the plane with an aisle-full of passengers behind, you don't have to retrieve and refasten the hook—an operation that not only takes time but usually requires two hands.

(e) **Gripping hanger locks which operate on ordinary hangers.** Rather than just a loop to put the hangers through, you need some mechanism which will hold them tight; so the hangers don't slip around or even worse fall out, wrinkling your clothes. The grip lock should work on ordinary hangers, so you can pack clothes directly from your closet without having to change hangers. The best bag will have two separate grip locks side by side at the top, so that by placing one hanger on one and the next on the other, you can fit more hangers into the same thickness.

(f)   A C-shaped zipper opening for the main hanging compart-ment, rather than just a straight zipper down. A C-shaped zipper allows you easy access to your full-length garments. Instead of having to unpack everything at your hotel, you can hang your bag in the closet and take the clothes out as you need them.

(g)   Nylon, self-healing zippers, which never rust, stick or, most importantly, snag your clothes.

(h)   A shoe-compartment with outside access, which will allow you to avoid getting mud or shoe-polish on your clothes when storing or retrieving your shoes. Outside access is also a lot more convenient than fishing through the hanging clothes trying to undo a zipper at the bottom.

After several years of searching I finally located a nylon bag which had all of these things. It's the 4250 Series Hartmann H4 Continental Hangbag made out of coffee-colored nylon "Fisherman's Packcloth" treated with Teflon. There are 43-inch and 48-inch length versions. Try it, you'll like it.

3.   Locks. The suitcase should have a combination lock so you don't have to carry extra keys with you. A combination lock is also harder to pick than a key lock. With a lock on your case, you won't have to worry about your valuables when you're away from your seat in the plane.

For the garment bag I recommend buying small combination pad-locks which not only can be used to lock some of the compartments of the case but, when you're sleeping in an airport, can also be used with the strap on the garment bag to lock both your garment bag and your suitcase (through the suitcase's handle) to an airport chair. The padlocks I use are Prestolock and are available for $7 to $10 at good luggage stores. If you can't find them, contact Presto Lock, Inc., at (201)340-1000.

I'm Sorry but Size Really does Matter

Each airline has its own specific carry-on limits. However, these limits often underestimate the actual space available and are seldom strictly enforced. Generally, for 737 aircraft and larger, the suitcase will fit under the seat if it is within 9" X 14" X 22", or in the overhead compartment if it is within 14" X 21" X 36". To fit in the cabin closet, the garment bag generally should be within 4" X 23" X 45".

If you want to be safe, following are the more specific airline limits.

Box 4-1.		U.S. Airline Carry-on Limits			
Airline	**No.Pieces**	**Weight**	**Under**	**Over**	**Garment**
Alaska	2	No limit	8x15x23	10x17x36	4x23x45
Aloha	1	20lbs all	8x14x36	40"total	Fit
America West	2	No limit	45" tot	45" total	54" tot
American	2	70lbs ea.	9x13x23	9x20x26	Fit
Braniff	2	No limit	9x13x17	9x13x17	—
Continental	2	No limit	9x14x22	10x14x36	4x24x45
Delta	2	40lbs ea.	45"	total	each
Eastern	1	70lbs	45"	w/7-1/2"h	4x21x40
Hawaiian	1	No limit	8x10x16	40" total	40" total
Midway	2	70lbs all	45"	total	all
Northwest	2	No limit	9x14x20	10x14x36	Fit
Pan Am	1	70lbs	45 total	9x13x23	Fit
TWA	2	70lbs all	45 total	8x16x21	—
United	2	50lbs all	9x14x22	Fit	Fit
USAir	2	40lbs all	45"	total	all

Be warned, however, that the limitation may be less on (i) aircraft smaller than a 737; (ii) if the aircraft is crowded (either at the flight attendants' discretion or according to a set formula, *e.g.*, more than 50-percent full); or (iii) on long-distance international flights. On the other hand, the flight attendants will often allow more carry-on in first class and business class, and, if the flight is uncrowded, in economy. In addition, you can often legitimately carry-on more than one or two bags as long as their combined weight and dimensions do not exceed the above limits.

The Loopholes in the Carry-on Rules

Different airlines' conditions of carriage have different exceptions. However, generally carry-on restrictions do not apply to a purse, an overcoat, infant's food (if you've got a kid), an infant's safety seat, a camera, a reasonable amount of reading material, an umbrella, a walking stick, a pair of crutches or other prosthetic device, or, for a few airlines, a briefcase and a foot rug. On TWA there's also an exemption for up to ten pounds of citrus fruit in a net bag. Most, as a matter of common sense, also allow you, if you've got an infant, to take on a small carry cot, changes of baby clothes, blankets and diaper bag. In addition, on international flights, you can usually take on any duty-free items acquired since check-in.

Some people desperate for space (as occurs when returning from holiday with new purchases) have used these exceptions to expand their effective carry-on limit—bringing on, in addition to their normal carry-on bag, an extra-large purse, a large camera case (with something other than a camera inside), an overcoat (with the pockets stuffed), a diaper bag (filled with clothes and a camouflaging layer of diapers on top), several books bound together with a carrying strap and a duty-free bag filled with their dirty laundry.

The biggest loophole in the carry-on rules is their failure to restrict the clothing you wear. Theoretically you could wear a suitcase-full of contents on your body and then, after you board the plane, take everything off and store it in the overhead rack. To be safe, however, you may want to wait until after takeoff before disclosing you're not quite as obese as you look.

The Problem with Wheeled Suitcases

To pull a wheeled suitcase behind you on a leash, you've got to be a fairly self-confident person. Wheeled suitcases, you see, are much like pocket electric fans—eminently logical and practical, yet for some indefinable reason, embarrassing.

One of my friends, on my advice, bought a wheeled suitcase but after his first trip gave it up. One difficulty, of course, was the hillbillies posted throughout the airport who, as he went by, pointed in amazement, guffawed and made noises as though they were calling a dog.

More serious for my friend, though, were the corrugated surfaces on the floors at the beginning of escalators or people-movers, placed there, he was sure, specifically so the wheels on his case traveling over them would produce an exceptionally rude noise—without fail causing everyone within fifty feet to turn and stare at him suspiciously.

"Looking back on it now," he told me later, "I can see I just didn't have enough self-confidence. A self-confident man wouldn't have kept trying to explain to people fifty-feet away exactly what'd made the noise."

I saw my friend the other day in Kansas City, sweating and panting as he lugged his heavy suitcase from one end of the terminal to the other to make a connection.

"One arm may now be longer than the other," he told me, "but at least I can sleep at night."

The Best Luggage for a Day-Tripper

It's not unusual nowadays for a business flyer to take a thousand-mile day-trip. A lawyer from New York will go to Minneapolis for the day; or a banker in Chicago to Miami. In that situation the most the business flyer needs to pack is his or her work papers, a good book and, in case a change of schedule requires an overnight stay, a small emergency toiletry kit and a fresh shirt (underwear and socks, as all experienced business flyers know, can be turned inside out). There's no reason to take a suitcase and/or a garment bag.

From a practical standpoint, the ideal piece of luggage for such a day-trip is a zippered, nylon knapsack. It's lightweight, secure and easy to carry. Unfortunately, though, most business travelers find nylon knapsacks embarrassing. I don't know why this is. Perhaps businesspeople are embarrassed by the appearance of practicality.

Recently I've noticed that, despite this, some businesspeople, especially the younger ones, have begun to use knapsacks. Even among them, however, there seems to be a slight uneasiness. Rather than wear the knapsack over both shoulders (which distributes the load evenly and allows both hands to be free), they hang it by the right strap over their right shoulder and grasp the strap near the top with their right hand. They just don't seem to have the self-confidence to go all the way.

If you're someone who'd be mortified to be seen carrying a knapsack by even one strap while wearing a business suit, a good compromise would be a leather briefcase with a detachable shoulder strap. It allows you to carry the load on your shoulder and to have both hands free for periods of time (before the strap slides off), and it doesn't look like a nylon knapsack. Most importantly, just before you get to your meeting, you can detach the strap and hide it inside your briefcase so that none of your business associates will have any suspicion that you might be a practical person.

The Best Luggage for Checking

If you are to check your bags, you should use luggage which you will not mind never seeing again.

To increase your chances of seeing it again and in the same number of pieces in which it was when you checked it, I suggest that your luggage also:

1. Be made of a heavy duty nylon, which is more resistant to tearing and abrasion than canvas or vinyl and impossible to dent like molded metals and plastics.

2. Use zippers and locking buckle-straps rather than clasp locks built into the edge of the case. The latter easily pop open when the case is dropped, and if the case frame is bent, can be impossible to put together again.

3. Have at least two reinforcing straps which go all the way around the case. If your bag doesn't come with them, they can be obtained separately from any good luggage shop.

4. Have dual strap handles which are extensions of the reinforcing straps. The dual handles should lock together with a grip pad, so that baggage loaders won't take the bag by just one handle. Avoid any handles which are connected to the case by swivel pins or other small pieces of metal; the first time the baggage handler tries to swing the case up into the plane by the handle, the handle is likely to break off.

5. Be of a square rather than rounded design, so that your luggage will stack easily on the baggage handler's cart. According to baggage handlers, rounded luggage is the main cause of luggage falling off the cart—not counting, of course, poor eye-hand coordination, inadequate driver training and excessive drinking.

6. Have built-in wheels recessed with the axle below the surface of the case. Wheels which are mounted at the end of one-inch tubes on the bottom of the case catch in conveyor belt connections, cart flanges and just about anything else they come within twenty feet of. This causes not only delay but also occasional de-wheelings, forcing you to exit baggage claim pulling your crippled, listing suitcase behind you on its leash to the general hysterics of the surrounding hillbillies.

7. Have a bolted-on identification-tag window. In my experience, any bag which lets its identification tags dangle about is likely to be quickly neutered.

8. Look old and beat up. Your suitcase, that is. Ask yourself, if you were a thief and needed one more bag to make your quota for the day, which would you choose: the new, monogrammed, suede-leather La Filani with polished brass fittings? Or the old piece of crud held together with chewing gum and string? It's common sense.

If common sense is not your *forte*, don't worry. After one or two flights, your La Filani will look like an old piece of crud anyway. Lighter colors are best. The least little contact with the rubber conveyor belt or the tarmac and they will display long black dueling scars for the rest of their lives.

9. Have bright orange reflective strips stuck on it. These strips not only help you identify your bag at a distance but also keep others from mistaking it for theirs.

Of course, I realize that there are people who are so concerned with impressing the bellboy at their hotel that they would find it impossible to put bright orange reflective strips on their luggage. Such people, rather than having unfashionable luggage in their possession, would apparently prefer having their luggage fashionable and in the possession of some myopic tourist from Des Moines.

They don't seem to realize that the average bellboy would be much more impressed being given a large tip for carrying luggage which appeared to be made out of night detour signs and luminous mudflaps than he would being given nothing at all for not carrying bags which were no longer there.

Box 4-2.	U.S. Airline Domestic Free Checked-Luggage Limits		
Airline	**No.Pieces**	**Weight/Bag**[1]	**Dimensions In Inches**[2]
Alaska	2	70lbs	1st<62;2nd<55
Aloha	2	70lbs	1st<62;2nd<55
America West	3[3]	70lbs	Each<62
American	3[3]	70lbs	1st<62;2nd<55;3rd<45
Braniff	3[3]	70lbs	1st<62;2nd<55;3rd<45
Continental	3[3]	70lbs	1st<62;2nd<55;3rd<45
Delta	3[3]	70lbs	1st<62;2nd<55;3rd<45
Eastern	3[3]	70lbs	1st<62;2nd<55;3rd<45
Hawaiian	2	70lbs	1st<62;2nd<55
Midway	2	70lbs	1st<62;2nd<55
Northwest	3	70lbs	Each<62
Pan Am	2	70lbs	1st<62;2nd<55
Southwest	3	70lbs	Each<62
TWA	3[4]	70lbs	1st&2nd<62;3rd<45
United	2[3]	70lbs	1st<62;2nd<55
USAir	3[3]	70lbs;3rd 40lbs	1st<62;2nd<55;3rd<45

1 Note that the weight limit is for *each* checked bag. Since each passenger can have two checked bags, if each bag reaches the 70-pound maximum, the total allowed weight will be 140 pounds.

2. "Dimensions" means the sum of the greatest height, width and depth of the case.

3. Carry-on bags must be subtracted from this figure to produce the number of bags which can be checked. Carry-on bags are subject to the carry-on limits above.

4. Carry-on bags in excess of one must be subtracted from this figure to produce the number of bags which can be checked. Carry-on bags are subject to the carry-on limits above.

Note: Children under age two who are flying free usually have no checked baggage allowance.

Beyond the Free Baggage Rules

If you exceed the free baggage rules, it doesn't mean you can't check your bag. A bag which exceeds the above limits will usually be carried at an additional charge, provided the item does not exceed certain outside limits.

> **(a) Weight.** For the smaller domestic airlines, the maximum weight limit is generally 70 pounds; for the majors, 100 pounds, with some going up to 150 pounds.

> **(b) Size.** Maximum dimension limits for most are 80 inches, with a few at 100 inches, 115 inches or 160 inches.

Luggage in excess of these maximum limits must be sent air freight at a much greater cost.

Loopholes in the Domestic Checked Baggage Rules

Each airline's conditions of carriage have detailed checked-baggage rules which should be available to your travel agent. If you have difficult items of baggage it pays to read these rules before you choose your airline. When you do, be on the lookout for the following four major loopholes.

1.   Checked carry-on. Most people think the domestic checked baggage limit is two. In fact, as demonstrated by the above chart, for many of the airlines one of your carry-on bags can also be checked—increasing the limit to three. Technically, your carry-on limit must then be reduced by that bag; however, the boarding pass collectors at the gate usually do not bother to determine whether you've checked an additional bag. So, as a practical matter, you can normally check three bags and still have your full allowance of carry-on.

2.   Free special equipment. Skiing equipment and wheelchairs (one often follows the other) can usually be carried free as additional luggage. In addition, many airlines allow a single item of sporting equipment used in fishing, bowling, golfing and shooting to exceed the free-baggage weight and dimension limits; however, for most of those, the item is counted as one of the two or three bags otherwise allowed. Needless to say, some nonsporting passengers have been known to take advantage of the latter exceptions by using oversized sporting-equipment cases to carry their clothes in.

3. Free military bags. Duffel-type bags carried by military personnel are usually allowed as one of the free checked bags even though they may exceed the weight or dimension limits.

4. Special items exceeding maximum limits. Scuba diving equipment, bicycles, surfboards, sailboards and vaulting poles, although not allowed as free baggage, will often be accepted as excess baggage even though they exceed the absolute maximum limits for luggage discussed above.

5. Nonenforcement. The biggest loophole in the domestic checked-baggage limitations is that despite all the precise rules, they're seldom enforced. As long as your bag doesn't look unusually large or heavy, the airlines will check it without a murmur. Be warned, however, international flights are another matter.

How to Make Sense of the International Excess Baggage Rules

There is a myriad of different excess baggage rules in international travel. However, these rules can generally be separated into one of two groups: (i) a restricted form of the US domestic rules known as the "piece" method" or (ii) a version of the IATA rules known as the "weight" method".

1. Piece method. The piece method is used generally on flights within, to and from the United States. "Piece" method is a bit of a misnomer since there are weight limits as well; but the weight limits are so high (usually 70 pounds per bag) that you are unlikely to reach them if you stick to the dimension limits on the bags. The dimension limits generally follow those for US domestic flights with the following exceptions:

(a) Only two bags can be checked.

(b) The combined dimensions of the two checked bags must meet some limit, such as the sum of the greatest outside dimensions of each not exceeding 106 inches.

(c) Children under two paying a ten-percent fare are allowed one checked bag with total dimensions not greater than 45 inches, plus one folding stroller.

2. Weight method. This is the method used generally for flights of non-US airlines which do not start or end in the United States. Here the airlines are concerned only about the total weight of the bags (including, theoretically, carry-on). They're not concerned about the number or size of bags because the weight limit is usually set so low that if you have more than two suitcases of a normal size, you're likely to exceed the limit with just the weight of the empty suitcases. (Well, almost.)

Most foreign airlines follow some variation of the IATA rule which sets a weight limit of 44 pounds (20 kilograms) for the *total* of all an economy passenger's bags *(including carry-on)*—which is considerably less than the piece-method weight limit of 140 pounds (two times 70 pounds). In addition, children traveling on ten-percent tickets are given no luggage allotment at all, other than possibly a folding stroller. If you fly business or first class, though, the limit is usually increased up to 66 pounds (30 kilograms) and 88 pounds (40 kilograms) respectively (though that is still much less than the economy-class piece-method limit.)

How to Avoid the Change of Method Trap

Although the general rule is that the weight method applies to non-US flights, sometimes a foreign airline will apply the piece method when flying from the US and the more restrictive weight method when flying back to the US. So you could fly out with your 140 pounds of free baggage and get hit with 96 pounds of excess baggage when you bring the same luggage back on the same airline!

Likewise, if you take a connecting flight at your foreign destination, it's likely the connecting airline will follow the more restrictive weight method, clobbering you with 96-pounds-worth of excess baggage charges.

If you don't fly a lot, try to plan your flights to avoid those airlines which follow the weight method. If you fly a lot and can't afford the luxury of choosing such airlines, then the only answer is either to keep your total luggage weight below 44 pounds or to become expert at sneaking an extra bag onto the plane—an art discussed in more detail beginning at page 218.

The Guiding Principle of Packing for a Plane Trip

Once you've acquired your luggage, you then have to pack it. What you will pack depends on where you are going, what you will be doing and how long you will be away. You will pack differently for a two-week holiday in the Caribbean than a one-day winter sales meeting in the upper Midwest. At least I hope you'll pack differently. You'd look pretty weird on the beach at St. Martin in a fur coat and galoshes. Even weirder on the speaker's podium at the St. Paul Hilton in bikini briefs and thongs.

When packing your bags for any trip, concentrate on the single principle which must override everything: Pack as little as possible.

If you don't pack as little as possible, you won't be able to travel light; and if you don't travel light, then, as mentioned before, a large number of the airline passenger strategies and tactics in this book will be totally worthless to you.

How to Pack a Minimum of Clothes

1.   Plan to wash your clothes. Hard as it is for some travelers to accept, your hometown is not the only place in the world where you can get your clothes washed or cleaned. If you're going for a ten-day trip, therefore, you don't have to take ten pairs of underwear. You can have most hotels and resorts clean your clothes during the day or overnight, or, if you're concerned about the expense, you can do it yourself with a packet of Woolite in the sink (squeezing the damp clothing in a towel for fast drying afterwards).

Generally, no matter how long you are going, there is no reason to pack more than three days worth of clothes: one set to wear, one to have cleaned during the day and one as a backup in case you miss a day's cleaning.

2.   Choose only those clothes which are absolutely necessary. When you pack each item, ask yourself, "Do I really need this?" For instance, T-shirts worn under dress shirts are not necessary. Suit vests are not necessary. For most skirts, slips are not necessary. If you've got the proper carry-on luggage, a large purse is not necessary. On most winter business trips, hats, mufflers, galoshes and gloves are not necessary. Unless you're particularly offensive to your associates, the time you'll spend standing out in the cold during a business trip is minimal. A good overcoat with warm pockets is enough.

3.   Choose those clothes which can serve double duty. For example, your suit trousers should be able to double as slacks (which usually means they shouldn't be pinstriped or dark blue). Or, if you're a jogger, take running shoes which can double as casual shoes—*i.e.*, those colored light brown or white rather than a methyl-orange with purple stripes. A lightweight turtleneck can be casual or dressy depending on whether it is worn with jeans or a formal jacket. Reversible sweaters, jackets and belts are ideal.

4.   Choose clothing which can be mixed and recombined. Base your clothes around complementary color schemes. Each sweater should be able to go with each of your shirts or trousers. Stick to muted, solid colors for your major items of clothing. Avoid garish plaids, stripes, *avant-garde* graphic designs and pictures of mass media stars on your clothing—particularly if you are in finance. Likewise stick to simple styling. Avoid faddish extremes. You don't want people to notice when you are wearing the same thing again and again.

5.   Use small, lightweight accessories for variety. Differently patterned and colored belts, socks, handkerchiefs and ties for men, and belts, stockings, scarfs, jewelry and hair bands for women, can make the same basic outfit look radically different each day if those items are the primary source of color.

6.   Choose items of clothing which can be worn more than once without washing. This means clothes of medium dark tones, which don't show the dirt as much as blacks, whites and pastels, and clothes with at least 50-percent synthetics for wool-type fabrics and 66-percent synthetics for cotton-type fabrics so they will be wrinkle-resistant. To the extent you can wear items more than once without washing, you will need less backup clothing while your other clothes are being washed.

7.   For protection against the elements, use lightweight clothing, such as cashmere sweaters, nylon Windbreakers or raincoats, or, for very cold weather, nylon-tube puff jackets. Not only is such clothing lightweight, but it can be folded and compressed into very small areas. To help pack the puff jackets, you can buy a small nylon pouch with a drawstring and a zipper into which the rolled puff jacket can be pressed like a sleeping bag. (Note, if you carry a small collapsible umbrella, you probably won't need a raincoat and rain hat as well.)

When Variety is Not the Spice of Life

When you are traveling, the idea is to give the appearance of variety to those you meet, not to yourself. So, if you're going on a business trip alone and you'll be meeting different customers each day, you don't need variety.

On such trips I'll usually wear my suit and pack only an extra pair of matching suit trousers. If the trip is long, I'll try to keep my suit coat off as much as possible to keep it neat and have one pair of the trousers cleaned every other day.

Four Easy Ways to Cut the Size and Weight of Your Toiletries by 70 Percent

1.   Use a small, nylon, drawstring toiletries bag rather than a square, leather toiletries case. The former is lightweight and easily molded into any spare space in your case, while the latter is both heavy and inflexible.

2. Take along only the supply necessary for the trip. Transfer shampoos, moisturizing creams, after-shave, makeup remover, saline and purified water to smaller containers. If you don't have a small container handy, then before you pack your large container, drain it of any amounts you're unlikely to use.

3. Choose the toiletry method which requires the least paraphernalia. Use tampons rather than pads. Use long-wearing contact lenses or, at least, the kind which can be disinfected with chemicals rather than a cooking case. Use an all-in-one makeup lotion rather than separate foundation, powder and cream.

4. Use smaller versions of each item. For instance, instead of a bulky aerosol, use a roll-on deodorant, a tube of shaving cream or a pump-action hairspray. Instead of a full-sized toothbrush, take a traveling version which folds up into the handle; it not only will be more compact but also prevent your plaque from establishing colonies on the other items in your toiletries bag.

Note, if you've got better things to do with your life than searching for and/or preparing smaller versions of your toiletries, there is a quick and easy way to do it. A company called Travel Mini Pack has miniaturized versions (all under three inches) of the more commonly available toiletries. Call them at (914)429-8281 for a catalog. They'll even sell you a travel bag to put everything in.

Traveling with Electrical Appliances

Let's face it. Irons, hair dryers, hair stylers, electric shavers, *etc.*, are not going to help you travel light. Not only are they generally heavy and bulky, but when you travel internationally, you've got to either carry a converter or look for a repairman who speaks English. With a little forethought you ought to be able to do without them. Wear fiber-blend clothes which drip dry. Use a plastic disposable razor. Dry your hair with a towel. If you're going to be traveling a lot, get a haircut that doesn't require special styling.

If, despite this advice, you are one of those people who don't feel comfortable unless they're carrying a small appliance store with them when they travel, then at least get a miniaturized version. Look in your travel store for the Stowaway line by Black & Decker. If you can't find it, call Black & Decker at (301)583-3900 for the nearest retail outlet.

Good Sources of Other Miniaturized Travel Items

For other miniature items, such as shoeshine kits, folding rain hats, inflatable clothes hangers, foldaway tote bags, sewing kits, converters, clothes brushes and pocket electric fans, look for Travel Aids at a good travel store or call Traveler's Checklist at (203)364-0144 to order a catalog.

Reducing Your Paper Weight

Whether you are traveling on business or pleasure, you are likely to be carrying some books, journals, files and other accumulations of paper. As with all packing, your ruling principle should be to bring only what you will need on the journey. The trick is to realize that what you will need is often only a small part of the information contained in the publication or file.

So, for example:

1. If you have a reference book, such as a flight or travel guide, instead of bringing the whole book, bring just a Xerox of the relevant pages which you will need on your journey.

2. If you need to read several trade periodicals, (i) tear out the articles you want to read on the plane, or, conversely, (ii) tear out the pages you've already read and want to leave behind.

3. Rather than bringing along a weight-lifter's Filofax, bring along a small sheet of paper. On one side put your important numbers—bank accounts, credit cards, passports (including place and date of issue), social security, insurance policies, glasses prescription, blood group, clothing measurements of potential gift recipients and the numbers for reporting stolen credit cards. On the other side, a list of the names, addresses and phone numbers of the fifty people you are most likely to call or write. Strip down the information to the essentials you wouldn't know from memory (*e.g.*, putting in only the person's first name, street address, zip code and local number, leaving out the city, state and area code). Leave some space to add numbers as you go along.

Got the idea? All it requires is a few minutes planning before each trip. The few pounds saved may not seem like much now. But when you've been traveling all day, it will seem like a lot.

Two for the Space of One

If you are traveling with a close companion, save space by sharing toiletries, equipment and items of clothing.

If your companion is of the opposite sex, the sharing can add considerable spice to your journey.

Four Convenient Items to Wear During a Flight

1. A small pouch wallet with a zipper along the top and a loop on the back so that it can fit on your belt. This type of belt wallet has two major advantages:

(a) **It's less likely to get lost during the flight.** Attached to your belt, it's not going to slip out like a loose wallet in your coat or rear pants-pocket may do. And since you can get into a belt wallet without having to remove it from your clothing, you're not going to mislay it.

(b) **It's easier to use when you're strapped into your seat.** Most people put their coat in the overhead rack during the flight. If you have a wallet in your coat and have to pay for drinks or earphones on the flight, you've got to undo your seat-belt, stand up and fish around in the overhead rack. With a wallet in your rear pants-pocket, you're no better off; you've got to undo your seat-belt, squirm around indecorously with your hand shoved down under your sweaty rear pocket and finally come to a grunting half-stand before you can remove it. With a belt wallet, all you need do is unzip the top and take out the money.

2. A shirt or blouse with a pocket, so when you take off your coat at your seat, you have somewhere to put your pen and, if you are really organized, either:

(a) **A three-by-five, narrow-lined loose-leaf notebook,** which, with appropriately small writing, will hold as much as a large notebook but take up considerably less space with considerably less weight; or

(b) **Some of the 1-inch-square, yellow 3-M Stick'ums and a collapsible 3-inch ballpoint pen** for taking emergency notes when you would otherwise have to get get a large notebook and pen from your case under the seat. The important Stick'ums later can be stuck onto the relevant pages in your notebook.

3. A wristwatch in which the hour can be changed separately from the minutes and seconds, so you can easily reset the time when crossing time zones. (Not counting, of course, places like India, where the time zone is a half-hour off from the rest of the world. Some people just have to be different, don't they?)

The watch should also have an alarm so you can wake yourself on the plane if you wish to freshen up before landing. (Unfortunately, the background noise in most airplanes makes it very difficult to hear a beeping watch alarm. When I wish to use mine, I put my watch around the end of the armrest and, if I'm sleeping sitting up, raise the armrest until its end is near my ear.)

4.   Around your neck, under your shirt, a pair of plastic earphones from your last flight. What? You mean you actually handed them back when requested?

Just kidding. I certainly don't want to advise you to commit a misdemeanor just to avoid paying for the movie on a plane. However, if you should ever find a pair of such earphones lying on the street somewhere, you would probably not be committing a crime or breaching any contract if you used the earphones on a subsequent flight. Most airlines' conditions of carriage do not provide for a charge if you use your own earphones. Those that do, such as those of United and Northwest, provide for a charge only if you use the earphones to watch the movie, not if you use them merely to listen to the audio entertainment. How the airline can tell which you are listening to—particulary if you keep your hand on the tuning knob—I don't know.

If your found-on-the-street earphones are a different color than the ones given out on the flight and you're not interested in arguing the finer details of the airline's conditions of carriage, you might bring your earphones out only after the lights go out for the movie; in the dark, as you're undoubtedly aware, colors disappear and the flight attendant will be unable to tell your earphones are a different color from the others.

How to Remember What to Take on the Trip

Following are four easy steps which should guarantee that you take everything you should on your trip:

1.   Permanent list. Keep in your suitcase a permanent checklist which includes everything conceivable you could take or ever have taken on a trip. The purpose of this list is to remind you of anything which might be necessary on the journey you are now taking.

2.   Temporary list. A week or so before you travel, start making a separate list of unusual things you will need on your trip, *e.g.*, gifts, business presentations, or whips and chains.

3.   Prepacking. Store your basic travel items, such as your toiletries, in your suitcase. To keep the contents up to date, every time you return from a trip, immediately refill the shampoo bottle and replace the razor and any shaving soap, deodorant or toothpaste which has a quarter or less left. The replaced items you can use up at home.

4. Role playing. After you have gathered everything together and checked it against the list, go through your trip in your mind, trying to picture at each stage what you will be wearing and using.

"Okay, she's lying there. I'm standing over her wearing my paisley silk ascot, my yellow, Oxford-cloth, button-down shirt, my French, natural-shouldered, peach cashmere sports jacket, my knee-high black silk socks, my Italian brown loafers with leather tassels and my orange-polka-dotted, 100-percent cotton, extra-large boxer shorts.

"Let's see, now. . . . Oh, yes. . . . And over the boxer shorts, my white-belted, double-knit polyester blue slacks.

"Yep. With just a little role playing before packing, I've managed to turn an ordinary sales presentation into a really great one."

How to Pack Things into Your Luggage

Once you've gathered everything together, lay it all out on a flat surface, such as your bed. Now you're ready to pack it into your luggage.

Here are certain simple tips that you should keep in mind.

1. Be sure to pack only the bags you are taking on the trip. Putting your things in the bags you are leaving at home will not do you any good. (I told you the tips were simple, didn't I?)

2. Pack in your under-the-seat suitcase your valuables and those things which you will need immediately. That way, if you get into a situation where you have to check your garment bag, you can survive if the garment bag is lost. (Among the items you might put in your carry-on suitcase is a photo of your garment bag, to aid you in submitting a claim to airline when it's lost.) If you think you might have to check both bags, *e.g.*, on a small plane, you should pack your valuables in a nylon knapsack or envelope inside your case so you can remove them quickly when checking the bag.

3. Pack in the garment bag those items which wrinkle easily, so you don't have to be concerned about proper folding. The garment bag puts only a single, forgiving fold in the middle and allows you to soften even that fold by hanging the bag on the plane. Put the hanging items which wrinkle easiest into the garment bag first so that they will be farthest away from the bend of the bag. To fit more in, layer several items of clothing on the same hanger.

4. Roll your stockings and underwear in the sets in which they will be used. For instance, men can roll one pair of socks inside a pair of underwear; women, a bra and a pair of panties inside a pair of pantyhose.

5. Wrap fragile items inside socks and put them in the center of the case, protected by clothing on all sides.

6. Put smaller items inside your shoes.

7. Put your shoes in a plastic bag in order to keep your clothes clean and your shoes shined. The better garment bags usually have a separate shoe compartment at the bottom of the bag.

8. Leave some air in any liquid containers so they will not leak in the lowered pressure of the aircraft.

The Expert Way to Avoid Wrinkling when Packing Your Clothes

Ideally all your items that wrinkle easily will go in your garment bag and your other items will go in your under-the-seat suitcase. Occasionally, however, you may find you have to pack wrinkleable items in a suitcase. In this event, there are a few basic rules:

1. Fold your clothes so that if creases appear, they will not stand out, either because they're hidden or because they emphasize the basic lines of your garment. For example, fold jackets and skirts so that most of the creases are vertical. Fold shirts so that most of the wrinkles are in the back. Don't fold pants at the knee, or skirts at the hem; the crease will be too noticeable. Turn your clothing inside out before you fold it so that the crease will be on the inside.

Figure 4-1.   Folding a Shirt

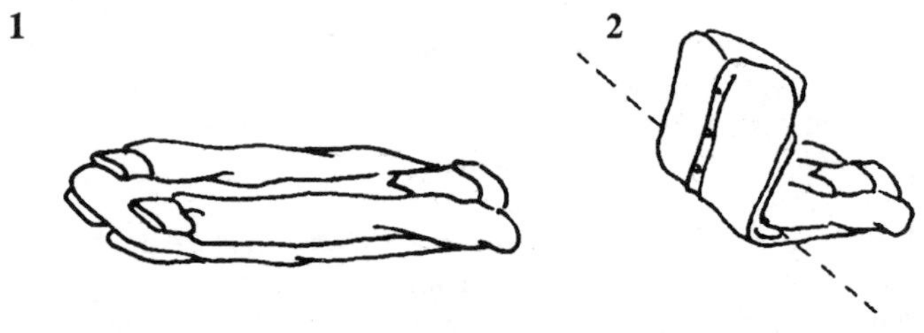

Figure 4-2. Folding A Jacket

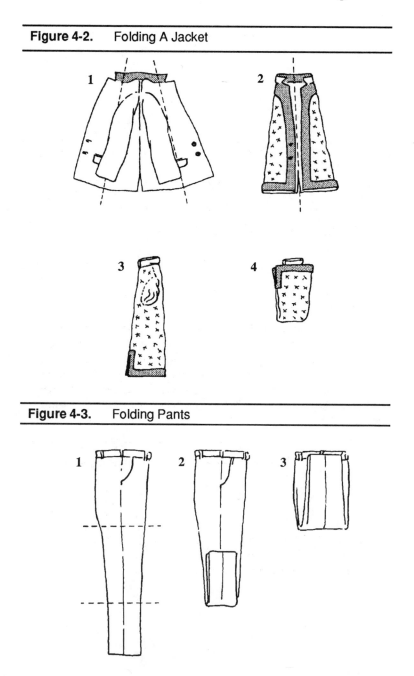

Figure 4-3. Folding Pants

Figure 4-4.   Folding A Dress

2.   Cushion the folds so that any creases will be less sharp. There are two major ways of doing this. One is interfolding, in which all your items of clothing are placed half in the case at various angles, one on top of the other, and then the second half of each item is folded in. (See illustration below.) Airline flight attendants use this technique a lot. It's quite effective in preventing creases as long as you want to take all of your items out of the case at once and don't mind spending a few minutes trying to figure out how to untangle everything.

Figure 4-5.   Interfolding

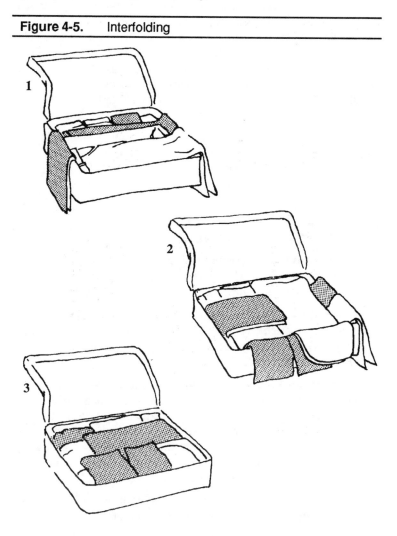

The other way of cushioning the folds is by putting something in them. Some people use tissue or plastic bags (the latter hold some air which provides a cushion). I use my socks and underwear. For particularly wrinkleable pant legs or sleeves you can stuff the cushioning inside the clothing itself.

3.   Pack heavy and irregularly shaped items such as shoes at the bottom of the case, so they are not resting on top of your clothes. Bottom means the bottom when you are carrying the suitcase, not when it is resting on your bed. If you put your heavy things on the "bottom" when the case is resting on your bed, then when you lift the case by the handle, the heavy things will slip down the side, scrunching up your clothing. (Putting the heavy items at the real bottom also makes the case better balanced for carrying.) Pack small items which wrinkle easily, such as neckties, at the top just under the handle of the suitcase where they will ride on top of everything else.

4.   Pack tightly. Wrinkling can be caused as much by clothes slipping around as by folding. Use rolled up socks and underwear to fill in the spaces around your major clothing items. Your case should have straps to hold the clothing firm.

Four Tricks for Getting Rid of Wrinkles when You Arrive

Most good hotels have a quick pressing service. If you're subtle enough, so do most private homes where you might be staying. However, if such services are not available, then I recommend the following four tricks:

1.   Carry special wrinkle removers. At least two are on the market. One is a portable electric hand steamer available from Traveler's Checklist at (203)364-0144. The other is an aerosol spray available from Travel Mini Pack at (914)429-8281.

2.   Hang your clothing up as soon as you arrive. With heavier clothing the weight of the material itself will remove many wrinkles. To avoid hanger creases in your pants or skirts, carry a small plastic pant/skirt hanger (most hotels do not have them) or, even more lightweight, a couple of large safety pins to attach your pants or skirts at the top to the hotel hanger. You can hang more than one item of clothing with a single pant/skirt hanger or set of safety pins.

3.   Hang the more wrinkled items in the bathroom with the door closed and run a steamy shower for fifteen minutes. The warm steam will relax the fibers and the weight of the clothes will pull out the wrinkles. You can assist the process by pulling gently on the bottom edge. Allow the clothes an hour or so to dry before you put them on.

4. Put pants, sweaters and skirts between your mattress and box springs. A night of bearing your load will flatten them out. If your clothes are severely wrinkled, go to the bar downstairs and try to pick up the most obese member of the opposite sex you can find.

What to Wear on Long Plane Trips

Usually the constraints of packing light will determine what you wear on the plane. However, if you have enough luggage space and your flight will be long and arduous (such as a 23-hour flight from New York to Sydney), you'll want to wear something you don't have to strip off your body with wallpaper remover at the end of the trip.

I recommend (whether you are a woman or a man) wearing a designer tracksuit over a muted, patterned T-shirt, supplemented by a turtleneck sweater.

1. Tracksuit. A tracksuit does not bind you at the knees, crotch, elbows and waist (the latter area particularly important since your abdomen tends to expand with the reduction in air pressure in the cabin). In addition, a tracksuit is less likely to wrinkle if you curl up to sleep. Finally, if the tracksuit is nice enough, you can use it as casual wear at your destination.

2. Layering for temperature. Stripping to the T-shirt or adding the sweater allows you to easily and tastefully adjust to the changes (i) in your own body temperature which occur as you move through your circadian rhythms and (ii) in the cabin air temperature which occur as the flight attendants continually overshoot the mark on the air-conditioning control knob.

3. Heavy socks. You can wear almost any kind of shoes because, once your feet begin to swell during the flight, you will take your shoes off. I recommend a pair of heavy socks to keep your shoeless feet warm when you're sitting in your seat, and protected when you're walking about the plane. If the plane appears particularly cold, you can put on one of your ordinary pairs of socks first, under the heavy socks, to give yourself more warmth.

4. Boxer shorts rather than briefs (for women as well as men). Being looser, boxer shorts are not only less binding than briefs but also take considerably longer to achieve a state of crusty putrefaction. This latter aspect is particularly important if you have to wear them the next day turned inside out.

The Best Way to Avoid Your Suitcase Getting too Full on the Trip

Quite simple. Mail your acquisitions back.

If you think you might be accumulating items on your trip, take along a few large self-addressed manila envelopes and have the hotel mail the items home. This technique is particularly good for conference and trade-fair brochures.

Likewise, if you're buying gifts, ask the store to mail the items home for you.

When traveling abroad, there is a $50 per donee per day duty exemption for goods mailed back to the US; thus, to the extent you have accumulated dutiable items abroad in excess of the $400 returning-resident exemption (see discussion of US customs rules at page 301 below), you will save duty by mailing the excess items back rather than bringing them with you; and this saving, assuming a normal duty of ten percent, is likely to be greater than the cost of the postage. To qualify for the exemption you need to meet the following conditions:

1. The gifts have to be to someone other than you or someone you are traveling with.

2. The packages must be sent to an address other than your own.

3. The package must be marked "Unsolicited Gifts under $50", with your name as donor, the nature of the gift and its fair retail value. If you exceed the $50 limit, the *whole* value of the gift, including the first $50, is subject to duty.

4. The gifts cannot not contain alcoholic perfumes valued over $5, tobacco or alcoholic drinks. Under US law it is illegal to mail alcohol, anyway.

5. You can consolidate gifts to different donees in the same package. But if any gift exceeds the $50 limit, all the gifts will be subject to duty.

6. The "per day" limit applies to receipt by the recipient, not mailing by you; so you must insure that none of your gifts arrive on the same day.

Note, if you are mailing items from a developing country, be sure you see the postal clerk cancel the stamp. In countries where a dollar a day is a good wage, uncanceled stamps are often stolen to supplement incomes.

CHAPTER FIVE

WHEN AND HOW TO GET TO THE AIRPORT

When to Arrive at the Airport Despite What the Airlines Say

The airlines advise their passengers to arrive at the airport early—generally an hour before a domestic flight and an hour and a half before an international flight. You and I know, of course, that this advice does not apply to us. It applies to those other people, the ones with a low tolerance for uncertainty and/or a desire to please those in authority. *We* can arrive later.

You can cut the suggested period by a third and still have plenty of time to make the flight. That is, the hour and a half can be cut to an hour; the hour, to forty minutes. The extent to which you can cut it further depends on six major factors:

1. What the airline's gate-appearance deadlines are. Each airline has a specific deadline by which the passenger is supposed to be at the gate. A passenger missing these deadlines is subject to losing his or her place to a standby or, if there are places available, his or her right to a nonsmoking seat (see page 269 below). For most domestic flights the deadline is ten minutes before departure; for international, 30 minutes. As most of the airlines' conditions of carriage are written in terms of "appearing" at the gate, the fact you are standing in line should be enough.

A significant difference occurs in that some of the airlines, such as Delta, require you merely to appear at the departure gate by the deadline *ready for check-in*, while others, such as American, require you to appear at the departure gate by the deadline *having already* obtained a boarding pass. If your airline is in the latter category, then you will have to get to the airport earlier in order to be certain of obtaining a boarding pass by the gate-appearance deadline.

Note, if you are thinking of getting to the airport really early, most airlines have a time limit *before* which they will not accept your luggage or check you in. Generally this time limit ranges from two to four hours before departure.

2. Whether you have a preassigned seat. If you have a preassigned seat, normally you don't have to check in early in order to get the seat of your choice. However, for a few airlines, if you don't check in at least 30 minutes before departure (in the case of American, for instance) or appear at the departure gate at least 30 minutes before departure (in the case of Delta), you are subject to losing your preassigned seat. Even though you might lose your preassigned seat on these airlines, however, you still won't lose your reservation for the flight itself, unless you fail to appear at the gate at least ten minutes ahead of departure.

3.   Whether you have a preissued boarding pass. With a preissued boarding pass, you don't have to check in early to avoid getting stuck in a last-minute line trying to get a boarding pass. For most airlines, you still have to meet the ten-minute gate-appearance deadline (30 minutes for international flights). For at least one, Northwest, you merely have to be on the plane five minutes before departure. However, for a few, such as American and Delta, if you have a preissued boarding pass for a domestic flight, you actually have to appear at the gate *15* minutes before departure—five minutes earlier than if you didn't have a preissued boarding pass.

4.   Whether you need to check your bags. If you have only carry-on luggage, you can get to the airport much later because you don't need to worry about your luggage missing the plane. This is particularly true on most domestic flights and some foreign flights where those without luggage to check can bypass the long lines at the lobby check-in counters and go directly to the gate to get their boarding pass.

If you do have to check your bags, then it's best to get to the airport at least 30 minutes before your flight departs—otherwise you have a much greater likelihood of your bags being lost. In fact, many airlines refuse to accept bags less than 15 to 20 minutes before flight time, or, if they do accept them, will require you to sign disclaimers of any liability and/or pick up the cost of delivery from the destination airport to your destination accommodation.

5.   Whether you have to buy your ticket. If you are going to buy your ticket at the airport, most airlines require you to have *applied for* or, in the case of some airlines, *obtained* your ticket by at least 30 minutes before the departure time (60 minutes for international flights). Merely being in line by that time is not enough.

6.   How fully booked the flight is. The airline will ordinarily give you this information over the phone the day of the flight. If the flight is lightly booked, you know that even if you miss the ticket-purchase and gate-appearance deadlines above, you'll probably still be able to get on the plane. At the other extreme, if the flight is heavily overbooked, you know you need to get to the airport even earlier than the stated deadlines in order to avoid being bumped.

The Advantages of Showing Up
at the Airport as Late as Possible

Assuming the flight is not fully booked, then, in addition to cutting down your time waiting around the airport, there are three advantages to showing up at the airport as late as possible.

1.   Shorter lines. Since, most of the other passengers will already have checked in, you're unlikely to have to wait in line at your flight's counter. Of course, if the counter is handling other flights than just yours, you may have a problem—but nothing which can't be solved with a sufficiently loud voice and pushy manner.

2.   Last look. You'll be able to have the last look on the computer screen to see how the seating has developed and choose a seat as far away from the other passengers as possible—which in economy, of course, is always a good idea.

3.   Preferred baggage treatment. If you're bold enough, your checked baggage will be treated preferentially. I discovered this by accident once when I had to travel with a troglodyte who obstinately refused to use carry-on luggage (*i.e.*, my wife) and found myself checking in late (checking in late being another inevitable feature of traveling with my wife). We were so late that the airline refused to check our bags. So instead I took the bags to the gate myself. There the gate staff naturally prevented me from taking the bags into the plane but, at my urging, took the bags down the steps to the baggage handlers loading the hold.

Not only did I cut down substantially on the risks of my baggage being lost and/or mangled on the way from check-in to the plane but discovered, lo and behold, when we got to our destination, that the last bags in at departure were the first bags out upon arrival.

The One Thing You Should Always
Do Before Going to the Airport

Before you go to the airport, call the airline and see if the flight has been delayed or canceled.

If it's been canceled, you can make alternative reservations from home before leaving.

If it's been delayed, ask the reservations clerk whether the gate-appearance deadline has also been pushed back. The conditions of carriage of some airlines, such as Delta and Northwest, provide specifically that the gate-appearance deadlines are shifted with the departure time. Others, however, refer only to the "scheduled" departure time and make no explicit provision for shifting the deadlines.

If the airline reservation clerk indicates the gate-appearance deadline has been shifted, ask for his or her name and see if a note can be placed next to your name in the computer indicating you will show up by the later time. If the reservation clerk can't tell you that the gate-appearance deadline has been shifted, and there's a danger of overbooking or subsequent cancellation, you'll want to meet the original deadline to preserve your rights—even though that may mean a long wait at the airport.

The Best Way to Get to the Airport

Most people today miss flights not because of what goes on in the airport but rather because of what goes on trying to get to the airport.

There is no foolproof way to make it to the airport on time.

Generally, the fastest way to the airport is to take a taxi, but not always.

1. Mass transit. Some airports, such as Philadelphia International, Washington's National, Chicago's O'Hare, Atlanta's Hartsfield, Frankfurt/Main International and London's Heathrow, have billion-dollar fixed-rail mass-transit systems which sometimes, during rush hour, can beat a taxi.

New York's JFK Express system can't beat a taxi even during rush hour. It runs only about once every twenty to thirty minutes and, as is true of the New York subways generally, stops sporadically to rest on the line for no particular reason. When the subway finally reaches the last station, it's on the wrong side of the track; everyone has to wait while the train goes past the station and then backs up onto the correct side. (Sitting on the train, watching this, you can't help wondering what kind of qualifications it takes to be a metropolitan transport designer.) Once off the train, the passengers are transferred to buses, so they can get a taste of the airport's rush-hour traffic, and then are dropped off serially at JFK's terminals in an order that always seems to leave my terminal until last.

All in all, not a very satisfactory experience.

2. Helicopter. Under special conditions, a helicopter service to the airport can beat a taxi. The first and perhaps most important condition is that a helicopter service to the airport be available. Unless this condition is met, a taxi will win every time.

To give the helicopter service a fighting chance, you need to be able to get from where you are to the local helicopter pad. In New York this usually means catching a cab—and, after you've caught the cab, outarguing the driver as to why you shouldn't let him drive you to the airport instead.

That's not all. The helicopter has to leave when you want. If it leaves only every 30 minutes and you arrive at the heliport a minute after the previous one left, you'll have to add 29 minutes to your trip time.

In addition, although the helicopter will cover a given distance faster than a taxi, it won't get you to your destination faster if it goes somewhere else first. In New York, for instance, the helicopter used to triangle out to La Guardia Airport first, in order to hang around for a while, dropping off and picking up passengers and waiting to get permission to take off for JFK. Fortunately, that practice has since been stopped.

Even when the helicopter finally gets to the airport, it doesn't mean you've arrived at your destination. In New York, unless you're flying TWA (which is the terminal at which the helicopter lands), you're going to have to walk or take one of the sporadic shuttle buses to your departure terminal—adding up to half an hour to your journey.

So unless you're a tourist from Iowa interested in a postcard view of Manhattan or a nostalgic ex-Vietnam door-gunner with a good imagination, you probably ought to skip the helicopter.

3. Other methods. Buses, hotel vans, rental cars, limousine services (including those sometimes provided *gratis* to first- and business-class passengers) and private automobiles not only are no faster than a taxi in traffic but because of their various peculiarities actually take longer to get you door to door.

The buses, vans and limousines run on a fixed schedule and pick their passengers up and drop them off along a fixed circuit; unless you happen to be at the last hotel with a flight leaving at just the right time from the first terminal, a bus, van or limousine will take longer than a cab. Rental cars and private automobiles, of course, don't run on fixed schedules but they require time for you to park and then for you to walk or catch a bus to the terminal. Water taxis (which run at Boston's Logan and New York's La Guardia) end up being little better since they also have fixed schedules and require bus or van connections at either end.

If you get stuck using any of these nontaxi vehicles, leave for the airport with plenty of time to spare. For instance, if you've spent the night at an airport hotel and are taking a morning flight out, rather than eating breakfast at the hotel and then taking the van to the airport, take an early van to the airport and eat breakfast there. Once you're at the airport, you can have a leisurely breakfast without worrying about the vagaries of the hotel van and make your flight with time to spare.

Of course, having eaten breakfast at the airport, you may no longer be in any condition to make your flight—but then that's a different subject. (See *The Secret of Good Airport Eating* below at page 166.)

The Best Sources of Airport/City Ground Transportation Information

By far the best source for the frequent traveler is the pocket-sized *How To Get From The Airport To The City All Around The World*, by Norman Crampton, published by M. Evans and Company, Inc., ISBN 0-87131-536-X. Cost: $4.95. Published annually, it contains a listing of the various modes of ground transportation (including parking) and their costs for each of 360 airports worldwide.

If what you want isn't available there, try *The OAG Travel Planner and Hotel and Motel Guide* (there are North American, European and Pacific Asia editions, all issued quarterly), which gives all ground transportation from airports except for taxis. North American cost: $94. Call them at (800)323-3537 or (800)942-1888.

If you want more up-to-date and/or detailed information on a particular area, contact the relevant airport authority to see if they have any information. In California, there's the *Airport Ground Transportation Directory* covering 23 California airports and available free from Cal-Trans, Division of Aeronauics, at (916)322-3090, and in New York, a tollfree information number maintained by the Port Authority of New York and New Jersey, (800)AIR-RIDE.

Tricks Which Increase Your Likelihood of Getting a Taxi Quickly When Going to the Airport from the City

1.   The round-trip trick. If ordering the taxi by phone, tell the dispatcher you want to go out to the airport, pick up a package and return immediately. This will make your fare more attractive than other airport fares because the driver won't have to sit in the long line of taxis at the airport waiting to catch a fare back. When you get to the airport, tell the driver you changed your mind about returning and give him a nice tip.

It's usually best to do this after you've gotten out of the cab.

2.   Luxury-hotel shift. If it's not rush hour, go into the nearest luxury hotel, come back out and ask the doorman to get you a cab; there's usually a line of taxis there. If there isn't, he should have a preferential phone number.

3. Flow games. If it is rush hour, avoid the luxury hotels (they're the last to get taxis at that time) and:

(**a**) wait at an intersection where you can get two streams of traffic rather than just one;

(**b**) try to pick the one-way street or the side of the two-way street that's going opposite from the most popular destination, so you'll catch the empty cabs coming back;

(**c**) if you are traveling with a partner and you're at an intersection, each of you head up one of the streets against traffic so you can "upstream" anyone else waiting at the intersection; and

(**d**) if the route to the airport is not hopelessly jammed (as it usually is in Boston), then:

(**1**) display your bags conspicuously so the taxi will think it's likely you're going to the airport; and/or

(**2**) hold up a small, preprepared posterboard sign reading, "I NEED A TAXI TO THE AIRPORT!"

The latter move, a sign, is surprisingly effective. Cabs give you preference over the other people waiting near you. Full cabs going by come back after dropping off their passengers. Some even stop and pick you up before dropping off their passengers.

I should note, however, that despite the effectiveness of such a sign, some people find it embarrassing to be so direct. They feel that holding up such a sign somehow destroys their image of casual sophistication. To people like that, it is much more important to be standing around on a sidewalk looking casually sophisticated than it is to get to the airport on time.

The Best Airport Parking Advice

The best advice regarding parking at the airport is don't.

As I mentioned above, driving your own car to the airport and parking it is slower and less convenient than taking a taxi. Its only advantage is cost. And even that is not always true. The cost of parking your car at the airport on long stays often exceeds the cost of taking a taxi. Especially when you take into account the theft of your car.

Or at the very least, the expense of replacing your broken side window and stolen radio-cassette player.

Most airports have two types of parking: long term and short term. The former is a euphemism for "cheap and inconvenient"; the latter, for "expensive and less inconvenient".

If you're someone who will do anything for money, has time on his hands and is interested in taking a self-guided tour of the lesser known parts of the airport, then long-term parking is for you.

Why people park in the long-term lots, I don't know. Certainly, they can't be interested in saving money. The amount of gasoline they eat up looking for the lots would take care of that. Even when the lots are nearby, the costs of driving to the airport and parking in the economy lot are still much more expensive than taking a bus.

Possibly these people consider arriving at the terminal in a bus *declasse*. But then, if that's true, they shouldn't be parking in the long-term lots because that's exactly how they'll arrive—in a dusty, broken down, third-world bus with "ECONOMY LOTS" emblazoned on its sides.

How to Find the Cheapest Parking Lots

The cheapest parking lots are usually those which are off the airport. The lower price is not only because they are farther away but also because they don't have to pay a franchise fee to the airport authority. Because they don't pay a fee to the airport authority, however, the airport authority is not likely to tell you about them if you call.

Unfortunately, most of the national and international guides mentioned above at pages 27 and 133 don't give you information on off-airport parking because the guides are aimed at passengers who do not live in the area and who, therefore, are not likely to be parking their own car.

Occasionally you might see a billboard or magazine ad or receive information from an airline club or airline passenger organization which has a discount parking arrangement with a cheaper lot. However, the only certain way of finding out about the lots is to look in the local yellow pages under "Automobile Parking", "Parking Lots or Garages", "Airport Services" or some similar title, and then call to determine the prices and shuttle-bus frequencies.

Some Parking Do's and Don't's

If you must drive your car to the airport, the following do's and don't's may be of some assistance.

1. If you're in a rush, call the airport before you leave to see if your terminal has valet parking. Valet parking is the fastest way to park. Unfortunately, it's also the most expensive. If you are flying first or business class, it may be provided free with your ticket.

2. When driving in the parking area, have a healthy skepticism about the arrow signs on the road. Their primarily purpose is to make you go the long way around. Going against them occasionally will give you an advantage over other drivers when searching for the empty spaces; it also will add considerable excitement on the blind corners.

3. If the lot is likely to fill up after you, park closest to the exit. When you return, you'll be able to get out of the lot more quickly—especially if you return during the evening rush hour.

4. If you are parking in a garage, park next to a concrete support. You are less likely to have your car banged by the door of a neighboring car.

5. If the parking area is mostly full, park in the first space available. Don't drive around looking for a closer-in place. The additional walking time caused by parking at the first space available is usually much less than the time it takes to find a closer-in space. If no convenient space appears immediately available, drive as quickly as possible to where there are most likely empty spaces—*e.g.*, on the top floors of a garage or the outer limits of a lot—and park there.

6. Back into your space. Because it's the front wheels which do the steering, it's easier to back into a parking place than to drive in head first. In addition, when you leave the space, you'll be able to drive straight out, which will be both easier and safer for entering traffic—especially if it's rush hour when you leave. Finally, if you back in, you're are more likely to notice if you left your headlights on when you leave.

7. Cover up your radio-cassette player with a magazine. If the junkies aren't sure whether you've got one, they'll bust into another car instead.

8. Write down on the cover of your airline ticket where you car is parked. Your airline ticket is the last thing you're likely to lose on the trip. When you return, you won't have to spend a lifetime like Captain Ahab looking for your great white whale somewhere in a sea of parked cars.

9. Don't take your parking receipt with you. It's the first thing you're likely to lose on your trip. Instead, hide the receipt in the car.

Note: Some people say you shouldn't leave your receipt in the car because if a car thief finds it, he'll be able to take your car out of the lot. My own feeling is that anyone who breaks into my car to steal it before he's found my hidden receipt probably had enough foresight to get a receipt of his own from the dispenser before he started the job.

10. Carry window cleaner and paper towels in your car. When you return to your car, the windshield is likely to be filthy with dust and jet exhaust.

11. Don't say to the attendant when you are leaving the short-term lot after having been away for two weeks, "I just dropped my friend off and lost my ticket. Do I have to pay for the whole day?" Not only is this practice immoral and illegal, but, if you get away with it, which you likely will, it'll make you feel quite guilty afterwards.

Well, at least it would make *me* feel guilty.

An Architectural Solution to Jam Ups at the Terminal Curb

Most terminals are poorly designed for dropping passengers off. The usual system, parking parallel to the curb, works okay when there are only a few cars. But in the normal, crowded situation, it degenerates into a contest to see who can block the greatest number of cars without having his own car blocked.

There is usually a traffic warden in the areas where the cars are most jammed up. I'm certain there is some sort of cause-and -effect relationship here; but I'm not quite sure which way it works. Not that I believe we should hold the traffic warden responsible. After all, he or she has been given an impossible job—trying to stop all the cars from doing what inadequate curb design has given them no choice but to do.

If the terminal designers had more than a capon's brain among them, they'd design drop-off areas in which there were marked, wide, diagonal parking places slanting backwards into the curb. (See the "A" diagonals in Figure 5-1 below.) Cars would drive up and back into the diagonal parking places. This would more than double the number of cars which could park at the curb, give each driver freer access to the trunk and allow each car when it was finished to move off without being blocked by the others.

To provide even more space, a set of diagonal parking places could run along the side of the road opposite from the terminal curb. (See the "B" diagonals in Figure 5-1 below.) These diagonals would be slanted *with* the flow of traffic so that cars could drive directly into the parking space. On the other side of this set of diagonal parking places would be another road so that when unloading was completed, the cars could drive straight out of their parking places without having to back up.

Figure 5-1.   Hatched Terminal Parking

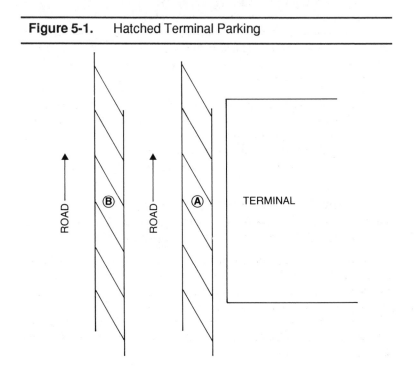

I doubt such a rational system will ever be employed by the airports, however. When I presented it once to the head of traffic of a major airport who happened to sit next to me on a flight, he laughed nervously and asked the stewardess if he could change seats.

I think the idea that I was using logic frightened him.

Special Tactics for Beating the Automobile Traffic at the Airport

If you are being dropped off at the airport and encounter traffic congestion, following are some techniques you could consider asking your driver to employ:

1. Airport jam ups. If the traffic is so jammed up your car can't get to the terminal by the normal way, it may be possible to either:

(a) Take a short cut through the short-term parking lot. Once a taxi I was in did this at JFK (where the short-term lots are in the middle of the oval on which the terminals are located); the time saved was well worth the two-dollar minimum parking charge. Of course, the taxi driver had turned into the lot by mistake—like most New York taxi drivers, road signs were a mystery to him—but I don't see why someone couldn't do it intentionally.

(b) Get dropped off at the nearest terminal which is uncrowded and walk to your terminal. This works best when you've got only carry-on luggage. Even when you don't, you can usually rent a baggage cart—the cost of which will be considerably less than the additional taxi charge you would have had to pay to get to your terminal.

2. Departure-level back ups. If the traffic to the departure level is backed up, try getting dropped off at the arrival level. You can get to the departure level by taking the escalator or elevator.

3. Curbside congestion. If your car can make it to the departure level, have it double park next to another unloading car rather than wait for an empty space next to the curb. You'll not only get unloaded much faster but your driver will avoid being trapped by other double-parking cars. If a traffic warden forces your driver to park next to the curb, have your driver back in diagonally so that the nose of the car will prevent anyone from blocking his escape.

How to Beat the Traffic-Warden When Double Parking

When your driver is double-parking at the terminal, he or she should do so just before the crosswalk. Since it's natural for cars to stop at the crosswalk, the traffic warden won't notice the car immediately.

While your driver gets out and goes back to unload the luggage from the trunk, you, stooping low so as not to be seen, can slip out of door, move around in front of the car and hunch over, peering intently at the pavement. If the traffic warden comes up to move the car on, your driver can then point to you and complain, "Officer, that person is blocking my way." The traffic warden will then leave your driver (who continues to unload) and stride up to the front to confront you. Just as the warden reaches you, look up with a pained expression and moan, "Officer! Can you help me? I was crossing the sidewalk and dropped my contact lens."

Nothing will freeze someone in his tracks faster than the announcement that a contact lens is lying somewhere near. Nine-out-of-ten traffic wardens will not only be unable to move their feet but at the same time be overcome by a powerful urge to bend down and study the pavement, trying to find the lens themselves.

If you happen to be unlucky and encounter the one-out-of-ten traffic wardens who responds to the announcement of a dropped contact lens by putting on a display of flamenco dancing, don't despair. Keep your cool and, at the height of the castanet solo, cry out, "Oh, dear God, you've smashed my lens," feign a heart attack and keel over "dead" on the road.

That's usually good for a minute or two.

By then your driver will have your luggage unloaded and you, now facing the threat of mouth-to-mouth resuscitation from the warden, can miraculously resurrect yourself, leap up and carry your unloaded luggage into the terminal, complimenting the dumbfounded official on his life-giving lips.

Three Things to Check When Checking Your Luggage at the Curb

Many airports, particularly in the United States, have facilities for checking luggage in at the curb (although you still have to go inside the terminal to get your boarding pass). If you are going to check your luggage, this is generally the most convenient way of doing it—not only because you don't have to carry your baggage so far but also because if, as usual, boarding passes are issued at the gate, you can bypass the slow lines at lobby check-in.

Note, if you are returning a rental car, consider going to the curbside check-in first to check your bags. It'll save you a lot of lugging.

When checking your luggage in at curbside, however, be sure to determine:

(a) **That your flight has not been canceled.** Checking your luggage onto a canceled flight is generally not all that convenient. At most major airport curbside facilities, the checker has a monitor showing him the status of the flights; since he doesn't issue boarding passes, however, he doesn't consult his monitor as much as the check-in staff inside. Take a look at his monitor yourself.

(b) That your flight has not been substantially delayed. If it has, you can often catch an alternative flight—in which case, unless you and your luggage are taking separate vacations, you don't want your bags to be on the original delayed flight.

(c) That the checker uses the correct destination tag with the correct flight number or numbers. Since, different from the inside check-in staff, the curbside check-in staff are usually handling more than one flight (and sometimes more than one airline) at a time, they are much more likely to make a mistake with your luggage tag. You have to watch them closely.

Note, some airlines are now allowing you to check your luggage for the flight at your hotel (*e.g.*, SAS) or at your car rental return (*e.g.*, at some airports, United at Hertz). The comments above on curbside check-in would apply equally to hotel or car rental luggage check-in.

What to Tip an Airport Porter

Many people do not use a porter at the airport to carry their bags for one simple reason: they don't know what to tip him. Very few airports post the charges and most people do not want to appear unsophisticated by asking the porter what they should pay.

Well, if you are one of these people, despair no longer. I have figured out exactly what the proper amount should be. Let me describe to you the process I went through.

I began by analyzing exactly what was involved. In the average trip the porter takes about thirty seconds to load my bags, one minute to carry it the fifty-some feet from the curb into the lobby check-in counter and thirty seconds to unload it—for a total of two minutes.

Assuming that the minimum wage for unskilled, manual labor with work clothes and trolley provided is $3.35 per hour, I calculated that the two minutes of labor were worth eleven-and-two-thirds cents.

Of course, I realized that this was not the amount that the passenger should pay. The porter, after all, recieves the elever-and-two-thirds cents from the airport authority as part of his minimum wage. What the passenger should pay is only the tip portion on that amount, *i.e.*, 15 percent or about 1.675 cents.

After first completing my calculations, I felt confident enough at last to hire an airport porter. That was at New York's JFK.

I can't remember everything the porter said to me when I handed him his tip. There was a lot in there about me having a canine maternal heritage—which I'm sure was quite mistaken.

What really got me was that when I'd paid the porter the tip, I'd purposely erred on the side of generosity by rounding the 1.675 up to two cents.

Since then, through trial and error, I've found that it takes about a dollar a bag before I stop getting comments about my mother.

I have to confess, however, that at that level, I feel I'm participating in some kind of regressive redistribution of income. I mean, these porters must be pulling in a hundred dollars an hour. And most of it unreported to the tax man. They should be paying me.

Box 5-1.	What to Tip Airport Porters Abroad

To get a breakdown on what to tip an airport porter as well as anyone else in foreign countries, I recommend *The International Guide For Tipping*, by Nancy Star, published by Berkley Books. ISBN 0-425-08905-3. Cost: $5.95.

Hints on Using Porters

If you are traveling light, you'll never need a porter. Occasionally, however, you will discover yourself traveling with enough bags for an army (see *How To Travel With Children* beginning at page 369) or having to cover a long distance quickly with heavy carry-on in order to catch a connecting flight. In that case, following are three tips which you may find helpful:

1.   The post-service power position. Don't negotiate the charge with the porter ahead of time. Wait until you get to your destination. That's when you're in the best bargaining position. Pay him a dollar a bag and walk away.

2.   The per-bag negotiating ploy. If you don't feel comfortable unless you've negotiated a price ahead of time, negotiate the price on a per-bag basis with all your bags on the ground. Once you've settled on a price, gather up as many bags as you can comfortably carry yourself and tell the porter you want him to carry only the remainder.

3. The price-per-yard locator. Occasionally you will need to get a porter inside the departure area—for instance, when you're making connections or have ended up at the wrong airline check-in desk (Air Malawi instead of Air Mali). In that case, don't wait around inside the terminal for a porter to pass by. Instead go outside to the curb. That's where they all hang out, waiting to catch the lucrative curb-to-counter trips. (The curb-to-counter trips are the shortest and hence, at a flat rate per bag, the most lucrative on a per-yard and per-minute scale.) Have them load you up and then let them know for once they're going to have to work for their money.

When to Check in at the Lobby Check-In Counter

If you have bags to check and have not checked them at the curb, then you will have to check them at the lobby check-in counter. If you have only carry-on luggage, then it is usually best to by-pass the check-in counter and go directly to the gate to get your boarding pass. Since no luggage is checked at the gate, the lines move much faster.

Even with only carry-on luggage, however, it can be advantageous to get your boarding pass at the lobby check-in counter if the lines are reasonable and:

(a) It's important to check in early—for instance, because the plane is likely to be crowded and you want to avoid being bumped or assigned a poor seat, or you're standing-by for a flight and your time of checking-in determines your priority. The lobby counter commences check-in often several hours before the podium at the gate does, and even when they're both open for check-in, it will take time to walk to the gate.

(b) When it's too late to get a reservation by phone and there are two possible alternative flights at the end of different concourses. Checking in at the counter saves you a lot of shoe leather and sweat if the first flight you try happens to be full.

How to Determine Which Line at the Check-In Counter Has the Slowest People

As we all know, the quickest line is not necessarily the shortest line. A lot depends on the people who make it up. If the people in your line are disorganized, argumentative or plagued with problems, your line will be slow no matter how short it is. Correctly gauging the "slowness rating" of people standing in line is an art which can come only from years of experience. However, the following general observations about airport check-in lines may be helpful:

1.   Travelers with only one bag are generally faster—not only because there is only one bag to check but also because the ability to travel with just one bag shows the people have an ability to plan ahead, which means they're less likely to have last-minute problems.

2.   Inexperienced travelers are generally slower. They're more likely not to know the routine or what type of seat they want, or to have packed away their tickets or passport, or to ask interminable questions of the staff. Some key indications that travelers are inexperienced:

(a)   They have a large documents folder which contains their ticket, passport, insurance, foreign money, *etc.*

(b)   Their passport is new.

(c)   They are talking excitedly in the line.

(d)   Their luggage is plastic, brand new and/or of a monstrous size.

(e)   They keep looking at their watch when there is still an hour to go before the flight.

(f)   They are accompanied by several nonpassengers seeing them off.

3.   A person with a major problem or a fussy person who sees everything as a major problem is as bad as five people in a line. Some techniques for spotting fussy/major-problem people:

(a)   There's no check-in clerk at the front of the line. (They're off talking to a superior about the problem of the person waiting there.)

(b)   Both the person at the front of the line and the check-in clerk are hunched over something on the podium.

(c)   Somebody in line is complaining to the person next to them, is looking worryingly through their tickets or otherwise appears upset. (In which case you should walk right up to them and ask them if they have a problem. If they're really a fussy/major-problem person, they'll tell you all about it and you can go to another line.)

4.   Several people who are traveling as a group will generally be faster than the same people traveling singly. This is particularly true of families since they let the father or mother handle everything for the group. As long as they can get a block of seats together, they put off deciding precisely in which seats they will sit until they get into the plane.

Four Techniques for Switching to a Faster Line

As everyone knows, whatever line you are in will always be the slowest. Or at least a large percentage of the time it will be. To mitigate this problem, may I suggest the following four techniques:

1.   Wait in more than one line at once. Many people, if they are traveling together, will have each person wait in a separate line; whichever one gets to the front first can check-in the others. Most people, however, don't realize that you can do the same thing if you are traveling alone. Two ways:

   (a)   Make a deal with the person behind you. You each wait in different lines, and whoever gets to the front first brings the other one in.

   (b)   Leave your bag. Tell the people behind you that you have to go to the toilet and ask them if they could save your place and watch your bag. Walk towards the toilets. When you're sure they're no longer watching you, circle back by a surreptitious route to another line a little out of sight and begin waiting there. As your original line moves forward, the people who were behind you will naturally move your bag forward ahead of them, keeping your place. If your bag beats you to the front, you can move back into its line. If not, you can pick up your bag after you hand your ticket to the counter staff at the front of the second line.

2.   Beat everyone to the new lines opening up. If all the lines are really long, have someone save your place and go prospecting for empty positions. Ask the check-in staff whether more personnel will be coming on and if so, when they should be arriving and which of the current empty positions they are likely to go to. Strange as it seems, there often is a logical basis to when and how the positions are staffed and most of the check-in personnel are aware of it and will tell you.

   After that, keep an eagle eye on the likely spaces. If a staff-member approaches one of the empty positions, immediately move in and ask him if he's opening up. Don't wait for him to turn his sign over or direct people there; by then it'll be too late.

3.   Disregard the signs over the counter. In your search for alternative lines, if there is no one in line at a particular counter, go there—even if the sign over the counter applies to a different flight or class of travel. When flying economy, I've often checked in at passengerless first-class or business-class counters.

4.   Crowd in line. In my opinion, to crowd in line in front of other people is going beyond the rules of the game. It's all right to take advantage of loopholes in the rules but not to break them. Nonetheless, in some countries, such as Germany, to crowd in line is expected practice. So if you're ever in such a country and absolutely have to get to the front quickly, may I suggest the following three techniques:

(a)   **Crowd where two lines are merging.** In that situation, none of the people are certain who is in which line and you can pretend to each line that you are in the other.

(b)   **Crowd in front of groups.** Groups tend to be inward looking and so the people in the forward part of the group will have their back to the front of the line. This means they're less likely to notice you crowding or to have taken much note of who's ahead of them.

(c)   **Put your bag in line first.** This technique can be used two ways:

(1)   Sneak your bag in first and then leave. Return a moment later, make yourself known, gesture to your bag as though it's been there for a long while and say, "Thank you," to the person behind you as though he's been saving you a place. This is particularly effective when a group is behind you because the person to whom you say, "Thank you," will usually assume that someone else in the group was saving your place.

(2)   Bring your bag in and place it just behind someone's bag, secretly reading, as you do so, his name and address off of his luggage tag. Leave before anyone behind can say anything. A moment later return with your second bag and, as you put it down, knock over the person's bag. "Oh, I'm sorry, Fritz," you say, loud enough for the people behind you to hear. He will turn to you with a smile as though you're an old friend he can't quite place. Quickly bend down, straighten up his bag and then say, "You know, that's a really nice pair of lederhosen you've got on there. Did you get them in Dusseldorf?"

The trick is to get the people behind to conclude you're a friend of the guy in front before the guy in front concludes you're some kind of deviate on the make.

Additional Options Open to Those With Only Carry-On Luggage

If you have nothing but carry-on baggage, you're likely to have several other line-beating alternatives open to you:

1.   Special carry-on counters. Some airlines, particularly the international ones, have separate lines for people with only carry-on. These lines naturally move faster than the luggage-to-check lines. On the intercontinental flights, where many fewer people travel with only carry-on luggage, these special lines are often hidden away at less obvious counters; so you may have to ask where they are.

2.   Ticket-purchase counters. If lines are really bad, you can go to the ticket-purchase counter and buy a new ticket for the same flight. Since the departure time is so close, the ticket-purchase staff will normally issue you a boarding pass right there for your new ticket. If there is no one waiting at the ticket-purchase counter, you can sometimes get a boarding pass even when not buying a ticket.

3.   Airline clubs. If you are desperate, you can go to the airline's club, write a check to join and check-in. (See **Whether To Join An Airline Club** beginning at page 160.) One person I know who did this then stopped the check when he got home assuming the airline wouldn't bother to come after him; they didn't.

4.   The gate. Of course, as mentioned above, on most domestic flights and some international ones, you can go straight to the gate and check in there.

The Best Way to Handle Your Baggage in the Check-In Line

Most people waiting in the luggage check-in line keep their bags gathered around them. Every time the line moves, they lift their bags up, move them a few inches forward and put them back down.

I've never understood why they do this. Before I get at the end of a check-in line, I always take my bag up and leave it at the front by the side of the ticket counter. That way I have to lift it only once again—when I'm putting it onto the conveyor at the counter.

Apparently the mass of luggage lifters don't seem to realize that when you start at the end of a line, you're extremely likely to end up at the front. They seem to feel they have to keep their luggage close by in case they're suddenly required to take off at right angles or in reverse or, for all they know, vertically.

How perilous life must be for them.

I hope you're not like that.

At least, not anymore.

Tips on Checking Your Luggage

1.   Check only those bags which you can live without for 48 hours. That is the period in which 98% of all lost luggage is recovered. Pack your carry-on luggage with those things you'll need immediately.

2.   Tear off your old baggage tickets. You want your bags to go where you're going this trip, not where you went last trip.

3.   Put durable luggage tags on your luggage. The tags should have your permanent business address and phone number on them. You should use your business and not home address—not only because it'll foil those potential thieves who read your label to determine you're not at home, but also because a business address will normally have someone there during the day to receive messages and lost luggage. (By the way, most airlines require that anything strapped to the outside of your luggage have a separate tag, in case it falls off in transit.)

4.   If you are to be at your destination for a day or more, you should add a temporary tag. These tags are available at most check-in counters. Put on this tag the address and phone number of your temporary destination plus the dates you will be there. If the bags are lost, the additional label will assist the luggage recovery people in getting the bag to you.

5.   Tape your business address, phone number and itinerary on the inside of your case. Sometimes the outside tags are torn off and the airline has to open the case to determine ownership. Also, if you lose your baggage check, merely having your name on a tag on the outside may not be enough to get out of baggage claim, since any thief could easily put his own tag on a bag.

6.   Lock your luggage. You not only want to prevent things from being taken out but also prevent drugs and other contraband from being put in. Some countries like China won't take checked luggage unless it can be locked. (On the other hand, it should be pointed out that under FAA pressure some international airlines flying into the US now require checked bags to be left unlocked so that they can be easily searched if X-rays reveal anything.)

7.   See that the correct airport destination tag is put on your luggage. For instance, it may be important to you that your bags go to DFW (for Dallas-Fort Worth) rather than DTW (for Detroit). The three-letter codes for your airports should be in the itinerary from your travel agent, your pocket flight guide, your *Airport Pocket Guide* or, failing all those, the *World Aviation Directory* at your main public library. Appendix One at page 385 contains the three-letter codes for most of the US airports.

8.   If you will have to change planes to complete your trip, make sure that the sequence of your flights reads on the tag from the bottom up.

Figure 5-2.   Connecting Flight Tag

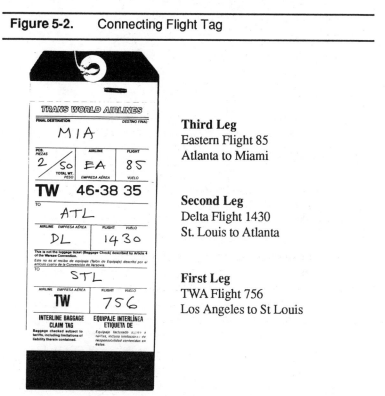

Third Leg
Eastern Flight 85
Atlanta to Miami

Second Leg
Delta Flight 1430
St. Louis to Atlanta

First Leg
TWA Flight 756
Los Angeles to St Louis

How to Choose the Best Airline for Your Fragile or Perishable Items

The best strategy for checking fragile or perishable items is, of course, not to check them at all. Carry them on board. However, if you have to check the item because of size or whatever, get a copy of each alternative airline's conditions of carriage and read the sections on fragile and perishable items. Some airlines definitely have better policies than others. A few of the things you should look for:

1. General rules. A few US airlines refuse to accept any liability whatsoever with respect to fragile or perishable items. The better US airlines follow versions of the old CAB rules which lapsed when deregulation occurred. These rules required the airlines to be liable for such items in one or more of the following situations:

(a) The item was packaged in an original factory-sealed carton or other such container designed to protect the fragile item. (Fragile items contained within a normal suitcase were excluded.)

(b) The damage was due to the airline's negligence and not to the inadequate packing, fragility or perishability of the items. In practice this meant that the outside of the case had to be damaged as well.

(c) The item was permanently lost (in which case the fact it was fragile or perishable would have been irrelevant).

2. Excess valuation insurance. A few of the airlines which admit liability for fragile or perishable items in the above situations will do so only if you have purchased special excess valuation insurance to cover the items. (See page 299 below.)

3. Definition of fragile or perishable. The old CAB rules also required the airlines to publish the list of those items considered fragile; so most conditions of carriage contain such a list, often extending, in some cases, far beyond what you and I would call "fragile". If your item is borderline, it's possible that one airline would consider it fragile or perishable while another would not. For instance, several of the airlines specifically exclude eyeglasses, contact lenses and reasonable toiletries from the definition of fragile; others do not. (Note, if you ever get into small claims court, it may be possible to argue that once a fragile item has been properly packed, it ceases to be fragile.)

4. Valuables. Most US airlines try to disclaim liability completely for certain valuable items, such as antiques, works of art, or electronic or photographic equipment, no matter what the circumstances. (See page 296 below.) However, certain airlines have more extensive lists than others. Also a few will cover your valuables if you buy excess valuation insurance. Check the various conditions of carriage to see if one of the airlines will allow the fragile valuables you have in mind.

Whether You Should Declare Your Fragile or Perishable Items to the Airline

Ideally you want to declare the item, have it accepted by the airline and marked "fragile" or "perishable". Then, if the item spoils or is damaged, you will have a good claim against the airline in small claims court since the airline was put on notice of the special situation yet still took the item under its care. To strengthen this claim, be sure to get written evidence from the airline that it is accepting the item in knowledge of its fragility or perishability.

The problem is if you declare the item, the airline may decide that it is not suitable for checking and require you to sign a waiver of liability before accepting it. For this reason, if there is a real danger of your having to sign a waiver, some people feel it's best to try to check the fragile or perishable item without declaring it. If you don't sign the waiver, these people argue, you won't be prevented from suing the airline later. They are aided in this argument by the fact that many airlines' conditions of carriage are so poorly written (as, no doubt was the original CAB rule) that it appears unless you sign the waiver, the airline will be responsible for all damage to a fragile or perishable item for whatever reason.

In my opinion, even if you are likely to have to sign a waiver, you should still declare the item to the airline. Unless the airline is put on notice that the item is fragile or perishable, you are not going to be able to claim that the airline should have been more careful with your bag. In addition, under most waivers you'd be required to sign, the airline would usually still be liable if its negligent actions would have damaged ordinary baggage as well. In other words, if your bag is crushed flat as a pancake, it shouldn't matter whether the items inside were fragile or perishable. Once you get to small claims court the line between action which would be negligent towards an ordinary bag and action which would be negligent towards a fragile item can often be blurred in your favor.

Note, a few airlines have waivers which attempt to exclude all liability for damage to fragile or perishable items, even if the airlines' actions would have damaged an ordinary bag. Many lawyers think it's questionable whether a court would enforce such a blanket waiver.

However, to avoid having to find out, try to avoid any airline which uses such language. (You can usually find an airline's waiver language in its conditions of carriage.)

Why, if You Have Excess Luggage, You Should Fly the Airline Which Uses the Piece Method

As discussed above at the top of page 112, the weight-method baggage limit is roughly only one-third of the piece-method limit. But that's not the only reason it's more expensive. Even if the limit were the same, the additional charge for baggage exceeding the limit is much higher under the weight method.

The standard IATA-designated charge has been one percent of the full one-way first-class fare per kilogram (2.205 pounds) of excess luggage. For instance, if you had 70 pounds (31.75 kilograms) of excess baggage on a San-Francisco-to-London flight and the IATA weight-method applied (which thankfully it does not), then based on a $3000 first class fare your excess luggage charge would be $30 per kilogram or approximately $952.50 in total. Under the piece method, your total excess luggage charge for many airlines would be approximately $60, or less than 1/15th of the weight-method charge.

Recently even the airlines have begun to recognize that the excess baggage charges under the weight method have been excessive. After conducting an extensive study, the International Civil Aviation Organization has recommended that the charges be reduced to one percent of the *economy-class* fare. In addition, more and more non-US airlines seem to be converting to the piece method. Experts predict that in a few years the piece method will be the worldwide standard.

In fairness, it should be pointed out that if you have only a small excess, the piece method can be more expensive than the weight method, since the piece method charges a flat rate for a band of excess weight. In the example above, if you exceeded 70 pounds, you could have up to another 70 pounds for a flat charge of $60. If your excess was only one pound, you would still pay the full $60. In which case, you would be paying at the rate of $60 per pound (or $132 per kilogram), much higher than the weight-method rate of $30 per pound.

How to Avoid Excess Luggage Charges

1. **Advance warning**. Before booking, check what the various airlines' limits are. Your travel agency should have access to this information on

its computer system. If not, you can always call the airlines and ask. If you think you may be close to the limit, go with the airline which is more generous.

2. Advance planning. If you know you will exceed the limit, then you can try to avoid the problem by:

(a) Sending the excess by another method of shipment early, such as by sea, so that it arrives when you are there;

(b) Leaving the item home and buying a new one when you arrive if the item is worth less than the expected excess luggage charge; or

(c) Pooling your excess luggage with fellow passengers who are under the limit. For many airlines, you don't have to bother allocating the contents among various bags; *the airline will pool the weight of any passengers' bags which are presented together for check-in, whether or not the passengers are officially traveling together as a group.* If you're traveling alone, ask someone in line who has only lighter luggage if they'd mind pooling with you.

3. Bluff. Just put your bags in and see what happens. Many times, if the plane is not full, the airline staff will not bother to check the weight and/or number of bags.

4. Unaccompanied baggage. If you are traveling under the weight system, ask the airline what the charge would be to send your excess as "unaccompanied" baggage. This is baggage shipped at 50 percent of the normal cargo rates—which often works out to be less than the weight-method excess baggage charges. Generally the airlines allow only an air passenger's personal items to be shipped this way. Usually included in the definition of personal items are portable musical instruments, type-writers and sport equipment. Items such as money, securities, tickets, documents, jewelry, watches, furs, films, cameras, perfumes, household furnishings, merchandise and sales' samples, however, are not allowed. In addition, several airlines require a minimum weight, usually between ten to 35 kilograms.

Unaccompanied baggage must be sent to the same destination that you are traveling to but, at the airline's discretion, may take a different route and a longer amount of time to get there. Once it does, you'll have to clear it through customs yourself (an aggravating and time consuming process) and pay any local duties and baggage-handling fees—which, on smaller shipments, may offset the savings over the normal excess baggage rates. So before using this method, you'll probably want to check out a few other alternatives.

5.   Mail. Go to the airport post office and find out the price of mailing your excess and unnecessary items to your next destination or home. If you send it surface mail, the charge may be quite reasonable for small amounts. In addition, if you are mailing it home you will be able to use the $50-per-day exemption, which, if you are near your $400 limit, may save you more in duty than the cost of the postage. (See page 126 above.)

6.   Excess baggage broker. Ask airport information whether there is an excess baggage broker nearby. Since most people do not use their entire free baggage limit, firms have appeared which purchase block amounts of unused excess baggage space from the airlines. You can often ship your excess baggage through a broker at half the cost the airline would charge you directly under the weight method.

7.   The lost-luggage trick. One person I know who was broke, success-fully tried the following. At the check-in desk, he stole a baggage-check tag from the container there and filled it out with his airline flight. Then he put the baggage-check tag on his excess bag, along with an address label giving his name and destination address and phone number. Then he took the bag down to his airline's baggage claim and left it on the carousel. When the airline baggage staff discovered the bag, they looked up his name in the computer as a recent passenger, assumed the bag had been misdirected and shipped it on to him for free.

Although demonstrating chutzpah, this technique is basically a form of theft and so, as far as I am concerned, not to be recommended. A better way to try to accomplish the same thing without actually committing a crime is to forget the baggage-check tag and use only the address label (filled out with your name, flight number, destination address and phone number). Instead of taking the bag to the airline, turn it in anonymously to Lost and Found. The staff there will read the address label and call your airline, which will then pull your name up on the computer and, if you are lucky, send the bag on to you for free as a goodwill gesture.

If not, you can pick your bag up on your way back or, if you really need it, arrange for it to be shipped at the lowest possible cost.

Where to Put Your Airline Tickets

While traveling, the safest place to keep your airline tickets is where you keep your money—in your wallet or if you're paranoid, in your money belt. The tickets are small and will fit easily in either.

Unfortunately, travel agents don't seem to want you to put your tickets in the safest place. Whenever they deliver your tickets, they've invariably put them in some gargantuan cardboard ticket folder which won't fit anywhere. To add heft, they stuff into the folder a multipage itinerary, triplicate invoice and half a pound of advertising circulars.

When this happens to me, I always remove my tickets from the folder—once I'm able to distinguish it from the other garbage there—and put it in my wallet. I don't mind if someone steals my itinerary, my invoice and my half a pound of advertising circulars; I do mind if they steal my tickets.

When I get to the airport, I take the naked tickets out of my wallet and hand them to the check-in clerk. She normally looks at me like I'm some sort of pervert and immediately clothes my tickets in a gargantuan billboard emblazoned with the name of the airline and with my first flight's ticket and boarding pass waving idiotically at passers by through a slit on one side.

"There," the ticket clerk's look seems to say, "try to put that in your wallet."

Not one for confrontation, I slip meekly away and once out of sight, throw away the ticket folder (unless it's also doubling as a boarding pass), fold up my first flight's ticket and boarding pass into my shirt pocket, put the balance of my tickets back into my wallet and mosey off towards the plane, satisfied that once again I have struck a blow for reason and good taste in airline travel.

What Happens if You've Got a Boarding Pass but No Ticket

You can't get on the plane. If you used the boarding pass but kept the ticket, you could use the ticket to take the flight again or get the normal refund for an unused ticket.

My sister once checked-in at the gate, got her boarding pass but neglected to get her ticket back from the agent. When she went to board, the same agent who had checked her in refused to let her on. Not only that, he began screaming at her, accusing her of trying to cheat the airline, and made a big display of calling the cops. After the plane left, they found her ticket in a pile on the podium.

So let that be a lesson. When they issue you your boarding pass, for God's sake, make sure they give you your ticket back. You don't want to give these crazies who work for the airlines an excuse.

CHAPTER SIX

HOW TO WAIT IN THE AIRPORT

The Major Problem with Airports

The major problem with airports is that they are inherently boring. Try to do paperwork or read a book and you find yourself constantly looking up, unable to concentrate. Try to watch TV (either in the bar or out in the passenger lounge) and the very same programs which at home you might have found interesting, now seem lackluster and hackneyed; you find it hard to keep your eye on the screen. The sense of ennui is everywhere—in the shops, the cafeteria, the rest rooms, the video-game parlor, even the local exhibit.

Local exhibits are a particular characteristic of small airports in the Midwest. They usually feature a locally-manufactured irrigation pump set up on a pedestal in a glass case; or a display in a wall case showing a bas-relief sugar beet with orange arrows emanating in all directions—to a candy bar, a piece of cake, a bottle of soda pop, *etc.*—like some kind of Junior High School science exhibit.

I remember one exhibit in particular, at an airport in Oklahoma, designed, no doubt, to encourage airline passengers to move to the state. It was filled with pictures of oil wells, power lines, miles of flat dry farm land and tidbits of information such as (I kid you not) that the Oklahoma state flower is the mistletoe, the state bird, the scissor-tailed flycatcher, and the state motto, the Latin for "Labor overcometh all things".

What in God's name was the Oklahoma state legislature thinking of? Mistletoe? Flycatcher? Work hard enough and even you can overcome the difficulties of living in Oklahoma?

Well, I guess at least it had the benefit of not being completely boring.

Of course, some airports depend on more than local exhibits to spark the passenger's interest. *USA Today* last year listed some unusual "high-flying delights" available at certain US airports. Top of the list: a used bookstore at Milwaukee's General Mitchell International, a popcorn stand at Greater Cincinnati International, a shoeshine shop at St. Louis' Lambert International, a Mexican nachos snack bar at Atlanta's Hartsfield International, and a fish store at Seattle-Tacoma International and Boston's Logan International.

Wait a minute. My heart! My heart! The excitement is just too much to bear.

Let's face it. The only way you're going to avoid the boredom of airports is to stay out of them.

How to Find Things You Need at the Airport

If you are a frequent flyer, the *Airport Pocket Guide* (discussed above at page 27) will show you where to find most of the important airport facilities, such as cocktail lounges, snack bars, restaurants, toilets, phone centers, luggage lockers, escalators, elevators, banks and information desks.

If you are not a frequent flyer, ask your travel agency to give you (along with all the other junk they put in your ticket folder) a photocopy of the relevant airport plans from their reference sources. If it's a good agency, it probably subscribes to the *Airport Pocket Guide* or some comparable publication.

If you arrive at the airport without an airport plan or the plan you have doesn't answer your questions, you can check three other sources of information:

(a) The courtesy phones, which are placed along the concourses;

(b) The airport maps, which are usually placed in the main lobby of the terminal near the entrances to the concourses and occasionally (in the more intelligent airports) at the entrance to the terminal itself; and

(c) The information desk, which is almost always in the main lobby of the terminal.

If you get desperate, you can call the airport authority directly at the number listed in the local phone directory. (See Appendix One below at page 385 which lists the phone numbers of all the major airports.)

Box 6-1. How to Tune In

To help fight the boredom at airports, some people travel with a small radio. If you are one of these people, you can find the station you want quickly by using a card-sized listing of all the AM and FM stations and their musical formats in 24 of the USA's largest cities and top tourist attractions. Order from Buick Radio Guides, P.O. Box 219-T, Ypsilanti, MI 48197. Cost: $4.50 for the set of 24.

How to Deal with Hare Krishnas

Airports attract true believers intent on proselytizing. It's not just that a large number of people pass through airports but that the people passing through airports are more likely to be far from home, lonely, rootless—in short, perfect targets for those who know they have the answer.

You see a lot of Hare Krishnas. A shaved head with a smudge of orange on the forehead, a bulky cardigan sweater over a dirty linen robe, sandals with socks (something no one else in the world would wear except perhaps an Englishman) and the ever-present book in their hand with the picture on the cover of some Indian god rising like a many-armed insect. They always seem to be trying to convert some young marine recruit. Perhaps the Hare Krishnas are attracted by the similar haircut and aura of stupefied blind obedience.

Assuming you are not interested in spending the rest of your life bouncing up and down on a sidewalk, beating a tambourine and looking generally goofy, then your goal when encountering Hare Krishnas and other such true believers is quite simple—get on past them as quickly as possible with the least amount of contact.

To accomplish this goal efficiently, you first have to understand that what makes these people such pests is not that they are out to get you—a lot of people you encounter in air travel are out to get you. What makes them such pests is that they genuinely believe it's in your own best interests if they succeed.

If you give them any sort of encouragement, no matter how slight, they will glom onto you like some sort of psychic leech. So when encountering Hare Krishnas and their ilk, you've got to forget everything your mother taught you about being polite. When they approach, look right through them; don't return their smile. Whey they ask you a question, don't respond. Don't tell them where you're from. Don't say you want to look at their book. Don't tell them your name. Believe me, they're not interested in any of your answers; they're only interested in slowing you down, so they can get a good grip on your mind.

Whether to Join an Airline Club

Most of the major airlines have private clubs which travelers can join. If you fly a lot, the cost (from $50 per year for Braniff's Business Club to $150 per year for TWA's Ambassador Club) is definitely worth it. Some of the advantages are as follows:

1. **More comfortable seating**, including desks to work at.

2. **Quieter surroundings**—the result of carpets, curtains, upholstery and a generally more civilized clientele. Hare Krishnas are not allowed without a membership card.

3. **Complimentary beverages and snacks.**

4. **Color television.**

5. **Convenient phones** at desks and/or armchairs, often with a partial soundproofing barrier in between. Some clubs now have credit-card-operated fax machines as well.

6. **Flight check-in.** If you have no luggage to check, then you usually may get your boarding pass at the club. Not only is the line much shorter but at many clubs you don't have to wait in line at all. Just give the staff your ticket with a note of what you want and go have a drink. When they've got your boarding pass, they'll page you.

7. **Flight reservations and ticketing.** Again the lines are much shorter and at many clubs nonexistent.

8. **Free baggage storage.** Although there is no cloakroom attendant, the significant cost of club membership is enough to screen out the typical baggage thief. Often, after arriving at a major hub airport, I'll leave my garment bag at the airline club while I make a day-trip on a commuter airline and then pick my bag up before flying out again to that night's destination.

9. **Conference rooms.** Many clubs have conference rooms which you can reserve for business meetings. This is particularly convenient for situations where customers are flying in from several places or where the only way to catch a customer is when he is passing through the airport.

Once, in New York, a potential client who was interviewing investment banking firms was unable to fit my firm in. I found out what airport he was leaving from and at the last minute arranged to meet him at the club run by the airline he was flying. The meeting resulted in an $800 million deal for my firm—well worth the $100 it cost me earlier in the day to join that particular airline club.

How to Choose an Airline Club

When deciding which airline club or clubs to join, in addition to checking that each of the advantages discussed above are available, be sure to check whether the club:

1.   Has a convenient distribution of clubs. Is the airline likely to have clubs at the airports from which and to which you will be traveling? Also, if you are interested in a specific club service, such as conference rooms, be sure to check which locations have that service. Often, the services are not available at all locations.

2.   Has convenient opening hours. A club at a given airport will usually open a few hours before the airline's first flight and close immediately after its last flight. If the airline has only one flight a day in the morning, the club will not be available in the afternoon and the evening when you may need it.

3.   Allows you to use the facilities even when you are not flying the airline that day. If it does (and most do), then you can sit in the lounge enjoying drinks, snacks and TV while waiting for someone to arrive on another airline or you can use the conference room (as I did above) for meeting out-of-town clients. Often, when the club of the airline I'm flying is overcrowded, I'll get my boarding pass at that club and then move to another, less-crowded airline club to which I also belong.

4.   Has reciprocal agreements with other airline clubs which allow you to use certain of the other clubs' facilities as well. Depending on the pricing, this can save you a considerable amount of money in membership fees. Warning: Be sure to check the small print to see just how reciprocal the agreements really are; they're usually limited to only certain locations.

5.   Charges for the use of conference rooms. Most don't unless you use the conference room for more than an hour or so.

6.   Provides free local calls from club phones. This seems minor, but when you're making a lot of local calls, you either have to carry a hundredweight of change around with you or bear the expense of the minimum credit-card charge per call.

7.   Provides free liquor. Clubs usually charge for liquor in domestic flight lounges but not in international flight lounges. There are exceptions both ways.

8.   Has a special flight-reservation number. Several clubs have special tollfree flight-reservation numbers that are less likely to be busy than the general reservation numbers.

9.   Has a message drop. Several clubs have formal procedures whereby phone messages, mail and express packages can be left for you at the club.

10. Cashes checks. Several of the clubs will allow you to obtain cash on a personal check guaranteed with a credit card at the club itself. Others require you to go out to the ticket-purchase counter.

11. Excludes children. Depending whether you're traveling with or without your family, this can cut either way.

Box 6-2.	US Airline Clubs		
US Airline Clubs			
Club[1]	**No. Loc.**[2]	**Fee Init**[3]	**Fee /Yr**
Alaska Boardroom (206)433-3315	3/0	$0	$75
Aloha Executive (800)367-5250	5/0	$0	$90[4]
America West Phoenix Club (602)273-2994	1/0	$0	$130
American Admirals Club (817)540-7716	22/2	$50	$100
Braniff Business Club (214)574-5454	1/0	$25	$50
Continental Presidents Club (800)525-0280 (800)231-0856 TX	11/1	$50	$80
Delta Crown Room (800)221-1212	30/2	$0	$125
Eastern Ionosphere Club (800)243-CLUB	21/5	$50	$80
			(continued)

Club[1]	No. Loc.[2]	Fee Init[3]	Fee /Yr
Hawaiian Premier Club (800)367-5320	7/1	$0	$75
Midway Metro Club (312)838-4500	1/0	$0	$50
Northwest World Club (800)328-2216 (612)726-3565 MN	19/8	$50	$110
Pan Am Clipper Club (212)880-1765	13/7	$25	$150
TWA Ambassadors Club (800)527-1468 (214)518-3224 TX	20/6	$0	$150
United Red Carpet Club (213)835-1507	17/10	$100	$100
USAir[5] USAir Club (800)828-8522	27/0	$25	$75

1. Where the special number is not a tollfree number you may be able to get general information through the airline's normal tollfree reservation number.
2. Domestic/International.
3. Initiation fee paid in addition to fee per year.
4. Or twenty revenue flights.
5. Could include up to an additional 12 locations owned by Piedmont, which is being acquired by USAir.

How to Sleep in the Airport

The boringness of the airport, the long and/or ungodly connection times, the number of delayed and canceled flights and the prevalence of jet lag mean that what a substantial minority of passengers want most of all in the airport is to sleep.

Unfortunately, this simple fact seems to have escaped the notice of most of the birdbrains who have designed our terminals.

The typical airport chair assumes every passenger is happy sitting in a upright posture. Where the chairs are joined side by side, their non-removeable armrests and/or high-ridged bucket-seats prevent the passenger from lying down.

If you find yourself faced with such chairs when you want to sleep, there are three alternatives open to you:

(a) Find a bed. Call the operator on the white courtesy phone and/or check at the information desk on the off chance the airport has someplace to sleep. There may be some areas hidden away out near the gates with wide, cushioned benches or couches. Or you might be in one of the few terminals which now provide sleeping facilities on a rental basis. For instance, the Bradley International Terminal at Los Angeles International has Skytel, a 13-room mini-hotel including both beds and showers. Cost: $8.95 for a half hour, $47 for eight hours. The Honolulu Airport Mini Hotel in the main terminal has $4-per-hour beds, and showers and baths for $7.50. For eight hours plus a shower the cost is $22.75.

(b) Sleep sitting up. Although this is not easy, with the proper technique it can be done. (See discussion of sleeping sitting up in the plane, beginning at page 253 below.)

(c) Sleep on the floor. The ideal spot for sleeping on the floor is often an unused gate near the end of a concourse. These areas are not only quieter but usually carpeted as well. Once you've found the spot, you'll want to assume a position that's both stable and comfortable, not putting too much pressure on any one part of the body. The best is to lie on your side in the prenatal position. Rest your head at a downward angle on your lower shoulder and bend you groundside arm at the elbow so your forearm drapes back over your neck. Put your other hand palm down between your lower thighs to take the pressure off the point where the insides of your knees meet.

This position, scientifically designed as it is, unfortunately is not a position in which the average businessperson would want themselves to be discovered by someone they knew. (I'm not sure precisely why this is. Perhaps it has something to do with the oft-mentioned businessperson's deep-seated fear of being though of as practical.) If you are a businessperson, however, do not despair. When you assume the floor-sleeping position, all you have to do is wear dark glasses and a false mustache, and no one will recognize you.

The Secret of Good Airport Eating

There are basically three types of eating establishments at the airport: those where you stand to be served and stand to eat—known as snack bars; those where you stand to be served and sit to eat—known as cafeterias; and those where you sit to be served and sit to eat—known as restaurants. Apart from whether you're standing or sitting, there appears to be very little to distinguish among the three. Certainly not the food.

In all three, the food is generally either reconstituted, canned, deep-fried, warmed over or a combination thereof. The only stab at freshness is a few pieces of bruised fruit and a Styrofoam bowl of brutally hacked lettuce.

The food is so unappetizing-looking in real life that many airport eateries have resorted to back-lit, full-color picture-menus on the wall, showing what the food was supposed to have looked like. Unfortunately, since the pictures never seem to get the colors just right, the resulting portrayal tends to be somewhat counterproductive.

Even without chartreuse and magenta cheeseburgers pictured on the walls, the decor of the average airport eating establishment is not particularly conducive to good digestion. Bright, flickering neon lights bathing everything in a slight purplish hue; hard, sharp-edged table tops made from Formica-covered slabs of unborn albino linoleum; cramped plastic seats designed to produce sudden excruciating back pain at the end of the regulation eighteen minutes and thirty-seven seconds allotted for your meal.

I'd like to let you in on a secret, however. Most of the major airports in the world do have at least one good restaurant. I mean, a good restaurant. Not just a cafeteria with waitresses.

Of course, it won't be a top restaurant. No top chef wants to be known as the man who cooks at the airport. And since locals find it too much of a hassle to go to the airport just for a meal, there's not enough potential repeat business to push a restaurateur to put in that extra bit of effort.

But the restaurant will be good. Soft lighting, table cloths, comfortable chairs, flowers, fine wines, black-tie waiters, a French-trained chef and not a single picture of a cheeseburger on the wall.

I say it's a secret, because for some reason these restaurants never seem to be properly advertised. They're usually stuck up on another floor in an obscure corner of another terminal and inadequately signed. So if you prefer this type of restaurant to the others, check with the information desk or courtesy phone to get the location.

One bit of warning: eat at one of these good airport restaurants only if you are on an expense account or have recently won the Irish sweepstakes. The cost of your meal could very likely exceed the cost of your plane ticket.

The Cheapest Place to Eat at the Airport

Most of the major airports in the world have employee cafeterias and snack bars. Some also have employee bars and lounges. These establishments are often run at cost or even subsidized by the airport authority.

Although intended only for employee use, many of these establishments don't screen their customers and most of those that do will allow friends of employees in as well. Some are quite convenient to the terminal; for example, one employee bar at Heathrow that an acquaintance of mine uses a lot is just across the road from Terminal 2. The employee cafeteria at National Airport is in the main passenger terminal at the bottom of the ramp leading down to gates 23, 24 and 25.

Try to befriend an airline or airport employee and find out where the employee cafeterias are and what type of screening procedure they have. If there is a screening procedure, ask your newfound friend to escort you in.

How to Deal with Your Luggage When Pushing Your Tray through the Cafeteria Line

If you have not followed the suggestions under *How To Pack For The Flight* above, then you have either to (i) leave your bags at your table—forcing you to keep craning your neck to make sure they're not being stolen; (ii) kick your bags along with your foot as you hold your tray with two hands; (iii) hold your bags with one arm as you balance your tray with the other arm; or (iv) stack your suitcases on the rack, put your tray full of food on top and carry the whole pile to your table with both hands. None of these alternatives, it must be said, will give you the image of someone enjoying a dignified life-style.

On the other hand, if you have followed the suggestions under *How To Pack For The Flight*, you should have no problem. If you don't want to take your luggage with you, you can secure it to your table or chair with the combination-lock. If you want to take your luggage with you, the garment bag, knapsack or shoulder-strap briefcase can be hung from your shoulder, and the wheeled suitcase can be pulled behind you by the leash hooked onto your belt. In either case, since you have both hands and both eyes free to concentrate on carrying your tray, you're much more likely to arrive at your table without having *papier-mache*'d an innocent by-stander *en route* with your meal.

How to Prepare Yourself for Airport Pay Phones

If you are someone who is likely to be using the pay phone in airports a lot, then it pays to pack the following:

1.   A 3-by-5, loose-leaf notebook as mentioned above at page 117. Standing at a public phone with little or no shelf space, trying to hold a large notebook in one hand, while you write on it with the other and simultaneously squeeze the phone between your ear and your shoulder, is not conducive to a good telephone manner.

2.   Your list of phone numbers on a single sheet as mentioned above at page 116. A large Filofax full of addresses presents all the same problems as the large notebook in paragraph 1.

3.   A briefcase which opens at the top and can be hung by a strap from the shoulder. It's much easier to access while standing at the phone than a hinged briefcase sitting on the floor.

4.   A pocketful of coins to make local calls or, where required, to raise the operator. Even where you don't have to use a coin, a coin-paid local call is often quicker and cheaper than using a credit-card.

5.   A telephone credit card number. Although most major airports now have phones which automatically read a VISA, MasterCard, American Express or other such card run along a slot on the front, these phones are often occupied. If you have a phone-company credit-card number, you can still dial direct on a regular phone by punching in the number.

6.   Non-AT&T access numbers. Although most major airports now have phones which at the push of a button will put you directly into a given system, these special phones also are often occupied. With the access number, you'll be able to use a regular phone to dial into your long-distance system.

What More You Should Do to Prepare Yourself for Making Calls from Abroad

Many US telephone-company credit-card numbers are valid for calls from abroad back to the United States. However, in order to make the call you have to raise the international foreign operator, who, in many countries, can take fifteen or twenty minutes to answer.

1. **Foreign local-access numbers.** To avoid the problem of foreign operators, AT&T and MCI each have local-access phone systems in many foreign countries. By calling a special local phone number, you can get into the AT&T or MCI system for your call back to the US. This allows you to bypass the foreign operator and pay US operator-assisted international rates, which are usually less than the foreign country's operator-assisted rates—but not necessarily the foreign country's direct-dial rates. (Note, these systems also allow you to bypass the often quite huge hotel phone surcharges on long distance calls.) Before you go, get the necessary foreign access numbers from USA Direct at (800)874-4000, ext. 333, or from MCI at (800)444-3333. Currently the AT&T system is in more countries and, in several of the countries, even has special airport phones.

Credit Card Calling Systems, Inc., also runs a similar system which allows you to charge your calls from overseas to any major US credit card using a US operator. The main advantage of this system is that it allows you to access US 800 numbers from abroad (although you have to pay for the call to the US). For local access numbers abroad, call (212)323-8030.

2. **Prepaid phone cards.** For calls between foreign phones, most US phone company credit cards are not valid and only a few countries, such as Britain, have credit-card-reader phones. However, in several countries, such as Britain, Italy, France and Japan, special pay phones can be operated on a prepaid magnetic phone card which you can purchase at the airport post office. You insert the card in the phone and can then direct-dial anywhere overseas without having to raise the international operator. This is particularly important in Britain where it's about as easy to raise the international operator as it is to get through to Dial-A-Porn at 9:30 on a Monday morning. The cost of the call is automatically deducted from your prepaid magnetic phone card.

3. **Post office telephones.** Some countries don't allow international calls to be made at all from pay phones. Instead they require you to go to the nearest post office (which runs the telephone monopoly) where they will make the call for you and assign you a booth when the call has connected. Often, payment can be made only in the local currency—no credit cards or collect calls are allowed. So if you're traveling to one of these countries and expect to use the pay phone to call abroad be sure to carry a lot of local currency with you.

The Problem of Touch

There is another problem with foreign pay phones which can be over-come only with years of hands-on experience. And I tell you about it only so you can better deal with the frustration it creates. This is the problem of your coin passing straight through the phone and out the coin return without catching in the mechanism.

Trying to maintain my objectivity on this matter, I am convinced that it is all a matter of touch. Those people who have grown up with a given system have learned with exactly what speed and force to insert the coin and accordingly have no problem; those who are new to the system haven't learned and so have a problem.

I base this conclusion on my experiences in England where the design of the some of the public phones puts a heavy premium on the coin lodging in the machine. In these, the older machines, the coin cannot be inserted until the person you're calling answers the phone. At that point, there is a loud beeping on the line and the caller has just a few seconds to insert the coin before the line is disconnected.

When I first used these machines, my rate of coin lodging was abysmally low (even discounting for the fact that I was often able to pass the coin straight through up to four times before the phone went dead). Panic, of course, may have had something to do with it. But I think it was more a matter of inexperience. My wife, who is English, could get her coins to lodge almost every time.

Now that I've been to England quite a bit and am much more careful about the pressure with which I insert my coins, I've noticed that a much higher proportion of them stay in the box. On a good day, it can be as high as one out of three.

Of course, I have to admit that English mechanisms generally do seem to require a lot more finesse in their operation than the mechanisms of other countries. Take, for example, the flushing of an English toilet. In the United States flushing the toilet is simple; you just pull the handle and the toilet flushes. In England, on the other hand, it's an art. Too little or too much pressure on the handle and nothing happens. You have to strike the perfect balance.

The English, who have grown up with their toilet handles, aren't even aware of it. It's the foreigners who encounter the problems.

The first time I had to flush an English toilet, I tried eight or nine times, each time getting more and more desperate, before finally having to call my wife in to help. It was humiliating. I was the only man in the

Heathrow Airport men's room who had to have his wife come in and pull the toilet handle for him.

"You Americans," I remember my wife saying, flushing the toilet on the very first try, "you just lack finesse."

Judging from their expressions, the other men in the lavatory couldn't have agreed more.

How to Get Information on the Operation of Foreign Phone Systems

If you're still in the US, call international directory assistance and ask them to find out for you. If you're lucky, they'll ask the foreign country's operator and let you know. If not, they'll give you the foreign phone company's number so you can call them yourself.

If you find yourself in a non-English-speaking foreign country's airport, staring at a strange-looking pay phone, don't despair. Nine times out of ten, somewhere there will be instructions in English on how to use the phone. If your phone doesn't have instructions in English, one of the ones nearby will; if none do, then the front pages of the foreign phone book should.

If you're in the one out of ten countries which don't have instructions anywhere in English, try to make out the number for the international operator and dial it. All international operators speak English. The international operator can then direct you to where you can get additional information in English.

Whether to Use the Airport Telephone Booth

Most inexperienced travelers when given the choice in an airport between a public wall phone and a public telephone booth will choose the booth. Experienced travelers are just the opposite.

Phone booths might make sense in the out-of-doors where they can protect you from the elements but inside the terminal they make virtually no sense at all. They are universally cramped, hot, stuffy and inadequately lit. Your bags won't fit inside. If you drop something on the floor, you have to be a contortionist to retrieve it. If you leave the door closed for more than 30 seconds, you start sweating profusely. If you leave the door open, the light goes out.

The only argument in the phone booth's favor is that with the door closed, the booth is marginally more soundproof than a wall phone. Thus, if you don't mind taking a steam bath in a coffin, you'll find it slightly easier to hear and slightly less likely you'll be overheard.

To the experienced traveler, soundproofing is not all that important. Since he's used to the background noise of airports, he can more easily screen that noise out. If the noise is particularly loud, he can use one of the amplified wall phones which are now readily available at the major airports; they have switches on the receiver which increase the volume. Finally, he realizes that sometimes the background noise can be helpful; locked up in a booth, he might miss an important flight announcement or page.

The experienced traveler is also less concerned about privacy. He knows that unless he's particularly loud, hysterical or obscene, most people aren't interested in what he's saying. Those using the wall phones next to him are usually concentrating too much on their own conversations to listen to his. Those walking by can't hear enough to understand. And even those who are interested are almost always complete strangers whom he'll never see again.

To guard against the slight possibility he might be overheard by someone he might not want to overhear, the experienced traveler speaking on the phone usually avoids proper names and adjusts his vocabulary so as to to cast his character in the best light—for example, using "Let's put it in and see if he has any objection" rather than "Let's try to sneak it through", or "Let's insure that our company gets top dollar for its services" rather than "Let's try to squeeze the most we can out of the sucker"—a salutary practice even when one is speaking in private.

How to Make Calls When You Don't Have Enough Money

1. Tollfree numbers. As you are probably aware, most major hotel, rent-a-car and airline companies have tollfree numbers (those beginning with 800). You should carry with you a list of the ones you're likely to use. The tollfree numbers of the major airlines and rental car companies are at the back of most pocket flight guides. You can also obtain them by calling tollfree directory assistance at (800)555-1212.

If you want to go whole hog, you can (i) purchase the *1988 Toll-Free Travel & Vacation Information Directory* by Pilot Books, cost: $3.95, ISBN 0-87576-135-6, or (ii) photocopy the 15 pages of travel-related numbers from your travel agent's *OAG Travel Planner* mentioned above on page 27.

Tip: To avoid charges, if you are accessing one of the alternative phone services, do it on a tollfree rather than a local number. This is especially important if you are calling from a hotel, since hotels have hefty surcharges on local calls.

2. Free phones. In most major airports the nearby hotels have set up a free-phone display in the terminal, consisting usually of a large illuminated board with a picture of each hotel on it, a map showing each hotel's location and a phone which will connect you with the hotel of your choice. This facility is particularly helpful if you've arrived without a reservation and most of the hotels are filled up; you can check a lot of hotels without any cost.

3. Collect calls. Most people are familiar with long distance collect calls but are not aware that local calls can also be made collect. As you have to raise the operator, such calls are more expensive than nonoperator assisted calls; but if you don't have any money, money is no object. When necessary, I have made collect calls not only to people who knew me but also to hotels and restaurants; the latter often have a policy of accepting such calls since the person calling is likely to want to make a reservation.

4. Call backs. If you have only enough money to make one short call (or if you're at a foreign airport where it'll be difficult to raise the international operator again), ask the person you called to call you back on their phone or, if you want to speak to someone else, ask the person you called to call that other person and ask him to call you.

Note: Be careful to check that your public phone will accept incoming calls; some of them won't.

Why the Tourist Rate for Foreign Exchange is so Much Worse than the Traders' Rate in the Financial Pages of the Newspaper

The tourist rate is based on the sale of legal tender, *i.e.*, paper money and coins, while the traders' rate is based on the sale of electronic money; and legal tender results in higher costs than electronic money for the following reasons:

1. Lost interest. The bank or other dealer cannot earn interest on the legal tender sitting in its tills waiting to be sold (as it can on electronic money).

2. Handling costs. The dealer bears much larger costs of shipment, storage and handling for legal tender than it does for electronic money.

3. Small amounts. Since the transactions for legal tender are usually smaller, the dealer's overhead costs are a higher percentage of the amount of currency bought or sold.

4. Time delays. Since it takes longer to account for and dispose of legal tender than electronic money, the dealer takes a greater exchange risk. With electronic money, the dealer can keep track of and thereby continually hedge or otherwise dispose of its net position in a given currency. With legal tender, the dealer often doesn't know until the end of the day, if then, what its net position is. More importantly, even when it does know, since the legal tender is in effect inventory, the dealer won't normally hedge the excess foreign legal tender right away but instead will try to sell it off to consumers over the following days. During this period the dealer has the risk that the legal tender's exchange rate could decline.

How You Can Get a Rate Closer to the Traders' Rate

1. Buy electronic money through a foreign currency trader. If you and/or your friends are going to spend a lot of money abroad (let's say, over $10,000), call the traders (not the tourist tellers) at a major money-center bank or brokerage house and negotiate a rate. Although US banks cannot maintain foreign currency accounts for customers in the US, you should be able to have the money held offshore for you through a foreign subsidiary or wired to a foreign bank. You can then write foreign currency checks against the account or, while you are in the foreign country, obtain foreign legal tender from the account at little or no charge.

If you are going this route, be sure to watch out for the following:

(a) The trader will expect payment in immediately available funds. A check won't do. As a practical matter that means you will be limited to trading with those institutions with which you already have funds on deposit, such as your bank or broker.

(b) The traders' rate is a matter of negotiation. Make sure you tell the trader you are comparing his or her quotes with those of other traders. Note, also, the higher the amount you want to convert, the better your rate is likely to be.

(c) The traders' quote is for "immediate delivery". If the market is clearly moving downwards, what looks like a low rate for delivery today could actually be a high rate for delivery three days from now.

In addition, often the traders take your payment on the day of the trade, in which case they are keeping the interest earned on it up to the date of delivery.

(d) All the charges which might be incurred for wiring funds or setting up accounts are quoted up front.

Note, as the traders now operate in a worldwide market, if you are purchasing a major currency (on which there are no exchange controls), it doesn't matter much in which country your traders are.

2.   Use your credit card for most foreign purchases. When your foreign charges reach the stage to be converted into dollars, they have been (i) transformed into what is in effect electronic money and (ii) combined with everyone else's charges into a million dollar sum. The credit-card company then usually negotiates a million-dollar conversion rate with an independent trader or settles interbank at that rate.

There are three major differences, however, between using your credit card and going directly to the trader yourself.

(a) Fees. Several of the card companies charge a one percent fee for making the exchange.

(b) Exchange rate date. For those which purchase their currency from traders or settle at the traders' rate, the rate is not set until the charges reach the credit-card clearinghouse, a process which can take weeks, even months. During this period, the currency could move for or against you.

(c) Use of money. Since the charges do take so long to clear, you don't have to pay for your foreign currency right away and hence can continue to earn interest on the money in your bank.

Note, the above advantages generally do not apply if you are using your card not to make a purchase but to obtain a cash advance in the foreign currency. In that case, the conversion takes place at the moment of sale at the seller's tourist rate rather than when the charge reaches the credit-card company. In addition, on most cards the customer is charged (i) a one to two-and-a-half percent fee and/or (ii) interest from the moment he or she takes the cash advance. If you use a card for such a cash advance, try to use one of the cards issued on a cash management or other interest-bearing account. There usually is no fee charged and the interest cost is the after-tax forgone earnings on your cash management account, which is usually considerably less than the now mostly nondeductible 18+ percent the credit-card company charges you.

The major problem with credit cards is that there are many parts of the world where they are still not accepted. For instance, in continental Europe, you usually can't use them for buying gasoline or for much of anything outside the metropolitan areas— particularly in Belgium, the Netherlands, West Germany, Switzerland, Yugoslavia and Turkey. Before traveling, be sure to check with your credit-card companies to find out the degree to which their cards are accepted in the country in question (as well as to increase your spending limit since you will probably be spending more than you normally do at home).

3.   Use traveler's checks. You can buy traveler's checks in US dollars or in the foreign currency (usually available only for the major currencies), and either way exchange them for foreign legal tender when you get abroad. Different from legal tender which must be held in inventory by the dealer before being sold or after being bought, traveler's checks have no value until they are issued and cease to have value as soon as the dealer gets a credit for those that are cashed. The result is the dealer's exchange risks and lost interest costs are less. However, because the exchange transactions are invariably small and based on daily rather than immediate currency values, the rates are still set significantly higher than the traders' rate.

Of course, against these savings should be offset:

(a)   Advance payment. You've got to buy your traveler's checks ahead of time and thus lose interest on your money.

(b)   Front-end fees. You usually have to pay a one to one-and-a-half percent commission to purchase the traveler's checks—although it may be possible to avoid this commission if you shop around. For instance, AAA members can get travelers checks free from American Express; Diner's Club members, from Citicorp.

(c)   Cashing fees. You may even have to pay a fee to cash the checks. This is less likely with the foreign-currency traveler's checks.

4.   Purchase your currency as close as you can to the heart of currency trading. The further away you get, the more the dealer is likely to have the various costs discussed above and the higher the rate he will charge. So try to buy your foreign currency in a bank rather than a hotel or corner *bureau de change*, and then in a money-center rather than boondock bank.

If you don't have time to shop around, look at the spread between the buy and the sell rate for the currency. If it's more than five or six percentage points, you're being screwed.

When it is Better to Buy Your Foreign Legal Tender in the Foreign Country

As a general rule, for the best price, you, as an American, should buy your foreign legal tender in the foreign country. There are several reason for this:

(a) **Cheaper costs.** It is less costly for the foreign dealer to obtain his own legal tender than yours. To obtain yours, he's got to either buy it from a broker or wait to obtain it from customers like you who are buying his currency.

(b) **World market in dollars.** As an American, you will be paying for the foreign money in dollars. Dollars are generally an easy money for the dealer to dispose of to brokers or other customers.

(c) **Hard currency premium.** If the foreign country has a soft currency, then the dollar, since it is still (if just barely) a hard currency, will be of more value in the foreign country than in the US—especially if you buy on the black market.

When it is Better to Buy Your Foreign Legal Tender Outside the Foreign Country

Despite the general rule, it is better to buy foreign money outside the foreign country when:

(a) **You're going to pay with coins.** Coins are generally only accepted in the country in which they were issued. Elsewhere they're just too expensive for a currency dealer to store and ship.

(b) **A domestic dealer has a surplus of a foreign legal tender which he finds difficult to unload.** For instance, if there were a lot of rich Arabs visiting the US, a currency dealer at JFK selling dollars to the Arabs would receive more Middle Eastern currency than the dealer could sell back to US passengers going to the Middle East. As a result the dealer might offer the Middle Eastern currency at a price lower than the price obtainable in the Middle East.

(c) There are exchange controls in the foreign country artificially holding up the value of the currency. This occurs most often in developing countries where the government fears the more politically active urban dwellers and army officers (who want to buy foreign goods and food cheaply) than it does the less politically active rural population (who want to export agricultural products for a higher price than that at which their products are sold domestically). If you are going to such a country, you are likely to get a better rate buying its money outside the country than from a government-controlled institution in the country. For instance, you can get a much better rate buying your Indian rupees in Hong Kong than you can at a bank in India.

In fact, in this situation it may be best to forget all the advice in the previous sections and try to make all your purchases with foreign legal tender acquired outside the country since wire transfers, traveler's checks and credit cards will all have to be converted at the higher, official exchange rate.

Note, however, if you purchase such controlled currency outside the country, it is usually illegal to bring it into the country. This is safer, however, than dealing on the black market once you get in the country, where there is the possibility not only of being arrested but also of being conned. In South America, for instance, when governments replace the existing legal tender with a new one in an attempt to fight hyperinflation, the old worthless notes often end up being sold to tourists on the black market.

Note, don't buy more of a controlled currency than you need since the currency-controlled countries usually require you to convert any excess money back when you leave and to account for any expenditures in between.

Note also, several countries, including some of the Communist block ones, not only don't allow you to take any of their money out of the country but also don't allow you to convert it back to your own currency. The result is that whatever amount of money you buy will have to be spent in the country.

If You Run Out of Money on Your Foreign Trip

If you run out of money on your trip, go to the US Embassy or consulate. They can arrange for your family or friends to wire money to the State Department, and then the local Embassy or consulate will disburse an equivalent amount to you, less a $15 charge.

If you can't get to an Embassy or consulate, call the Overseas Citizen Emergency Center at the Department of State at (202)647-5225.

Buying Things at the Airport Shops

When you're traveling, it's nice to buy something with a local connection to take back home—such as orchids from Singapore, sourdough bread from San Francisco, gravlax from Oslo or pre-Columbian figurines from Bogota. If you buy one of these presents from the airport, though, don't expect it to be genuine; the "Norwegian" gravlax, you'll find, is often Canadian, and the pre-Columbian figurine, no matter what certificates of authenticity you get, almost certainly will have been made in the back of someone's garage.

What never ceases to amaze me is how tasteless some of the items are in airport shops. Who buys these things? An ashtray from Rome's Fiumicino International with the picture of the Virgin Mary on it. (Can you see a devout Catholic stubbing out his smoldering butt in her face?) A postcard from the Dallas-Fort Worth Airport showing Dealey Plaza and the route the bullets took from the Book Depository to President Kennedy's head. (I swear I'm not making this up.) A pair of black, crotchless underwear from Las Vegas' McCarran International. (Are there really people out there who are aroused by having sex with somebody whose underpants are still on?) Polyester tea towels imprinted with cartoon maps, imitation car licenses stamped with a common first name, miniature dolls dressed in garish felt clothing, cheap china cups with off-balance decals, tin-plated teaspoons with plastic rosettes on the handle.

It's downright frightening.

The people who buy these things could be sitting next to you on the plane right at this moment.

Why and Where Duty-Free Theoretically Saves You Money

If you buy an item in a duty-free shop, you avoid any local sales tax, excise tax, duty and quotas which otherwise would have been applied in the country of the purchase. The key question in deciding whether to buy duty free, then, is what sales and excise tax, duty or quotas the item in fact would otherwise have incurred.

1. **Sales tax.** Most European countries have a sales-like tax known as the value-added tax (VAT) which can be quite high; but if you are a nonresident and leave the country with your purchase, the VAT is

refunded to you at the border. In that case, you don't effectively save any VAT by shopping in a duty-free shop. In the US, on the other hand, sales taxes are levied by the state and local governments and, as such, are seldom refunded when you leave the country; so you definitely save sales tax by shopping in duty-free.

2.   Tariffs and quotas. High duties and small quotas naturally correlate strongly with those industries which are being protected from the threat of foreign competition. Small quotas, of course, levy an indirect duty by lowering the supply of cheap goods, thereby raising the domestic price, often up to 30 percent higher. One of the main quota categories in the US are textile products governed by the infamous Multifiber Agreement.

Items with direct duties in the United States include textiles, shoes, leather accessories, cheap china tableware and cheap silver jewelry. Among these latter items, the highest US duty is 35 percent. In addition, certain imports from Communist countries can attract a duty as high as 90 percent. For most other dutiable items, however, including perfume, the duty is under ten percent.

3.   Excise taxes. High excise tax items correlate strongly with sins and luxuries, such as liquor, cigarettes and perfume. These taxes are often greater than the duty. For instance, the excise-like internal revenue tax on liquor in the US is $12.50 per gallon; on beer, $9 per gallon.

Box 6-3.	The Most Popular Duty-free Items Worldwide
Item	**% Of Total Duty-Free Sales**
Alcohol[1]	27.20%
Fragrances, Cosmetics & Toiletries[2]	22.60%
Tobacco[3]	14.70%
Leather Goods	5.2%

1. Of which over a third is Scotch whiskey and a little under a quarter is cognac.
2. Of which over half are women's fragrances.
3. Of which over 90 percent are cigarettes.
(Source: *Generation Publications*, Sweden, as quoted in *Time Magazine*.)

Why Duty Free Shops Don't Save You as Much Money as They Could

Added altogether the various tax savings of duty-free shops could be substantial. Unfortunately, the airport shops don't pass all these savings on to their customers. Part of this is because the shop, if it's an independent franchise, has to pay the airport authority a large fee. In Alaska, the franchise to run the duty-free shop (which has one of the highest *per capita* expenditures of any airport duty-free shop in the world, over $100) in the past has been auctioned off to potential franchisees for tens of millions of dollars. In effect, the state is collecting a large part of the potential duty, excise and sales tax back in the form of a franchising fee.

Duty-free shops owned by airports are just as bad. *Flight International Magazine* has estimated that duty-free sales account for up to 50 percent of all airport revenues. The less of the savings the airport passes on to the consumer, the more money it's got to subsidize its other operations.

Box 6-4.	The Ten Cheapest Duty-free Shops in the World As Nominated By International Passengers	
Airport	**% Of All Nominations**	**% Of Users Of Shop**
Amsterdam	33	50
Singapore	12	34
London Heathrow	8	10
Frankfurt	7	12
Hong Kong	5	11
Paris ChasDeG	4	7
Dubai	3	20
Zurich	2	5
Miami	2	6
Copenhagen	2	6
(Source: International Foundation Of Airline Passengers Associations.)		

How to Determine Whether a Duty-Free Price is Cheap

Answer: Prepare by pricing the likely items you might buy, first, in the United States and, second, in the non-duty-free shops in the foreign country.

Generally, in those areas which have very low duties and taxes, such as Hong Kong, the airport duty-free shops, while cheaper than most of the world's other airport duty-free shops, tends to be more highly priced than the regular shops in town. In those jurisdictions, then, you may be better off buying your items before you go to the airport.

In one recent survey, the best duty-free shop averaged 55 percent cheaper than ordinary shops in its nearby city. Others averaged only seven to eight percent cheaper. Many duty free shops had items which were more expensive than in their nearby cities.

Beware of the Hidden Costs of Duty-Free

1.   Conversion costs. You will incur a loss when you convert your dollars to the foreign currency to purchase the item—particularly if you have the duty-free shop do it for you.

2.   Taxes due in the US. Even when you buy an item in a duty-free shop, if you exceed certain limits, you will have to pay US customs duty, internal revenue tax (in the case of alcohol) and even potential state taxes (primarily in the case of alcohol and cigarettes) when you bring the items back into the US. (See discussion of US Customs rules beginning below at page 300.) Even worse, some states, such as Idaho and Oklahoma, won't allow the import of alcohol in excess of certain limits no matter what duty you pay. The US Customs' officials strictly enforce the state requirements.

3.   Taxes due in other countries. If you are taking items into another country, the situation is likely to be even worse. Generally other countries' duty-free exemptions are much lower. In the UK, for instance, the overall exemption is roughly one-tenth the US exemption. In addition, the rates of duty and other taxes imposed on imported items, such as value-added tax, are much higher. Current value-added rates in some European countries can be as high as 38 percent; but between now and 1992 they are gradually dropping to a range of 14 to 19 percent. (The duty-free shop should have a list of the current import exemption amounts for the country to which you are traveling.)

4.   Hassles. If the item is anything larger than perfume, you'll have to carry a plastic duty-free sack, in addition to your regular luggage. Apart from being generally inconvenient, the sack makes it more difficult for you to sneak an additional carry-on bag into the plane—particularly since duty free is often delivered to you at the gate—and, at the other end, can slow you down at customs and, at the very least, make you more likely to be stopped for inspection.

For a one or two dollar savings on a twenty-dollar item, is it really worth it?

Avoid Buying Electrical Appliances in Duty-Free Shops

1.   Voltage. For a large part of the world, there's the problem of the electrical current being at a different voltage.

2.   Repair. If something goes wrong, it's difficult to take the appliance back to the person who sold it to you for repair.

3.   Warranties. Although many internationally available products have warranties which can be honored at a variety of shops, often these warranties are limited to a specific country or group of countries. For example, because the US personal-computer market is so competitive, a Japanese-manufactured personal computer can often be purchased in the US for less than two-thirds the cost of that same computer in the UK; however, the Japanese manufacturers discourage UK residents from buying their computers in the US and bringing them back to the UK by making the warranty on the US-bought computer invalid outside the US—even though there are dealers selling the exact same computer in the UK.

Unless you can assure yourself on all of the above, wait until you get home and spend a little more.

When to Buy Duty-Free in the US Before You Leave

If you are going to be gone on your trip for a while, you might consider buying some items in the duty-free shop in the US. Before you do, here are some pointers:

1.   Buy items you will consume on your trip. To the extent you don't consume them and return with them to the United States, they will be subject *without any exemption* to duty as well as to some state taxes (and, in the case of alcohol, internal revenue tax). In other words, whereas there are exemptions from US duty for items purchased abroad, those exemptions do not apply to items purchased in US duty-free shops.

2.   US law makes it illegal for you to consume your own liquor on the plane. So unless you want to be a secret drinker, any duty-free you buy in the US will have to be entered, unconsumed, into the country of your destination, where, depending on the exemptions, it could be subject to duty.

3.   Without going abroad first, it's difficult to determine whether the US duty-free shop is cheaper. US cigarettes are almost always cheaper in US duty-free shops than elsewhere; on the other hand, UK scotch is also cheaper in the US, at least compared to the UK. For other things, though, you'll just have to make an educated guess based on the discount on the item from US prices outside the duty-free shop, the place of manufacture of the item, the country's relative economic development and the exchange rates. In fact, of all things, exchange rates are probably the most important. If the dollar has dropped against other currencies recently, then US duty-free shops are likely to be cheaper than the foreign ones.

Whether to Buy Duty-Free on the Plane

Most international carriers sell duty-free on their flights. Contrary to what you might think, this duty free is often cheaper than the duty-free shop.

According to one study by *Business Traveller Magazine*, in the past Air Malawi has been 30 percent cheaper than the duty free shop at Amsterdam's Schiphol Airport, traditionally one of the cheapest in Europe. Ethiopian and South African Airways, 20 percent less. Air France, Alitalia, Nigeria Airways, Olympic Airways and Air Portugal ten percent less.

Before you buy in the duty free shop, ask the airline check-in desk whether they can give you a price list of their duty-free items. Beware, however, once you get on the plane, you'll often discover they're out of the more popular listed items.

The Beauty of Duty-Free on Arrival

If you don't buy in the US or on the plane, you still may be able to buy at a duty-free shop on arrival in the foreign country. Whereas most countries have only duty-free on departure, there are now over 15 airports which allow you to buy on arrival before you go through customs, including Cairo, Rio de Janeiro, Sao Paulo, Khartoum, Reykjavik, Accra, Singapore, Kuala Lumpur and Moscow.

The advantages of duty-free on arrival are manifold. Less muscle strain. More room on the plane. Fewer broken liquor bottles in the cabin. Greater safety—not only from duty free items falling from overstuffed luggage bins but also from fire. One of the contributing factors to the Manchester, England, aircraft disaster was broken bottles of alcohol catching fire.

Duty-free on arrival can also lead to considerable fuel savings and hence lower fares. British Caledonian once estimated that if each passenger on its transatlantic flights carried an orange, the additional fuel cost per year would be approximately $350,000. If each passenger were instead carrying a duty-free bottle of booze, the additional cost each year would be twenty or thirty times that. *Flight International Magazine* estimated that there is a total of 72,000 tons of duty-free alcohol carried worldwide each year, costing an approximate 6.5 million gallons of fuel.

Despite these clear advantages of duty-free on arrival, don't expect to see it widely adopted. Some of the arguments put forth against it:

Argument 1: Having the passengers shop for duty-free on arrival will slow up their exit from the airport.

[More than the normally slow baggage retrieval does? Come on, who are you kidding?]

Argument 2: Because people will have some place to go other than baggage claim, customs officers will find it more difficult to guess which flight someone was on. This is important to the customs officers because they tend to target those flights coming from areas where returning passengers are likely to have purchased a lot of dutiable bargains.

[What the customs officers are really concerned about, of course, is that they may have to give up the easy pickings among relatively harmless, vacationing bargain hunters and start focusing on the more difficult-to-catch drug dealers.]

Argument 3: If passengers know they can get duty-free on arrival, the airlines will lose some of their inflight duty-free sales.

[This is not just a loss for the airlines but also for the flight attendants. The reason the attendants are always running up and down the aisle pushing duty-free at you is that they get a substantial commission on their sales. You can be sure to see their union at the hearings battling against duty-free on arrival no matter how safe and economical it is.]

Argument 4: Duty-free on arrival competes unfairly with local merchants who have to pay taxes.

[If duty-free on arrival increased the total amount of duty-free purchased, then this argument might hold some water. But more likely all it does is replace purchased-abroad duty-free with duty-free purchased in the US. The net effect on the local merchant is the same.]

Notice something about all four of the above arguments put forth against duty-free on arrival?

Yes, that's right. They talk about the interests of the airlines, of the flight attendants, of the airports, of the customs men and/or of the local merchants. But not one of them even mentions the interests of the airline passenger.

But, then, what else is new?

How to Conduct Business in the Airport

No longer are airports just places to go through on your way to business meetings. Now they are becoming centers of business in and of themselves.

Many of the major ones now provide most of the facilities a modern businessperson would need. For instance, Mutual of Omaha Service Centers, which are in 16 major US airports, provide photocopiers, typists, telexes, faxes, personal computers, express mailing, electronic mailing, notary services and conference rooms (not to mention travel insurance, foreign money exchange, emergency cash, airline ticket pickup and baggage and garment check).

These new business facilities now mean you can, in effect, have an office away from home. Instead of wasting your time drinking in the bar or playing the video games or reading a racy novel, now you can be in there grinding out the memos for the home office.

Naturally I hope you'll keep the existence of these facilities secret from your boss.

How to Get an Extra Day on Your Luggage Locker

It's not all that easy to get a luggage locker. Some airports, through the fear of bombs, don't have them. Others that do, often have too few for the demand. Even when there are available lockers, you often find that they are designed primarily for a midget's hand luggage.

Let's assume, however, that you find a good locker and want to leave your bag in it for more than one day while you take a brief side trip. The notice on a locker usually states that the rental is for only 24 hours. If you go over that limit, your luggage supposedly will be removed and taken to a special storage facility, from which you can retrieve it by paying an additional fee.

As the lockers are inspected only once a day, however, you can get almost 48 hours if you put your luggage in immediately after an inspection is made—since the inspector has to inspect your locker twice before knowing your bag has been there more than 24 hours. (Normally the inspector collects the money in the till at each inspection; if the inspector finds your door locked but no money in the till, he or she knows your bag's been there since the last collection.)

The trick for getting longer than 24 hours is to call the locker people on the courtesy phone and find out when they inspect the lockers in your area; if they won't tell you, ask one of the airport guards. Then add 24 to the number of hours between when you put your luggage in and the next inspection. That's how long you will have. If you put it in just after the most recent inspection, you'll have almost 48 hours before your bag is removed.

How to Store Your Luggage for Free

If the lockers are all full, there may be a few other places you could leave your bags for a charge. For instance, almost all European and a few US airports have special "Left Luggage" windows where for a small fee you can check your luggage in and retrieve it whenever you want. As mentioned above, many US airports now also have business centers which do the same thing.

If none of these are available to you or you don't want to pay to store your luggage, then you have three alternatives:

(a) **Using your padlock, you can lock your luggage briefly to a chair in the general waiting area.** Always tell someone what you are doing, however, and even then never leave your luggage for more than half an hour. You may return to find your bag has been removed by a bomb-disposal robot to an unused runway and is currently dodging bazooka shells from the National Guard.

(b) **If you are a member of an airline club, you can leave your luggage in their cloakroom.** If you want to store it for several days, the staff will often put your luggage away in a special place or at the very least keep an eye on it for you. After notifying the staff of your intent to leave it there for several days, fix it to the luggage rack in the cloakroom with your padlock.

(c) Clear your bag of all airline tags, put a home address label on the outside and turn it in to Lost and Found. To make sure they don't ship it off somewhere, call them on the phone, identify the bag and say you will be down to pick it up in an hour, or tomorrow, or whatever.

Whether to Buy Life Insurance at the Airport

Do you buy special life insurance every time you get in your car to go for a ride?

No?

Well, your risks of dying in a car are much higher than your risks of dying in a plane. (See *So Should You Be Afraid Of Flying?* below at page 342.) So there's no reason to buy special life insurance every time you get in a plane. Your normal life insurance should be enough.

If such logic doesn't satisfy you and you still want special life insurance, charge your airline ticket to a major credit card. Most provide substantial amounts of free life insurance if you die due to an accident on transportation purchased with the card. Call your own card company to determine the amounts.

CHAPTER SEVEN

HOW TO GET ONTO
THE PLANE

How to Find Your Gate Before it's Announced

The airlines often know hours in advance to which gate a flight is assigned, but they avoid passing this information on to the passengers until just before departure. The two main reasons for this secretiveness are (i) the airline doesn't want passengers on a later flight clogging up the gate during the departure of an earlier flight, and (ii) last-minute changes in air traffic may result in a different gate being assigned than originally intended, causing confusion and/or irritation in passengers who went to the originally-announced gate.

Occasionally it's important for you to know your gate before it's announced. For instance, you may want to be first in line at the gate podium to stand by for a flight. Or you may want a few hours of sleep and feel you are more likely to wake up in time if you are at your departure gate. To find out your gate, you should take the following steps:

(a) If your airline has only a small operation at the airport, you can look for the airline's normally-assigned gates in the schematic map of the airport posted on the wall of the terminal or in the *Airport Pocket Guide* mentioned at page 27 above. That will narrow it down for you.

(b) Go to your airline's general area and ask the airline staff there from which gate your flight normally departs. They usually know.

(c) To confirm the gate, call the airport (not the airline) on a pay phone and ask. If they are hesitant, you can tell them you have a bad leg and you want to know whether the gate is so far away you'll need a wheelchair to get there.

These three steps should give you a pretty good idea where your gate is. However, be sure to stay alert. Refer to nearby flight monitors periodically to see if delays or congestion have caused the gate to be changed at the last minute.

Common Flight-Announcement Errors
Made by Inexperienced Passengers

1.   Watching the announcement board rather than a flight monitor. Announcement boards are those large flight-announcement systems in airport lobbies which operate on mechanical principles not too different from a slot machine. Although easier to read, they are much slower than monitors at reporting new information. If you want to beat your fellow passengers to the gate, watch a monitor rather than a flight announcement board.

2. Confusing the departures' monitor with the arrivals' monitor and *vice versa.* The standard of monitor labeling in airports is abysmal. Often the only labeling is the tiny copper plaque masquerading as a TV brand-name which is glued just beneath the screen; the average passenger, intent on reading the information displayed on the screen, is sure to miss it. So before reading a monitor always ask yourself first, "Is this an arrivals' or a departures' monitor?"

3. Not watching long enough. Some monitors can't fit all a flight's information in at once so they show first one part and then, ten seconds later, the other. An inexperienced traveler looking at the first part may conclude that a gate hasn't been assigned yet and turn away before the second part comes on, giving the gate.

4. Not continuing to check the monitors after announcement of their flight. Flight gates sometimes change after their first appearance on the monitor. If you've got a long walk to the gate, you should always continue to check each monitor which you pass to see if the gate has changed.

5. Failing to check the flight posted at the gate. Occasionally the gate staff are operating from a different gate than shown on the monitor. Or, more often, you have gone to gate 16B, which is on the lower level, when you should have gone to gate 16A, which is on the upper level. When you arrive at the gate, you should confirm that the flight is posted on the board behind the podium. If it isn't, ask the staff. The fact that your flight is not up on the board or, even more disconcerting, that another flight is up in its place, does not necessarily mean you have the wrong gate. More likely the gate staff is still dealing with a previously scheduled flight which has not yet left.

If (i) your flight's not up on the board at the gate, (ii) there's no staff around and (iii) it's fifteen minutes before your flight takes off (half an hour on international flights), go to a nearby podium of the same airline and ask them to find out from their central office what's wrong. Don't just sit there like a mushroom waiting for someone to show up.

The Real Meaning of "Last Call"

When a monitor or public address system announces last call for a flight, inexperienced passengers conjure up the image of a railway conductor blowing his whistle just before the train departs, and take off running for the gate. In fact, "last call" in the airline context means not that the flight is about to depart but rather that the deadline for check-in is about to lapse (after which the passenger with a reservation is subject to losing his or her seat to a standby). Since the deadline for check-in could be ten to thirty minutes before departure, if your flight is not crowded, there's no reason to take off running on the announcement of last call. You'll have plenty of time to get onto the plane before it departs.

Flight Departure Time in Fargo, North Dakota

Catching a flight out of Fargo, North Dakota, is by definition a pleasurable experience. ("It's a nice place to raise children," a local told me once—a statement I couldn't help associating with the description of a prospective blind date as having a "wonderful personality".)

If my one experience at the airport there is anything to go by, however, you have to be very careful about timing your arrival.

Having finished my business meeting in Fargo early, I noticed in my *Pocket Flight Guide* that there was an earlier flight out. Arriving at the gate ten minutes before the scheduled departure, I discovered the door already closed and the plane taxiing away.

"Hey," I said to the ticket-taker at the gate, "that plane's not supposed to depart until four o'clock."

"What time is it now?" the man asked.

As he had a watch of his own, I was a little uncertain why he was asking me but I answered anyway. "Three-fifty."

"Right on schedule," the man said with all the pride you might expect from someone wearing a burgundy-colored polyester uniform with a striped chartreuse shirt and bright orange tie. "Ten minutes of taxiing, and the plane ought to leave the ground right at four o'clock."

"Uh-huh," I said, lowering my eyes (his outfit made him somewhat difficult to look at straight on). "If that's the way you define departure, why don't you tell people the flight is at three-fifty?"

"Are you kidding?" he said. "Then we'd have to close the gate at three-*forty* and a lot of people would miss the plane."

To this day I remain convinced that there was a hole in the man's logic; but, try as I might, I have yet to be able to find it.

Box 7-1.	Causes of Flight Delays

Weather	67%
Air Traffic Control Volume	13%
Airport Volume	11%
Runway Construction	4%
Equipment	3%
Other	1%

Measures only delays of 15 minutes or more. Excludes mechanical delays (whether before or after leaving gate) plus gate delay problems, *e.g.*, failing to load passengers, baggage or food fast enough.
(Source: FAA.)

Why the Airlines Always Fail to Announce Delays Adequately

It is a general rule of air travel that the airlines do not announce delays until very close to flight time and then, when they do, they severely underestimate the amount of delay.

To some extent this can be explained by the fact that some delays are unforeseeable. A check just before departure discovers some minor mechanism doesn't work, or a bottleneck develops in refueling or revictualing, or the ticketing computer suddenly goes down. However, most delays are reasonably foreseeable hours in advance. A violent storm is moving in. Air traffic congestion has been building all day. A runway is being repaired. An incoming flight took off an hour late. A malfunction was spotted in the aircraft while the incoming flight was still in the air.

So why don't the airlines tell you earlier and more accurately about these delays? There are three possible answers:

(a) The airlines want to make sure the passengers are all at the gate ready to go if the delay turns out to be shorter than expected. If the airlines gave out a reasonable estimate of every delay, then in those situations in which the delay turned out to be shorter or even nonexistent, departure would have to wait while the passengers were summoned back from all over the airport.

(b) The airlines are afraid that passengers will switch to a competing airline's flight if they learn the real extent of the delay.

(c) The airline flight announcement staff get sadistic pleasure out of stringing the passengers along.

I don't know which of these answers is (or possibly are) correct. I do know, however, that not one of them, as usual, has anything to do with the comfort, convenience or dignity of the airline passengers themselves.

How to Board a Flight which has Departed

The tendency of an airline to underestimate delays can go so far as to result in a premature announcement of departure.

Sometimes when I've been trying to make a tight connection, I've noticed that the departure monitor indicates a flight has departed when, in reality, it's still sitting at the gate loading passengers. I assume this is because the flight-announcement communications center presumes departure on schedule unless notice of a delay is reported by the gate, and the relatively short delays which occur during loading are not reported.

For this reason, if you are minutes late for a gate, don't give up merely because the monitor indicates the flight has departed; there's a good chance it hasn't.

Your Chances of Encountering a Delayed Flight

Some random statistics from the DOT *Air Travel Consumer Report*:

(a) The best airlines have only about one out of sixteen flights delayed fifteen minutes or more; the worst, one out of three so delayed.

(b) The best airports have only about one out of sixteen flights delayed fifteen minutes or more; the worst, one out of three.

(c) At the worst time of day for the worst airport, more than one out of two flights are so delayed.

(d) There are approximately forty flights which are regularly late more than 80 percent of the time. The average delay of those flights: roughly three-quarters of an hour.

Conclusion: If you take just a few trips, the odds are against you encountering significant delays. If you take more than a few trips, the odds are in favor of you encountering significant delays.

Your Chances of Encountering a Canceled Flight

According to the statistics below, the best airline in the continental US cancels only about one out 100 flights; the worst, about one out of 30. In Hawaii, the figures are roughly one out of 13 and one out of nine.

Box 7-2.	Airline Flight-Cancellation Records	
Airline	**%Canceled**	**One Out Of**
Delta	1.0	100
Southwest	1.2	83
USAir	1.4	71
American	1.8	56
Alaska	1.9	53
United	2.0	50
TWA	2.1	48
Northwest	2.4	42
Midway	2.5	40
Pan Am	2.7	37
Continental	3.0	33
Eastern	3.3	30
Aloha	7.6	13
Hawaiian	10.8	9

(Source: Salomon Brothers.)

Conclusion: Unless you are a very frequent flyer, your chances of being on a flight that is canceled are fairly low.

The Government Rules Governing Flight Delays and Cancellations

The government does not penalize the airlines or require them to compensate you if your flight is delayed or canceled. This is true even if the airline cancels your flight purely for economic reasons, *i.e.*, there weren't enough passengers.

Only if the airline cancels a given flight so many times that there is a question whether the flight is any longer really a "scheduled" flight will the Department of Transportation step in; and then it is highly unlikely there will be a fine.

Back in the summer of 1987, when flight delays were in the press, the Secretary of Transportation announced that airlines were to be fined $1,000 for each flight which was late more than half the time. However, to this date, despite the fact the DOT's own *Air Travel Consumer Report* lists each month approximately forty flights which are late more than 80 percent of the time, the DOT has never actually imposed a single fine.

What Your Rights are if Your Flight is Canceled, is Delayed or Otherwise Fails to Meet its Schedule

Any rights you may have will be in the airline's conditions of carriage. Looking at the excerpts from the conditions of carriage which are in the small print at the back of your ticket, you will see that the airline does not guarantee its schedules. However, if you look at the full conditions of carriage under the heading, "Schedule Irregularities," you usually will find the airline has admitted some obligations towards you.

Note: a "schedule irregularity" normally is defined not only as a delay or cancellation but also as a missed connection, a flight diversion or a published change of schedule which the passenger was not notified of.

1.   Alternative flight. Generally, if there is a schedule irregularity, the airline will put you on the next available flight to the same destination city (although not necessarily the same airport) and, if no seats are available on that flight in your class, they will put you in a higher class at no additional cost.

If the next alternative flight is a competitor's, the airlines differ as to (i) whether they will put you on the competitor's flight and (ii) whether, if no seats are available on the competitor's flight in your class, they will put you on at a higher class at no additional cost. Some airlines will do it only if they caused the schedule irregularity; others if they caused it or if you missed the flight because of the schedule irregularity of an incoming connecting flight of another airline; and still others will do it for all schedule irregularities except those due to the failure to notify the passenger of a change of schedule.

Naturally, airlines do not go out of their way to steer their passengers to a competitor's flight. So if the airline appears to be steering you towards its own, less-convenient alternative flight, you should ask to look at the conditions of carriage and see what your rights are to get on a competing airline's flight. For those airlines which pattern their conditions after the old CAB rules (see page 35 above), the provisions on schedule irregularities are in Rule 240.

If you don't have time to look at the conditions, quote Rule 240 anyway. "According to Rule 240, you're supposed to . . . ." Even if the rule doesn't support you, the airline staff may be sufficiently intimidated to put you on a competing airline in first class.

(Note: On foreign airlines the cite should be to the substantially similar IATA Resolution 375(d).)

2.   Refund. Under most conditions of carriage, if the airline cannot put you on an alternative flight, you can request a refund under the involuntary refund rules discussed above at page 94. This is true even if your ticket is marked nonrefundable.

Two finer refund points which may be of advantage:

(a)   Acceptable alternative. Under most of the conditions of carriage, the offered alternative transportation has to be acceptable to you. So if a delay caused you to miss the meeting which was the reason for your trip or *if the delay is so great that a competing flight the airline refuses to endorse your ticket over to will now arrive earlier,* no alternative flight offered by the airline would be acceptable and you could claim a full refund.

Be aware, however, that a few of the conditions of carriage, such as USAir's, say only that the airline has to offer alternative transportation, not that it has to be acceptable to the passenger. If that is indeed your airline's policy, then if you refuse the offered alternative flight, your refund would be limited to what it would be had you failed to appear for the flight.

(b)   Required delay. Assuming your ticket is with an airline which states that the alternative flight has to be acceptable to you, how long does the flight have to be delayed before you can ask for a refund? According to a literal reading of most conditions of carriage, any delay in the schedule is sufficient to trigger the "schedule irregularity" provisions. As a practical matter, however, the delay should be long enough that you have a good reason not to go ahead with any alternative flight the airline may offer.

3.   Amenities. Under the old CAB rules which lapsed when deregulation occurred, if a flight was delayed for four hours, diverted or canceled, and the airline failed to give you reasonable notice of the possibility, then:

(a)   The airline would pay for a three-minute phone call or a 15-word telegram from you to anywhere in the US.

(b)   If you would have gotten a meal on the plane and the flight was delayed beyond the normal meal time, the airline would provide a free meal.

(c)   If you were stranded in a city not your home, destination or stopover point between 10:00 P.M. and 6:00 A.M., the airline would provide you a hotel room.

(d) The airline would pay for the cost of transportation between the airport at which your were stranded and your hotel or home.

Some conditions of carriage, such as Alaska Airline's, substantially follow the old CAB rules. Those of most of the majors, however, give you a right to certain amenities only if your flight is diverted or if you are an invalid, elderly, an unaccompanied child or similar extraordinary case. Several, such as American Airlines', give you no right to amenities in any situation.

If, before you leave for the airport, you suspect bad weather may be approaching, get your travel agent to look at the various conditions of carriage, to book you on the airline which has the most liberal provisions and to give you a photocopy to take along. Failing that, be prepared to stand in line with the two-hundred other passengers who are waiting to read the airline's single copy of the conditions of carriage.

The Best Procedure to Follow if Your Flight is Delayed

1. Don't trust the airline. Call the airport authority and ask them about the flight delay. They are more likely to tell you exactly what is happening.

2. If your flight is an international flight in a small airport, don't go through passport control; there are usually significantly fewer facilities on the other side.

3. If you suspect the delay may be substantial, go to the telephone and book a seat on the next available flight whatever the airline and then another reservation on the next available flight on your airline. (You can get this information either from your pocket flight guide or from your travel agency on its 24-hour emergency number.)

4. If the delay turns out to be substantial, ask the gate staff of the delayed airline to endorse your ticket over to the other airline. If the fare on the other airline is higher, the staff may refuse to so so. Demand to see the airline's conditions of carriage (or try citing Rule 240 blind). If the conditions don't support you, then ask to have the ticket refunded. Even if your ticket is restricted, the staff may go along as a matter of good will.

5. If the airline makes a reservation for you on an alternative flight and issues you a new ticket, make sure you have a confirmed

reservation, *i.e.,* the status box is marked "OK". Once you have a confirmed reservation, you can always stand by for an earlier flight.

6. If the delay takes you past mealtime or into the night, ask for whatever amenities you think are fair. As a standard of fairness, refer to the old CAB rules above. Even if the conditions of carriage don't give you a right to those amenities, the airline staff often has a great deal of discretion as to what largess will be distributed to stranded passengers. Foreign flag carriers, for instance, generally give their passengers no rights to amenities whatsoever in their conditions of carriage, but in most situations provide full CAB-type amenities as a matter of policy.

7. If the staff still refuses to provide you amenities, keep your meal, lodging and phone receipts and send them to the airline's home office. Someone there may have a more charitable view.

8. If you bought special travel insurance or have it as a matter of course through your credit card, check if it has a travel-delay benefit. Some policies will provide reimbursement up to $25 to $50 a day in delay-caused costs.

The Best Procedure to Follow if Your Flight is Canceled

The procedure is basically the same as above for delay, except this time you go directly to the phone to make a reservation as soon as you hear the word cancellation. Don't bother to hang around waiting for any prevarication.

After that you can go through the other steps above at your leisure.

Note, if in booking your reservation you find that a more convenient flight is fully booked, ask the gate staff at the canceling airline to book you on the more convenient flight. It may be fully booked only because your airline reserved a block of seats for its canceled passengers.

All Hope Abandon, Ye Who Enter Here

If you've ever boarded a plane which is then substantially delayed on the runway, you'll know the true meaning of Dante's inscription over the gates of Hell. The airline at last has got you in its grasp and there's nothing you can do to escape an eternity spent in indefinite waiting.

A friend of mine, though, points out that your situation is not entirely hopeless. You could start smoking in the nonsmoking section or otherwise intentionally violating the airline rules, or, if you find that a bit too extreme, you could try screaming, "Good God, I've got the bubonic plague!"

Unless you're at La Guardia on a Friday evening, however, the time you save by getting off the plane will probably by offset by the period you'll have to spend locked up in a police holding-pen or in an airport-authority quarantine cell.

Hints on the Use of the Luggage Trolley

If you've been following the recommendations of this handbook, you won't have a need to use a luggage trolley. Traveling light, you'll easily be able to carry your bags with you. Your garment bag will hang by a strap from your shoulder and your suitcase will have built-in wheels.

On the other hand, if you're one of those people who aren't comfortable unless they're carrying half their home with them when they travel, let me give you a few hints on how to use the trolley:

1. **Finding stored trolleys.** To locate a trolley, first ask yourself where is the most inconvenient out-of-the-way place the trolleys could be stored. Nine times out of ten, that's where they'll be. Who places the trolleys in such places, I don't know. I suspect it's either the baggage porters, who are trying to increase their business, or, more likely, the trolley-retrieval personnel, who are trying to cut down on the number of trolleys they have to retrieve.

2. **Finding a free trolley.** To get a trolley for free, go to the various barriers beyond which people cannot take their trolleys. Security is a particularly good place. Also, at the start of escalators. In fact, just about any place within fifty feet from where the average person might have loaded up his trolley.

3. **Negotiating escalators.** If you are confronted by a down escalator, don't try to put your loaded trolley onto it unless you're interested in trying to set a new Olympic downhill tobogganing record. You'll find it safer and more dignified to locate the elevator which the terminal designer has hidden off in some corner and take that to the next floor.

4. **Reading instructions.** If you have a modern trolley, read the instructions before using it. Some of these new ones can be folded into different postures to make them more suitable for different types of luggage. Some can even be folded into the shape of a wheel chair—a great aid when traveling with the very old, the very young or the very lazy.

5. Steering the trolley. If in doubt, push rather than pull the trolley. Although this will not necessarily allow you to steer any better, it will substantially increase the chances that when the trolley collides with somebody, that somebody will not be you.

I find that whether I push or pull the trolley, it invariably ends up drifting sideways, often with each of its four independent wheels vibrating like mad, each attempting to take its part of the trolley off in a different direction. I consider it important in these situations to at least pretend that I'm still in charge, and, above all, to avoid any sudden exclamations such as "Look out! It's alive! It's alive!" to the horrified onlookers scattering before me.

How to Get Driven to the Gate

Most airports and/or airlines have electric carts for driving the infirm and the important from check-in to the gates. At some places, these carts hang around at the entrances to the concourses waiting for passengers. At others, they have to be requested on the courtesy phone or at the check-in desk.

If you are a good enough actor, you can, as I often have at Heathrow's Terminal 3, just walk up to a cart driver, look like somebody important and direct him to take you to your gate. I usually give the driver a tip at the end of the journey.

If you're concerned about the morality of pretending to be important, then may I suggest you instead try pretending to be infirm. A bad foot is usually the easiest. Don't worry about taking off your shoe and putting all your socks on your foot to make it look swollen; an understated, painful limp is enough. No cart driver would dare refuse to take a cripple, no matter how unimportant looking.

Note, at smaller airports, rather than being driven in an electric cart, you'll be pushed in a wheel chair. It's not as fast as a cart or as convenient for carrying luggage but, if you're lazy enough, it's still a heck of a lot better than having to walk there yourself.

How the People-Movers Divide Humanity

Airport "people-movers" (also known as "moving sidewalks" or "travelators") divide all humanity into two groups: those who look at the people-mover as a way of getting to the gate in the same time with less effort, *i.e.*, those who *stand* on the people-mover, and those who look at the people-mover as a way of getting to the gate in less time with the same effort, *i.e.*, those who *walk* on the people-mover.

This difference in approach to people-movers reflects, I think, a much deeper difference in approaches to life: those who wish just to coast through and those who wish to get ahead.

How a Stander Should use the People-Mover

If you are a person who stands on the people-mover, I have the following advice:

1.   Stand on the right. Almost all airports, including those in England, direct those standing on the people-mover to do so on the right so that those walking can pass on the left. (This is because most people are right-handed and, therefore, are more secure holding onto the railing with their right hand.) You should stand on the right not only as a courtesy but also as a matter of your own self-interest, since people standing on the left are, at the very least, subjected to abuse from and often simply knocked down and run over by walkers.

2.   Don't lean too heavily on the handrail. For some reason, these never are going at the same speed as the surface under your feet, so if you lean on them, you will soon find the top half of your body preceding or following the bottom half of your body to such an extent that you will become an object of ridicule.

3.   Beware of the timid when getting off. The "standing" side of the belt tends to have a disproportionate number of nervous nellies. As you approach the end, therefore, it's not unusual to find the person in front of you backing up, elbows raised, the back of their hands in front of their face, as they contemplate the terror of stepping from a three-mile-an-hour rubber belt to the stationary ground.

Once, an elderly woman in front of me became so paralyzed with fear that she wouldn't let go of the two handrails. When her feet came up against the plate at the end of the belt and stopped, the upper half of her body continued on, following the rubber handrails forward and then sharply down and around, somersaulting her onto the floor, on which she lay, in a supine position, for quite a few moments, a dazed expression on her face, as I and the others behind me stepped over her as best we could.

How a Walker Should use the People-Mover

If you are a person who walks on the people-mover, I have the following advice for you:

1.   **Walk fast with a heavy step.** Those blocking you in front are more likely to hear you approaching and get out of your way.

2.   **Warn the blockers to move before, rather than after, you reach them.** If you're bearing down on them as you speak, they're much more likely to respond quickly.

3.   **Instill terror in the blockers.** Phrase your warning not in terms of a request, such as "Could you let me by, please?" or an order, such as, "Stand to the right, please," but in terms of the simple announcement of the approach of an irresistible force: "Coming through!"

4.   **If you can't become part of the solution, don't become part of the problem.** If you can't bring yourself to ask two side-by-side blockers to move over, move over yourself and stand to the right. Do not wait patiently behind the blocker on the left, hoping he or she will notice you and move. If you do, a walker behind you will be blocked by three people instead of just two.

5.   **If the people-mover is crowded, don't use it.** The three-mile-an-hour assist in speed will be more than offset by the inevitable delays due to blockers.

6.   **If you have a trolley, do not take it onto the belt unless the belt is absolutely clear.** All you need is one wide suitcase ahead of you and you will be unable to get by.

7.   **Make sure that the people-mover will let you off before your gate.** The airport usually posts directly over the entrance to each section of the people-mover a list of the gates being served by that section, and on either side of the entrance a list of the gates which are bypassed by that section. If you make a mistake and discover yourself gliding past your gate, don't get hysterical and begin waving your arms about wildly and crying to the gate staff to save you. Instead, just lift your bags up onto the moving hand-rest a little behind you, sit your buttock up onto the hand-rest, swing your legs over and drop to the ground. It shows so much more finesse.

Which Side to Walk on in the Concourse

Each country has its own convention about which side of a sidewalk you should walk on. In the United States, people walk on the right. In Australia, they walk on the left. In England they walk all over the place, saying, "Sorry," to each other.

When arriving at a strange airport, please take a moment to study the pedestrian traffic before striding off. Except in England, there is usually a discernible flow which, if you follow it, will cut down significantly on your head-on collisions.

Some Thoughts on the Security Screening Strategy at Airports

Since the early 1960's when the hijacking of airplanes began (the very first one, by the way, being from Cuba to the United States, not the other way around), airports have had some method of screening passengers and their carry-on luggage for weapons. The theory has been that the airlines could best prevent hijackings by preventing potential hijackers from taking weapons onto the plane.

Security screening has not been without its costs—to the airport and the airline (which must pay for the equipment and security staff) and to the passengers (to whom security screening is yet another obstacle between them and their flight).

You know what it's like. Long lines of passengers waiting to put their luggage through the system. Oversensitive detectors which you have to go through again and again, each time removing something more—the change from your pockets, your metal belt buckle, your steel-framed glasses, the fillings in your molars—until at last, to the applause of the passengers waiting behind, you're given a clean bill of health, or more likely, are taken to one side and made to stand in the crucified position as a small detector is passed over your body, beeping in the most peculiar places.

And then there's the insensitive security staff, who, after ripping through your carefully packed case, hold up a copy of some of your more personal reading matter for all to see and exclaim, "Holy mackeral! Will you look at this?"

Then they turn to you and ask, "Is this yours?"

Just once you'd like to have the courage to say: "Yeah, and that's me on page 32 with the electric cattle prod." But all you do is lower your head sheepishly and mumble something about a joke gift for a friend.

Anyway, my point here is not that there are significant costs to the current security system; that's obvious. My point is that those costs exist because the strategy of the security system is all wrong.

The way to prevent hijacks is not by trying to prevent anyone from taking a gun onto a plane but by doing just the opposite—by issuing a gun to each passenger as he enters the plane.

No hijacker would dare try to take over the flight. He'd have several hundred bullet holes in him before he got halfway out of his seat.

And after that, when the passengers realized he was trying to hijack the plane, he'd really get shot up.

Box 7-1.	Largest FAA Fines Of US Airlines for Security Lapses	
Airline		**Fine**
United		$216,000
Northwest		$157,000
Delta		$113,000
American		$96,000
Continental		$79,000
Eastern		$67,000
TWA		$63,000
USAir		$58,000
Pan Am		$51,000
Alaska Air		$31,000
(Source: FAA.)		

How to Get through Security Quickly

Occasionally when you're late for a plane, you need to get through security quickly. The following suggestions may help you:

1. Don't wait in line. Instead, go to the head of the queue, tell the security staff you are late for a plane, put your luggage on the conveyor and walk through the security system. You might get a few dirty looks from fellow passengers, but it's highly unlikely the security staff will stop you.

2. Put everything possible onto the screening-machine belt. It'll save the delays caused by manual examination.

3. Open up and/or turn on any equipment which must be manually examined. For instance, if you've got a lap computer which is opaque to X-rays, you should open it up and turn it on to demonstrate it is real before handing it to the examiner. Otherwise the examiner will waste a lot of time trying to figure out how to do it him- or herself. (By the way, you do not need to worry about the security machine affecting your laptop. It is magnetic fields, not X-rays, which corrupt data.)

4. Remove all metal items from your body and put them in the plastic tray before you go through the detector. If the detector wouldn't have picked up the metal anyway, you haven't lost much time since you still have to wait for your hand-luggage to come out of the machine. If the detector would have picked it up, then you've avoided the delay of going back, removing the items and coming through again.

5.   Do not pack anything in your case which might be mistaken for a weapon. The primary culprits are umbrellas and odd-shaped camera equipment. Instead put these items on the conveyor belt by themselves. The X-ray picture will be clearer and if the security officer wants a manual inspection of those items, he can do so without opening your bag.

In this regard, do not use lead envelopes to protect your film. Either the security X-ray will not be able to pentrate them (in which case you will be delayed while the officer does a manual inspection) or, at more and more airports, the operator will merely turn up the power until it does penetrate (ruining your film more than if you hadn't used a lead envelope).

Box 7-4.   Hazardous Items

Except for toilet articles and medicine (up to 75 ounces), it is illegal to carry on board or check in your luggage any of the following hazardous materials:

(a)   Aerosols, including polishes, waxes, cleaners and degreasers.

(b)   Corrosives, including cleaners, acids and wet-cell batteries.

(c)   Flammables, including paints, thinners, lighter fluid, adhesives and liquid-reservoir lighters.

(d)   Explosives, although small arms ammunition may be checked if securely packed in a hard box.

(e)   Radioactives, including uninstalled pacemakers and radiopharmaceuticals.

(f)   Compressed gases, including mace, oxygen or divers' tanks.

(g)   Loose book matches or safety matches not on your person.

The civil penalties can be up to $10,000. The criminal penalties up to $25,000 and/or 5 years in jail.

You've been warned.

6. Don't overpack you luggage. If your bags are searched, not only will the officer's search be longer and more disruptive but you will also need more time to repack afterwards.

7. Don't have any wrapped packages, such as presents, in your luggage. The security staff may have to unwrap them to look inside. If going somewhere for Christmas, take the wrapping paper separately.

8. As the signs say, do not in any circumstances make jokes about carrying weapons. The security staff have no sense of humor.

Electronic Equipment You Definitely Should not Turn on in the Plane

Most cassette player/recorders, AM radio receivers and laptop computers create no problems in air travel; many FM radio receivers and televisions, however, do. They can affect the airplane's navigation system. So, whatever you do, don't turn your FM radio receiver or television on in the plane—especially if your pilot is in the middle of an instrument landing. Your program may have a different ending than the one intended.

How a Standby Can Increase His or Her Chances of Getting on the Plane

Occasionally, when you arrive at the gate, you find you can't get a boarding pass immediately because the plane is overbooked and the gate staff is waiting to see how many of the passengers with preissued boarding passes (and hence priority over you) will show up.

In this case, you should take one or more of the following steps:

1. Hand the gate staff your ticket, since that will determine your standby priority.

2. Go immediately to the nearest phone and make a reservation on the next most convenient flight, making sure to ask how full that flight appears. If there's no other convenient flight, then you know you've got to use all your efforts to get on the existing one.

3. Ask the gate staff to give you a written statement of their boarding priorities. In the US, they're required to do so by law. Look in the statement and see if there is anything which could conceivably apply to you. Generally the US airlines deny boarding on a last-come-first-bumped basis. However, many of them make certain exceptions. Most, for example, will give preference to the old, the handicapped, the infirm and unaccompanied minors, to the extent the airline feels such passengers would suffer an undue hardship. A few will, in addition, give preference to first-class, business-class, full-fare or connecting passengers. Others add a general catchall provision covering passengers who, in the opinion of the airline staff, would suffer undue hardship.

Those airlines which have the general undue-hardship provision usually add a clause to the effect that business emergencies will not qualify as an undue hardship. Beyond that, though, the definition is up to the staff member. In practice, an undue hardship usually means a family emergency, such as seeing a dying relative or attending a funeral.

4.   If you don't qualify under the explicit priority exceptions, make an appeal based on an undue hardship. Despite the priority guidelines, the staff often have some practical discretion to bend the rules. If possible, your appeals should be made to the head of staff at the gate, quietly, to the side, out of earshot of the other passengers, in all sincerity and humility. Public exclamations of outrage and self-importance will only have a negative effect. After all, the staff aren't responsible for the overbooking.

5.   If you're flying economy and priority is given to business or first class, see if you can upgrade your ticket. Since you're undoubtedly past the deadline for ticket purchase, the airline needn't allow you to upgrade but sometimes they will. (Note, if after upgrading your ticket, you find you can get on only in economy class, you can get a refund of the difference from the airline after the flight.)

6.   Find someone in the waiting area who has a boarding pass and buy it. Young singles and students are good prospects. If you buy just the boarding pass and not the ticket, you need pay only for the person's priority rather than for the flight itself. If the ticket is restricted or nonrefundable, you'll probably have to buy both the pass and the ticket and refund yours when you get home.

7.   If you have a confirmed ticket, make sure the airline asks for volunteers. US airlines are required by law to solicit volunteers to give up their seats to other confirmed ticket holders in return for compensation (usually a free travel voucher plus some money). Some European airlines do this as a matter of policy. If you're on a foreign airline whose policy is not to do this, it won't hurt to ask the staff to make a request for you.

8.   If you are absolutely desperate, you might consider forgery. A friend of mine claims he did this when he had to get to his brother's wedding. As each standby passenger handed in his ticket, the gate staff wrote the time on the ticket envelope and put it at the bottom of the standby pile. Taking note of the style of writing, my friend moved away from the podium and wrote on his ticket envelope a time which put him just after the one on the top of the pile. Then, when no one was looking, he dropped the ticket envelope on the floor behind the counter for the staff to find, which they did. If the handwriting had been questioned, he'd planned to say that the lobby-check-in staff had written the number; sometimes priority is determined by time-of-arrival there as well. But nobody questioned a thing.

My friend's "forgery", of course, didn't affect the airline. The same number of people were bumped as before. Instead the forgery resulted in another person being bumped who otherwise wouldn't have been. Before employing this technique, then, you'd want to be sure that you in fact will suffer significantly greater hardship from being bumped than the person you are replacing. If not, forging the check-in time would be grossly unfair.

What are Your Rights if You are Involuntarily Bumped

There's nothing illegal about airlines overbooking flights. Most flights are overbooked an average of 20 percent; during holidays they can be overbooked as high as 70 percent. Normally it causes no problem because the overbooking is exceeded by the number of no-shows. (Yep, that's right, hard as it is to believe, sometimes up to 70 percent of vacation travelers are no-shows.)

If you are involuntarily bumped on a US-originating flight, however, you do have certain rights.

1. Original ticket. You get to keep your original ticket and either use it on another flight or have it refunded.

2. Next available flight. Similar to the delay and cancellation situations above at page 196, the airline is usually obligated under its conditions of carriage to try to put you on the next available flight arriving at your destination at no cost to you (other than surrendering your original ticket).

3. Compensation. In addition to putting you on the next available flight, the airline also is required by the DOT to pay you compensation for your inconvenience equal to the lesser of (i) twice the one-way fare to your destination or (ii) $400, unless:

(a) the alternate flight is to arrive within one hour of your original flight's arrival time, in which case you receive nothing; or

(b) the alternate flight is to arrive more than one hour but not more than two hours (four hours on international flights) of your original flight's arrival time, in which case you receive the lesser of (i) the one-way fare to your destination or (ii) $200.

4.   Immediate payment. The law requires this compensation to be paid on the spot, unless you're rushing to catch an alternative flight—in which case the airline has to pay you within 24 hours. The airline often will offer you in lieu of the money a free travel voucher. (Make sure the travel voucher allows you to book a reserved seat and is not just for standby.) Although the offered travel voucher is usually worth significantly more than the money, you have the right to demand the money if you wish.

5.   Written statement. When you are bumped, the airline is required by law to give you a written statement describing all your rights (as well as the airline's bumping priority rules); so be sure to demand one.

Exceptions to the Denied-boarding Compensation Rules

To obtain the legally required compensation above:

(a) You must have had a confirmed reservation and have met the airline's advance purchase deadline.

(b) You must have reconfirmed (if required), checked-in at the gate within the period required by the airline's conditions of carriage and met the airline's passenger-acceptability requirements.

(c) You must have been bumped for a reason other than the airline substituting for operational or safety reasons (but not economic reasons) a smaller plane for the one originally scheduled.

(d) The flight from which you were bumped must have:

(1) been one originating in the United States (inbound international flights, therefore, don't count);

(2) been a regularly scheduled flight (charters, therefore, don't count);

(3) employed an aircraft with seating for more than 60 people;

(4) not been canceled; and

(5) been deliberately oversold by the airline.

How to Ask for More

The above compensation is only the *minimum* required by law. This means:

(a) **The airline's conditions of carriage may be more generous.** For instance, many of the airlines waive the small-aircraft exception or give a flat $100 in the case of small aircraft.

(b) **You are free to negotiate or sue for a higher amount.** If you feel being bumped cost you more than the minimum required or if your flight is one of the exceptions in (d) above pursuant to which the airline is not required to offer anything, the law does not prevent you from obtaining more.

If you plan to ask for more than the minimum required by law, it is best not to accept the compensation offered by the airline. If you are not certain or decide later to ask for more, return what you have received in the form received. If you cash the check or use the flight voucher, you probably lose your right to collect more.

Compensation for Being Bumped Outside the US

If you are flying from outside the US, what you receive as bumping compensation depends mostly on airline policy—often a policy which does not appear in the conditions of carriage.

US airlines tend to follow the US rules. European airlines tend to follow the voluntary code of the Association of European Airlines. This latter code provides that if the airline doesn't get you to your destination within four hours within Europe (six hours for other flights), the airline will pay you generally:

(a) the lesser of (i) one-half the one-way fare and (ii) approximately 150 British pounds (converted into other European currencies at the exchange rate of January, 1979), *plus*

(b) all reasonable accommodation, meals, telephone and similar expenses incurred due to the bumping.

Under the European rules, "flight" is defined merely as the leg you are on, not all the legs to your ultimate connecting destination.

Other airlines follow proposed rules set out by IATA or by the International Civil Aviation Organization, which are basically modified versions of the European and US rules. Other airlines compensate you only for your out-of-pocket expenses up to a limit of $50 or $100 per day. Still others simply deny that the passenger deserves any compensation whatsoever for being bumped.

Usually the rule followed by the airline is set forth in its conditions of carriage.

Some Fine Points of the US Denied-boarding Compensation Rules Which May Be to Your Advantage

1. Difference in definition of arrival time. In determining whether you meet the the required one-, two- or four-hour alternative-flight arrival minimums for purposes of calculating your compensation (if any), the DOT regulation compares at the time the compensation is being arranged:

(a) when your alternative flight "is planned to arrive", with

(b) when your original flight "is planned to arrive".

To the extent either has been delayed, the delay will be taken into account in determining whether you meet the required minimums.

The written statement the airline is required to give you at the airport, however, compares at the time the compensation is being arranged:

(a) when your alternative flight is planned to reach your destination, with

(b) the *"scheduled arrival"* or *"originally scheduled arrival time"* of your original flight.

In other words, according to the written statement, while a delay must be taken into account in determining the arrival time for the alternative flight, it's *not* to be taken into account in determining the arrival time for the flight from which you were bumped. So, for example, if the flight from which you were bumped was originally scheduled to arrive four hours earlier than the currently planned arrival time of the alternative flight, you will receive full denied-boarding compensation even if, because of a four-hour delay, your original flight is planned (at the time compensation is determined) to arrive at exactly the *same* time as the alternative flight.

If your original flight has been delayed substantially, therefore, you should base your argument for compensation on the written statement handed out to you and not refer the airline staff back to the conditions of carriage.

2. Arrival time for a connecting flight. A flight is defined as all the legs from the point of the bumping to your next remaining stopover or destination. A stopover means a deliberate interruption of a journey by the passenger, scheduled to exceed four hours. So in determining one-, two- and four-hour arrival times, you must look beyond the remaining connection points to the final point. This can cut both ways. For instance:

(a) If your first leg of your alternative flight arrives within an hour of the originally scheduled leg but thereby misses the connecting flight so you arrive at your final destination over four hours late, you get compensated for being over four hours late.

(b) If your alternative first leg is two hours later but you still can make your connecting flight and arrive at your final destination at the originally scheduled time, you get no compensation.

If you find yourself in a paragraph-(b)-type situation, you're under no obligation to educate the airline staff. If, in the confusion, they confine themselves the first leg only, well so be it.

3. Comparable alternative flight. If the alternative flight has to be acceptable to the passenger, then you could refuse the comparable flight (*e.g.*, because you've missed the meeting which was the reason for your trip) and receive full compensation because no comparable flight *acceptable to you* was provided. The problem is the DOT regulations have been sloppily drafted and do not say explicitly that the alternative flight must be acceptable to the passenger. However, the text does lend strong support to that argument in two ways:

(a) The DOT rules define a "comparable" flight as one "provided" to the passenger at no additional cost. The fact that a flight is *offered* does not mean it's *provided*. For the airline to actually provide the services to you, you've got to use it.

(b) The DOT rules also state that as an alternative to a comparable flight, the airline can arrange "for *other* transportation *used by the passenger* at no extra cost to the passenger". The term "*other* transportation *used by the passenger*" implies very strongly that a comparable flight must also be "used by the passenger" to qualify.

Certainly as a matter of basic justice, if no flight is acceptable to you because the reason for your trip has been ruined by the bumping, then you shouldn't have your denied boarding damages reduced just because the airline offers you a flight which would be of no use to you.

4. Value of a flight. The value of your bumped flight is the applicable one-way fare, including any surcharges and air transportation taxes (including the current eight percent Federal tax on air travel), less any applicable discounts. It is not one-half of the round-trip fare, which may be considerably lower.

5. Value of connecting flights. The flights which go into determining the value of your compensation are all the legs from the point of the bumping to your next remaining stopover or destination. (See definition of stopover above in paragraph 2.) So if you are bumped on a connecting flight, you should:

(a) include the value of the one-way fares for the remaining legs which are part of the connection, rather than for just the leg on which you are bumped; and

(b) determine that value by adding up the one-way fare for each leg rather than taking the overall one-way fare from the first to the last point, which usually will be considerably lower.

6. Bonus compensation. A few airlines offer additional compensation for full-fare passengers who are bumped. United Airlines, for instance, offers, in addition to the normal compensation, two first-class tickets to anywhere in the contiguous 48 states. Significantly this provision is not in the part of the denied boarding section dealing with compensation but in the part dealing with boarding priorities (Section 245(C)(1)).

7. Proper information to volunteers. Technically, if the airline asks you to volunteer to give up your seat, but fails to tell you (i) that you might be bumped involuntarily and (ii) what compensation you would be entitled to if you were bumped involuntarily, then they can't bump you. (DOT *Regulations* Section 250.2b.) So, for instance, if they offer you $100 to get off the flight but neglect to tell you that you can get $400 if you are bumped involuntarily, they can't bump you. Unfortunately, one, the airline usually includes the information required in (i) and (ii) in the card it hands out to prospective volunteers. Two, there's no sanction against the airline if they violate this rule. And, three, arguably all the airline has to do is ask you to volunteer again, giving you the proper information, and then bump you. Nonetheless, if you're grasping at straws, you just might be able to sow enough confusion with this provision to get yourself on board.

Four Things to Make Sure of Before Accepting an Airline Offer to Give up Your Seat Voluntarily

The amount an airline pays passengers to voluntarily give up their seats in an overbooked situation is purely a matter of negotiation between the airline and the individual passenger. If a lot of passengers are willing to give up their seats, you'll get less than if no other passengers are willing to give up their seats. In the latter situation, the airline's opening offer can usually be improved upon. It's unlikely, however, that the final price paid will ever exceed the maximum price which the airline would have to pay to an involuntarily bumped passenger.

The airline's offer will probably be to put you on the next available flight plus give you a free ticket and sometimes cash. Before you accept the offer, determine:

(a) What the next available flight is.

(b) Whether you'll have a guaranteed reservation on that flight (and any subsequent connecting flight).

(c) What restrictions there are on the free-flight voucher being offered, *e.g.*, is it standby only, is it blacked-out at certain holiday periods or, most commonly, is it valid only for reservations made within 24 hours of the flight. (Note, the guidelines of the National Association of Attorneys General discussed above at page 64 require the airlines to tell you of any such restrictions before you give up your seat for the ticket.)

(d) What out-of-pocket expenses you are likely to incur, such as meals, hotel rooms, telegrams or cab fares, because you have given up your seat.

Armed with this knowledge, you can then determine whether the airline offer is worth it.

When Most Airlines Will Refuse to Transport a Passenger Despite the Fact There are Seats Available

As mention earlier at pages 95-96, the conditions of carriage of all airlines allow them to refuse to transport certain ticketed passengers. Among the passengers usually listed are those who:

(a) Refuse to permit search of their person or property for explosives or weapons. (Note, read literally, this provision does not include searches for other things.)

(b) Refuse to produce identification upon request.

(c) Fail, on international flights, to have the proper travel documents.

(d) Are disorderly, abusive or violent.

(e) Are barefoot. (Some airlines intelligently exempt passengers five years or younger.)

(f) Appear intoxicated or under the influence of drugs.

(g) Are known to have a contagious disease.

(h) Have an offensive odor, such as from a draining wound.

(i) Are unable to sit in the seat with the seat-belt fastened (except for those airlines which allow passengers on stretchers).

(j) Are mentally deranged or incapacitated (though most airlines will accept one escorted, non-dangerous mental patient per flight).

(k) Are carrying a weapon.

(l) Are manacled and in the custody of law enforcement personnel.

(m) Are unwilling or unable to abide by the no-smoking requirements.

(n) Are both blind and deaf, unless unaccompanied. (A few airlines allow such persons on alone if they can communicate through some device.)

(o) Would require unusual or unreasonable type of assistance or medical treatment *en route*, unless accompanied. (See more on disabled passengers beginning below at page 353.)

Additional Reasons Some Airlines Will Refuse to Transport a Passenger Despite the Fact There are Seats Available

Some airlines also list as unacceptable those passengers who:

(a) Are under seven or 14 days of age.

(b) Are pregnant and due within seven or 14 days, unless a recent doctor's certificate says it's okay.

(c) Cannot control their bodily functions.

(d) Are clothed in a manner that would cause discomfort or offense to other passengers.

(e) Engage in action that might jeopardize the safety of the aircraft or any of its occupants.

(f) Refuse to comply with any seating requirements.

(g) Attempt to interfere with any member of the flight crew in the pursuit of their duties.

So if any of the descriptions above in this section or the previous one might apply to you, be sure to read the relevant portion of the conditions of carriage before booking your flight. (Rule 35 in the old CAB form.)

The Best Time to Board the Flight

After all the passengers have their boarding passes, they sit around the gate, waiting. When the gate staff announces that the flight will begin boarding, the inexperienced and experienced passengers suddenly separate.

The former leap up *en masse* and crush themselves against the door to the skyway, while the latter remain sitting, waiting for the line in the skyway to disappear so they can leisurely stroll onto the plane to their assigned seat.

I might point out that the airline, in an attempt to discourage such an uncalled-for display of human dignity by the experienced passengers, has arranged the waiting-area seating so that no one will have a view down the skyway. In order to see whether the line's gone down, therefore, the experienced passengers have to get up out of their seats and stand at the entrance—which, were they to think about it, is almost as much trouble as standing in line.

Not satisfied with that, the airline has also made sure the skyway has a major bend a third of the way down so that the last two-thirds are not visible from the entrance. This means the experienced passengers have to hang around the entrance to the skyway, biting their nails, trying to guess when they should enter. (Too early and there'll still be a line. Too late and the plane door will have been closed.) Almost inevitably the experienced passengers crack, rush down the skyway, turn the corner and find themselves at the end of a still very long line.

In my opinion, when the flight announcement is given, you should ignore the smirks of the experienced passengers and join the inexperienced passengers in their stampede toward the door. The earlier you get onto the plane,

(a) the more valuable storage space there will be in the overhead rack and in the foot space under the unoccupied middle seat;

(b) the more pillows and blankets there will be available on the seats and in the overhead bins; and

(c) the more magazines there will be in the rack.

More importantly, if necessary, the earlier you try to get on the plane, the more of a chance you will have to sneak your additional carry-on bag into the cabin.

Why more of a chance? Read on.

The Ethics of Sneaking Your Extra Bag onto the Plane

Naturally, it's important that passengers not be allowed to carry onto the plane a greater size or number of bags than can be easily stored in the cabin. To the extent baggage can't easily be stored, the more likely it is that the passengers' escape during an emergency will be blocked.

For the experienced flyer traveling only with carry-on, the US domestic two-bag limit is ideal. Under this limit, the experienced flyer can bring on both a suitcase which fits under the seat and a garment bag which fits in the overhead compartment, in the closet or, on some 747s, in the special power-assisted garment-bag lifter in the central section.

The problem occurs when an airline attempts to limit carry-on to just one bag. Experienced travelers, now forced to check their garment bag, suddenly lose the freedom and speed of traveling with carry on and become hopelessly mired in the "tragedy of checked luggage" discussed earlier in this book. No wonder, then, that so many experienced travelers, when confronted with a one-bag limit, will do everything in their power to sneak their garment bag on.

Whether it is ethical to do so depends on balancing the loss of freedom and speed against the reasons the airline has for imposing the one-bag limit. Generally, the airlines give three reasons:

(a) The plane is small and hence doesn't have the cabin space for more the one carry-on bag per passenger. To me, this is a valid reason why you shouldn't sneak your extra carry-on into the cabin. However, that doesn't mean shouldn't at least *try* to sneak your bag on. Since the door of a small plane is so tiny, you don't have to worry about succeeding in getting your garment bag on; but since you're stopped at the door of the plane (rather than at the gate), you're more likely to be able to convince the attendant to allow you to put your second carry-on directly into the cargo hold and pick it up from there as you leave the plane.

(b) The flight is crowded, so there's not enough room to store both bags. Theoretically this would seem to be a strong reason. As a practical matter, though, to my knowledge, almost no experienced traveler has ever been on a normal-sized plane where they haven't been able to find space somewhere for their small suitcase and garment bag.

Of course, sometimes there is space only because other passengers have obeyed the one-bag limitation. However, that doesn't necessarily make the result unfair. Generally, the passengers who carry on only one bag either:

(1) don't have a second carry-on bag (in which case the limit is irrelevant); or

(2) have at least one other bag which is too large to carry-on (and hence are already hopelessly mired in the tragedy of checked luggage anyway).

In other words, those passengers for whom carrying on a second bag means not checking any bags at all have a greater right to carry on a second bag than those who are going to check at least one bag anyway.

(c) The flight is international. This, the most common reason, makes no sense at all. International aircraft are just as spacious as domestic ones. True, international airlines are more likely to have long-haul flights and thus be more concerned with weight; but then a garment bag isn't going to weigh any less in the cargo hold. I don't know any experienced travelers who have qualms about smuggling their garment bag on here.

Smuggling a Garment Bag Past the Check-in Counter

Often, especially on international flights, you must begin the process of sneaking your garment bag into the cabin back at the lobby check-in counter. There, while showing your passport and getting your boarding pass, you'll engage in the subtle practice of psychological misdirection, *i.e.*, creating the impression in the airline counter clerk that you have only one carry-on bag when in reality you have two.

This misdirection is accomplished through a very simple technique. When the counter clerk asks you how many bags you have, you lift one of your bags up, look her or him straight in the eye, and say, "One."

Misdirects them perfectly every time.

You don't have to worry about the clerk leaning over the counter to see if you're telling the truth, because you know the clerk is highly unlikely to be able to see your garment bag hidden ten-feet away behind a post.

Sneaking Your Garment Bag Past the Gate

There are many techniques for sneaking a garment bag on. Here's my favorite.

Let's say I'm waiting at the gate for an international flight on which I'm allowed only one carry-on bag. I've got my trusty under-the-seat suitcase and my garment bag. My mission is to get the garment bag past the ticket-taker at the door to the skyway.

When the first boarding announcement causes the inexperienced passengers to rush towards the door, I leap into the midst of the crush. Using the other passengers' bodies as a screen, I push myself towards the door jamb opposite the ticket-taker with my large garment bag hung from a strap over my outside shoulder, my under-the-seat suitcase in my outside hand and my boarding pass clutched in my inside hand.

When I get to the door, I assume the bovine countenance of an inexperienced passenger and lift my boarding pass into the air, forcing the ticket-taker to look up, away from my bags. As he repeatedly tries to grab hold of my pass, I weave it from side to side like a drunken moth.

The trick is to keep the pass high enough so that the ticket-taker can't quite grasp it but low enough so he doesn't give up hope altogether.

Once the ticket-taker starts leaping in the air with his arm fully extended, I quietly begin backing my bags around through the door. As soon as I'm through, I lower my hand and mercifully let the poor man tear off the stub. Then, as he turns back to be engulfed by the flood of inexperienced passengers (now impatiently waving their boarding passes in the air in monkey-like imitation of me), I fade innocently backwards down the skyway into the plane.

Pure artistry, you'll have to agree.

What to Do When You Get Caught Sneaking Your Extra Bag on

On occasion, I get caught. When that happens, I never point out to the staff that they'd let me take the extra bag on when I'd last flown the airline. Only a simpleton would expect an airline to be swayed by an appeal to consistency.

Instead, I say, "Okay," turn around and head back towards the terminal.

A few moments later, when I'm sure the boarding attendants' attention has been diverted, I creep back into the waiting area, look for a passenger who doesn't have a bag and try to persuade him to carry my garment bag for me.

I might say this is *not* the easiest thing to do. I find the reaction of most passengers I approach is to shake their heads in fear and edge away from me. I try to convince them it's not a bomb by saying I'll board the plane with them. A few of the braver ones, seeing the logic of this, then respond, usually by talking about "drug-smuggling" or by becoming uppity about having checked their own bags just so they wouldn't have to lug anything onto the plane.

That's when I have to muster all my powers of persuasion.

"Yes, I always check my bags, too," I say. "It's just that this time I've got to make a tight connection at the other end. If I miss it, it's 16 hours before the next one. I wouldn't mind except my mother's likely to be dead by then. She's lying in the hospital in agony in the final stages of cancer, crying for her little boy whom she hasn't seen in 25 years."

Let's face it; when it comes to sneaking your bags onto the plane, you must know no shame.

After all, this isn't a game.

How to Board through a Skyway

On most flights in a major airport the passenger gets from the gate to the plane through a skyway. This telescoping funnel bears an unsettling resemblance to the cattle-chute at the entrance to a slaughterhouse:

apprehensive, mooing passengers being herded down the ever-narrowing passageway toward their unknown fate. It's not a reassuring image.

Like the slaughterhouse cattle-chute, the skyway does have one major virtue: It doesn't require a lot of decision-making on the part of those inside. Once you enter the skyway, you're pretty sure of getting to the doorway of the plane without many substantial detours.

You should be alerted, however, that there are some skyways—used primarily for boarding wide-body planes—which are of a higher degree of complexity. About halfway down, these skyways will suddenly fork into two passageways, one marked "A" and the other marked "B".

If you encounter this situation, which fork should you take?

In my opinion, it is best to take the one that offers you the biggest piece of cheese—unless there are electrodes attached, in which case you should definitely take the other one.

In the absence of such clues, I suggest you first pause to analyze the situation. In most cases, one of the skyways will go off to the front side door of the plane just behind first class, while the other will go off to the rear side door in the middle of the economy section—although occasionally, when the ground staff have forgotten to put up a chain, the rear skyway will go off into thin air, leading to quite a pile of unobservant economy-class passengers on the tarmac below before the oversight is corrected.

To determine which passageway leads where, try to remember where the plane was positioned when you entered the skyway. Then, looking at your seat number, estimate where your seat is. If your seat is clearly in the rear of the plane, go to the passageway leading to the rear. Otherwise, take the passageway leading to the front door. Even if the front door is a little further from your seat, a good part of the distance will be through the wide aisles of business class where it's much easier to carry your luggage.

What You Should Definitely Not Do When Boarding through a Skyway

I know it's tempting but when you get near the plane-end of the skyway, do not under any circumstances play with the levers and knobs on the skyway control panel. I can tell you now there are only six ways the skyway can go and all of them will lead to a delay of your flight:

1. **If you lower the end of the skyway,** all the boarding passengers will fall out onto the tarmac.

2. If you raise the skyway, all the boarding passengers will fall back into the terminal.

3. & 4. If you move the skyway to the right or the left, many of the boarding passengers (if they're lucky) will end up on the nose or the wing of the plane—which, of course, would violate FAA safety standards for takeoff.

5. If you move the skyway straight back, the result will be somewhat better—as a few of the boarding passengers will be able to leap over the gap into the plane. A substantial number, however, particularly the old and the infirm, will invariably not make it and end up hanging by their fingers from the bottom edge of the plane's doorway, delaying departure considerably.

6. If, instead of all of the above, you merely thrust the skyway straight ahead, the passengers should still be able to board quite easily but, as the plane will be lying on its side, the pilot will find it difficult to taxi down the runway with sufficient speed to achieve liftoff.

How to Walk across the Tarmac

Sometimes the passenger has to walk outside on the tarmac and up a set of portable stairs to get to the aircraft door. Except at smaller airports (which have no skyways), it seems this walk-across-the-tarmac method is used only when the weather gets bad.

Although skyways are supposed to protect passengers from the elements, they unfortunately are much more prone than passengers to breaking down in bad weather. When the sky is sunny and clear and you don't need them, skyways operate perfectly. Come the 30-below ice storms, and they immediately freeze up and sensibly refuse to go out.

Crossing the tarmac to the plane can be quite an adventurous experience. It's not just the excitement of trying to protect yourself from the wind and rain, from the noise of nearby jet engines and from the mini-trucks whizzing around; it's also the excitement of trying to decide which plane is yours. Having come down a spiral staircase from the boarding lounge, you're totally disoriented, like someone who's just been whirled around at the beginning of blindman's bluff. You look up and see, out across the tarmac, two planes, both the same size, each with the same markings. There's no way to tell them apart. No ground staff to show you which is which.

In this situation you've got to depend solely on the laws of probability. Choose the plane on the left. If you do so, you can feel secure in the knowledge that with a sufficient number of such choices over a long enough period, you're likely to be correct at least 50 percent of the time.

I know I have.

If you choose wrong, be philosophical. It's not everyone who can fly to Lubbock, Texas, by mistake 16 times in a row.

How to Ride to the Plane on a Transporter.

Sometimes, when the aircraft is a long way away, the passengers are taken across the tarmac in a motorized transporter. If this should ever happen to you, before entering the transporter try to determine whether it is a LIFO model (*i.e.*, Last-In-First-Out) or a FIFO model (*i.e.*, First-In-First-Out).

Most airport standing-only transporters with large doors in the middle are LIFO models. The last one into the transporter at the terminal is usually the first one out at the plane. With these, you hang back during loading and get on only at the last moment.

If a LIFO transporter has a few seats, do not take them. They're usually far inside where you'll be trapped. Plus if you sit down, you'll find it hard to keep your suitcase from being stumbled over by the other passengers and, as the transporter turns the corner, you'll find you're being hit in the face by garment bags hanging from the overhead bars.

When encountering FIFO transporters (usually ones with a primary entrance next to the driver and lots of seats on a long aisle), do just the opposite; get in as quickly as possible and sit near the front.

Sometimes it's not easy to tell immediately whether a transporter is LIFO or FIFO. Take for example, the mobile lounges at Washington Dulles Airport (also at Jedda and occasionally at Charles de Gaulle) which take you directly from a sealed second-story terminal port directly to the aircraft door; these transporters have large doors and steering wheels on both the front and rear ends of the vehicle. Only experienced passengers can tell which the driver will use. (At Dulles it's almost always the end which you entered.)

A similar problem exists with transporters which have wide doors on either side. The fact the driver picks you up through the right door doesn't mean he won't drop you off through the left. If you were the last in through the right door, you're not going to be the first out through the left door.

The technique used by my brother in situations like these is to enter the transporter, stand near the middle and spend the trip across the tarmac hunched over, straining to look through the windows, so that he can figure out a few seconds before everyone else which door will be used as the exit.

A more sensible person, of course, would have obtained this information from the driver upon entering the transporter, thus releasing the mind for more mature and important preoccupations during the ride; but not my brother.

Getting Past the Guardian Angel

The primary job of the flight attendant at the aircraft door is to enforce the airline's rigid class system. As the passengers arrive, the flight attendant, like a smiling angel on the Day of Judgment, divides them according to their intended destinations. A blue boarding pass envelope: to the heaven of first class. A brown one: to the purgatory of business. A red one: to the hell of economy.

On many of the narrow-body planes, the torture of the condemned is increased by their being made to pass through first class on their way to the depths—one last vision of what could have been theirs had they been willing, while they were on earth, to give away all of their worldly goods in order to obtain the salvation of a first-class ticket.

If you are attempting to carry an additional bag onto the plane, don't worry about the flight attendant at the aircraft door stopping you. He or she will be too busy making sure everyone knows their place (and will assume that any excess luggage problems have been taken care of at the gate). Just hold your boarding pass up and away from your bags as you did at the gate and do nothing to bring your baggage to his or her attention.

A Brief Synopsis of the Passenger Classes

1. **First class.** First class is characterized by wide seats with elevated leg rests and deep reclining backs, gourmet food served on china with silverware and a table cloth, and ever-present, personal service from the flight attendants. This class is populated primarily by wealthy Arabs, frequent-flyer upgrades and off-duty airline employees flying free.

2. **Business class.** In the early days of flying, there were only first class and economy. With deregulation, however, airline fares began to plummet and many of those people who used to travel by bus began to show up on airplanes. Business class was created by the airlines as a kind of expensive economy class in which the primary benefit was not that there were free drinks, better earphones and slightly more room but rather that

the loud-mouth drunks, mothers with squalling babies and teenagers with blaring ghetto-blasters wouldn't be able to afford the fare.

3.   Economy class. To describe this class as a snake pit is perhaps going too far. It is merely the mass class—the class in which all things have been reduced to a lowest common denominator: the seating, the service, the food, the earphone entertainment system, the toilets, the . . .

Yeah. It's a snake pit.

4.   Super-economy class. In this class all that the passengers get is a seat. No food service. No drinks service. No earphone entertainment system. Surprising as it may seem, the airlines don't charge more for this class than they do for ordinary economy. They apparently don't realize that the attractions of the food, drink and entertainment in ordinary economy class are such that most people would willingly pay to avoid them.

How an Economy Class Passenger Should Behave When Due to Overbooking He or She is Given a Seat in First Class

Occasionally, due to overbooking, an economy class passenger will be bumped up to first class. Although the passenger will have paid for only an economy class ticket, he or she will usually be treated as any other full-fare first class passenger. In return for this treatment, all the airline asks is that the passenger take pains not to betray his or her lowly class origins.

Accordingly, if you are ever bumped from economy to first class:

(a) Do not announce to everyone around that you're actually an economy class passenger and don't belong in first class. Few people do. And those that do don't want to sit next to those who don't.

(b) When the stewardess addresses you by name—without your having introduced yourself—and asks you—without your having pushed the call button—whether there is anything she can do for you, don't reveal your total and utter amazement. She got your name from the passenger list and she's being solicitous only because, different from economy class, the first-class stewardess' relationship with her passengers is governed by something other than crowd control.

(c) Don't ask the stewardess to bring you an elevated footrest like the ones your fellow passengers have. Your footrest, like theirs, comes from a hidden position under your seat. Just reach down, grab hold and within an hour or two you'll have it unfolded into the correct position.

(d) When you're handed a small zippered bag containing miscellaneous toiletries, don't say, "Hey, what's this?", ask your seatmate, "Hey, did you get one of these, too?", open the case, hold up the miniature toothbrush, comb and razor, and say, "Hey, will you look at that?" and then ask the stewardess when she comes by whether you can take the case and contents home after the flight. Instead, put the case quietly in the seat pocket in front of you and, later, when you go back to the lavatory, take the case with you to gawk at in private while you're sitting on the toilet.

(e) When the stewardess gives you a pair of stretch slippers and a blindfold, do not put the blindfold on immediately. It's supposed to be worn only when you're sleeping.

(f) When the stewardess hands you a pair of earphones, don't complain that its plastic tubes have withered away. Earphones in first class are electronic; those "withered tubes" are wires. Insert the thin metal plug into the tiny hole in the end of your armrest and listen.

(g) When the stewardess serves you a drink, don't try to pay her. Drinks in first class are free—or, more precisely, they're free for you. For the full-fare passenger, they've been paid for in advance at the rate of roughly $100 a drink. Do not point this out.

(h) When, at mealtime, you're served two small pieces of toast with a thimbleful of caviar, onion and egg shavings, don't exclaim, "Hey, is this all?" Unlike economy-class meals, which are served all at once on a tray, meals in first class are served serially in many courses, one at a time.

In short, in order to appear as an ordinary first-class passenger, keep your mouth shut, take things as they come and, above all, maintain the appearance of complete indifference to your amazing good luck. Remember that the main pleasure of first class comes not from experiencing the superior accommodation, cuisine and service, but rather from acting as though these things are nothing out of the ordinary.

CHAPTER EIGHT

THE BASICS OF CABIN LIFE

The Best Row to Sit in on the Plane

What is best for you depends on what factors are most important to you:

1.   Rapid departure on arrival. Since most planes exit their passengers from the front, row by row, obtaining a seat near the front will get you out the quickest.

2.   Health. Naturally you will want a row in the no-smoking section. In addition, since the fresh air circulates from the front to the rear, you'll want a row near the front—unless the section in front of you is smoking, in which case you will want a row about a third of the way back to allow drifting smoke to dissipate.

3.   Smooth ride. Seats over the wing give the smoothest ride; those at the back, the bumpiest.

4.   Movie watching. To be able to see the picture clearly yet not suffer eyestrain, you'll want a row about two or three back from the screen. In any case, you'll want to be particularly careful to avoid those rows next to the galleys which have no view of the screen at all.

5.   Seat reclining. The row all the way at the back and the rows just in front of emergency-window exits often do not recline all the way.

6.   Spreading out. Generally rows at the rear, in the smoking section or which have some seats blocked out for the use of flight attendants are less likely to be occupied.

7.   Legroom. Certain rows have more legroom but they also carry certain costs.

> **(a)   Main door entrance area.** In my experience, although these seats do provide greater leg room, the toilets or galleys invariably open onto them, which then attract a mob of drunks or desperately-waiting toilet-users to trip over your feet—not to mention a peculiar amalgam of smells.

> **(b)   Bulkhead.** The bulkhead has the legroom without the crowds and also no seats in front to recline into your lap. On the other hand, there's no under-the-seat storage space and, worse, the adjoining seats are usually occupied by mothers with small children. If the children are not crying, puking, peeing, fighting or growing appalling snot mustaches on their upper lip, they're trying to get your attention so they can brag about their pathetic little accomplishments.
> "I can count to ten. And tie my shoelaces, too."
> "Great, kid. Here's the Nobel Prize for Physics."

(c) Emergency window exit rows. These have the legroom with the under-the-seat storage and without the crowds or small children (the latter are generally not allowed in these rows at all). However, these rows are not entirely without their little problems. For instance, recently, as a plane was taxiing away from the gate, an excitable novice passenger actually opened the emergency exit window next to him so he could wave to his friends in the terminal. Needless to say, the guy was Italian.

These emergency rows also seem to attract a disproportionate number of hysterics, who cling to the exit window and ask you over and over again during the flight whether flames should be coming out of the back of the jet engine like that.

What they would do if you said no? Exit the plane at 30,000 feet?

8.   Special needs. Some of the major ones:

(a) Nonambulatory. You'll want the seats designed for non-ambulatory passengers and which are close to the special toilets for the disabled.

(b) Children. You'll want the bulkhead to give them floor space to play on and/or a row close to the lavatories with diaper-changing facilities. If you have an infant, another reason to have a bulkhead row is that on some airlines there are special bassinets which fix to the bulkhead wall.

(c) Carry-on luggage. If you have a lot, you'll want a row closest to the closets and garment-bag power-lifters.

(d) Sensitivity. If you want peace and quiet or have a sensitive nose, you'll want a row away from the toilets and galleys.

How to Know the Number of the Row You Want

Although a few flights have "open seating" (usually where the plane is small or a shuttle, or the computer has broken down), on most flights nowadays you have to choose your seat before you enter the plane. Since even the same types of aircraft will have different seating configurations on different airlines, you cannot rely on your favorite seat having the same number from plane to plane.

Fortunately, most of the information you'll need is available from a good travel agency; all you need to do is ask for it. If you are a frequent traveler, the *Airline Seating Guide* mentioned above at page 42 is by far the best source. In addition to the configuration of each airline's aircraft, the *Guide* shows which seats are nonsmoking, have the most legroom, don't fully recline, have no view of the movie, are reserved for disabled passengers, are next to seats blocked for airline staff or are close to disabled or diaper-changing lavatories, luggage storage, galleys, smoking sections, movie screens or airphones.

The Good, the Bad and the Ugly: or Should You Choose an Aisle, a Window or a Middle Seat?

1. **Aisle seat.** Sitting in an aisle seat has three advantages:

    (a) Less embarrassment. During the flight you can get out without making your fellow passengers get up.

    (b) Immediate access to luggage. When the plane lands, you can get your luggage out of the overhead bin immediately.

    (c) Quicker departure. You can take off down the aisle while it is still unblocked by exiting passengers.

2. **Window seat.** Sitting in a window seat has three advantages:

    (a) View. This is primarily of appeal to inexperienced travelers. Experienced travelers know there's not much to see—what with the dust scarring and window fog—and in any case they've seen it all before. (Hint: For the best possible view make sure your seat (i) is not over the wing and (ii) is on the shady side of the plane.)

    (b) Pillow support. If you want to sleep, you can lean your head against the wall (and get your brains vibrated for free).

    (c) Less disturbance. You won't have to get up when other passengers want to leave the row nor will you be bumped by people walking down the aisle.

3. **Middle seat.** Window seats and aisle seats are the opposite of each other. The advantages of each demonstrate the disadvantages of the other. Middle seats, on the other hand, have all the disadvantages of window seats and aisle seats with none of the advantages. You've got no view, you've got no place to rest your head, you've got to get up when the window-seat passenger wants to get out, you've got to make the aisle-seat passenger get up when you want to get out, you've got no immediate access to the overhead bin and the aisle-seat passenger prevents you from making a quick departure on landing.

About the only advantage is that middle seats have been designed to have the largest under-seat storage space, but this is more than offset by the fact that the middle seats have not been designed for anyone with arms and legs.

Why I Think the Aisle Seat is Probably Best

I'll be the first to admit that the aisle seat isn't a bed of roses. In the first place, you're fair game for the flight attendants, who roam up and down the aisle, waiting for you to start dropping off to sleep so they can run over your foot with the service trolley, or for you to put a drink in your hand so they can bump your elbow.

This latter disadvantage can be mitigated by choosing a seat which is on the same side of the aisle as your dominant hand. In other words, if you are right-handed, sit on the right side of the aisle, so that when you're taking a drink or a forkful of dinner, your right elbow will not be the one bumped.

There are other problems as well. On a lot of planes there's a metal bar curving in from the aisle under the seat in front of you, the sole purpose of which seems to be to prevent you from fitting your carry-on case underneath. And it's somewhat of a pain to have to get up to let your seatmates in and out.

All these inconveniences pale, however, before the central inconvenience of the window and middle seats: There's no way to get out without disturbing the person or persons between you and aisle, and, through some profound law of nature, such person or persons are invariably the kind that even the most severe claustrophobic would be hesitant to disturb— *e.g.,* a seven-foot, manic depressive in a coma or a 300-pound, arthritic with a heart condition. It isn't until several hours into the flight, when your bladder literally gets too big for your britches, that you're finally able to build up the courage to ask them to let you out. And then they make such martyrs of themselves getting up from their seats, you spend the rest of the trip in the toilet, so as not to make them get up again to let you back in.

Why the Central Section of a Wide-Body is Best

Assuming you are going to sit on the aisle in a wide-body, then it is better to sit on either aisle seat of the central section than on the aisle seat of either outer section.

1.   Less crowded. Since inexperienced travelers prefer window seats, you are less likely to have anyone else in your row in the central section (where there are no window seats). If there is only one other passenger in your row, he or she will be on the opposite aisle, leaving several free seats in between to store your carry-on bags, to maintain your privacy or to allow you, after take off, to move inside in order to avoid being bumped by people walking up and down the aisle.

2.   Less disturbance. Each row in the interior section has two exits rather than one. If there is one other passenger in your row, he or she won't have to climb over you to get out. If the plane is packed and there are four-across seating, you'll have only one inside seatmate who needs to crawl over you to get out.

3.   Better movie-watching. If you attempt to watch the movie, the sociopaths walking up and down the aisle will not block your view of the screen.

4.   More sleeping room. Perhaps most importantly, if your row is empty, you can lift up the armrests and stretch out four-across to sleep. (See *The Best Way to Sleep on the Plane* below at page 252.)

How to Increase the Chance of There Being an Empty Space Between You and Your Partner

As most flyers know, when two people are traveling together, the ideal seating arrangement is an aisle and window seat with an empty middle seat between. If the flight is not crowded, merely booking the window and aisle seat will probably insure that the middle seat is empty since middle seats are so undesirable.

If you're concerned that the flight might be crowded, however, there are several ways you can increase the chances that the space between you (or if you're traveling alone, next to you) will be empty.

1.   Choose a less desirable row. For instance, the last row in the section is generally undesirable because the seats don't recline and it's so far from the exit.

2.   Reserve opposing aisle seats. Even if the middle seats next to each of you are full, you'll have an empty space between you.

3.   Pay for the center seat. I have an aunt and uncle who find this a way to get business-class space at a lower price. They report having encountered the following problems, however:

(a)   **Split locations.** If you buy the tickets before you can obtain an advance seat assignment, then when seat assignments occur, the airline may end up scattering the three seats all over the plane. Make sure you get in writing the airline's promise to put the three seats together.

(b) Delayed check-in. The boarding pass computer is usually not set up to issue a boarding pass for an empty reserved seat. You'll probably have to go to the manager to get it.

(c) Poachers. Once you get on the plane, other passengers who want to get out of their section into yours (for instance, to avoid smokers, to watch a different movie or to allow their lap baby to have a seat) will keep trying to force themselves into your empty middle seat.

4.   Reserve the center seat. A friend and his wife regularly reserve the seat between them in the name of "Mr. Jones". This prevents the seat from being claimed until the seat reservation is canceled due to the failure of Mr. Jones to purchase a ticket by the appropriate deadline, usually 30 minutes before the flight. If they want the seat reservation to last longer, my friend and his wife purchase a full-fare ticket for Mr. Jones and, on those airlines which terminate seat reservations 30 minutes before the flight, go ahead and obtain a boarding pass for him. Only when Mr. Jones fails to turn up at the gate-appearance deadline is the seat subject to being filled. Note, as mentioned above, even though Mr. Jones obtained a boarding pass, my friends are able to obtain a full refund on his unused ticket.

5.   Employ the "imaginary infant" trick. Occasionally my friend and his wife have utilized this trick on domestic flights when they didn't want to buy a ticket. When he and his wife book their flight, they tell the airline that they will be traveling with an infant (although in fact they won't). Infants can normally travel for free on domestic flights as long as they don't have a guaranteed seat; if the flight is full, they have to be carried on an adult's lap. When my friend and his wife get their aisle and window seat assignments, they request that the airline put a "block" on the middle seat for their infant. (See discussion below at page 374.) This means that the seat, although not reserved, will be the last seat filled in the plane. Because the block is visible only to the seat-assignment staff and not to flight attendants, nine times out of ten the airline never discovers that my friend and his wife don't have an infant.

I imagine this technique would work on an international flight except that my friends would have to purchase an infant ticket for ten percent of full fare. To keep the block on for the longest time, they would then have to obtain a boarding pass for their imaginary infant, which would require them to produce a passport for the infant. They could possibly borrow the passport of some friend's infant, since the passport will not be stamped or anything. But, there comes a point where you begin to wonder whether it's really worth it.

Personally, I don't feel the reserving or blocking of seats for imaginary passengers is proper. Rather than taking advantage of a small loophole somewhere, it is somehow a breach of the trust inherent in the system—similar to the difference between figuring out how to get something wholesale and shoplifting. If a lot of people start reserving or blocking seats for imaginary passengers, the airlines, in response, will eventually change the system to make it much less convenient for everyone. For instance, the airlines might require us to buy a ticket before we can reserve a seat, or require us to present identification before we can receive a boarding pass, or might do away with the blocking of infant seats altogether.

For that reason, before reserving or blocking seats for imaginary passengers, think long and hard about how important it really is to you to be sitting next to an empty seat.

Which Seats Are the Safe Seats on the Plane

Short answer: There are no "safe" seats on the plane.

Depending on what you are trying to avoid, however, some seats are safer than others:

(a) **To avoid being squashed on impact,** sit anywhere further back than the wing.

(b) **To avoid having your neck broken in turbulence,** sit anywhere but in the back of the plane, since the back of the plane is the furthest from the center of gravity. While only one out of 20 *crashes* occur while the plane is at its cruising altitude, eight out of 20 *injuries* occur during that period—primarily from turbulence.

(c) **To avoid being burned to a crisp in a fire**, sit away from the engines, since fire is usually caused by the fuel lines breaking. This means sitting at the front if the engines are at the rear and the middle, or at the front and rear if the engines are in the middle. Ideally you should be next to an exit door.

(d) **To avoid being sucked out of the plane when the exit doors open in midflight,** sit as far away from the exit doors as possible.

(e) To avoid being suffocated in poisonous smoke, sit as close to the exit doors as possible.

In other words, when you get in the plane, first decide which way you want to die and then choose your seat accordingly.

The Difficulties Involved in Finding Your Seat on the Plane

Passengers don't always read their boarding passes correctly. A common error is to mistake the gate or flight number for their seat number. Even when they do read the boarding pass correctly, however, the airlines do not make the task of finding their seat easy.

The general rule, of course, is that the rows are numbered from front to back and the seats lettered from left to right (looking forward). The pitfalls are in the exceptions to this rule:

1. Superstitious deletions. Most airlines leave out row thirteen (or more precisely they call row thirteen row fourteen) in consideration of certain passengers' primitive beliefs.

2. Separate compartments. The numbering from the last row in one compartment to the first row in the compartment behind is often not consecutive. As many as six to eight row numbers can be left out. Some airlines appear to be leaving imaginary rows for the area taken up by the galleys and toilets in case they want to change the configuration. Others appear to be assigning certain row numbers to start each section, no matter how many fewer rows were in the previous section.

3. Confusing de-confusers. Some airlines leave out seat "I" on wide-bodies—probably because it could be confused with the number "1". In these aircraft, the letter "H" is followed by the letter "J".

4. General misalignment. On wide-bodies the row numbers in the four- or five-abreast central section are often slightly behind or ahead of those in the window sections. Thus, you have to be sure to check the row number posted on the side of the aisle on which your seat is and not on the row immediately across the aisle.

What to Do About a Defective Seat

Very often when you get to a seat you will discover it's defective. The reclining back will not stay up. The tray table slopes into your lap. The earphones don't work or do so through only one ear. The reading light is out or misaimed. (Note: To prevent you from discovering the reading light and entertainment system problems until it's too late, most airlines leave them turned off until after takeoff.)

If you discover that your seat is defective, stop a passing stewardess and tell her exactly what is wrong. It will amuse her.

If there are no other adequate substitute seats available in your class, try demanding a seat in a higher-class section. If the defect is serious enough and the flight attendant is in a good mood, you may get it.

How to Change Seats on the Plane

If, after arriving on the plane, you discover you have an undesirable seat and see a more desirable, empty one available, take it immediately. Do not ask the flight attendant for permission. The flight attendant will only tell you to wait until after takeoff and by then the seat may be filled by last-minute standbys.

If, after moving to a more desirable empty seat, someone does show up with a boarding pass for that seat, suggest they take your old seat instead. That person may not care which seat they have or, if they do, they may be a much more accommodating person than you are.

In the event there are no desirable empty seats around, you might consider approaching other passengers about a trade. A middle seat is virtually impossible to trade, unless you have a sex object of some sort sitting next to you. A window seat, however, can often be traded to an inexperienced passenger.

Find such a passenger in an aisle seat who appears to be traveling alone and ask him if he'd prefer to sit where he could look out the window. Mention specific scenic opportunities, such as icebergs being born off the Greenland glaciers (on Europe-US routes), or Mt. Witney and Death Valley, the highest and lowest spots in the continental US, seen in a single view (on coast-to-coast flights). If your descriptions of these sights are sufficiently glowing, you'll not only get the guy's better seat but receive his blubbering thanks as well.

The Art of Settling In

Once you've found your aisle seat, cornered a supply of pillows and blankets, stored your luggage (laying your coat on your case in the overhead rack so it won't get crushed by those who'll come after you) and staked out your seat with sufficient debris to discourage any squatters, you'll notice the fasten-seat-belt sign urging you to sit down.

Don't do it.

If one of the inside seats has been assigned, you'll only have to get up again when your seatmate arrives. Even if no one takes the inside seat, sitting on the aisle during loading is a dangerous business. Flight bags and purses swing out from the shoulders of passing passengers to bash you in the face. Large pieces of luggage, resisting all efforts of a neighboring passenger to squeeze them into the tiny space you've left in the overhead rack, fall onto your head in revenge.

If you're not going to sit down, however, you can't just stand around the aisles and get trampled.

The answer is to gather up some reading and go to the toilet.

This course of action has a couple of advantages. In the first place, absent some peculiar emergency, you're unlikely to be trampled in the toilet by the other passengers. In the second place, now, before the flight starts, the toilet is at its best. There are no lines, no trash, new soap, and paper cups in the dispensers. While waiting, you can use the latter to fill up on water as protection against the dry air in the plane.

The airline, of course, doesn't like people taking refuge in the toilet during loading, so it lights up a return-to-seat sign there whenever the plane is on the ground. I find the sign provides just that extra bit of light I need for my reading.

Once you feel the plane begin to move, peek out of your cubicle to see if the aisles are clear. If they are, then you can get up and placidly return to your seat through the bruised and battered remains of your fellow passengers.

What to Do Immediately Before Taxiing and Takeoff

During taxiing and takeoff, you should follow the airline's advice:

1. Make sure your seat belt is buckled. Experienced passengers, as the flight attendants love saying over the public address system, wear their seat belts not only during taxiing and takeoff but during the rest of the flight as well. Experienced passengers know what maniacs these airline pilots can be.

2. Be certain to bring your seat back to the upright position. This will allow the person sitting behind you to put his head between his knees in the event of a crash.

Why anyone would want his head between his knees in the event of a crash, God only knows. It's certainly not a position I'd want to be found dead in.

3.   Put your tray table up. This is not always the easiest thing to do, particularly if you've put anything in the seat pocket behind the tray, but it's well worth the effort. In the event of a crash, not only can you put your head between your knees (if you're into that sort of thing) but also avoid having the upper part of your body severed at the solar plexus.

Instead, it'll be severed at your waist by the seat belt.

4.   Store your luggage under the seat in front of you. In the event of a crash, your suitcase might fly free and you'd have a terrible time trying to recover it—particularly if, as is likely, it happens to lodge two-feet inside the upper back of the passenger in front of you.

Unstored luggage also creates another problem—which it shares with the reclined seat and the lowered tray table. All three things tend to block the foot space in front of or, in the case of the reclined seat, behind the seat. In the event of a serious crash, the passengers would be forced to walk on the seats to get out, which would lead to the upholstery being soiled.

5.   Put your armrests down. Some people think this requirement arises either (i) because raised armrests could, in the event of a crash, come smashing down, stripping the shoulders off the unwary, or (ii) because lowered armrests would provide the passengers with some lateral support if the plane suddenly began doing cartwheels on the runway. In my opinion, these are not the reasons. The lowered armrest is, instead, the last line of defense in the event of a crash. If, contrary to all the rules, your fellow passengers have left their luggage unstored, their seats reclined and their tray tables lowered (so you have to get out by climbing on the seats), you'll be able to step on the armrests and thus avoid soiling the upholstery.

6.   Extinguish your cigarette. In the event of a crash, the air conditioning is likely to go out. If you're puffing on a cigarette, the cabin air will quickly become quite smokey, thereby increasing substantially the chance of lung cancer among the nonsmoking passengers. This danger is especially acute if, following the crash, you and the passengers are soaking in jet fuel. Recent studies have indicated that inhaling ignited petroleum products can have a significant carcinogenic effect on lung tissue.

How to Behave During Taxiing and Takeoff

An experienced traveler never acknowledges a takeoff when it is occurring.

During the interminable taxiing, when it appears the pilot has decided to drive to the destination instead, when everything and everyone is bouncing around, when the overhead compartment doors are springing open and when strange crashes are emanating from the galleys, the experienced traveler doesn't look up.

As the engines roar and thrust the plane forward, the experienced traveler doesn't pause to glance out the window, take a deep breath or grip his armrests more firmly.

When the plane banks steeply so that one side is looking straight down at the ground and the other, straight up at the sky, the experienced traveler continues reading or talking, exactly as before—even if, at the time, the plane is not yet airborne.

The experienced traveler, in short, is as cool as a cucumber.

Inexperienced travelers, of course, might be tempted here to make some additional comparisons between the experienced traveler and a cucumber which would not be particularly conducive to the cause of mutual understanding.

My point is not that the experienced traveler is unaware of the dangers of takeoff but rather that, realizing he's powerless to do anything about it, he's decided that pretending to be a vegetable is the only sane course open to him.

How to Deal with Your Seatmate

The airlines, using the latest computer technology, are now able to select mutually incompatible seatmates for almost everyone.

For me, the telltale sign that the computer's done it again is when I return to my seat after my settling-in retreat to the bathroom and discover my prospective seatmate watching the flight attendants' safety demonstration.

No, I'm not making it up. There actually are people who watch the flight attendants' safety demonstration.

You can imagine where *they* rank on the personality scale.

To sit next to them is to court an agonizing, lingering death through unremitting boredom. Not because they won't talk but just the opposite: because they won't stop talking. Endless, droning drivel about Junior League baseball, dog-grooming, lawn-mowing, matchbook collecting and other such appalling hobbies.

The trick, I've discovered, is to never let a conversation begin.

While the guy's still trying to figure out from what part of the ceiling the oxygen masks will drop, I slip into my seat, pull out some papers, put them on my lap and, as he turns smilingly towards me, begin scribbling furiously. I know I mustn't look up, no matter what. Not when he clears his throat for the fifth time. Not when he leans over to try to read my scrawl. Not even when the airline, realizing it's a critical time for me, tries to make me stop writing by taxiing down the runway on pogo sticks. I must continue to pretend to be engrossed in my work, oblivious to the eyestrain and wild pen marks on my leg.

After takeoff, when I've pulled the tray table down and put my papers on it, I can usually fend the guy off relatively easily until the next major hurdle: drinks service.

Having studied the sociology of these matters in some depth, I know that once my seatmate gets a drink in his hand, he'll find it impossible not to speak—even if it's just to his reflection in the window. And I, likewise, will be confronted with an almost irresistible urge to respond.

When the trolley arrives, I jam my peanuts packet into my pocket and gulp down my drink with my left hand, while I continue scribbling like mad with my right, never once lifting my head (no matter what my seatmate says to himself), repeating over and over in my mind, "Think of the consequences, think of the consequences, think of the consequences."

If I can keep my concentration until my seatmate's glass is empty, I'm usually rewarded with an hour or so of leisurely doodling—during which time I must prepare myself mentally for the really big test: meal service. Meal service—when, with my tray table covered completely with plastic wrappers and food, I will have to perform the impossible—scribble and eat at the same time.

It's not easy, I tell you.

When dinner arrives, I, continuing to write with my right hand, lift my papers into the air with my left so the flight attendant can put my food tray down. Then I lower my left hand a little at a time until the bottom of my papers rests on the back edge of the tray and the top of the my papers leans against the back of the seat in front of me.

When, out of the corner of my eye, I notice my seatmate turning back to focus his attention on the arduous job of opening his plastic utensils packet, I spring into action. Without taking my eyes off what I've written, I lay down my pen, release my papers and in the brief moment it takes for my papers to bend in the middle and start sliding down behind the table, I remove the plastic wrappers, take out my silverware and cut up all my food.

I've become so practiced at this procedure that I usually can finish the job, catch my bending papers with my left hand and begin scribbling again with my right before my seatmate is even aware he's missed the opportunity to engage me in conversation.

From then on it's merely a matter of waiting. Each time my seatmate puts some food into his mouth, I quickly drop my pen, pick up my fork and shovel in a few mouthfuls. No matter how much effort the poor guy puts into hurriedly swallowing his food, I'm almost always writing again before his mouth is sufficiently unobstructed to speak.

As you might imagine, it isn't long before the man's spirit has been totally broken.

Realizing he's met his match, he resigns himself to having to wait until his next flight to find someone to bore to death.

What to Ask for at Drinks Service

When the flight attendants come around with the drinks trolley, I ask for just water. This has three major advantages.

(a) In the first place, water is the most efficient way to fight the dehydration caused by the dry air in the cabin. (In most jet aircraft, your body will be losing moisture at twice its normal rate.)

(b) In the second place, water is one of the few things in economy class which is free.

(c) In the third place, because it's free, the flight attendants never have it on the drinks trolley and have to go back, muttering, to the galley to get it; this gives me the chance to steal a few extra packages of peanuts off the trolley so I can stay alive until meal service.

Usually, when the flight attendant is in the galley getting my water, I also swipe a can of orange juice from the trolley to store away to have with my meal. Of course, there's normally a later drinks service designed specifically to go with the meal but for some unknown reason, perhaps a deeply held belief by airline management in the virtues of deferred gratification, I've never known the mealtime drinks service to occur until long after all the passengers have finished eating.

When ordering your water, always ask for lots of ice. The ice acts as a sort of rationing device which, by taking time to melt, forces you to spread out your water consumption over a longer period. Do not become impatient and try to suck the ice cubes after you've drunk the water around them. Airline cups are specifically designed so that ice cubes will stick on the bottom, coming unstuck only after you've tipped the cup upside down over your mouth and given the bottom a strong enough whack to send the ice bouncing off your teeth onto the floor.

If you want to order something other than water, be sure to avoid the following:

> **(a) Carbonated beverages,** Because of the low pressure in the cabin, your intestine can swell up by 20 percent or more. Air bubbles expanding out of your drink will only exacerbate this condition.

> **(b) Coffee and tea.** These are diuretics, *i.e.*, they increase the amount you urinate, so they both increase your dehydration and make you have to get up from your seat more often.

> **(c) Alcohol.** Alcohol increases your dehydration, upsets your inner ear and, at the reduced air pressure in the cabin, is 50 to 100 percent more powerful in reducing your oxygen consumption and making you drunk. In addition, wine (especially sherry and port) contain histamines which aggravate head congestion, increasing the danger of ear trouble on descent.

So to be safe, stick with water, juice, and carbonated beverages which you've left open until they've gone flat.

The Best Way to Open Your Peanuts Package

The instructions on the peanut packages recommend that you try to rip open the bag by gripping the seam on the upper edge on either side of a tear mark and twisting in opposite directions. The difficulty with this method is that the resistance of the foil usually requires some pressure to overcome and then suddenly evaporates as you tear through the sealed portion, causing you to tear straight down both sides of the bag, spraying the contents over the floor.

The proper method is to pinch the opposite flat sides of the bag just below the seam and, by rocking the heels of your hands together with the bag in between, gradually pull the seam apart from the inside out. The resistance disappears slowly and no dangerous tear is created in the foil.

What to Eat on the Plane

Please, don't think I'm one of those people who spend their time attacking the taste and appearance of airline food. I mean, why beat a dead horse?

I long ago learned to accept as a fact of life the lowest-common-denominator versions of the gourmet which airlines feed to their passengers: Breakfasts composed mainly of various manifestations of cholesterol injected with artificial coloring. Snacks consisting of imitation meat and stale bread sandwiches in which all the taste has been concentrated in a tiny pickle of uncertain origin. TV dinners of overcooked lasagna, chicken Kiev, fish with shredded almonds or sirloin tips with rice, garnished with a bulletproof roll, some kind of aerated dessert and the remains of vegetables which were put on to boil when the passenger originally booked his or her flight.

The best I can do are the following three hints:

(a) Taste. Try to order those things which common sense tells you are most likely to survive reheating in a microwave, *i.e.*, stews, casseroles and ragouts, and avoid those things which cannot, *i.e.*, almost everything else.

(b) Sanitation. There isn't much you can do here. I have been assured by airline personnel that the risk of ptomaine poisoning and salmonella from an airplane meal are less than you'd encounter going out to a restaurant. Whether this is because restaurant food is more likely to be contaminated or because restaurant food is more likely to be eaten, I couldn't say.

Certainly the airline rule prohibiting the pilot and copilot from eating the same meal on the plane gives one pause for thought.

(c) Physical comfort. Choose foods which do not exacerbate the problems of dry air and low air pressure. For the former this means basically avoiding salt. (Scrape those peanuts clean before you eat them.) For the latter, it means avoiding those foods which can cause gas, such as beans, cabbage, onions, apples, cucumbers and melons, and eating lightly.

Along the same lines, avoid chewing any gum. Besides lowering substantially the appearance of your IQ, the continual chewing causes you to swallow much more air than you normally would, aggravating the pressure in your stomach.

How to Order a Special Meal

Most airlines will provide special meals, such as kosher, Hindu, Moslem, Oriental, Soul, bland, vegan vegetarian, lacto-ovarian vegetarian, lactose-restricted, diabetic, low-calorie, low-sodium, low-cholesterol, gluten-free, high-carbohydrate, high-protein, weight watcher, fruit salad, seafood casserole, barbecue, pizza, cold cuts, children's meal, hamburger and french fries, and combinations thereof. Generally you have to order the meal several hours in advance of the flight, although occasionally I've done it successfully a half-hour before the flight. Be sure to check with your airline to see what is available.

Box 8-1.	Advance Notice Requirements for Special Meals
Airline	**Advance Notice**
Alaska	24 hrs
America West	24 hrs
American	6 hrs; kosher 12 hrs
Continental	24 hrs
Delta	6-24 hrs dep'g on type
Eastern	8 hrs
Hawaii	48 hrs
Midway	24-36 hrs dep'g on plane
Northwest	8-24 hrs dep'g on type
Pan Am	2-8 hrs
TWA	24 hrs
United	6-24 hrs dep'g on type
USAir	72 hrs

Many people order special meals on the theory that specially prepared food will taste better than the mass-produced variety. Whether this theory is correct or not, however, is difficult for me to say. Although I have several times ordered vegetarian meals, I have seldom eaten them. Not because of a fear of the taste but because almost always the airline has forgotten to put the special meal on the plane.

If you order such a meal, then from the moment you enter the airport until meal service occurs you must take advantage of every opportunity to remind the various airline representatives along the way of your order. Be especially certain to have the check-in staff check that the meal is noted in their computer and to have the flight attendant at the door of the aircraft confirm that it is on board.

If, after going through all this, you still have an ordinary meal slapped onto your tray table, it may be best to eat it. More than once, I've pointed out to the serving flight attendant that I'd ordered a vegetarian meal, only to have her whack her forehead, scurry off in the direction of the galley and twenty minutes later come back with a tray full of overboiled vegetables looking suspiciously like uneaten leftovers from the other passengers' ordinary meals.

How to Get at Your Food

Much of the adventure of airline eating is in trying to remove utensils and food from their packaging without spilling them all over the floor. The airlines and/or their caterers have designed airline food packaging without a thought to the poor passenger who has to deal with them. Let me give you a few examples:

1. The cellophane packet containing your napkins and cutlery. How in the hell is an inexperienced passenger supposed to know how to open this thing? There are no instructions. It's only through trial and error that you eventually discover that you're supposed to slide the packet vertically down over the knife until the top of the packet is pierced. Even then, when you pull the wrapped napkin out of one end, the salt, pepper and plastic stirrer invariably fall out the other.

2. The cup-like containers of liquid with foil sealed over the top. These things are deadly. For two reasons:

(a) Because of the reduced air pressure in the cabin, if the initial opening is made where there is liquid rather than air, the contents will explode out of the container all over your lap. With experience you learn to tip the container back slightly before you begin opening it.

(b) Even when you tip the cup-like container so the liquid is away from the lid, if you use the necessary force to push the lid back while pulling on the cup with the other hand, at some point the resistance of the lid suddenly evaporates and the pulling hand sloshes what's left of the contents of the cup into your lap. Some highly coordinated people can avoid the sloshing by holding the container against their knee and pulling the lid off with their other hand, using a gentle rolling motion. Me, I just hold the container flat on my tray and cut a hole in the lid with my knife.

3. Vacuum-sealed plastic, such as that around the appetizer cheese. The plastic is so tough, there's no way to tear it. The best I've ever been able to figure out is to put it on my armrest, slice it lengthwise with my Swiss-Army knife and then squeeze the contents out onto my cracker.

4.   Salt and pepper tubes. You know, those small tubes set inside the corrugations of a tiny piece of cardboard which you're supposed to break upwards in the middle before gently sprinkling the contents over your food. Unfortunately, since the airline always fills the tube more than half way, when you break it upwards in the middle, a large glop of the excess contents invariably falls straight onto your plate. The only way to defeat this is, before opening, to skewer the small piece of cardboard on the end of a pen and whirl it about so that the contents are evenly distributed at either end of the tube.

5.   Main course heat covers. The difficulty in removing this cover stems not from its being sealed (it isn't) but from its being too hot to touch. Anything you try to use as a potholder, such as your napkin or shirttail, becomes soiled with the bits of the meal which are clinging to the edges of the cover. You could wait for your meal to get cold, I guess. If you're like me, however, having waited four or five hours for the meal to be served, you'll probably try to put your knife underneath and tilt the lid off—only to have it continue on over in a backwards, dead-man's fall, knocking over your drink, squashing your dessert and creating more general destruction than a mere ton of bricks.

How to Get up From Your Seat During Mealtime

No doubt once you've opened all your food containers, you've found yourself so occupied attempting to keep the mountain of trash from sliding down the tray table into your lap that trying to get up from your seat has never crossed your mind.

If it ever does cross your mind, however, let me suggest how to do it.

Carefully take the air sickness bag out of the back of the seat in front of you. Load it with the wrappers and lids. Put it on the floor. Grasp the food tray with your right hand. Keeping the tray level, lift it up about a foot, steadying your body with your left hand, and stand, pushing the tray table up with your knees. Turn towards your seat and move backwards into the aisle, letting the table fall. Replace the tray. And you're free.

Well, if not free, at least you're in the aisle.

The Secret of the Toilet Sign

This useful device is seldom mentioned in the flight attendant's spiel at the beginning of the flight and so most inexperienced passengers miss it. It's a small sign at the front of each section which lights up, "Toilets Aft Occupied," when there are no free toilets at the rear of the section.

If you're not desperate and prefer sitting in your seat to standing around the entrance to the lavatories wondering how so many people could've died simultaneously behind the locked toilet doors, wait until this sign indicates a toilet is free before you get up.

How to Overcome the Problem of Toilet Protocol

On wide-bodied planes the toilets are arranged on either side of a small corridor running between the two aisles, each aisle invariably having its own line of waiting passengers. In this situation, what's the accepted priority? Do the aisles alternate sending passengers into any of the toilets which open up or instead does each aisle have first claim on the toilets on its half of the corridor?

You'd think the airlines would post a guide. But they don't. As a result, passengers spend a conspicuous amount of anguish and time in silent-film "after-you-no-after-you" routines or, on flights to and from New York, in shoving contests at the toilet door.

Other than organizing a general plebiscite on toilet protocol among all the passengers at the beginning of the flight (which the few times I've tried it has not met with considerable success), the only solution is to look out for number one. In my case, this means going for the "alternating" rule since for some reason the toilets with dead bodies in them always seem to congregate at my end of the corridor.

I find that if, just before my turn, I step into the middle of the corridor to get myself a cup of water from the dispenser there and, as a door begins to open, rush over, slopping large amounts of water towards the opposing aisle and crying, "Alternating rule! Alternating rule!", I can usually make it inside before the other passengers (who've fallen back in disarray to avoid being drenched) are able to regain their composure.

How to Master the Problem of Toilet Soap

In case you might be getting the impression that I'm a bit neurotic, let me say that over the years, the portion of my worries which are centered around going to the bathroom in an airplane has actually declined dramatically.

For instance, in the early days, after pulling my pants up, I'd spend a significant amount of time agonizing over whether to risk contamination by washing my hands with the used soap on the basin or to contribute to ecological wastage by opening up a clean soap package from the dispenser.

Since then I've become much more sophisticated: now I don't bother to wash my hands at all.

If you've encountered this same dilemma about the soap, then I think you should consider taking the same approach—although from personal experience I can tell you it's probably best if you refrain from announcing your newfound sophistication to anyone with whom you happen to be shaking hands.

The Toilet Trap

Once you've finished in the toilet, you troubles are not over. You still have to get out. If there are accordion doors on the airplane lavatory, this may be near nigh impossible.

Accordion doors take a lot of skill and practice to operate. If you ever find yourself having difficulty opening a set from the inside, take my advice. Rattling them back and forth in a panic is not the way to handle the problem.

Just remain calm. Don't get excited.

Somebody will discover you eventually and let you out.

Probably the cleaning staff after the plane has landed.

How to Operate the Call Button at Your Seat

Be assured that the call button does work, sometimes. Primarily those times when it's been pushed by accident. Then it is that the stewardess will appear almost immediately and seek to embarrass the hapless passenger who has made the mistake.

Inexperienced passengers often confuse the call button with the light switch. Both are on the inside of the armrest and both are rectangular in shape. Of course, one has a black outline of a flight attendant on it while the other has the picture of a glowing light bulb; but then inexperienced passengers aren't known for their powers of observation.

Of course, when the right button is pushed intentionally, the correlation between that push and the arrival of the flight attendant is so close to random that it's difficult to speak of any sort of causation. In my experience, you're just as likely to get a flight attendant to appear by drawing a hexagram on the floor around you as you are by pushing the call button.

Needless to say, if it makes you feel better to see a causal relationship, I'm not one to condemn it. After all, everyone needs to feel he's got some control over his life. But, personally, I've given up the use of the call button. Now if I want something, I simply wait to hail the first flight attendant who walks by—or, if I can't afford to wait the hour or two required for that to happen, I get up and go get what I want myself.

If you do intend to use the call button, please be aware of two things:

(a) On some planes the call button can shut itself off if pushed a second time. Thus, if you repeatedly push the button in order to call the stewardess and do it an even number of times, you'll end up with the call signal off.

(b) When the call signal is on, a small light will be illuminated on the outside of the lower part of the aisle seat or on the panel which contains the reading lights and air vents above the seat. Be sure to check after you push the button that this light is on.

How to Interpret the Real Meaning of the Seat-Belt Sign

Most people assume that when the fasten-seat-belt sign comes on, the airline is concerned solely with the safety of its passengers. In fact, this is not always the case. Often the airline is concerned solely with the convenience of its cabin crew, as, for example, when the sign is used as a method of keeping the passengers in their seats during drinks or meal service so the flight attendants can more easily get up and down the aisles.

Even when the signs are used primarily for the safety of the passengers, there are many different degrees of urgency.

Despite the general advisability of obeying the seat-belt signs (after all, it's the law), there are times when it's important to get up, say to get something out of your overhead bin or to go to the bathroom. (The latter is particularly advantageous when the seat-belt signs are on, since then the lines will be much shorter.) At these times, most passengers will balance their need to get up, against their perception of the seriousness of the safety risk. In doing so, they normally take four factors into account:

1. How was the seat belt sign announced? If it just came on without announcement or was announced by the head flight attendant, the safety risk is probably fairly low. If the captain announced it (with a prediction of imminent turbulence), the safety risk is higher.

2. Is the plane in fact experiencing turbulence at that time? If not, you're probably safe for at least a brief stand.

3. Is there a drinks or meal service going on? If so and the factors in 1 and 2 above indicate low risk, then it is likely the sign was activated for the convenience of the staff and not for the safety of the passengers. Even if the factors in 1 and 2 above indicate risk, however, the fact the crew are still in the aisle with drink trolleys shows that the risk cannot be terribly high. When the risk is very high, the captain will order service to be suspended.

4.   Are the no-smoking signs on? On a domestic flight of two hours or less the no-smoking sign is required to be kept on all the time (see discussion at page 268 below). However, if you are on any other type of flight and the no-smoking signs come on at any time other than takeoff and landing, the plane is very likely facing serious trouble and you should in no event get out of your seat.

The Best Way to Sleep on the Plane

Do you remember in the days when wide-bodies were first used? If a flight was partially full, the airlines used to spread the passengers out all over the plane.

About ten years ago, maybe fifteen, the airlines decided to abandon this practice after an industry-wide study revealed that the only ones who found it convenient were the passengers.

Nowadays, in partially-filled planes, the airlines cram the passengers together in the front of each section. Together—so that the flight attendants won't have to take as many steps. In the front—so that the passengers won't get restive staring at the mass of empty seats in the rest of the section.

Strange as it sounds, this practice of the airlines has opened up an opportunity for sound, comfortable sleep by those willing to take advantage of it. The trick is to use the empty seats in the back.

When you enter the plane, immediately head for the back, choose an empty center row, lift all the armrests and lie down flat.

To secure possession, it's usually best to close your eyes right away and proceed to look as dead as possible. I've found that even those occasional people who have an assigned seat in the row will be put off by the appearance of a dead man lying there. Especially when there are so many other corpseless seats nearby.

Assuming you've been able to keep your empty row, the real test comes when you have to sit up—for example, for takeoff or for a meal—leaving the other seats in the row temporarily empty. For some reason, it's just at these points in the flight that some of the more intelligent sardines begin to wonder what the hell they're doing jammed in at the front and start eying the wide-open seas behind them. To keep them at bay, move to an interior seat so you can better dominate the row and spread all your belongings across the row to give the impression that your whole family has just dashed off to the bathroom.

The Secret Sleeping Compartment in a 747

If you can't get an empty center-section row, there is a secret sleeping compartment in every 747 section—the floor behind the last row of seats. While usually that space in economy is somewhat cramped, the equivalent space in business is fairly comfortable.

The Hard Way to Sleep Sitting Up

Of course, it's not always possible to get an empty row. Often when the plane is full and the secret sleeping compartment is filled with flight attendants' bags, you'll have to sleep sitting up.

My technique for sleeping sitting up is to put my right elbow on a pillow on the armrest with my right forearm vertical, place a pillow on my open right hand and rest my cheek on it. In this position I usually find that I can go to sleep quite easily.

Of course, in this position I usually find that my right forearm can go to sleep quite easily as well.

In and of itself, a lifeless forearm isn't so bad. After all, there's no feeling or anything.

The problem, if you want to call it that, is the slight embarrassment I tend to feel the fourth or fifth time I awake with a start to discover that my moribund hand has slipped out from under my chin and flopped fingers-up with a thud on my neighbor's lap.

It's not so much the initial look of shock in the guy's abruptly opened eyes. It's more the subsequent look in his eyes when, yet once again, I reach over with my good hand and, uttering profuse apologies, slide my unconscious arm off his person like some kind of dead snake.

I get the feeling, I don't know, that he's beginning to suspect me of certain motives the suspicion of which would be warranted only if my hand had landed fingers-down.

The Easy Way to Sleep Sitting Up

In many good airport shops and luggage stores now you can purchase an inflatable pillow collar which is ideal for sleeping sitting up. The pillow collar is basically a small crescent-shaped air mattress which fits around the neck, supporting the head in a near-upright position. Because it's deflatable, the pillow collar can be stored away easily in your carry-on luggage.

I find the pillow is most comfortable if I only partially inflate it and put it on backwards so the bulk of the pillow is under my chin. It allows me to lean back further and provides more comfortable support.

If you can't find a pillow collar in the airport shops, call the mail order house, Norm Thompson, at (800)356-6000 or (800)331-1000 for Alaska and Nebraska, and ask for item number 9139. Last time I looked the cost was $10 each.

By the way, in addition to the pillow, you might also consider packing a hotel do-not-disturb sign to keep the flight attendants away. Some people also like to pack eyeshades and earplugs to block out distractions; however, if you are like me, you will probably find that wearing eyeshades and earplugs ends up being more of a distraction than the lights and noises they were meant to block out.

What the Future Holds in Store for the Rich

If you are willing to pay for it, a few airlines, such as Philippine Airlines, now provide sections with full-length single beds in the upstairs first-class compartment of many of their 747s.

The Airbus A-340, due to enter service in 1992, will have air-conditioned containers in the cargo section which will contain beds, a changing room, a refrigerator/bar and an entertainment system. Initially these containers will be only for the crew but there's no reason they couldn't eventually be used by passengers as well. Ultimately, in the same way that the very rich used to have their own railroad cars, they will now have their own airplane containers to travel around the world in luxury.

Meanwhile you and me will still be elbowing it out in steerage.

CHAPTER NINE

THINGS TO DO
ON THE PLANE

Why You Should Never
Become Bored on a Plane

It's actually quite difficult to become bored on a plane.

To start with, on most long flights the airline puts on five major events designed specifically to keep you from getting bored: The safety lecture. The drinks trolley. The meal service. The movie. And the subsequent rush to beat the queue at the toilets.

If those weren't enough, the airline intersperses these spectaculars with entertaining public addresses from the captain, regaling the passengers with the height and speed of the aircraft or the view of the lights of some distant city which can be seen only from the other side of the plane.

And that's not all. There's much, much more.

For instance, there's the magazine rack. In there you can regularly find such soul-stirring items as a two-month old issue of the *Peoria Businessman*, sixteen copies of *Popular Stamps* and the bottom half of a 1973 *Field & Stream*.

After reading those several times, you can turn to the seat back in front of you. It has loads of thrilling stuff:

- The airline's complimentary magazine of comparative plagiarism, with its clearly recognizable excerpts lifted from *Rent-A-Car Digest* and *Optimistic Travel Agents' Monthly*.

- The fold-over of safety instructions (known in the trade as the "Stations of the Crash") portraying hapless passengers pathetically trying to protect themselves against airline ineptitude.

- The directions for use on the air sickness bag, which you can spend hours translating into English from the original euphemism.

- And, last, the most fascinating reading material of all time: the 'OCCUPIED' card.

Such poetic economy.
'OCCUPIED'.
You can't put it down.

If you should ever tire of reading, though, there's always your plastic earphones. Many the hours I've spent trying to keep them from twisting out of my ears. Even after you've achieved the requisite precarious balance, several more hours can be taken up searching for the hole to put the plug into.

Once your earphones are hooked up, you've not only got five whole channels devoted to music for the tone deaf but two additional channels which are nothing but talking. The first is the Comedy Show, featuring scratchy recordings of early-American-TV situation comedies with the controversial portions deleted. The other is the Newsmaker's Forum, which specializes in in-depth interviews with the Postmaster General and the President of the International Hamster Society.

If you fly a lot, of course, you get to know these channels by heart. I find trying to say the words a split second before they come onto the tape can add a lot of spice to my trip.

Sometimes, when all this excitement becomes too much for you, you find yourself driven to real feats of daring. Throwing caution to the wind, you actually begin to talk to your seatmate.

Always looking out for your interests, the airline at times like these arranges for your seatmate to be a High School athletics coach from Orlando, Florida, who, without fail, rewards your interest in him with a spirited dissertation on baseball statistics.

If he goes on long enough, very amusing changes take place. Your brain inflates with stale air. Your eyes fade away. Your smile takes on a life of its own. And, perhaps the most humorous of all, your ears fall off.

Never fails to produce a pause in the baseball statistics.

But don't worry. Even now, you're not in danger of becoming bored. After a brief point and chuckle, your helpful seatmate will invariably continue on exactly where he left off.

What You Should Take onto the Plane with You to Fight Boredom

The best things to fight boredom on the plane are those things in which you can become totally involved.

1.   Reading matter. To become totally involved, you need a book, rather than a magazine, and it should be a book which really interests you, rather than something you think you ought to read, like *War and Peace*. For most people such a book will either be a self-improvement manual or a thriller with lots of exotic sex. Try to get about a third of the way into the book before you leave on your trip. This will not only let you know ahead of time whether the book is in fact interesting but also, if it is, will help you to become immediately involved as soon as you open the book on the plane.

2. Cassette player. Music, foreign language lessons and taped radio variety shows and interviews are nice but, for most people, not totally involving. As with the reading matter, you'll need something full-length and of real interest. Some people like taped self-improvement courses, available through mail order or the airport shops. Others like cassettes of plays or read-aloud books, also available at airport shops and from most local libraries. (If your local library doesn't have a tape section, look in the phone book for libraries for the blind.) Occasionally there are good plays you could record off of National Public Radio.

One hint: because of the background noise in the plane, use earphones which have a cup over the ear—rather than the normal foam-circle or earhole varieties.

3. Electronic games. Any adult game store will have a plethora of these. For the sanity of nearby passengers, it's best if you get one that doesn't beep like a digital watch alarm every time you press a button. I like best the electronic chess games. They're not only totally involving but can be switched off and used to play with your seatmate, if he or she is interested.

Learning To Be as Blind and Deaf as an Experienced Airline Passenger

Most experienced airline passengers are so used to air travel they no longer hear or see those flight sights and sounds which strike terror into the heart of an inexperienced passenger. If you are an inexperienced passenger who wants to appear as blind and deaf as an experienced passenger, following are some of the major sights and sounds you will have to learn to ignore:

1. At the gate:

(a) The whirl of the skyway lowering to keep level with the plane which is sinking as passengers and baggage are loaded.

(b) The banging of baggage being loaded into the belly of the plane.

(c) The steam and condensation on the luggage rack coming from the overhead air vents.

(d) The lights flickering when the plane disconnects from the ground electrical source and changes to its onboard auxiliary unit.

(e) The alarm bell as the skyway is withdrawn.

(f) The noisy under-the-floor air conditioning units suddenly being turned off before the pilot starts the engines.

2. **During taxiing:**

(a) The captain starting the other engine after taxiing out of the gate.

(b) Fuel collecting in the lower sections of the engines and sometimes smoking.

(c) The bouncing of the plane on the irregular surface of the airfield, including the runway lights that mark the center of the strip.

(d) The grinding of new brake pads when the plane comes to a stop.

(e) The wing appearing to come apart as the pilot checks the flaps and slats for takeoff.

3. **During takeoff:**

(a) The wheels dropping down to the full extent allowed by the shock absorbers when the plane leaves the ground.

(b) Improperly-stowed meal trays falling out of an open door in the galley.

4. **After takeoff:**

(a) The vibration of an out-of-balance tire in the air before the wheels are retracted.

(b) The wheels being braked and folded into the belly of the plane and then the wheel doors closed.

(c) The engines cutting back after takeoff as the pilot tries to avoid too much noise over populated areas.

(d) The plane banking up to 25 degrees to set the proper course.

(e) The whine of the hydraulic engine retracting the flaps and slats which had been extended during takeoff to give the wing more lift.

(f) The fans in the galley and toilets suddenly being turned off when air-pressure in the plane is high enough.

5. **During flight:**

(a) Condensation running along the back of the wings like a fuel leak.

(b) Light coming out of the back of the engine from the combustion inside.

(c) The wings flapping up and down in turbulence. (The 747's wings can flap as much as ten feet.)

(d) The plane bouncing around in turbulence. (The 747 can take twice the G-forces you can. By the time the turbulence-generated G-forces start to tear the plane apart, you'll be dead twice over.)

6. **During descent:**

    (a) The engine power cutting back and the plane descending.

    (b) The captain changing the navigation lights at the ends of the wings from blinking to constant to avoid distractions.

    (c) The increasing bumpiness as the spoilers on top of the wings are lifted to disrupt the airflow and deprive the plane of lift.

    (d) The thump of the landing gear going down.

    (e) The whine of the flaps being deployed to slow the plane.

    (f) Vapor forming behind the spoilers and flaps.

7. **During landing:**

    (a) The screech of the wheels hitting the ground.

    (b) The squeal of the brakes and the jerkiness of the anti-skid brake-release mechanism.

    (c) Occasionally a wobble of a tire going flat.

    (d) On planes, such as 727s, with engines in the tail, the coughing of the center engine as it fails, with the slower speed, to get enough air through the "S" vent.

    (e) The reversing of the engine jets to slow the plane down.

If you are an inexperienced traveler, study the above list, count off each sight or sound as you encounter it and after that, you, too, can find airline travel boring.

Why the Captain's Address Should be Banned

During almost every scheduled flight the captain will make an address to the passengers over the plane's public address system. The purpose of this ritual is to make the passengers more comfortable by making the captain look more human.

Well, as a passenger, I can tell you that the last thing that'll make me feel comfortable is a human captain. To reverse Alexander Pope: "To be human is to err." And who wants a captain who errs?

Not me. I want a machine. Someone who sticks to his job in the cockpit and doesn't waste his time blathering over the public address system, or even worse, in person, wandering down the aisle.

"Is everything all right?" I remember a wandering captain asking me once when I was sitting in economy.

"How in the hell should I know?" I said. "You're the one who's supposed to be flying the plane."

Any pilot who shows his face in the passengers' quarters should be told immediately to get his fanny back up front and keep his eyes on the road. I mean, would you let your taxi driver climb into the back seat with you to discuss the weather while the cab was barreling down the New Jersey Turnpike?

A serious problem with the captain's address over the PA system is that it always seems to come during the most interesting part of the film or audio program. His announcement automatically cuts off the sound on the entertainment system but does not stop the entertainment system from running. The result is that when the sound comes back on, it begins two or three minutes further on from where it cut off.

To add to the irritation, the sound track doesn't come back on immediately after the captain finishes but only after a five- or ten-second delay, during which short period an inexperienced passenger can achieve a remarkably high state of agitation thinking that the crew has forgotten to turn the sound system back on.

How can it be that the airline manufacturers, which can work such amazing electronic miracles as computer-operated automatic pilots, can't design an announcement override which cuts off both the sound and the running of the film or tape when the captain begins speaking and turns it back on immediately when he finishes? Is this a case of insuperable technological difficulties or one of massive indifference to the comfort and enjoyment of airline passengers? You tell me.

Judging from their vocal presentation, most pilots have personalities you could store meat in. ("I've seen more life in a dog's fur," is how one friend of mine put it.) Dry, monotonous, unimaginative, humorless.

Which is okay with me. The last thing I want is a pilot who wears a lampshade on his head, trying to get laughs from the stewardesses.

To me, displays of *any* emotion in the captain's voice can be unsettling. For instance, when, on management instructions, the captain adds that extra bit of sincerity while thanking his passengers for flying with the airline, I invariably begin to wonder whether those who are not flying with the airline know something I don't.

Even totally unemotional voices can conjure up images of pilot unsuitability: a strange accent, an improper word usage, a phlegmatism of delivery bordering on stupefaction. So unless it's absolutely necessary, I feel it's better for everyone if the pilot remains a voiceless abstraction.

Barring emergencies, the only information the pilot needs to disseminate to the passengers is the estimated time of arrival and the weather at the destination. This could be done through the chief flight attendant. Everything else could be easily dispensed with.

Take the pointing out of landmarks. Firstly, only a small portion of the passengers are ever in a position to see these landmarks clearly, *i.e.*, those passengers sitting at the window on the correct side. Secondly, only a small portion of those are interested. Thirdly, of those who are interested, what they can see from such a height—a mountain, a lake, a city—is usually quite indistinguishable from any other mountain, lake or city of the same type. Fourthly, to the extent what they might see is unique—such as the Manhattan skyline or an erupting volcano— they don't need someone to point it out for them to recognize it. Finally, if there ever was something most of the passengers on the plane really wanted to see, the last thing you'd want would be for it to be announced; the next thing you knew, everyone would've run to the side to look, and tipped the plane into a vertical sideslip which even the Red Baron would have difficulty pulling out of.

Another thing which can be easily dispensed with: the captain's comments on air turbulence. Anything he says will cause you to lose confidence in him.

Say, after thirty minutes of severe buffeting, during which once or twice your stomach has tried to kiss your brain, the captain finally comes on the public address system:

"It appears, ladies and gentlemen, that we've been experiencing some clear-air turbulence."

"Brilliant," you think. "What amazing deductive powers. And it took him only half an hour."

Of course, what the pilot says over the PA is probably not what he's really been thinking. What he's really been thinking is something more like: "Holy molely!!!"

Not something, no matter how appropriate, the average passenger wants to hear the captain of his airplane scream over the loudspeakers.

But then a more reassuring comment such as, "Ladies and Gentlemen, you'll be happy to know that I've at last regained control of the aircraft," is unlikely to increase your confidence in the pilot either.

No, it's best if the captain, like God, says nothing at all, leaving us to project into the cockpit our hopeful image of an all-seeing, omnipotent intelligence.

And One More Pet Peeve: Aisle Pacers

On every flight there will be a passenger who will react to the confines of economy class by pacing continually up and down the aisle like a caged animal, bumping the sitting passengers' shoulders or stepping on their feet or blocking their view of the movie screen. Occasionally the pacer will stop at the front of the section and turn to survey his or her domain, with an expression eerily combining the self-conscious and the detached— as you might see on the countenance of a caged gorilla at the zoo, a distant, primitive ancestor peering at you across the eons of time.

The provocativeness of the pacer's expression at this moment is, I believe, the main reason airline passengers are not allowed to bring guns onto the plane.

To be fair, not all aisle pacers can be categorized as gorillas. I've noticed, for example, that a lot of first-class passengers go for walks through the economy section. My impression is they're motivated by a kind of *noblesse oblige*, a feeling that they should show themselves to the lower orders as evidence that not all sectors of the airplane are marked by degradation and hopelessness.

Occasionally a first class passenger will engage in conversation with an awe-struck discount flyer or, curious as to what kind of movie the airline shows the masses, will sit down briefly to watch. He never likes to stay long, though, as there's always the danger that the economy class passengers, desperate for their meal service, will gobble up his trail of breadcrumbs—leaving him unable to find his way back to civilization.

How to Use the Airfone

Most major US aircraft now have Airfones, public telephones which can be used by passengers on the plane. If you have never used such a phone, following is some brief instruction:

1.   Insert your credit card in the slot. Don't lift the cordless phone. Wait for your credit card to be verified. Okay, now you can lift the cordless phone.

2.   Don't panic. I know your credit card is still in the machine. When you finish the call and replace the phone, you can get it back.

3.   Take the phone to your seat to make your call. You could stay at the wall socket or go into the lavatory, but then all your seatmates would not be able to listen to you whispering sweet nothings to your significant other.

4.   When the person you're talking to suddenly begins giving you bakery truck delivery instructions and then sinks into a whirlpool of static, don't despair. The Airfone operates on radio waves not telephone lines, and the FCC has yet to assign a separate frequency for air-to-ground telephone service.

5.   Remember that depending on the speed and direction of the plane, each domestic call is limited by the distance between ground stations to approximately 45 minutes or, at a $7.50 charge for the first three minutes and then $1.25 per minute thereafter, $60. International calls are at twice the domestic rate.

6.   Be happy for small mercies. The next generation will have phones on the back of every seat. (Three Pan Am Shuttles have them already.) And there'll be computer jacks for transmitting and receiving information with laptop computers, stock quote terminals and fax machines.

No longer will there be anywhere for you to hide from the totalitarian communications monster that is taking over the world.

How to Avoid Being Airsick

With modern wide-body planes which fly at higher altitudes, the turbulence you encounter on most flights will be less than you encounter taking a cab over the potholed roads leading to JFK.

If you are subject to motion sickness, you probably will have taken a motion sickness medicine before getting on the flight. I like the Transderm-Scope patch which you place behind your ear or Bonine tablets, which supposedly are less likely to cause drowsiness than some other preparations. If you can't get any medicine and are at home, try a teaspoon of powdered ginger mixed in water.

If you haven't taken anything and the flight attendants won't provide it (technically they're not supposed to give out any medicines other than aspirin), then I suggest the following:

1. Press the Nei-Kuan acupressure point. This point lies three finger-widths up the underside of the arm from the crease of the wrist on your dominant side. I know this sounds flaky but I've tried it and it works. Doctors in Scotland have used it to combat morning sickness in pregnant women and had an over 80-percent success ratio. It has also been used by doctors in Belfast to reduce post-surgery nausea. Recently some travel suppliers have begun marketing special wristbands with a pressure ball sewn in which accomplishes the same thing; the enclosed instructions recommend that the bands be worn on both wrists.

2. Close your eyes. You want to avoid any conflicting signals between your eyes and your inner ear.

3. Recline your seat, put a pillow behind your shoulders and lay your head back. Since the inner ear can cope with lateral movements better than it can with vertical movements, you want to make the primarily vertical movements caused by turbulence appear to your inner ear as lateral movements.

4. Open the overhead air jets and aim them directly into your face. The increased oxygen and coolness will fight your nausea.

5. Do not take aspirin. Although aspirin normally combats nausea, it also upsets the inner ear, making the problem worse.

6. Do not drink alcohol. It irritates the stomach and changes the specific gravity of the fluid in the inner ear. At high altitudes, alcohol has up to twice the effect it does at sea level.

7. Hold the air sickness bag close. This is not merely a matter of consideration for your seatmates. Scientific studies have shown that one of the major factors contributing to throwing up is worrying about in what or on whom you will throw up when you do; having the bag handy reduces this worry and hence the likelihood of your using it.

8. Get it over with. If you think it is inevitable before the flight is over that you will throw up, then go into the toilet as early as possible and stick your finger down your throat. It'll save you a lot of worry, cut down on your suffering and insure you will not add more than your share to the general unsightliness of economy class.

Economy Class Syndrome

Believe it or not, medical specialists have actually discovered a medical complaint called "economy class syndrome" (ECS). According to the British medical journal, *The Lancet*, the symptoms can appear several weeks after flights as short as three hours. The syndrome can result in anything from minor body pains and shortness of breath to heart attacks and strokes.

Doctors suspect that cramped legroom in economy class combined with dehydration interrupts the blood flow which causes clots, cutting off the supply of oxygen to various parts of the body. This may account for the results of one study which showed that 18 percent of sudden deaths on airplanes are due to blood clots in the lungs.

The medical specialists reported that the syndrome most often affects smokers, heavy drinkers, those whose feet don't reach the floor (because the seat puts more pressure on the backs of their legs), the elderly and those with a predisposition to coronary heart disease. But it also can affect normally healthy people, in some recorded cases causing them to develop pneumonia-like symptons due to blood clots in the lungs.

The best ways to fight ECS: drink nonalcoholic beverages, don't smoke, take aspirin to thin your blood and exercise on the plane.

How to Exercise on the Plane

The best type of exercise on a long flight is to get out of your seat, go to the back of the plane (or, if you're shy, into a toilet cubicle) and engage in traditional calisthenics, such as touching your toes, reaching for the sky and running in place. Avoid doing jumping jacks if you're in the lavatory.

If you can't or don't want to get up, there are certain sets of exercises you can do in your seat.

Before you start, be sure to inform your seatmate of what you intend to do. This will prevent him from thinking you're having some sort of seizure, which could lead to his attempting to wrestle a pencil sideways into your mouth to keep you from choking on your tongue—always an embarrassing mistake for both parties.

The exercises are as follows:

1.   Tighten and release, one group at a time, the muscles in your shoulders, back, buttocks and thighs.

2.   By raising your thighs, lift both feet six inches off the floor and rotate them first in one direction and then in the other.

3. Reach up repeatedly toward your overhead light with one arm and then with the other as though trying to block out the light.

4. Bend forward with all your weight, press your crossed forearms onto your knees and, keeping your toes on the floor, repeatedly lift your heels as high as possible.

5. Sitting up, arching your back, repeatedly roll both shoulders forward and then back, first together and then one at a time.

6. Pretending you are on skis, push your knees to the right and your heels and hands to the left. Lift your feet off the floor, and swing your knees to the left and heels and hands to the right. Repeat twenty times.

7. Sitting back, lower your head as far forward as you can. Then, still facing forward, lower it to the left. Then, to the right. Repeat several times.

8. Lay your head back, with your mouth hanging open, and, arching your back, look as far back on the ceiling as you can.

9. With your right hand grab the back of your left armrest and pull your upper body around until you are looking behind you. Hold for ten seconds. Repeat in the other direction.

10. Place your right hand on your left shoulder and your left hand on your right shoulder, and hug yourself. Lean forward as though giving someone a Latin lover kiss. Repeat several times.

11. Sit up slowly, turn towards the aisle and tell the crowd looking at you that you've finished your exercises, so they can all go back to their seats.

The Invasion of the Lung Snatchers

Nothing is spookier than to be sitting in the smoking section of the plane after takeoff when the no-smoking sign at last goes off. Suddenly, all around you, your fellow passengers, staring dully ahead, like people whose minds have been possessed by secret invaders from outer space, simultaneously reach into their pocket, take out a small pack, remove a white paper tube filled with dried vegetable matter, stick it in their mouth, produce a flame from a lighter, set the end of the tube on fire and suck the resultant alien smoke into their lungs.

It's the near unison of the thing which is so spooky. Fifty cigarette packets crackling. Fifty fingertips bursting into flame. Fifty gray clouds of pollution expanding outward. Fifty doomed human beings, paying unconscious obeisance to the evil force which is feeding on their body.

The real problem with these nicotine addicts, of course, is not that they're destroying their health. (The faster the better as far as I'm concerned.) The problem is that their mindless activity threatens to destroy the health of everyone else around them as well.

"For your seat assignment today, sir, would you like smoking or passive smoking?"

On the aircraft, passive smoking is even worse because at the lower air pressure nicotine has up to double its normal power. In addition, because these is less oxygen in the air, not only is there more carbon monoxide produced by the tobacco burning but there is less competing oxygen passing into the lungs. The result is not just lung cancer but eye, throat and lung irritation and, for 30 percent of the people in one test, even headaches.

Assuming you are one of the more than 80 percent of US airline passengers who do not smoke, the overriding question you will face is how to protect yourself against these particulate-matter generators on your flight. To answer that question you need to know, first, what are the rules of the game, and, second, what strategies you can employ within those rules.

The US Rules Governing Smoking In Airlines

1.   There is no smoking on domestic scheduled commercial flights between two points within the fifty states, Puerto Rico or the US Virgin Islands, excluding those flights to or from Hawaii or Alaska which are over six hours long. For purposes of this law:

   (a) **The term "flight" means any single nonstop leg of a flight.** Each nonstop leg stands or falls on its own, if you excuse the pun. For instance, the fact that you might be on a seven-hour one-stop flight to Alaska won't allow you to smoke if the two legs are each three-and-a-half hours. Or if, due to prevailing winds, the flight out takes more than six hours, while the flight back takes less, you'll be able to smoke on the flight out but not on the flight back.

   (b) The six hour period is measured by the scheduled flight time in the *OAG Flight Guide* (not the more up-to-date computerized reservation system). The fact a flight is delayed beyond six hours will not turn a nonsmoking into a smoking flight. Also the fact that you are switched due to cancellation or overbooking from a flight of over six hours to one of under six hours (*e.g.*, because the new flight makes intermediate stops) will not allow you to smoke.

(c) **Nonscheduled flights are exempt.** Examples: charter flights and travel clubs.

(d) **International flights are exempt.** However, if an international flight has a US leg, that leg will not be exempt, even if the airline is a foreign airline (despite the fact such an airline is allowed to carry a passenger between two US points only as part of the passenger's international flight).

2. **For all other domestic commercial flights** (whether scheduled or unscheduled), there is no smoking of cigars or pipes at all. In addition, there is no smoking of cigarettes:

(a) **On aircraft designed to seat fewer that 30 passengers** except on-demand air-taxi services (because the air ventilation systems on smaller aircraft generally are not as effective).

(b) **Whenever the aircraft is on the ground** (because the air ventilation systems don't work as well there).

(c) **Whenever the ventilation system is not fully functioning.**

(d) **In the aisles, galleys or toilets** (because of safety considerations). In 1973 116 people died in only four minutes during a fire caused by some nicotine addict leaving a burning cigarette in the toilet rubbish bin.

(e) **In no-smoking sections.**

(f) **During takeoff and landing** (because of safety considerations).

3. **If there aren't enough seats to accommodate nonsmokers who have reservations, the airline must expand the size of the no-smoking section.** Standbys are not protected nor are those who fail to comply with the airline's deadline for checking in. Nonsmokers do not have the right to choose which nonsmoking seat (or even type of seat) they will be assigned.

4. **The flight crew must act to keep passengers from smoking in the nonsmoking sections.**

5. **A passenger could be liable for a civil fine** of $1,000 for violating the no-smoking signs; $2,000 for tampering with the smoke detectors in the toilets. Several passengers who violated the rules have found FBI agents awaiting them on arrival. In one case in California, the pilot made a special stop to have two stubborn smokers arrested.

How to Avoid the Nicotine Addicts on the Plane

As a practical matter, only a few domestic flights to Hawaii and Alaska are likely to exceed the six-hour limit. So most of your concern with avoiding smokers will be on international flights.

1. Fly those airlines which have banned smoking. The government no-smoking requirements are only a minimum. A few airlines, such as Northwest and Delta, have gone beyond to ban smoking on all their North American flights. Others are likely to follow. Since the smoking ban affects almost all domestic flights, it's an administrative headache for the airlines to maintain special smoking rules for the remaining flights. A ban on smoking also produces significant savings in cabin and air-filter cleaning and even in fuel. (Over a ten year period a jumbo jet can build up a ton of nicotine tar on the interior which takes about 57,000 more gallons of fuel a year to carry.) Finally, a ban on smoking helps avoid burn damage to seats, carpets and, ultimately, the whole aircraft caused by tobacco junkies accidentally dropping their cigarettes.

Outside the US, as well, more and more airlines are banning smoking. Air Canada, British Airways, Virgin Atlantic and Singapore Airlines have instituted bans on smoking on many of their flights.

2. Break your flight into segments of six hours or less. For instance, rather than taking a nonstop flight of seven hours to Hawaii, take a one-stop flight which has two legs of three and a half hours. This will increase your trip by a half hour but will avoid seven hours of breathing recirculated smoke.

3. If you can't find a smoking-banned flight, fly the airline which gives the nonsmoker preference over smokers. This is not a problem with US carriers, since all airlines must expand the nonsmoking section to accommodate nonsmokers, even if it means disadvantaging smokers. Most foreign carriers, however, fix the percentage of smoking and non-smoking seats before the flight and will not expand the nonsmoking section to take account of an increased number of nonsmokers.

4. Fly the international airline which has the largest percentage of nonsmoking seats. The ratio of nonsmoking to smoking seats changes radically from country to country. Western European airlines generally provide at least 50 percent nonsmoking seats. African, Far Eastern and East European carriers provide as little as 20 percent. Before you book, ask the airline or, if you are a frequent traveler, consult the international edition of the *Airline Seating Guide* discussed above at page 42.

5.   Tell the stewardess you have a respiratory or allergic reaction to smoke. Even East European airlines don't want a passenger having an apoplectic seizure on their plane. If you present a convincing enough case, the airline staff will probably do everything they can to get a passenger in the nonsmoking section to switch with you.

The Best Defense Against Smoke Drifting from the Smoking into Nonsmoking Section

Unfortunately, smoke drifting from the smoking section into nonsmoking section specifically does not violate most airline rules. So you will have to fend for yourself. Among the better fending tactics are:

1.   Sit in a forward seat. The air-conditioning system of the airplane causes the air to circulate back through the plane. So you want to get as far in front of the smoking section as possible. Unfortunately, if you are in economy, some of the smoke from the rear of the business section drifts back into the nonsmoking economy section. So ideally the best position is about a third of the way back through the economy section.

2.   Use your overhead air jets, if your plane has them. Not only will this provide you with more fresh air but also, if you are in the last row of nonsmoking (just before the first row of smoking), you can aim the three overhead air jets towards the back to help keep any eddies of smoke from drifting forwards.

3.   Stay close to the floor. Smoke rises, so many passengers who really dislike smoke try to keep their heads low. Perhaps you've noticed them on their way to the toilet, crawling down the aisle on their hands and knees, cursing the poisonous fog suspended above them.

4.   Use a gas mask. Let's be frank. If you want to avoid completely the inhaling of carcinogens on the plane, this is the only effective way. It's what I do.

Normally, of course, I don't put the mask on until the no-smoking sign goes off. Occasionally, however, if I'm worried about the effects of all the tobacco junkies trying to get their last-minute fix in the airport lounge, I'll put my mask on there and wear it straight through the boarding process.

You should see the airline staff frantically searching their rule books on this one.

And the other passengers. They're not especially comfortable about sharing their plane with someone who has the head of a praying mantis.

Still, I don't let it bother me. I know that twenty-five years hence, when they're all dying of lung cancer, they'll suddenly realize I was right. It's better to be weird than dead.

Special Rule for Nonsmoking Businesspeople

If you are a businessperson and thus naturally afraid that a gas mask might make you appear too practical, try instead one of the light, disposable, fiber masks used by hospital and construction workers. These masks can be obtained from medical supply stores and some of the better drugstores. If you feel self-conscious, just explain to your fellow passengers that you've got an allergy to smoke. To put them at ease, draw a big friendly smile on the mask.

Enforcing the No-Smoking Rules

Occasionally smokers will light up in the nonsmoking section. This happens most often when the nonsmoking section has been expanded after the smokers have booked their seats.

Don't confront the smokers directly. These people are dangerous. Their craving for the weed has warped their minds. Even worse, where the nonsmoking section has been expanded to include them, they're likely still to be under the impression that they've got a smoking seat.

The best approach is to quietly ask the flight attendant to tell the smoker to quit. In the US, by law, the flight attendant is required to do so. If the flight attendant refuses, go to another, and another, and finally up to the captain.

If the captain refuses, then, wait until the smoker has sated himself, so he's in a good mood, and then explain the situation as politely and objectively as you can. If he refuses, then you'll just have to move, put your head on the floor or whip out the old gas mask.

Some Other Dangers in the Cabin Air

Smoke isn't the only danger in the cabin air. Some of the others:

1.   Lack of humidity. Jet aircraft draw their air from outside the plane. Above the clouds there is very little water vapor. As a result, on most US airlines, the humidity of the air is down to five or even two percent at high altitudes (versus at least 30 percent in normal temperate-zone air).

Most airlines generally do not have humidifiers because they don't want to carry the extra weight of water required.

To help avoid this dryness:

(a) Fly some of the pre-400 series British Airways 747s, which do have humidifiers. Although their humidifiers have proved unreliable and difficult to maintain, the airline has at least tried.

(b) Drink lots of water.

(c) Don't eat much. It takes a lot of fluid to digest food.

(d) Avoid diuretics, such as coffee, tea or beer, which make you urinate a lot.

(e) Avoid alcohol, which dehydrates your body.

(f) Avoid salts.

(g) Don't wear contact lenses on the plane.

(h) Use a cold cream on your face.

(i) Travel with people who sweat a lot.

2.   Lower air pressure. When the air is taken from the outside, it is at a very low pressure. The power of the engines is used to compress the air but normally is unable to compress it below the air pressure one would experience on top of a five- to eight-thousand-foot mountain.

With lower air pressure, less oxygen can make its way into your lungs and the hemoglobin cannot be fully oxygenated. The lower air pressure also makes alcohol, nicotine and carbon monoxide much more of a problem. Finally, it also causes your stomach and intestine to bloat up.

3.   Positive ions. The air in US airlines is filled with positive ions. They make you feel irritable, headachy. Negative ions make you feel good. They can be found around waterfalls, seaside and mountains. Nuclear submarines and spacecraft are fitted with ionizers for producing negative ions. US aircraft are not. If you feel lousy on airplanes, consider carrying a battery-operated ionizer with you.

Additional advantage: the ionizer will make smoke particles cling together and fall to the floor.

4.   Ozone. Ozone is a form of oxygen which is a more powerful oxidizing agent than regular oxygen. It has a light chlorine smell. It scars lung tissue, which worsens respiratory diseases and can cause breathing problems, especially for the very young. It also makes the eyes sting and the throat itch. Boeing offers catalytic filters on some of their very long-haul jets which solidify the ozone; their shorter-haul jets don't have them. Drinking a lot of liquids will help fight the ozone affect.

5. Stale air. The ventilation system on planes is often inadequate. The average system might have the capacity to move 20 cubic feet per passenger per minute. A full flight with a third of the passengers smoking, however, may need a rate of over 50 cubic feet per passenger per minute to avoid irritation.

To make matters worse, the ventilation system is often not operated at full capacity in order to save fuel. Whereas at full capacity the air might be completely changed every two to four minutes, at low capacity it could take up to eight minutes. If you suspect this is happening, complain to the flight attendant. The captain, who controls the flow, has a separate circulation system in the flight deck and may not be aware that the air is becoming stuffy in the cabin. At the very least, on US flights, you should be able to get him to put the no-smoking sign on, since by law smoking is prohibited when the ventilation system is not fully functioning.

To save power, some of the newer aircraft, such as 757s and 767s, can recirculate up to half the cabin air—air which in the old planes would have been vented to the outside. This means that when the recirculation system is operating at full capacity, half of what you're inhaling will have recently been exhaled by someone else. Since the recirculated air is filtered and mixed with fresh air, however, it is probably better than the old system in which all the air was originally fresh but, when it was necessary to save power, circulated at half speed. In the old system, when the circulation was reduced, unless you were sitting near the intake vent, probably all the air you were breathing was unfiltered previously-used air. The real problem is that although the newer aircraft are fitted with these recirculation systems, most airlines are finding them too expensive to use; so when they need to save power, they simply cut down the rate of circulation as before.

Note, to obtain at least the feeling of circulation (as well as some personal control over your air flow and temperature), choose those airlines which have configured their aircraft with the personal air jets above your seat. These vents, known as "gaspers" in the aircraft manufacturing trade, are optional on certain planes, such as 747s and 767s. Ask your airline ahead of time whether your plane will have them.

6. Airborne diseases. This happens most often when the ventilation system is not operating at full capacity. In one well-known case reported by the National Academy of Science, an airline in Alaska sat on the ground for three hours with the ventilation not working. Before the flight began, one of the passengers had an active case of flu. Within three days, three-quarters of the passengers reported they had contracted a virus.

7. Noise. Studies have shown that the constant din of the engines increases fatigue and, if it's loud enough, damages the hearing.

8. Cosmic radiation. These rays are much more prevalent at the higher altitudes. Smashing through your cells, they probably increase the chances of cancer and birth defects. And there is also evidence that they can suppress your immune system.

All in all, then, airplane cabins are probably one of the least safe environments to which you may be exposed during the normal course of living.

Emergency Medicine

Although flight attendants will not normally dispense any medicines other than aspirin, they will normally ask if there is a doctor on the plane. A recent FAA rule requires the airline to carry an emergency medical kit, including certain prescription medicines for persons suffering from heart attacks, insulin shock and acute allergic reaction. If you're fortunate enough to fit into one of these categories, you can get free medicine on board.

How to Pick Up Sex Objects on the Plane

There are, of course, an infinite number of approaches to picking up a woman or a man on the plane. Unless you're Robert Redford or Faye Dunaway, all the really good approaches have one element in common. After initially selecting your target, you must go back to your seat and sit there for an hour before doing anything more.

Why?

Because you've got to give the target time to get bored. Once the incredible boredom of flight has overwhelmed them, they'll be much more open to any approach you might make.

Even then your approach should be indirect. Most people are afraid of getting stuck in a conversation on the plane where there are no avenues of escape. So you have to present your approach as something other than an invitation to conversation.

My technique, before I was married, of course, was to pull out a travel backgammon set and ask, "Do you know how to play backgammon?"

It didn't matter what they answered. If they said, "yes," I'd say, "Let's play."

If they said, "no," I'd say, "Let me teach you."

Either way, nine times out of ten, they'd end up playing.

The beauty of this approach is that you are promising relief from boredom that does not involve the strain or dangers of a forced conversation. You're merely asking the person to play a game of backgammon, something she or he will find interesting and enjoyable in itself. As you play, a conversation will naturally develop.

If you're lucky, the conversation which develops will not merely be verbal.

The Best Ways to Make Love in an Airplane

As this book is intended to be a comprehensive guide to everything an air passenger may encounter, it is necessary for me to cover a subject which some may find offensive. If you are a person with high moral standards, please skip the balance of this section and go on to the next chapter . . .

Last warning . . .

You still here?

Uh-huh. So much for high moral standards.

Let me start the discussion by saying that an airplane is one of the more uncomfortable, inconvenient and unsuitable places to consummate a relationship. Like the back of a galloping horse, about its only attraction as a place to make love is its novelty.

Well, almost only. A Lufthansa stewardess I know claims there is another attraction. According to her, in the lowered air pressure of the cabin, certain key parts of the body expand and your sensitivity is increased. On the other hand, she points out that you may not appreciate this increased size and sensitivity as the lack of humidity in the cabin tends to dehydrate.

The major reason that an airplane is unsuitable for making love, of course, is the lack of privacy.

One of my friends recommends using a blanket to gain some privacy. While I can see how it may be possible for you and your lover, sitting upright in your seats and covered with a blanket, to use your nearside hands to good effect without being discovered, it seems to me you'd still have to be quite careful to restrain the amplitude of your arm motions—especially if, at the time, someone happens to be sitting in the seat between you.

Likewise, if you want a more traditional consummation, you and your lover could, I guess, spread out under a blanket in an empty center-section row or, if you're really desperate, in the aisle. But I find it hard to believe that merely being covered by a blanket can mitigate the danger that someone, trying to maintain the decorum of the plane, might dowse you both with a bucket of cold water.

When you examine the problem logically, there are really only two ways to gain the privacy necessary for making love on a plane: (i) buy up a whole section of the cabin (the upstairs first-class compartment of a 747 would be ideal), or (ii) lock yourself and your loved one into a toilet. Which you choose, of course, depends what kind of person you are.

Assuming you are toilet person (I mean, let's face it, the nontoilet people took my advice and quit reading this section after the first paragraph), following is some helpful advice recently offered to me by a friend who prides himself on his membership in the mile-high club.

"Wait until the seat-belt sign is on," he told me. "You're less likely to be disturbed. If you're in a wide-body, use the lavatories designated for disabled passengers or diaper-changing mothers (you can find them in the *Airline Seating Guide*); they're usually the biggest."

"Once you're inside the lavatory," he continued, "you've got two basic choices of method. Efficient or romantic. The former is basically that which you can effect without unduly wrinkling, tearing or soiling your clothes, bruising your elbows and knees, making odd-angled scuff marks high up on the wall, or leaving telltale signs scattered about the lavatory."

"And what is that method?" I asked him, somewhat at a loss to visualize precisely what it might be.

"Kissing," he said.

"Kissing?" I repeated.

"Yes, kissing," he said. "It's a well-known fact that kissing can be just as physically satisfying to your partner as sexual intercourse, especially if your aim is not all that accurate."

I considered this for a moment. "So that's the method you use?"

"No," he answered. "I use the romantic method." And he went on to describe it in some detail.

Before passing this description on to you, let me say first that my friend's definition of "romantic" appeared to be somewhat limited; as far as I could tell, the term as he used it meant basically any position in which he and his girlfriend ended up face to face.

Let me also say that I had some difficulty following the details of several of my friend's rather intricate clinical variations on the basic theme. Occasionally it appeared to me that his limbs, hips and neck were so intertwined with those of his girlfriend that some kind of homing device would've had to be installed for the act of lovemaking to be consummated.

Nonetheless, I did come away from my conversation with two basic lovemaking positions which I now pass on to you, so if you ever find yourself having to engage in this activity in an airplane lavatory, you won't waste a lot of time trying to figure out the best way to do it.

Even though you've obviously failed the high moral standard test, I unfortunately have to describe these positions in as oblique a manner as possible so as not to offend my publicist who feels a straightforward discussion of lovemaking positions would not be suitable in a handbook on airline travel.

Okay. Now imagine you have a Daddy bee. He flies into the lavatory and . . .

No, this isn't going to work.

I know, I'll describe just half of the couple for each of the two positions. In fact, to make it even more innocent, I'll describe the one who is taking the more passive part. Following the general principle of face to face, you'll have to fill in the rest with your imagination.

Position One: The man is sitting on the seat, leaning back slightly.

Position Two: The woman is half-sitting on the basin ledge, legs off the floor.

There, you've got it. I've fulfilled my obligation to comprehensiveness—hopefully without bringing on the decline of the West. Now I can go on to more conventional subjects.

Except for one final problem which must be addressed: What do you do if, when you and your lover leave the lavatory together, there is a long line of curious passengers waiting outside?

If you are someone who's not easily embarrassed, my friend advises that a simple cry of "Next!" will probably suffice.

If, however, you wish to create the impression that you were in the toilet for other than lovemaking purposes, he suggests that as you leave you turn to your partner and say something like, "I told you that was the flush knob."

Or, "Let that be a lesson to you. Lift the lid from now on."

Or, "The next time you get your zipper stuck in the soap dispenser, ask somebody else for help, will you?"

Any of these comments, he says, should keep the other passengers scratching their heads for quite some time.

CHAPTER TEN

HOW TO END YOUR FLIGHT

The Best Way to Pop Your Ears When Descending

It is much more difficult for your ears to adjust to the change in pressure when the plane is going down than when it is going up. Many people employ a variety of techniques: chewing gum, sucking candies, yawning, swallowing, jiggling their fingers in their earholes or, I'm not kidding, putting Styrofoam cups filled with hot, damp paper towels over their ears. While such techniques are highly successful at making their practitioners into objects of fear and amazement in the eyes of their fellow passengers, they are not always successful at popping the ears.

If you want to have a 100-percent success rate at popping your ears, then, you should employ the Valsalva Maneuver. In this technique, you pinch your nose, close your mouth and blow against your cheeks with gradually increasing pressure until your ears pop. If you pop one ear but not the other, you blow again, releasing your grip slightly on the nostril on the side of the popped ear; this will keep the pressure from getting too high on that side but still allow you to pop the ear which needs it.

Because the Valsalva Maneuver employs some force, there is a slight risk that it will damage your ear. However, the Maneuver can't be that dangerous, since it's universally used by scuba divers, who face a much greater change in pressure under water than you are likely ever to face in a plane. Unless you're congested, the Valsalva Maneuver should be safer than not having your ears pop at all. Unrelieved, the pressure can become so great that it causes serious bleeding in the ear.

The only time that the Valsalva Maneuver has ever failed for me (or, more precisely, succeeded but only at the cost of filling my inner ear with mucus) was when I had a cold. For that reason, if I feel a cold coming on, I always take a decongestant before I fly. I also carry in my toiletry kit a small mentholated inhaler for expanding my nasal passages during descent.

If you are suffering from ear, nose or sinus problems, you should, of course, consult your physician before you get on the plane, let alone employ the Valsalva Maneuver.

Hint: If you've had problems popping your ears before and plan to sleep on the plane, be sure to be awakened before descent. When you are sleeping, you swallow less than when you are awake. Plus, being asleep, you are less aware of any ear pain. By the time you awake you could be in serious difficulty.

Why You Should Stay on the Plane During a Stop

Occasionally your flight will make several intermediate stops before you arrive at your destination. If the stop is primarily to pick up new passengers, it's not worth deplaning since you will almost immediately have to reboard. If the stop is for refueling and supplies, then you've got more time. In that case, boredom, curiosity or a desire for fresh air, exercise, better drinks or more comfortable seating might encourage you to deplane.

My advice: Don't. It's hardly ever worth it. For a variety of reasons:

1.   Once you get off, you normally cannot get back on until the plane is ready to board new passengers. This could be an hour, or, if difficulties are encountered in refueling or restocking, several hours. If it's the middle of the night, you may not appreciate having to hang around the gate trying to stay awake in order to hear the call.

2.   There is generally nowhere off the plane where you can sleep comfortably. If you stay on the plane, you can pull up the armrests of the now-empty neighboring seats and sleep four across, confident that you won't miss the plane when it takes off.

3.   The terminal, particularly in some developing countries, may actually be worse than the plane: hot, humid and totally uninteresting. It doesn't take long for scuffed plastic seats, scum-covered toilets, cheap shiny trinkets and chipped bottles of warm Coca Cola to lose their allure.

4.   During the longer stops, cleaners often come through the plane. Unless you're there, they may throw away your loose papers and possibly walk off with your valuables. For that reason, if you are going out of the plane, be sure to put your papers and valuables in your suitcase and lock it.

5.   If there is open seating or a mixup in the seat assignments and you can't reboard ahead of the new passengers, you might return to find your seat taken—and in the unwritten folkways of airline travel, possession is nine-tenths of the law. Putting the "OCCUPIED" card in your seat before you leave may help but only if you can get the poacher to stand up so it can be seen. (In fact, you're unlikely to be able to find an "OCCUPIED" card; with improved computerized seat reservations, fewer and fewer planes provide them any more.)

6.   Very occasionally you will forget to take your boarding card with you or, worse, lose it while you are in the terminal, and have to engage in a huge palaver to get back in the plane. Inevitably, of course, you'll make it on board but not without a significant loss of time and good will.

So unless you're desperate, stay on the plane.

How to Get out of the Plane Quickly

If you have only carry-on luggage, then the faster you can get out of the plane, the faster you can be on your way. The problem is that those passengers who have checked their luggage have no incentive to get out quickly. (Whether they get off fast or slow, they'll still have to wait a half hour in baggage claim.) And it's those passengers who will inevitably be positioned between you and the airplane's exit door.

To make matters worse, it's those passengers who are most likely to have carried half a ton of stray garbage onto the plane (usually in plastic bags) which they immediately on landing will plop into the aisle to form a near insurmountable barricade.

If you think you're going to have to run such an obstacle course, then the best thing to do is try to get to the front before the plane lands. As the plane is descending, tell the flight attendant in your section that you have a tight connection to catch (throwing in your dying mother in the hospital if necessary). The flight attendant will sometimes let you walk down the aisle to the front as the plane finishes taxiing.

If you can stand being condemned over a public address system before several hundred unsympathetic people, you can try walking down the aisle during taxiing without permission. However, look out if you're in certain narrow-body planes; often when you get to the front, you'll find the vengeful flight attendant has decided to exit the passengers from the drop door in the tail.

If you're in a wide-body, the aisle on the side opposite the exit door is usually the fastest. Those in the center section will tend to exit into the aisle on the exit-door side, jamming it up. In addition, if you are in economy, a flight attendant will ordinarily be blocking the front of the aisle on the exit-door side in order to let the business- and first-class passengers off first. Sometimes the flight attendants do the same for the other aisle, but often they don't, in which case you'll be able to reach the exit by walking through the front galley to the door.

Understanding the Foreigner
Lines at Passport Control

In the major airports of most countries there are separate lines in passport control for foreigners and nationals. You can tell the lines for foreigners: Those are the ones that are four times as long and ten times as slow as the ones for nationals.

Some people say that this difference in line length and speed is due to the fact that the passport control staff naturally scrutinize foreigners more strictly than they do nationals. For instance, in England, a few years ago, young Pakistani women claiming to be married to English residents were actually being physically examined at passport control to determine if they were virgins. (I mean, talk about slow lines.)

Personally, however, I don't think this stricter scrutiny (which certainly does occur) is the real cause of the foreigner line being longer and slower. The real cause is understaffing. Despite the fact the authorities know foreigners will be scrutinized more strictly, they don't put on adequate passport control staff to do the job.

Why not?

For a very simple reason. Foreigners can't vote. They've got no say. So, like disenfranchised people everywhere, the foreigners in passport control are treated like slaves, subject totally to the whim and convenience of their masters. Held in uncomfortable quarters. Herded from place to place. Kept in the dark about what is happening to them. Made to play the supplicant, in constant fear of bringing upon themselves, by unguarded word or deed, arbitrary judgments and penalties.

So what, if foreigners have to wait two and a half hours in line? Nothing they do can affect the passport control staff. The only people against whom the foreigners can retaliate are those who have to go through the "foreigner" lines back in the foreigners' own country. And the net effect of such retaliation when practiced by all countries is merely to increase the waiting time of all foreign airline passengers everywhere.

As I see it, the simplest solution to the problem of the long foreigner lines at passport control—and one that I've been advocating for some time—is to merge all the nations of the world into a single state. Then there wouldn't be any national borders for passengers to cross and the officious twerps who run passport control would be out of a job.

It is a measure of the lack of concern our elected representatives have for the international airline traveler that not one of them, to my knowledge, has suggested legislation to create such a state.

No wonder we have to resort to guerrilla warfare to get what we want.

How to Beat the Long Foreigner Lines at Passport Control

Despite the blatant discrimination against foreigners at passport control, there are some things you can do:

1.   Fly the foreign airline. When flying to a foreign country, use the foreign country's airline. Nationals tend to fly their own country's airline.

Thus, there will be fewer non-nationals like you on the plane and so fewer people in the non-national passport control line.

2. Use the foreign airline terminals. Similarly, in large airports with more than one international terminal, consider going through the transit lounge to another terminal which serves primarily the national airline of that foreign country and exit passport control there. If you are unfamiliar with the layout of the airport, ask the flight attendants on your plane or consult your *Airport Pocket Guide*.

3. Bluff you way through the line for nationals. By this I don't mean you should pretend you are a national—in Beijing, for instance, pulling the outside edges of your eyes back, trying to look Chinese. That seldom works. Rather I mean you should pretend you're stupid. That's a lot easier to do. "Gosh, was I supposed to be in another line?" (To be safe, have someone save your place in the foreigner line.)

4. Link up with a national you met on the plane. This helps you get through the national line not because friendship with such a national will be clear evidence to the passport officer of your lack of intelligence but because, since the national can vote, the passport officer will not want to offend him or her by prohibiting you from going through the nationals' line. To show the necessity of your getting through with your "friend", get your friend to say that you're taking him or her home in your rental car.

5. Get to the foreigner line first. Try at the very least to get ahead of the other foreigners from your plane. This means that (i) you should be the first off the plane and down the concourse and (ii), at those airports where you have to pick up checked baggage before approaching passport control, you should have no checked baggage.

6. Choose the fully-manned two-window booth. Often there will be several lines, each one feeding into a separate passport control booth. Each booth often has two windows, one on the left side and one on the right side. Sometimes both windows are manned; sometimes only one is manned. Be sure to choose a line which leads to a booth with both windows manned. A line leading to a booth with only one window manned will go at half the speed of one leading to a booth with two windows manned.

How to Fill out Landing Cards So as to Avoid Problems at Passport Control

When flying into most foreign countries, you are required to fill out a landing card. Usually the flight attendants will pass the cards out before descent. If your plane has begun its descent and you have not received a card, ask the nearest flight attendant. Often they forget.

When filling out the card, observe the following hints:

1. Normally there is only one card required per family. Each member of the family will not have to fill out a card. If in doubt, check with the flight attendant.

2. Print in easy-to-read block letters. Sloppy writing will only lead to questions at passport control.

3. Keep everything simple and definite, again in order to avoid additional questions at passport control.

(a) **When the form asks where you are staying in the country, give only the first place you will stay;** don't bother with the subsequent places. If you don't have a place to stay yet, ask a fellow passenger for the name of a local hotel and put that name down; if you are questioned on it (which is highly unlikely), you can truthfully say that is where you *intend* to stay.

(b) **When asked for your place of birth, just put the country—** unless the card specifically asks for more. Most of the passport control staff couldn't care less in what city you were born. Even worse, in some non-Western countries, they're likely to think the name of the city is the name of a country and spend quite a while trying to look it up in their manual.

(c) **When asked for your occupation, try to reduce it to one simple, easily understood word.** For instance, don't say, "Professor of Applied Mathematics" or "Speech Therapist," say, "Teacher." Don't say, "Real Estate Agent" or "Insurance Broker," say, "Salesman." More specific words are likely either to confuse them or to raise red flags.

4. Be aware that other countries may have different conventions or forms of notation from the US.

(a) **Most countries write the date "day/month/year" rather than "month/day/year".** (The "month/day/year" convention, by the way, is the way the English used to write their dates two hundred years ago. Somehow the Americans got left behind.) To be absolutely clear, I usually write the month's abbreviation instead of its number.

(b) Many countries' forms will place the family name in a different place. US forms tend to put the last name first on the forms. Others put it last. Still others will actually put it penultimate. Be sure to read the form carefully.

(c) Different countries have different descriptions of the same part of a name: for instance, the first, Christian, given or proper name, versus the last, family or patronymic name or surname. If you aren't entirely sure which is which, ask the flight attendant.

5. If the form has carbon copies, make sure all the copies are legible. If not, you'll have to stand aside at the passport control desk to fill it out again.

Note, after you have completed the form, the best place to put it is inside your passport, since you will have to give both to passport control. Often, you have to fold the form to fit it inside your passport; in all my years of traveling, such folding has never created any problems for me.

If you don't get a landing card on the flight, do not despair. Passport control always has plenty. If there is a line at passport control, as there usually is, you will have plenty of time to fill out the card before your turn comes.

How to Deal with Passport Control Staff

Passport control staff can be quite intimidating. They'll stare at your passport, stare at you, stare at the passport. The Soviet passport control staff are particularly good at this staring procedure—usually bringing in nearby leather-jacketed KGB types to join in. The idea, of course, is to see if they can rattle you, get you to betray any nervousness.

Most passport control staff employ similar techniques. In Munich, for instance, I've noticed they tend to ask the same question again after I've answered it. I've also seen them photocopy my passport.

To avoid creating problems, you should react as follows:

1. Never volunteer anything. Only speak in answer to the officer's questions. Volunteering implies you are nervous about something.

2. Answer all questions simply, directly, without qualification or elaboration. As when you filled out the landing card, use easily understandable words. When they ask you what you are doing in the country, just say "business" or "pleasure". The more you elaborate, the more questions you will provoke.

3.   Never, I repeat, never, try to be funny. In the first place, seeing hundreds of people a day, the passport officer has undoubtedly heard your joke before. In the second place, the officer is trained to be suspicious of anyone trying to jolly him up. That's why passport officers never smile. You come in cracking jokes and you'll end up being examined in detail.

4.   Never complain about the passport procedures. In the first place, the officer dealing with you can't do anything about the procedures. In the second place, his only concern about the procedures is how they make life uncomfortable for him, not for you. You're just one of the fifty-plus quota an hour he's got to get through before he can have his coffee break. Wasting his time with your complaints will just make him hostile.

5.   Look the officer in the eye. Passport control staff usually put great store in the eyes. They believe that by looking deep into a traveler's eyes, they can read his soul. This is horse-manure, of course; but you've got to play along. Look them in the eye as long as is comfortable. When you finally look away, do it for an apparent reason, such as to adjust your bag or to glance at your ticket.

A Case Study: Getting Through Passport Control in Canada

Several years ago, before the free-trade agreement, Canada was suffering one of its periodic bouts of anti-American xenophobia. Fearing that the US was taking over the economy, Canada was making it difficult for American businessmen to enter the country. They seemed particularly hard on those in finance.

A Wall Street investment banker friend of mine, flying into Canada to make a presentation to some potential clients, made the mistake of describing himself to the passport control officer as a "financier". He was immediately surrounded by several beefy immigration officers and taken into a side room. There, after some hostile questioning, he was forced to make his presentation to the assembled officers.

He said it was amazing. For over forty-five minutes he went on describing the intricate tax, accounting and mathematical aspects of a billion-dollar cross-border financing of a power plant, to a group of guys who, altogether, couldn't have had more than one forehead among them.

At the end of the presentation, one of the officers raised his hand and asked what was, in his protectionist's mind, the key question: "Why can't Canadians do this type of finance themselves?"

My friend told me that, try as he might, he couldn't think of an answer that wasn't impolite.

He packed up his briefcase and caught the next flight home.

The next week one of his associates returned to give the presentation to the client. This time, on the advice of a Canadian affiliate, he gave his occupation as "salesman" and got through passport control with no trouble.

Apparently "salesman" was a job the Canadians recognized they clearly could not do themselves.

How to Deal with Passport Control Staff in Basket-Case Countries

In many of the poorer, developing countries of the world, there is often an additional problem: corruption. Generally the amount of corruption increases in direct proportion to the amount of poverty.

If you're being taken care of by a tour agency or a local customer, you're probably okay. If you're on your own, though, you're a fair target.

White, clearly-Western people have an advantage. Passport control staff realize Westerners are harder to get bribes out of because (i) Westerners often don't realize what is being asked and (ii) when they do, they tend to get morally outraged. In addition, thanks to colonialism, there is a residual feeling that white Westerners must have ties with those in authority.

The trick, when entering passport control in one of these countries, is to try to position yourself just in front of a more attractive target so that the staff will want to hurry you by in order to get to him. From experience, the more attractive targets are ones which look local and prosperous (but not so prosperous as to have close friends in high places) and have a lot of baggage (which invariably means they are carrying contraband they don't want to disclose). In West Africa, for instance, local Lebanese businessmen are ideal.

If you are to be dunned, you will know because the authorities will ask you to step into a back room. Don't try to argue against the minor infraction they have discovered, no matter how absurd. Once you've got to this stage, it's too late. Instead, listen quietly to what they say and then reply, "I'm sorry. Being a foreigner I didn't know. What can I do to solve the problem?"

If this fails to bring out a price, listen a bit more and then say, "Perhaps I could pay a fine here rather than going to court."

Remember, never use the word "bribe" or indicate a payment is being made to them personally to drop the case.

Accompany this latter statement by pulling out a five dollar bill. That will probably get things going.

If they ask for more that five dollars, it's best to become obstinate. Say that five dollars is all you can afford. If they press you, ask to speak to John Smith, the US Consul General, and give them his phone number. (Before going to one of these countries, it is a good precaution to learn the name of the current consul general; asking to speak to him by name has much more impact than asking to speak to "someone at the US Consulate". Also, please note, it is the *Consulate* which deals with the problems of citizens abroad; the *Embassy* deals only with diplomatic matters.)

Seeing that you are obstinate and that there may be trouble with higher authorities if they detain you, the passport control staff will probably start lowering their price. Continue being obstinate until the price gets to a range you think reasonable; then, with a great display of reluctance, pay it and leave.

How to Survive Baggage Claim

The easiest way to survive baggage claim, of course, is not to check your luggage.

Even then you're not home free. Some airports require all passengers, including those with carry-on, to exit through baggage claim. Occasionally, airport security staff will mistake your carry-on for checked luggage and ask you to show your claim check. Be sure to have identification on a permanent-looking tag and on the inside of the bag as well.

If you do check your luggage, then some of the following hints may help you avoid the major pitfalls:

1.   **Don't stand around waiting in baggage claim.** Unless you've been delayed in passport control, your bags will not arrive until twenty or thirty minutes after you arrive in baggage claim. Use this time to do other errands, such as arranging for a rent-a-car or searching for the place where the luggage trolleys are hidden.

2.   **Don't waste your time trying to figure out which of the potential carousels your luggage will be on.** Not that it's impossible to do. A given airline or arrival gate might normally use a given carousel; or you can sometimes tell which by looking at the airline tags on unclaimed luggage on a carousel. It's just that there's no advantage in knowing ahead of time.

3.   **When your flight number is posted, don't rush over to the carousel, trying to get a front row position.** You won't get your bags any quicker. Five minutes later you'll still be standing around in a crowd, being stepped on and jostled, as you wait for the carousel to begin

rotating. You may even look up to discover that in the interim your flight has been switched to another carousel.

4.   When the bags starting coming, stand about five feet back from the start of the carousel. Here you will have the space to move around and to park your trolley yet still be in a position to get your bag as soon as it comes onto the track. Although there will be people between you and the carousel, you will be able to see the bags coming onto the track—either because the end of the loading belt is elevated at that point or because the ground-level strip-curtained entrance door is set back a few feet from the passengers. As soon as you glimpse your bag coming onto the carousel, you need only thread your way through the crowd, saying, "Excuse me, I need to get my bag," grab it and return to your trolley.

5.   Don't panic when your bag has not yet appeared but no new bags are appearing on the carousel. As long as there are still a lot of passengers standing around waiting for their bags, the chances are your bags are still in the plane waiting to be loaded onto the carts.

6.   If you have odd-shaped or odd-sized luggage, look for a special odd-shaped luggage section. Baby strollers, cardboard boxes and even unfolded garment bags are often placed on the ground near the carousel. If you don't see it, ask the baggage handlers or porters.

Concerning an Incorruptible Absolute

As Albert Einstein so aptly demonstrated, there are very few absolutes in the universe. One of them is that the speed of light appears constant no matter what the relative speed of the observer. Another is that two bags checked together will never come out of baggage claim together.

If your first bag comes out near the beginning, it is certain that your second bag will come out near the end—assuming, of course, that it comes out at all.

I know this doesn't jibe with common sense. But like Einstein's Theory of Relativity, it's been proved beyond doubt by experience.

The Moment You Know You
Shouldn't Have Checked Your Bag

All the passengers have picked up their luggage. All except you and a family from Winnipeg, standing at the carousel, watching a lonely string-tied cardboard box revolve slowly around the track.

Your Pierre Cardin bag has been lost.

Or stolen.

"But wait," you say to yourself.

You move closer.

"That cardboard box. There's something . . . ."

You peer inside the box.

It's the remains of your bag!

Quickly you lift the cardboard box off the carousel. There's a note Scotch-taped to the side.

"Fell off the luggage cart," it says.

You peer inside again.

"Doing what?" you ask yourself. "A hundred and twenty miles hour?"

Don't Worry: You are Not Alone

The Department of Transportation requires reporting of "mishandled bags"—a vague concept which some airlines interpret variously to include lost, damaged, late and lost-and-found items. These reports show that an average of one out of 140 passengers has a mishandled bag in the US—a figure which is approximately the same as the average for airlines worldwide compiled by the International Civil Aviation Organization.

Box 10-1. Mishandled Checked Baggage On US Airlines		
Airline	**%Passengers Reporting**	**One Out Of:**
TWA	1.165	86
Continental	0.758	131
USAir	0.738	132
Delta	0.715	140
Northwest	0.700	143
Alaska	0.673	149
American	0.665	150
United	0.663	151
Eastern	0.640	156
America West	0.634	158
Southwest	0.387	258
Pan Am	0.295	339
Average	0.715	140
(Source: Department of Transportation.)		

Why So Many Bags are Lost Now but Why Things May Get Better in the Future

The number of airline passenger flight miles has gone up 86 percent in the last ten years. On top of this, peak loads have gone up even faster due to the increased use of wide-bodies, the introduction of the hub-and-spoke system and the competitive bunching of flights at given flight times. Baggage handling facilities have not kept up.

At the end of 1987, new International Civil Aviation Organization security rules came into effect for purely international flights. These rules require every checked bag to be matched with a passenger before the flight leaves. Bags which don't match will usually be removed or subjected to special scrutiny, such as X-raying.

In order to comply with these rules, the major international airports have introduced the automation of baggage handling based on machine-readable tickets, boarding passes and luggage tags. Although the ICAO rules apply only to international flights (they don't even cover the interlining of bags between domestic and international flights), the automation is being expanded beyond the ambit of the ICAO rules.

Once the bugs are worked out and the systems standardized (IATA has agreed on a standardized bar code), the amount of lost and damaged luggage should decline substantially.

What to Do When You Get Your Bag

If your bag was not locked or if it had breakable items inside, then immediately open the bag to check for pilferage or damage. Once you get home, you will have a much more difficult time proving to the airline that the contents were stolen or damaged.

In any case, be sure not to throw away your ticket stub and baggage checks until you've had a chance to look inside. You'll need them to prove that you actually checked luggage on the flight in question.

What to Do if Your Baggage is Lost or Damaged

If your bag doesn't appear at baggage claim, or appears in a guise considerably further down the hierarchy of fashion than when it began its trip, or you open it up and discover some contents are missing or damaged, you should:

(a) **Immediately find the airline's baggage officer or roving baggage staff member in the baggage claim area.** Under many airlines' conditions of carriage, you've got only four hours to notify them of loss of or obvious damage to baggage. In the case of unobvious damage, many of the airlines require notice within 24 hours. American Airlines goes even further; its conditions state that "[a]cceptance of baggage by the bearer of a claim check without filing a written complaint shall constitute evidence of delivery by American of your baggage, with all original contents, in good condition".

(b) **Once you find the right person or place, ask for a form to fill out.** Nothing can get done until you fill out a form. Don't waste time complaining to the staff member. He sees hundreds of lost bag cases every day and couldn't care less.

(c) **Don't, I repeat, don't take the form home to fill out**—even if you have seven days, three weeks or 45 days to file a written claim. (For the appropriate limit look at the small print on the back of your ticket or ask to see the airline's conditions of carriage.) You want to make sure that you've got everything you need now to get things started.

(d) **Fill out the form.** In the process, be sure to:

(1) **Check that the form you are filling out is not just a report of your lost or damaged luggage but also embodies a claim for damages.** Some airlines have two different forms, particularly in the case of lost luggage. If the form is not a claim form, ask for one and fill it out as well. In the case of lost luggage, the airline may not allow you to submit the claim form until your luggage has been determined to be permanently lost; however, by filling out the form immediately, you can go over any points you don't understand with the airline staff as well as be put on notice of anything you will need later when you do submit the claim form.

(2) **If your bag is lost, describe not only the bag but its contents as well.**

(3) **If the bag is damaged, describe not only the damages to the bag but to any contents as well.**

(4) **Keep your ticket stub and baggage claim tag.** Don't give it to the lost luggage staff unless the form notes this and is signed

by the staff member. Try to get the staff member to make a photocopy instead. As mentioned above, you will need the stub and baggage claim as evidence you checked the luggage on the flight.

(5) Check if the form requires a notarized signature and if it does, see if a witnessing by the airline staff member is sufficient.

(6) If your luggage has been lost, be sure to request in writing that it be delivered to you when found. Ideally the form will have this request in it.

Note, if for some reason you fail to notify the airline or submit a claim before the appropriate deadline, don't give up. Most conditions of carriage allow the deadline to be waived if you can show good cause.

What Sort of Compensation You Can Expect from the Airline if Your Bag is Lost or Damaged

Once you've turned your form in (remembering to keep a copy for yourself with a note of the name of the airline employee with whom you're dealing), you can reasonably expect the following:

1. **If your bag or its contents have been damaged:**

    (a) The airline will pay for repairs or do the repairs itself (often lending you a replacement in the interim); or

    (b) If an item can't be fixed, the airline will pay you the item's depreciated value. Often the airline will take off ten percent for each year you've had the item.

2. **If your bags have been delayed:**

    (a) The airline's airport staff will pay you initially a small amount for emergency supplies while they look for your bag (although some require you to submit claims afterwards to the home office). The amounts are small because almost all bags are recovered within hours, and most of those in the first few hours. The airline will naturally pay you less if you are at home. If you can show special circumstances, such as needing to rent a tuxedo or sporting equipment, the airline will sometimes pay more.

    (b) The longer the bags are lost, the more the airline will pay. However, if you start buying major items of clothing, the airline may reimburse you for only half the cost, or when your bags are found, pay you the full amount on the condition that you give them the new clothes.

(c) If the airline finds your bag, it will usually ship it to the door of your home or your away destination if you're still there.

Note, the proposed Airline Passenger Protection Act of 1987 discussed above at page 18 provided that if the passenger's bag was delayed (i) two hours or more, the airline would provide a free one-way space-available ticket for the same journey; and (ii) more than 24-hours, a round-trip space-available ticket for the same journey. If a replacement bill is ever proposed, lobby your Congressman to include this provision.

3. If the airline declares your bags permanently lost, the airline will pay you the depreciated value of the bags and their contents. Sometimes the airline can take as long as six months to declare your bags permanently lost. Even then, before it pays you, the airline will probably:

(a) Require you to fill out a new claim form. Make sure that you meet any new deadlines and keep a copy of all submissions.

(b) Demand receipts for the contents of your lost bag, especially expensive items.

(c) Take a few months to jerk you around, trying to beat you down on the estimate of value.

You still want to check your luggage next time you fly?

Special Limitations on Liability for Lost or Damaged Baggage

The conditions of carriage of most airlines provide that no compensation will be paid with respect to the following:

1. Consequential damages. Some conditions of carriage, such as those for Eastern, provide that the airline will pay for "direct" damages but not "consequential" damages. Although the line between the two is often hard to draw, generally direct damages cover out-of-pocket expenses you have to incur to repair or replace (permanently or temporarily) the property, while consequential damages cover all other losses. To avoid having to draw the line, consider flying those airlines, such as Southwest and Midway, which give you an express right to recover consequential damages as well.

2. Wear and tear. Most airlines' conditions of carriage except normal wear and tear to your bag, including scuffs and dents which do not affect its function as luggage.

3. Valuables. What is a "valuable" varies from airline to airline. Generally, however, the conditions of carriage list money, securities, jewelry, silverware, photographic and electronic equipment, samples, works of art, antiques, medication and irreplaceable items. A few airlines will cover valuables if you have bought excess valuation insurance. (See discussion beginning below at page 299.)

4. Fragile items. This was covered above at page 150 under *How to Choose the Best Airline for Your Fragile or Perishable Items.* In practice, most airlines will refuse to pay for fragile items if the outside of the bag shows only minor damage and the items were not packed in a special container. If the item was not fragile and the outside of the container shows no damage, the airline will also refuse to pay—not because of fragility but because there is no hard evidence that the airline caused the damage. Note, the definition of fragile can include the luggage itself, *e.g.*, a cloth or cardboard container.

5. Delayed perishables. This was also covered earlier under the *Fragile Or Perishable Items* section referred to above. The exception does not apply if the perishables are permanently lost; so if your perishables are substantially delayed, see if you can push the airline to call off the search and have them declared permanently lost.

6. Late-checked baggage. If you checked your luggage in late, *e.g.*, less than fifteen minutes before the flight, several airlines will not pay any compensation for delay even if the delay lasts several weeks. Others, as mentioned earlier, exclude only delays caused by putting the luggage on a later flight and refuse to pay for the delivery from the arrival airport to your destination. In the latter case, you may want to wait around for the next flight to see if your bag comes in.

7. Unclaimed baggage. Many conditions of carriage absolve the airline of responsibility for your bags if you were on the same flight as your bags and failed to claim the bag immediately or within a certain deadline, *e.g.*, thirty minutes of arrival of the flight or of the bags being made available. This limit probably applies only to loss or damage occurring after the pickup deadline; however, as a practical matter, if you show up at the carousel late and find your bag missing, you are going to find it tough to prove the bag was never there. For that reason you should always be sure to pick up your bags as soon as you can.

Note, if you take too long to pick up your bags, most airlines will store your bag in an area near the carousels and then after four or five days (one in the case of United and three in the case of Delta) will send it on to be stored in an airport baggage warehouse. While the bags are in an airline storage area, under general bailor-bailee rules the airline should be responsible for damage or loss to your bag occurring after it took your bag back into its custody. This argument will be particularly strong if, as some do, the airline tries to charge you for the storage.

8. Nonrevenue passengers' baggage. Some conditions of carriage exclude liability for the baggage of nonrevenue passengers. Although theoretically this could apply to someone flying on frequent-flyer coupons, it is intended to apply only to those working for the airline or who have been given a free flight for some other reason. As discussed above at page 48, frequent-flyer coupons are not free in any real sense.

Absolute Limits on the Airline's Liability for Domestic Baggage

If your checked bags are lost, delayed or damaged on a flight:

(a) between points in the US (excluding the domestic leg of a connecting or direct international flight); and

(b) on an aircraft of over 60 seats or on a smaller aircraft included in the same ticket with such an aircraft,

then the airline by law need not pay you more than $1250 for all (not each) of your bags. This limit applies not only to normal checked baggage but to any baggage otherwise delivered into the custody of the airline.

If your carry-on bags are lost or damaged on a domestic flight, there is no government-mandated limit of liability. However, most airlines' conditions of carriage state that the airlines will not be liable for any loss or damage to carry-on. If the carry-on is lost or damaged because the plane crashes, some of the better airlines will specifically allow you to claim under a general damage limitation. (See discussion of general liability limits beginning on page 378 below.)

Absolute Limits on the Airline's Liability for International Baggage

If your checked bags are lost, delayed or damaged on an international trip (including the domestic leg of a connecting or direct international flight), most countries follow one or other version of the Warsaw Convention (see discussion at page 379 below). In the most common version, the limit for checked baggage is 250 Poincare gold francs per kilogram, which, at the fixed rate of 12.5 francs per dollar, works out to $20 per kilogram, or $9.07 per pound. Some airlines assume your bag weighs 70 pounds (32 kilograms), resulting in a compensation limit of approximately $640. Others actually weigh it and note the weight on your ticket. The small print on the back of your ticket will normally say which procedure your airline follows.

For carry-on luggage, the limit under the most common version of the Convention is a flat 5000 Poincare gold francs, which, at the fixed rate of 12.5 francs per dollar, equals $400 per passenger.

In 1975 an amendment to the Warsaw Convention was proposed in a meeting of the signatories in Montreal. This proposed amendment, known as the Montreal Protocol, changed the measurements from Poincare gold francs to International Monetary Fund Special Drawing Rights (SDRs) at the then exchange rate. For checked luggage the limit then became 17 SDRs per kilogram and for unchecked luggage, a flat 332 SDRs. Since the dollar value of SDRs fluctuates from day to day (see page 379 below), the dollar value of the limit depends on which day you claim or are paid. Fortunately, the value of the dollar has fallen relative to its value in 1975, so the limits under the Protocol are slightly higher than under the old rules. Unfortunately, since the Montreal Protocol has not yet been fully ratified, not many countries follow the new limits. The US certainly doesn't.

Whatever limit applies, remember it is only an upper limit. You still have to prove damages to collect.

One Way to Decrease the Likelihood of Reaching the Absolute Liability Limit

Most conditions of carriage limit claims for lost or damaged luggage or contents on a *per-passenger* basis, not a *per-bag* basis. Since the chances of losing two bags are significantly less than those of losing one, you decrease the likelihood of reaching the limit if you allocate your possessions among your bags so that each bag is under the limit.

In fact, for most airlines, you don't even need to limit yourself to your own bags. Under most conditions of carriage, the property covered includes all the passenger's personal property in the custody of the airline, whether or not the passenger checked the property himself. Therefore, theoretically, if two passengers got together and packed each of their bags half with one passenger's contents and half with the other's, if one of those bags were lost, each of the passengers could claim up to a total limit of $1250 on their half or a total of $2500 for the bag.

I don't know of any passengers who have tried this, but one of the airline's conditions of carriage specifically prohibits the practice, suggesting the airline probably lost in small claims court on the issue at least once.

A Possible Way to Double the Absolute Liability Limit

For a few airlines, if (i) your bags are lost on an interline connecting flight, (ii) you can't tell which airline is at fault and (iii) your claim exceeds the limit, it may be possible to take both airlines to small claims court and before a favorable judge, collect the amount from the airlines jointly, applying the limit to each rather than both. After all, the purpose of the arbitrary limit is not to prevent you from collecting on a valid claim but to protect the airline from paying large amounts of damages. As long as no one airline has to pay in excess of the limit, the purpose of the law is being maintained.

Unfortunately, most airlines are aware of this possibility and put in their conditions of carriage that if blame cannot be apportioned, the limit will apply to the total you collect from all airlines. Even worse, the conditions go on to state that the limit applied will be the lowest applicable to any of the airlines involved. So, for instance, if you fly in on an international flight where the limit is $640 and switch to a domestic flight where the limit is $1250, and it can't be determined which airline has lost your bag, your limit will be $640.

Note, for the latter airlines, a similar rule also applies for items excluded from liability. So if one of the airlines disclaims liability for antiques and the other doesn't, the disclaimer for antiques will apply to both.

(For a further discussion of possible loopholes in the Warsaw Convention and similar limitations on liability, see page 380 below.)

Excess Valuation Insurance

For either domestic or international flights, you usually can increase the maximum limit by buying "excess valuation" insurance from the airline. The premium ranges between half a percent to two percent of value. Some airlines will also allow you to purchase the insurance to cover certain valuables which otherwise would be excluded from liability. If you have valuables you wish to cover, be sure to check (or have your travel agent check) the various airlines conditions of carriage on this point.

Excess valuation insurance covers your bags only while they are in the custody of the airline. You can purchase broader baggage insurance from the insurance counter at the airport.

It is possible that your baggage is covered under your homeowner's insurance or, if you purchased the ticket with your credit card, under insurance provided automatically with the credit card. (See page 88 above.) Be sure to read your homeowner's policy and call your credit card company before leaving home.

What a Returning US Resident Need Declare for US Customs

If you are a returning US resident, you must declare all items acquired abroad and in your possession at the time of your return, including:

(a) Articles you purchased.

(b) Gifts to you while abroad.

(c) Repairs or alterations made abroad.

(d) Items you've been requested to bring home by another person.

(e) Articles you intend to sell or use in your business.

You have to declare the article at the price you paid for it or, if a gift, at the estimate of its fair retail value. Even though you may have used the item, you still have to declare it at its purchase price; if there has been significant wear or use, the customs officer may thereafter make an appropriate reduction in its value for customs purposes.

A written declaration will be necessary in one of the two following situations:

(a) You exceed your total exemption (see below) or one of the specific exemptions for alcohol, cigarettes or cigars (see below). If the value of all your items is less than your exemption plus $1,000, you'll only have to write down the total value.

(b) You have items not intended for your personal or household use.

Otherwise an oral declaration can be made.

The Returning US Resident General Duty Exemption

1. $400 limit. If you are a returning resident of the United States and have been abroad at least 48 hours, then you may bring in free of duty articles intended for your personal or household use totaling $400 (based on the fair retail value of each item in the country where acquired).

2.   Alcohol and tobacco. Within the $400 limit you will still have to pay duty, to the extent any of the articles exceed the following limits:

(a)   liquor: one liter (33.8 fluid ounces)

(b)   cigars: 100

(c)   cigarettes: 200

3.   State taxes. As mentioned earlier at page 182, there are also separate state limits on the amount of alcohol and cigarettes, which can be brought in free of state tax or, in some cases, at all.

4.   Rate of duty on excess. The first $1,000 above your exemption is taxed at a flat ten percent. Thereafter, it depends on the scheduled duty for the item. Most items have a duty of less than ten percent. Of those which are higher, jewelry has a duty of 27.5 percent while items from most Communist countries can have a duty as high as 90 percent.

5.   Family members returning together to the United States may make a joint declaration and combine their personal exemptions, even if the articles acquired by one member of the family exceeds the personal exemption allowed. Children get the same exemptions as adults (except they get none for alcoholic beverages).

6.   Thirty-day limit. You can claim the above exemption only if you have not already claimed the exemption (or any part of it) within the preceding 30-day period.

7.   Short-term exemption. If you can't claim the exemption because of the 48-hour or 30-day rule, you can claim a flat $25 exemption and, within that, 50 cigarettes, ten cigars, 150 milliliters (four fluid ounces) of liquor or 150 milliliters (four fluid ounces) of alcoholic perfume.

More Generous Exemption Rules

Generally, there will be a more generous exemption in the following circumstances:

1. Certain US possessions. If you're returning from the US Virgin Islands, American Samoa or Guam, generally you get (i) an $800 exemption of which not more than $400 can apply to merchandise acquired elsewhere, (ii) an alcohol limit of five liters of which at least four must be purchased and one produced in those possessions and (iii) a five percent flat rate duty on the first $1,000 excess.

2. Certain preferred countries. The US has granted special exemptions or reduced rates of duty under the Generalized System of Preferences or similar programs to items brought in by US residents returning from certain developing countries, Caribbean countries or Israel.

3. US government employee. US government and military employees generally have a more generous exemption.

4. Non-US resident. Non-US residents on a short visit to the US generally have only a $100 exemption but can exclude most personal possessions (except alcohol and tobacco) that they're going to take back out with them.

Items Which are Totally Exempt from US Duty

Totally exempt from any duty when entering the US are the following:

(a) Articles purchased abroad which are the growth, manufacture, or product of the United States and have not been processed or enhanced in value while abroad (subject to the liquor, cigar and cigarette limits above).

(b) At least 100-year-old antiques.

(c) Signed, limited edition (usually less than ten) works of art—as long as the person who made the work is a professional artist rather than a craftsman. Rugs usually don't qualify; tapestries, however, do. (Give you any ideas?)

(d) Drawings and paintings done entirely by hand.

(e) Books. (But see below for pirated editions of copyrighted material.)

(f) Binoculars, opera glasses and field glasses.

(g) Natural pearls, loose or temporarily strung without a clasp.

(h) Postage stamps.

(i) Diamonds, cut but not set.

(j) Exposed film.

(k) Furniture, carpets, paintings, tableware, linens and similar household furnishings (excluding personal items) if they were available for use in a household abroad in which you were a resident member for at least one year.

(l) Animals and pets, except as prohibited below.

Items which are Totally Prohibited from Entering The US

Other than things you would expect, such as narcotics, dangerous drugs, pornographic materials, endangered species and pests, the following items may not be brought into the US:

(a) Most fruits, vegetables, meats and poultry. On the other hand, commercially labeled, cooked and canned items not requiring refrigeration and hermetically sealed can be brought in. And bakery products and all cured cheeses (the latter subject to a $25 limit) are also allowed.

(b) Absinthe.

(c) Liquor-filled candy.

(d) Lottery tickets.

(e) Dangerous toys.

(f) Hazardous articles, such as fireworks.

(g) Toxic or poisonous substances.

(h) Switchblade knives (unless you have only one arm).

(i) "Pirate" books, records, tapes or computer programs infringing US copyright.

(j) South African Krugerrands.

(k) Certain types of monkeys.

(l) Fake trademarked items which the manufacturer has requested US Customs to seize, *e.g.*, Rolex, Louis Vuitton, Gucci and Yves St. Laurent.

(**m**) Genuine foreign-made US-trademark-registered items in excess of one of each type of article per passenger every 30 days. Such articles usually include cameras, musical instruments, tape recorders, watches and perfume.

(**n**) Iranian rugs exported from Iran after October 29, 1987.

Items Requiring a License to Import into the US

Many items can be imported only if you obtain a license first. For a few of them, a license will not normally be granted. Some of the more important licensable items:

(**a**) Firearms.

(**b**) Personal merchandise from North Korea, Vietnam, Cambodia or Cuba in excess of $100, or any such merchandise from Libya or Nicaragua.

(**c**) Narcotic or habit-forming medicines in excess of a reasonably prescribed amount.

(**d**) Biological materials (such as disease organisms).

(**e**) Cultural property (such as pre-Columbian art).

(**f**) Wildlife.

(**g**) Items made from endangered species.

(**h**) Certain wildlife products, especially those which are illegal in the country of origin (such as zebra-skin wallets, tortoise-shell jewelry, leopard-skin pillbox hats or snow leopard coats).

(**i**) Any products from whales, walruses, narwhals or polar bears.

(**j**) Plants, cuttings, seeds, plant products and, believe it or not, any accompanying dirt (for which you have to obtain a separate license).

Where to Get More Detailed Information on US Customs Rules

As the above demonstrates, if you are going to do anything unusual, you will have to check the details of the customs rules. Write the Department of the Treasury, U.S. Customs Service, P.O. Box 9407, Washington, DC 20044 and ask for the following free booklets: No. 512, *Know Before You Go* (for US residents); No. 511, *Customs Hints for Visitors (Nonresidents)*;

No. 518, *Customs Highlights for Government Personnel* (including military); No. 515, *GSP and the Traveler* (special exemptions for products from certain countries); No. 508, *Trademark Information for Travelers.*

If you intend to bring in food, write the US Department of Agriculture, Washington, DC 20250, and ask for publication No. 511, *Travelers' Tips.*

If you intend to bring in wildlife or wildlife products, write the National Fish and Wildlife Foundation, U.S. Interior Department, Washington, DC 20240, and ask for the publication *Buyer Beware.* This pamphlet is also available from the American Society of Travel Agents at (703)739-2782.

Why Casual Smugglers Find US Airport Customs Much Harder than European Airport Customs

If at the end of a holiday you discovered that the purchases you'd made exceeded the US duty-free limit, I'm sure you'd be anxious to declare that excess on your customs form and pay duty on it. After all, without US customs duties (and import quotas), US residents might be able to pay lower prices for currently-protected consumer goods, and the discipline of the market might force currently-protected US companies to become more efficient.

Nonetheless, it has to be admitted that there are people who, in the above situation, will try to smuggle their excess purchases through customs. These people, "casual smugglers" let's call them, face a formidable task—at least in the US.

There are two basic airport customs' systems in the world:

(a) The European model, in which a passenger (usually after going through passport control) has a choice of exiting through a red "something to declare" section or a green "nothing to declare" section. In the latter section, the passenger is stopped for an interview only on a random or suspicious-appearance basis.

(b) The traditional American model, in which every single passenger, whether he has something to declare or not, is interviewed by a customs officer (who in some airports is the passport control officer as well). There might be a red and a green line, but even in the green line every passenger is personally interviewed by a customs officer.

The European model is obviously much easier for casual smugglers to beat. All the smugglers have do is try to look innocent as they walk through the "nothing to declare" section" and they're unlikely to be stopped. Plus, if they are caught, it's easier to plead ignorance. ("Oh, I'm sorry but I'm red/green color blind.")

With the traditional US model, on the other hand, to get through, the smugglers have to be able to lie convincingly in the face of direct questioning from a customs officer—a much tougher proposition. And if, after lying, they're caught, they will have a much harder time pleading ignorance.

In addition, the penalties in the US for lying are severe. Smugglers are subject to (i) having their articles seized, plus (ii) paying a penalty of two to six times the normal duty, plus (iii) if they're really egregious, paying a criminal penalty.

Fortunately for smugglers, US customs recently announced that due to the dramatically increased volume of international traffic, the major US airports will be converted to something like the European system over the next few years. Customs officers will depend on computerized profiles to try to catch smugglers.

Tricks of an Inveterate Casual Smuggler

Personally, I have never smuggled anything knowingly through customs. And I would never advise anyone else to smuggle something through customs. True, in my opinion customs duties and quotas are usually special-interest measures which indirectly cause significant damage to the general public interest. But they're the law and, as the law, should be obeyed. In addition, the amounts of duty (at least in the US) are usually so low that any potential savings hardly seem worth the effort or the risk.

Nonetheless, purely as a matter of intellectual curiosity, I do find it interesting how smugglers go about their business. In preparing for this book, I've had extended conversations with one casual smuggler who regularly smuggles small amounts through customs. Why he does it I don't know. He doesn't need the money. It seems to be a matter of pride in his own ingenuity.

On the assumption that you (as well as the customs authorities, to the extent they don't know) would find it interesting how he does it, I've set out some of his techniques below. All of them seemed to be aimed at giving him a colorable argument for customs, in case he gets caught, as to why he has not exceeded the exemption limit.

1.   The wear-and-tear ploy. As mentioned above, the customs rules state that any item purchased within the last twelve months is to be declared at its purchase price. If the item has had significant wear and use before someone brings it into the US, the customs officer will make an appropriate reduction in its value. Logically, after one wearing the price ought to be reduced under the "fair retail value" test to the price at which a secondhand store could sell the item.

Unfortunately, logic is not something the average customs officer is particularly endowed with. To the average customs officer, fair retail value is a concept of Platonic, perhaps even Marxist dimensions, which has nothing to do with the price that a willing buyer and a willing seller would agree on. To the average customs officers, if the item was sold for one price when new, then it should sell for the same price when used—unless the item has experienced visible physical deterioration. In other words, designer dresses which were worn only once should be selling in second-hand shops for their original price.

To avoid getting into this argument, my casual smuggler friend, when making his declaration uses his estimate of the wear-reduced value as the value of the item. Technically he should use the original price but, if he's caught, he merely says that he assumed that by "fair retail value" the law meant "fair retail value".

If his estimated value is under $1400, he also points out that the Customs Declaration form talks in terms of "the total value of all goods . . . purchased or acquired abroad" without any discussion of how he's supposed to arrive at that value. If his estimated value is over $1400, he has greater difficulty with this argument because then the form requires him to list each purchase in a special section in which he is instructed to give the "price paid, or for gifts, fair retail value".

2.   The per-person spread. The excess value rules are usually on a per-person basis. So if my friend is over the limit, he tries to find other passengers on the plane who are not over the limit and will take his excess in for him. He normally looks for nonresidents on short visits to the US since, as long as they can claim that the item is personal and they will be taking it back out of the country, generally there is no duty. (Note, my friend points out that alcohol, tobacco and perfume do not fall into this exemption.) Whoever my friend gets to carry the item in must be willing to say that the item is theirs.

3.   The foreign-receipt fraud. When my friend buys something abroad, he gets the shopkeeper to give him a receipt for a lower amount. Many shopkeepers in foreign countries are happy to give him such a receipt since it allows them to defraud their own government on their income and sales taxes.

According to my friend, to make this technique work, (i) the item should be unusual and (ii) the price should not be absurdly low. The customs people are on the lookout for this practice and have a databank of foreign prices for the more common items. My friend is also very careful to destroy any documents, such as credit card slips, which might evidence a higher price. To be absolutely safe, he normally pays for such items only in cash.

4. The domestic receipt fraud. If my friend knows before he leaves the US that he intends to buy an item abroad identical to one owned by a friend of his in the US, he gives a check to and obtains a US receipt from his friend for that item at a fair market price before he goes. When he returns with the new item, he then states that it's the same one he bought from his friend in the US before he left. Needless to say, this works only on items which do not carry serial numbers.

A hint for nonsmugglers: If you are leaving the US with an expensive, new, US-purchased but foreign-made item, be sure to take your US receipts with you so that you can prove to the US customs authorities on your return that you did not purchase the item abroad. If you have no receipts, then on departure ask the customs people to register the item so you won't have to worry when you return.

5. The domestic label scam. My friend takes labels from his US clothing and sews them into his foreign clothing purchases. He says, however, in doing this he has to be very careful to:

(a) Use a sewing machine. The customs officers will be suspicious of hand-sewn labels.

(b) Get not only the manufacturer's label which appears behind the neck but also the fabric content and washing instructions label which often is sewn into the seam at the side. These are all required by law on any clothing sold in the US.

(c) Take the labels only from manufacturers which sell items in the US which are similar to the one he is buying abroad.

6. The previous trip story. If the item is clearly something which was purchased abroad, my friend argues that he purchased it abroad on a previous trip. Of course, he makes this argument only when:

(a) he in fact has made a previous trip within a reasonable time period (which would be evidenced in his passport); and

(b) he's able to get a foreign shopkeeper to predate his receipt to a date within that period.

Note, to get the maximum exemption, his prior entry has to have occurred more than 30 days before.

7. The general drunk. If my friend can't think of any particular argument as to why he is not over the limit, he'll spill some alcohol on his clothes before he leaves the plane and act as though he's drunk. He feels that to the extent he appears to have clearly diminished capacity, the customs officer will go easy on him for having forgotten to declare everything. He claims this technique works best if the value of his items do not exceed $1,400, since in that case the US form does not require him to list separately each article and its value. The customs officers apparently find it easier to forgive an oral mistake by a drunk than a written one.

8. The sloppy list. My friend will make an almost illegible list of foreign purchases including all the items in one column but leaving off one of the prices in the other column. At the bottom of the prices column he puts the total of the prices listed. A customs officer searching his bag will find every item listed but may miss that not every item has a price listed. If he does, he'll probably think it's an understandable mistake—particularly if my friend appears drunk as well.

Amazing, isn't it, what someone will go through to avoid a ten-percent duty? Phony labels. Phony receipts. Bald-faced lies. Feigned inebriation. Hopefully, my revealing these techniques here will help the US Customs Service to devise more effective counter techniques against them.

Taking Advantage of the Psychology of the Average Customs Officer

Unfortunately, Customs is going to have a tough time catching my friend because he claims to have developed a keen understanding of how their minds work. From this understanding, he's been able to develop two major approaches:

1. Avoiding a high profile. According to my friend, customs officers, like anyone else, want to employ their efforts where they'll have the greatest chance of success. Apart from using sniffer dogs or informers to uncover drugs and explosives, customs officers at the airport have little chance of catching the professional smuggler. The professional smuggler has sophisticated equipment and skills which make him difficult to detect. What the customs officers are looking for, therefore, according to my friend, are the easy pickings, *i.e.*, the families loaded down with mounds of luggage, returning from holiday in prime dutiable "bargain" countries.

To avoid fitting into this high profile, then, my friend employs one of three major techniques:

(a) **The "innocent flight" cover.** Customs officers are much more likely to suspect passengers getting off flights from Paris or Hong Kong than they are from Eastern Europe, where there isn't much worth buying, or a developing country where there is a preferential exemption from US duty (see above at page 302). When my friend comes in on a flight from a target country, he hangs back until a flight from a nontarget country comes in and then goes through customs with the passengers from that flight. He has to be very inconspicuous about hanging around the baggage claim hall, because the customs officers are on the lookout for just that sort of behavior. Normally he takes his luggage off the suspect-flight carousel and, in the midst of a crowd of passengers, takes it over to the unsuspected-flight carousel. When most of the passengers have cleared there, he takes his bag and departs.

By the way, my friend says he never opens his bags before presenting them to customs. Otherwise the customs officers watching baggage claim will immediately become suspicious he is putting in or taking out a forbidden item, and require him and all his bags to be searched.

(b) **The non-US-resident shift.** According to my friend, US customs officers (different from passport control officers) are much more likely to search US residents than they are non-US residents. Non-US residents on short business or holiday trips to the US are not likely to be bringing a large number of articles permanently into the US. So if my friend is traveling with a non-US resident, he asks that resident to bring the item in.

(c) **The sole-business-flyer masquerade.** Customs officers are much less likely to search passengers who are alone, dressed in a business suit and carrying a minimum of luggage. When my friend travels with his family, he, dressed in his normal business clothes, takes the more questionable items in a piece of carry-on luggage and goes through customs first. A few minutes later the rest of his family follows with the trolley full of harmless luggage.

2.   **Misdirecting the attention.** According to my friend, the psychology of customs officers is such that he can often get them to miss the relevant item. Among his techniques:

> (a) **The least-favored bag.** As my friend comes up to the customs inspector's position, he puts the bag he doesn't want inspected up on the platform and leaves the other one down on the ground. If the inspector searches at all, he invariably picks the one he thinks my friend is trying to keep from him, the one on the ground.
>
> Purely as a game, I've tried it myself several times. It's amazing that customs officers could fall for such simple child psychology.
>
> (b) **The duty-free liquor bag.** A similar technique my friend employs is to put the smuggled item in a duty-free liquor bag. Since it's so obviously the first place an inexperienced smuggler would assume the customs inspector would look, the customs inspector rarely looks inside. The few times that the customs inspector has looked inside and discovered the item, my friend avoided any penalties by claiming he thought that since he bought the item in a duty-free shop, it didn't need to be declared. (Once, according to my friend, when he was bringing in a ring for his wife, it fit perfectly inside the fist-sized indentation on the bottom of a duty-free wine bottle which was also in the bag, so the customs officer missed it completely.)
>
> (c) **The wheelbarrow diversion.** My friend named this one after the old joke about the man bringing a wheelbarrow of sand across the border each day: The customs officers search the sand each time but find nothing; years later it's discovered the guy was smuggling wheelbarrows. Analogizing from this story, my friend wraps soiled, foreign-purchased clothes around duty-free liquor bottles in his suitcase. The customs officers are so interested in discovering what's wrapped up inside that they miss the wrapping.
>
> By the way, my friend says the popular belief that the best way to smuggle something in is to wear it is not true. According to him, unless the item being worn looks clearly old and US-made, the inspectors are just as likely to inspect them on you as in your suitcase.
>
> (d) **The lost-bag trick.** My friend claims to have employed this once when he had about $800-worth of items he was bringing in (twice the exemption limit). What he did was put $400-worth in one bag and $400-worth in another, and then left one of the bags "by accident" on the wrong carousel. After he went through customs, he

complained to the airline about his lost bag. While they searched for it, he went home and unpacked. When the airline at last located the bag, they took it through customs for him (where apparently there was no record of how much else he'd brought in) and delivered it to his home for free.

I have to admire my friend for his ingenuity. But, as I said before, smuggling is a crime and, my friend, no matter how much he looks on his smuggling as a game, is committing a criminal act. Some day, somewhere, I fear, he's going to get caught.

CHAPTER ELEVEN

HOW TO GET THROUGH AND AWAY FROM THE AIRPORT

The Profile of the Best Place to Meet at the Airport

Most people meet arriving passengers at the gate or, if nonpassengers are not allowed in the gate area, then just outside the arrival concourse or, for international flights, the customs hall. By meeting the arriving passenger at these places, the greeters feel they are demonstrating the maximum affection and courtesy.

If you are to be the arriving passenger, however, you might demonstrate your own affection and courtesy by suggesting that your greeter does not wait for you in these places.

Do you really want him or her to stand around in a packed crowd for some time (for international arrivals, often over an hour) straining to catch a glimpse of you among the exiting passengers, unable to sit down, to go to the bathroom or to get something to eat or drink, for fear of missing you? Worse, what if your plane arrives early or your greeter arrives late? Then neither of you will be entirely sure whether you've missed the other or where you should meet now.

Planning to meet at the gate also creates other burdens on your greeters. First, they will have to walk a longer distance (from one end of the concourse to the gate and back)—a distance which you are to cover anyway. Second, since they have to allow time to find the gate, they either arrive earlier than they otherwise would or face a greater chance of being late at the meeting point. Third, after they have said they will meet you at the gate, they may discover that nonpassengers are not allowed on the concourse, in which case they wait fretting at the entrance to the concourse while you, unaware of the restriction on nonpassengers, wait for them at the gate.

If you are going to be met at the airport, therefore, it is much better if you choose a meeting place:

(a) **Where the greeters can sit.**

(b) **Which is a specifically described point.** (That way the greeters won't have to find you. You can find them.)

(c) **Which is as close as possible to the terminal entrance,** so they can arrive later at the airport and do a minimum of walking.

How do you find such a point? Read on.

How to Find the Meeting Place Which Fits the Profile

Most European terminals have a specific "Meeting Point" which has the characteristics described in (a) through (c) above. When you get off the plane, all you need do is follow the signs marked "Meeting Point".

Few US airports, unfortunately, have yet adopted this civilized system. Thus, in the US, you are likely to have to pick a point based on either the personal knowledge of you or your friend.

If neither you nor your greeter are familiar with the airport, it's difficult to choose a place blind. Saying you'll meet at the closest seating next to the X rental car company, the Y airline ticket desk, the airport restaurant or the bar is dangerous. In the first place, there may be no such seating. In the second place, there may be more than one location for such things. For instance, the American Airlines ticket desks at Dallas-Fort Worth are spread over two terminals.

It's best, therefore, to try to pick a point the existence and location of which you can confirm before you leave. Three suggestions:

(a) **Look in the *Airport Pocket Guide*,** mentioned above at page 25. It shows the specific location of almost everything in the airport, including cocktail lounges and restaurants.

(b) **Look for an airline club.** Assuming one of you is a member, you'll be able to confirm its existence and location from your membership material. If your greeter is not a member but you are, you can usually arrange for your greeter to be admitted by calling ahead and giving your card number. Note, occasionally an airline will have more than one club at its home airport; so be sure to designate at which club location you are meeting. Note, also, that at some international locations, the airline clubs are on the gate-side of security and hence possibly inaccessible to nonpassengers.

(c) **Call up the airport authority.** Ask them to suggest a place to meet which conforms to the three requirements specified above. At the same time ask them how to go about having someone paged when you arrive at the airport, just in case the airport's description of the meeting point turns out to fit more than one place. (See the list of airport phone numbers in Appendix One at page 385.)

The Proper Way to Set the Time to Meet

Often the time it will take you to get from your gate to the greeting area is uncertain. This is particularly true with international flights where you are subject to the vagaries not only of baggage claim but also of passport and customs procedures. For that reason, if you have a single greeter, you should schedule free-time during which he or she can go to the lavatory, snack bar or phone without worrying about missing you permanently. For example, you could provide that the greeter may leave the meeting spot at will but, at the very least, will return precisely at each quarter-hour on the clock.

The First Things You Should Do after Landing if Your Flight has Been Diverted Because of Weather

1.   Ground transportation. If your intended destination is within reasonable distance for ground transportation, immediately upon getting off the plane, go to a phone and try to make a reservation for a rental car, bus and/or train to your intended destination. If you decide on a rental car, you can solicit some of the other passengers to share the cost.

2.   Weather report. After you've made your alternative reservation, call to find out the weather at your intended destination to get an unbiased forecast. There are at least three ways to do this:

(a) **The local weather number,** which you can obtain from telephone information by dialing the area code plus 555-1212.

(b) **American Express.** If you are an American Express cardholder, call 1-800-554-AMEX and ask for the weather at your destination.

(c) **WeatherTrak.** To reach this service which provides the weather in 400 cities worldwide, call (900)370-USAT, followed by the area code for the US city or the first three letters for the foreign city whose weather you want. For foreign destinations if you punch in the month, you can also obtain the average highs and lows in temperature, the currency rates, documentation required and travel advisories, if any. The cost is 75 cents for the first minute and 50 cents for each minute thereafter. To obtain more information about Weather-Trak, call (214)556-1122.

3.   The airline staff. Then, and only then, ask the airline staff what they plan to do. If they say they will send you to your intended destination by ground transportation and give you a precise early estimated departure time, hang around and take that. If not (for instance, if they're vague about what they are going to do, or definite about putting you up overnight), leave immediately via the alternative ground transportation you lined up on the phone.

What You Can Expect from the Airline if Your Flight has Been Diverted

When a flight is diverted to an unexpected location due to bad weather at your destination, most airlines, although not required to, will at least provide you with blankets, pillows and the meals which were prepared for the flight. Some will arrange for one free three-minute phone call, a free hotel and, if possible, free alternative ground transportation as mentioned above.

If the diversion is due to the airline's equipment malfunction, then they will usually take responsibility for all of the above, plus arrange for substitutes for any missed connecting flights.

If you aren't satisfied with what the airline is offering, follow the appropriate steps in the discussion about cancellation, delays and other schedule irregularities above at pages 195-199.

How to Prepare for Tight Connections

Making quick connections requires preparation.

1. **Before you left on your trip,** you should have:

    (a) Booked the nearest connecting flight, probably an on-line connection. (See discussion above at pages 6 and 21.)

    (b) Brought only carry-on luggage. (See discussion above at page 102.)

    (c) Obtained a copy of the airport layout. (See discussion above at page 27.)

    (d) Obtained information on the airport transportation system, *i.e.*, the routes, schedules and costs of the inter-terminal trams or buses. (See discussion above at page 27.) This is particularly important if you are making a connection to a nearby airport. If you know the precise schedule of the helicopter and/or the express bus, then as soon as you get off the plane you'll know which will get you there faster or whether you're better off getting a taxi or rental car.

2. On your flight you should check with the flight attendants or your seatmates for their recommendations as to the best way to make your connection.

3. On arriving, especially on international flights, your connecting airline very often will have a small podium outside the customs hall. You not only can check-in for your flight there but get advice on the best way to make your connection.

Some Hints on Making a Tight Connection

1. Walk rather than ride. If your connecting flight is in another terminal, sometimes it is quicker to walk than to take airport transportation. This occurs most often where the airport is on an oblong plan and either (i) the terminal you wish to go to is only a few doors down in the direction opposite to the flow of traffic on the oblong or (ii) the oblong is long and narrow with a parking lot or underground garage in the middle and the terminal you wish to go to is directly across the narrow part.

2. Stand near the door. If you do take an airport bus or tram to the next terminal and the bus or tram is crowded, you will get off quicker if you stand near the door with your bags. If you sit down, you'll have to fight your way through other passengers when it arrives at your destination. If you put your bag in the rack, you'll have to spend time pulling it out from under the other bags which naturally will have been dumped on top of it.

3. Take a taxi. If you are in a real rush, you can take a taxi from one terminal to another. However, unless you want interminable argument and delay, you should begin by offering the driver a huge tip comparable to the profit he could make taking you to town. Since airport cabs usually have to wait in line quite a while to pick up a passenger (sometimes several hours), they are not happy about wasting their pickup on a quarter-mile trip.

If there is a taxi dispatcher and he asks you where you are going, tell him somewhere in town. If you tell him another terminal, he may not allow you to get in the cab. Once you get in the cab, you can cut your own deal with the driver.

4. Call ahead. Whichever way you are getting to your next flight, if your time is very tight, ask the ground staff at your arriving flight to phone ahead to the gate of your departing flight to let them know you are coming. At the least this may keep you from being bumped by a standby; at the best, the airline may hold the plane for you.

Five Ways to Improve Your Chances of Getting a Taxi Quickly

Occasionally you will come out of the terminal and discover a long line of people waiting at the taxi rank and hardly a cab in sight. In this event, there are five major ways you can improve your chances of getting a taxi quickly:

1.   The share-a-ride gambit. Ask the people further up the line if they are going near your destination and, if so, whether they'd like to share a ride to cut their costs. If they say yes, then you can legitimately join them at the front of the line.

2.   The departure level. Go to the departure level where taxis drop passengers off and hail one there. This is quite advantageous to the taxi driver since he will not have to go around and come back into the arrivals area. It's also against airport rules. So you have to be very careful to do it surreptitiously, out of sight of the traffic warden and other taxis. Needless to say, the lighter you are traveling, the easier it is to be surreptitious. A five or ten dollar tip thrust immediately into the driver's hand can also do wonders.

3.   The separately-fed rank. At many airports all the taxi stands are fed via radio from a central taxi-waiting area. Theoretically, then, the supply of taxis is evened out among the various stands. However, at some airports, all or some of the taxi stands are fed from their own separate line of waiting taxis (as, for example, is the one on the western end of La Guardia). In this situation, there can easily be an oversupply of taxis at one stand and none at the other. So if your taxi stand has a long line of passengers and no taxis, the odds are you're better off going to another separately-fed taxi stand.

4.   Upstreaming. In the situation where taxis are neither separately fed or fed by radio from a central waiting area, you can improve your chances by walking or taking the airport van to the taxi rank closest to where the taxis enter the oval from the city. Even where the taxis theoretically are fed by radio from the central waiting area, in my experience when things get really jammed up, the system seems to break down and the taxis are sent out to pick up wherever they can—which naturally means the first terminal on the route.

5.   The less-crowded airline. Try to determine which airline or terminal is likely to be less crowded at the particular time and go there; its taxi stands should have the shortest lines. For instance, if you're at Heathrow in early evening, Terminal 1 Arrivals, which handles European flights, is likely to be crowded, while Terminal 3 Arrivals, which handles primarily transatlantic flights, is likely to be near-empty. Or last year, when Eastern's plans to cut most of its Kansas City flights were held up by a union-sought court injunction, the uncertain situation prevented a lot of people from booking flights on Eastern; the lower load factor was reflected in the taxi ranks fed by Eastern. Just review in your mind all the factors which might make some flights less popular than others (see discussion above at page 61), and you'll soon figure out if a less-crowded taxi stand is likely to exist.

Box 11-1.   A Comparison of Taxi Fares

One comparison of fares from the airport to town at over two hundred airports worldwide found the average fare per mile (not including tip) was $1.55.

The ten most expensive in the US on a per-mile basis were Boston, $3.67; San Diego, $2.75; Reno, $2.50; Norfolk, $2.33; Milwaukee, $2.29; Richmond, $2.14; Phoenix, $2.13; Newark-to-Manhattan, $2.03; Tampa and Anchorage, $2.00, and Louisville, $1.90.

The ten least expensive in the US on a per-mile basis were Chattanooga, $0.80; Mobile, $0.83; Fort Worth, $0.90; Dayton, $0.92; Albany, $0.99; Grand Rapids, $1.00; Houston and Dallas, $1.02; Youngstown, $1.07; Chicago-O'Hare and Cincinnati, $1.08; and Omaha, $1.10.

The most expensive trip from the airport to the city in the US was Newark to Manhattan: $32.50 for the 16-mile trip. The most expensive internationally was Tokyo International: $122.50 or approximately $3.06 per mile for the 40-mile trip.

(Source: *How To Get From The Airport To The City.*)

The Most Important Thing to Do to Avoid Being Cheated by Your Taxi Driver

The most important thing you can do to prevent being cheated by your taxi driver is to get an independent estimate of what the fare for your trip should be.

In the more enlightened airports, you will find an estimate of the cost posted on a sign near the taxi stand. However, you can't depend on all airports being enlightened. So before you leave on your trip, it's best to consult (or ask your travel agent to consult) *How To Get From The Airport To The City All Around The World* mentioned above at page 133 for the estimated fare.

If you find yourself on a plane to a strange destination without having consulted one of the above publications, try to find an experienced passenger on the plane who can tell you what the cost of a taxi into town should be. Failing that, ask someone in the airport.

Whatever you do, do not appear at the taxi stand until you have gotten an estimate of the fare from some independent source.

The Best Strategy for Dealing with Unmetered Cabs

Contrary to what you might think, where taxis are unmetered, as is the case in most developing countries, it's best to get into the cab without discussing the price ahead of time. If the driver wants to bargain, you'll be in a much better bargaining position after he's given you the trip— plus, when you reach your destination, you're likely to be at a place (such as your hotel, the office of business associates or the home of friends) where you can get independent advice and the taxi driver will not find a lot of support.

When you get to your destination, before the driver can say what the fare was, pay him what you know from your earlier research to be the rate (or if you couldn't find out, then what you think is a fair rate), get out of the cab and walk away. If you were just guessing at the fair rate and the guy follows you down the sidewalk waving his arms at you and screaming unintelligible obscenities, consider upping your payment a few pennies.

Techniques to Keep from Being Cheated in a Metered Cab

Where taxis are metered, the cheating takes several forms:

1.   The taxi which picks you up already has some time on the meter. You can protect yourself against this scam simply by requiring the cab driver to turn the meter to zero before you start.

2.   The driver will try to charge the meter rate to each person in the cab or to add all sorts of phony additional baggage, rush hour and other charges. You can protect yourself against these if you:

(a) Know ahead of time what the charge basis is. The book, *How To Get From The Airport To The City*, mentioned above at page 133, will tell you or your travel agent precisely what the basis of the charge is. You can ask your fellow passengers, but often they are not all that clear on the basis of the rates.

(b) Presume against the per-person basis or unusual surcharges unless you can see it in writing. Many places will add surcharges for baggage, more than two passengers or rush hour. Some places, such as Sun Valley, Idaho, and Springfield, Illinois, will charge a flat rate per person. And I'm sure there must be some place somewhere (although I've yet to encounter it) which charges a *metered* rate per person. Because such charges are exceptions to the normal rule, however, the taxi authorities, in order to prevent disputes between passengers and drivers, almost always require such charges be posted in an official notice in the cab. For that reason, unless you see such a notice, pay only the amount on the meter and walk away.

3. **The taxi will take a long, circuitous route to your destination.** You can protect yourself against this scam if you always make sure you:

(a) Know the normal route and ask the driver to take it. The easiest way to do this is to pick up a free map and free printed directions at one of the busier rental car desks. Or you can ask your travel agency to put in your ticket folder a photocopy of a local area map with the best route from the airport marked on it.

Before you leave the airport, establish which route you want the driver to take. If he argues for another route, ask him to show you on the map so you can see if it's longer. Note the agreed route there and then study it ostentatiously as he drives.

(b) If you don't know the cheapest route, ask the driver to take you by the cheapest route. If, at the end of the trip, the fare is significantly higher than what you know from your previous research to be the correct fare (or than what you think is a reasonable fare), you can then legitimately point this out to the cab driver, pay only the reasonable fare and walk away.

(c) Require a signed receipt. When you first get into the cab, tell the driver you will require a signed receipt for the journey, specifying the pickup and drop-off points. He'll be hesitant about going a roundabout route if he knows there will be a written record. Even if he's not, with a written receipt you are more likely to get satisfaction if you complain to the taxi authority.

Note, in some of the deregulated taxi systems, such as San Diego, Kansas City and Phoenix, the rate per mile will vary from cab company to cab company. So one cab's meter could show a higher fare than another's even though both took the cheapest route. Therefore, if you find yourself in one of these jurisdictions, try to quickly scan several waiting cabs for their posted per-mile rate before choosing one.

Case Study: Taking a Taxi from JFK to Manhattan

No cab drivers in the world are so determined and expert at overcharging their passengers than those on the route from JFK into Manhattan. After years of experience, I can just about manage to avoid paying for pre-existing time on the meter and, when there are other passengers, for more than my proportionate share of the proper mileage charge. If I'm extraordinarily vigilant, I can even prevent the driver from going to Manhattan via Philadelphia. However, I'm almost never able to get a New York cabby to take the shortest, cheapest route I want him to take.

To New York cab drivers, the only legitimate route from the New York airports to midtown or downtown Manhattan is by way of the Triboro Bridge. For those of you who are not familiar with the geography of New York, following is a schematic which will give you an idea what this means.

Figure 11-1. The Route From JFK to Manhattan

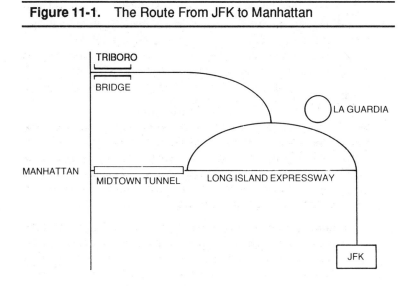

Even those with the most elementary knowledge of geometry can see that the Triboro Bridge is not the shortest route to midtown or downtown Manhattan. The shortest route between two points is, miracle of miracles, not the curved line but the straight line, the Long Island Expressway.

Now, I'm sure the average New York cab driver is unlikely to have read much Euclid. And I'm certain there are some who are so ignorant that they are simply unaware of any alternative route. (Those are the ones who, when they finally make it to 41st Street in Manhattan, require detailed directions on how to get to 42nd.) Most, though, have simply realized that the Triboro Bridge is the longest route they can take to the city which will not get them in trouble with the New York Taxi And Limousine Commission for overcharging.

When you try to get a New York cab driver to take an alternative route, he will resist in several ways.

One way is to argue that at that time of day the Long Island Expressway or Midtown Tunnel is jammed up. Needless to say, it doesn't matter what the time of day is. I've had the argument put to me at two o'clock in the morning on a Tuesday.

How these guys know the Long Island Expressway or Midtown Tunnel is jammed up is a mystery to me. Especially since they never seem to know when the Triboro Bridge is jammed up.

It's certainly possible that because of the number of cars or counter-rush-hour lane restrictions, the midtown route is more jammed up. But the way I see it, it has to be twice as jammed up as the Triboro Bridge route in order to justify covering twice the distance to avoid it.

If by some miracle, you're able to get a New York cab driver to agree to take you on the midtown route, do not assume that the battle is over. He probably doesn't understand. I mean, so few New York cab drivers today speak English. Who knows what the words, "Midtown Tunnel route," mean in Ukrainian? You're probably lucky not to be sodomized with a large cabbage at the first exit.

Even if your cabby does understand, he is likely to take a broad interpretation of your intent. This is the cabby who takes you to the Midtown Tunnel via the Triboro Bridge—or, at the very least, via the "great circle route" that passes by La Guardia.

Or your cabby may "accidentally" miss the relevant turnoff for the Long Island Expressway and end up at the Triboro Bridge that way.

This is a tough one to defend against. You've got to keep an eye on the road and continually warn the driver about upcoming exits without appearing too pushy. If you appear too pushy, then the driver is likely to respond by stopping at each exit along the road and asking you sarcastically whether he should take it. ,

"This one's to New England," he'll say. "That's somewhere near Manhattan, isn't it?"

Even if the driver eventually takes the fastest route, his stopping every quarter-mile to ask you directions will have turned it into the slowest route.

The ultimate defense New York cab drivers have against taking other than the Triboro Bridge route is to get "lost". Once they've got you off the beaten track, your skeletal rent-a-car map and skimpy knowledge of the topography of Queens is of no use. You're lost, too.

You could try a few plaintive cries of, "You've been a cab driver for forty-two years and can't find your way from the airport to the city?" but it's unlikely to do any good.

It's best just to resign yourself to having been beaten, sit back and wait for the Triboro Bridge to come into view.

How to Deal with Pirates

Pirate cabs, *i.e.*, unlicensed, unauthorized taxis, have one major virtue. Take one and you will learn the absolutely cheapest route into the city. Being unmetered, they operate on a prenegotiated flat-price basis, and thus their only concern is to get you into the city at the lowest all-in cost to them.

Apart from this educational experience, you should avoid pirate cabs. Their vehicles are much more likely to be unsafe and uninsured and their drivers more unsavory.

Since pirate cabs are illegal, they can't get customers by waiting in taxi ranks or putting up signs. Instead they have to send touts into the arrivals areas to solicit the passengers directly. If you come out of baggage claim and find someone saying, "Taxi? Taxi?" as he pulls you by the arm towards the exit, he almost certainly is soliciting for a pirate cab. Tell him you don't need a taxi because you've got a car picking you up, and, after he leaves, go find the legitimate taxi rank.

In some countries taking a pirate cab is a good way to get mugged or murdered. I remember flying into Bogota, Colombia, which ranks with Lagos, Nigeria, as one of the most violent cities in the world—four times the murder rate of New York City. Tired and jet-lagged I let myself be escorted into a waiting cab. As I entered, I realized that I hadn't seen any markings on the outside of the vehicle. Before I could get out, though, two burly passengers, locals, obviously not from the plane, got in on either side of me. The driver quickly started the cab and took off.

No one said a thing. The men on either side kept eying me, as though they were sizing me up.

What would you have done in this situation?

Well, I'll tell you what I did. I leaned forward towards the driver. "Senor, do you know where I can get a woman?"

"Yes, Senor," the driver said after a moment's thought. "I take you good place where you can choose many women. We go there now."

"I'd like that," I said. "Only I've got one problem. I don't have any money on me. I must go to my hotel first so I can cash a check. Will two or three hundred dollars be enough?"

Needless to say, he took me to my hotel.

Once there, of course, I "discovered" a message requiring me to meet immediately with some business associates and sent the cab driver away with a healthy tip.

Obviously, I don't know for sure whether I ever was in any danger in the Colombian cab. But if I was, my little ploy is the reason I'm alive today to tell you about it.

Why You Should Rise Above Your Station and Ride in a Limousine

Most people assume that limousines are only for the rich and famous. At the airport, however, that is not necessarily the case.

Airport limousines (I'm talking here about real limousines, not buses and other scheduled services which call themselves limousines) are often only 30 to 50 percent more expensive than taxis. If the cost can be divided among several people, the premium is bearable. Particularly when you consider the usual benefits of a limousine:

(a) If you book ahead, your personal limousine will be waiting for you when you step out of baggage claim; you don't have to wait in line.

(b) Even if you don't book ahead, the wait for a limousine is often much less than the wait in the taxi queue—because limousines are more expensive and less well-known to the traveling public.

(c) The seating will be more spacious and comfortable.

(d) You're charged a fixed price, so you won't have to be worrying continually about which route the driver is taking.

(e) You can pay by credit card or guaranteed check.

So next time you face a long taxi line, consider stopping by the limousine desk to see what's available.

How to Obtain a Rental Car Cheaply

Only a fool would rent a car at the full rates advertised by the airport rent-a-car companies. There are too many ways to get a car more cheaply.

1.   Use off-airport car rental companies. The national off-airport car rental companies often charge 30 percent and sometimes up to 60 percent less than the on-airport chains. Local off-airport car rental companies can be even cheaper. (The greatest savings, by the way, are usually in the larger, more luxurious cars.) The airport doesn't advertise these agencies because the airport receives substantial franchise fees from the car rental companies in the airport.

As these companies are located outside the airport, you have to call them to pick you up when you arrive and you have to spend time making the trip to their lot. On the other hand, since they usually have much shorter lines and since the national car rental companies generally now require you to take a van to their lots, you won't necessarily spend more total time renting a car from one of these companies.

Box 11-2. National Car Rental Companies

Company	800 Number
Normally in Airport	
Avis	331-1212
Budget	527-0700
Hertz	654-3131;
	522-3711 OK
National	227-7368
Normally Off Airport	
Agency	221-8666
Ajax	352-2529
Alamo	732-3232
American-International	527-0202
Dollar	421-6878
Enterprise	325-8007
General	327-7607
Snappy	669-4800
Thrifty	367-2277
Tropical	367-5140
United States Assoc'd	323-3024
Value	327-2501
Normally Off Airport and the Name Says it All	
Rent-A-Dent	426-5243
Rent-A-Wreck	423-2158

To find the local car rental agencies, you can consult the local yellow pages when you arrive or at your main library at home.

---

2. Claim an affiliate discount. The national car rental companies have such a plethora of discounts that you are sure to qualify for at least one. If you work for a major employee, belong to a major professional or recreational organization, use a major credit card, arrive at the airport in a major airline or belong to an airline club, you are likely to obtain a ten to 15 percent discount from one of the car rental companies. Check ahead of time with each company (and with your airline) to see if there is a car rental discount which might apply to you.

If you don't seem to qualify at first blush, all is not lost. Consider trying the following:

(a) Enroll for free in the car rental company's rapid rental system (see below) and/or its centralized billing system, and pick up a bonus discount.

(b) Store in your briefcase all your boarding pass stubs and/or ticket jackets from previous flights. When you discover a rental car company giving a discount to passengers of a particular airline, pull out the appropriate one. (If the ticket jacket isn't marked with the appropriate flight number, do it yourself.)

(c) Mention the name of any qualifying organization with which you have at least some connection. You don't have to emphasize that your only connection with X Company is that you own its stock or buy your electricity from it. Just say you want the X-company discount. Surprisingly, many rental car companies will not grill you further.

3. Claim a period discount. As with the airlines, there are off-peak discounts. Weekends (often liberally defined as noon Thursday to noon Monday) are off-peak for most airport car rental agencies. In addition, there are also discounts for using the car over a weekend or for seven days or more, or if the rental is paid in advance and/or is nonrefundable, or if the rental is booked as part of a holiday package through an airline or tour group before you arrive at the destination.

4. Compare flat rate charges. Some discount packages are based on a low flat rate plus low mileage charges while others are based on a high flat rate and unlimited mileage. If you intend to drive the car a long distance, the flat rate may save you a lot of money.

5. Try the "subcompact trade-up". If you always book a sub-compact (which is, of course, the cheapest), a good percentage of the time when you arrive at the rental car desk no subcompacts will be available so you will be given a larger car at the sub-compact rate. This is one time when it pays to be at the end of the line waiting to get a rental car.

6. Buy your own gas. Before returning your rental car, fill it up with gas. The rental car company's charge for gas is often twice the normal cost.

7. Know your miles from your kilometers. Many cars today have odometer LCD readouts which can be changed with the push of a button from miles to kilometers. There are reports of the unobservant writing the number of kilometers down in the rental form as though it was mileage, effectively increasing their mileage charge by a factor of 1.609. Check your readout carefully.

8. Ask the car rental company to give you all mandatory additional charges not listed in the price. Several car rental companies have been advertising one price and then adding on required charges such as a $5 gas refilling charge (to be added even when you return the car full) or an airport "tax" which is really the company's franchise fee to the airport. The National Association of Attorneys General has recently enacted guidelines which require the car rental companies to include all mandatory charges in their advertised price; however, since these guidelines are only recommendations to the various state enforcement authorities on interpreting the state's deceptive practices statutes, they do not have the direct force of law.

9. Avoid "insurance" charges. I use quotes here because much of what you might think of as car rental insurance is not. For instance, let's take "collision damage waivers". Under the common law, you would be liable to the rental company for damage to its car only if you were negligent or worse; you would not be liable for damage to the car arising from your innocent accidental acts or the acts of a third party. When you sign the car rental agreement, however, it includes a waiver by you of these common law protections so that you will be liable for any damage whatsoever to the car. The car rental company then offers, for a price known as the "collision damage waiver", to reinstate all or part of the protections you have just waived. Pretty clever, huh? Like the mob charging you "protection" money so they won't break your legs. It's insurance in only the loosest sense.

Even cleverer is that the car rental company often reinstates only some of the protections you've waived (*e.g.*, you're often left liable if the car is stolen) or hems in the reinstatement with so many restrictions that it's almost impossible for you to meet them. So you've got to take the time to read the small print.

The car rental agencies will push you hard to take out their insurance. And well they should—the premiums can often add up to 50 percent of the cost of the rental. That's why some of the clerks are paid commissions for pushing the insurance. One insurance industry source has estimated that the car companies make a 90-percent profit on their premiums for collision damage waiver alone.

If you have automobile insurance of your own, you may not need to take it out. More than half of such policies cover rental cars. Check yours before you leave. If your own automobile insurance does not cover you, it will probably be cheaper to amend your policy than take out the rental car company's insurance. The rental car rate for all insurance can be over $17 per day or a rate of $6,205 per year.

Also, many credit cards provide free collision insurance on rental cars rented with the card. (Recognizing how much the rental car companies have been gouging customers, the credit-card companies have been willing to forgo the 90-percent profit on the premiums in order to get more customers.) Some, like the TWA-sponsored Visa and the Merrill Lynch Gold Visa, provide this coverage for the full value of the car, while others do it only up to a certain limit. Check with your card company before you leave on your trip.

It is likely the car rental companies will soon be cleaning up their act with respect to insurance. The guidelines of the National Association of Attorneys General mentioned above recommended that states enact laws dealing with the problem of collision damage waivers. Many have responded by effectively relieving customers of liability for all but intentional collision damage. It is likely that in the future all car rental companies will assume responsibility for collision damage and no longer sell collision damage waiver insurance to their customers. Unfortunately, the only people to benefit from this will be those who would normally have taken out insurance. Because the car rental companies will lose the revenue from collision insurance premiums and/or customers' payment for collision damages, they will raise rental rates for everyone (including those people who normally didn't buy the insurance). To add insult to injury, the increase in rental will be subject to sales tax (which the "insurance" premiums themselves usually were not).

Note: if you are uninsured and incur damage to your rental car, be sure to check the rental company's bills for repairs. Recent investigations have uncovered massive overcharging.

How to Keep from Being Bankrupted

If you are not otherwise insured against third-party liability and must depend on the rental car company's coverage, be sure to check what the limits are for liability. Although most rental car companies will provide the minimum required by state law (usually a couple of hundred thousand dollars), only a few will provide liability coverage up to a more reasonable million dollar limit, and even fewer will couple that higher limit with uninsured motorist protection. Looking at the details of the insurance coverage may lessen the chances that some silver-haired PI lawyer will leave you in the poorhouse.

Note, if you are driving abroad, then almost certainly your US insurance will not cover you, and you will want to take the foreign rental car company's insurance package. If you are going to be in the foreign country for a while, you might consider taking out cheaper insurance with a local insurance company; however, in the more provincial countries (such as the US), car insurance is not available to nonresidents other than through a car rental company. Be sure to check what limits there are on the liability insurance in the foreign country. You may be pleasantly surprised. Different from the litigious US, automobile liability insurance in most countries has no upper limit.

How to Get a Rental Car Quickly

If speed is your major concern, then I suggest the following:

1. Join the car rental company's rapid rental system. Under these systems, all of your key information for the rental form is stored in the company's computer system. When you arrive to pick up your booked car, your information will have been already pulled out of the computer and printed onto a form for you. Some allow you to bypass the lines at the terminal counter and go directly to an express desk at the lot—sometimes with the driver radioing ahead so that everything is ready.

Some systems, such as the Avis Express system, are even faster. Assuming you qualify for the program, you are given your car number and its position in the lot before you even take your flight. When you arrive at the airport, you go straight to the car (bypassing any rental-car check-in) and there find your keys and the completed rental contract sitting on the seat. All you need do is sign the contract, give a copy to the guard at the gate, flash some identification and you're off.

2.   Choose the less popular rental car company. Apart from the case of the total bypass system above, the major delay in getting a rental car comes from excess passenger demand. You have to wait in long lines at the desk to fill out the necessary form or, even worse, the rental company has run out of cars and you must wait for one to be returned. These problems can be avoided if you take care to choose the less popular rental car company.

For instance, if a rental car company has a special promotion with the airline you are flying in on, then it's likely that many more of your fellow passengers will be using that company. Also, an off-airport rental car company will normally be less popular, even though it takes no longer to get to the off-airport company's lot than to an on-airport company's lot.

3.   Make a duplicate reservation. Of course, it's not always possible to know which rental car company will be less popular. Often, it's just a matter of chance. You arrive in the rental car area and find a long line at one of the national rental car companies and no line at the others. Some people I know, therefore, make duplicate reservations, and when they arrive, choose the company with the shortest line. Personally, I don't approve of duplicate reservations as a regular practice, because they have the potential for screwing up the system for everyone. However, if you have a very short amount of time to make an absolutely crucial appointment, you might consider it.

4.   Abandon your presumptions. After you've finished at the desk, never assume that the procedure will be the same as it was at the last airport or even as it was the last time you were in the current airport. Be sure that the counter clerk (i) gives you clear directions to the parking lot or van pickup point, (ii) tells you exactly where you car is and (iii) gives you the key or tells you where you will find the key. I don't know how much time I've wasted waiting for nonexistent vans, searching for my car by its license number because I didn't have its stall number, or turning the car inside out looking for the key.

The Secrets of Successful Hotel Courtesy-Van Usage

Many hotels, especially those near the airport, have courtesy vans to pick up guests for free from the terminal. If you intend to use one of these vans, keep the following tips in mind:

(a) If you are carrying your luggage, call the hotel as soon as you get off the plane. Don't wait until you've walked down the concourse and out through baggage claim. If the hotel asks you where you are, tell them you are at your airline's baggage claim. If you say you're at the arrival gate, they'll tell you to call back after you've gone through baggage claim or will delay sending the van out until they think you've collected your luggage.

(b) Ask exactly where the pickup point is. If they say outside portal X, ask them whether the van stops at the curb of the terminal or at a passenger island separated from the terminal by a traffic lane.

(c) Pin the hotel down as to precisely when the van is estimated to arrive. In my experience, statements such as "the van is just leaving now" are akin to "the check is in the mail". At the best, they're vague; and the worst, they're lies.

(d) When you get into the van, take your luggage inside with you rather than store it in the back. When you get to your destination, you'll be able to get to the reception desk ahead of those people who have to get their luggage out of the back. You're also less likely to have your bags stolen along the way.

(e) If available, take the shotgun seat. You won't have to worry about moving for or being blocked by passengers getting on or off at the other terminal stops. The driver is also more likely to let you put your bags inside if you take the shotgun seat since your bags will not be blocking the other passengers.

(f) If the driver requires your bags to be put in the back, ask him at that time if for a tip he'll take your bags to you in reception when he's done unloading the others. If he says yes, then you can skip waiting at the back for your bags and beat everyone else to reception.

(g) If there are two of you, then when you arrive at the hotel, one of you should get the luggage while the other beats everyone else to reception. There's no reason for both of you to hang around the van.

Note, if (i) your bags have been put in the back, (ii) the van is going to make subsequent stops dropping off and/or picking up passengers and (iii) when you get to your hotel, you're going to use one of the techniques in paragraphs (f) and (g) (so you don't need to worry about being first out the door), then sit on the back seat near the aisle. This not only gives you more leg room but also allows you to keep an eye on your luggage in the back during the subsequent stops.

Beware of "Airport" Hotels

Note that very few airport hotels are actually in the airport. Some are as much as fifteen miles away from the nearest terminal. Of those that are in the airport, only a few, such as the Miami International Hotel and the O'Hare Hilton, are within walking distance of the terminals. Most require a ride in a van or automated transit system.

For that reason, when choosing among airport hotels, be sure to ask exactly how far away each hotel is from the terminal at which you arrive and what form of transportation you have to take to get there. It could mean the difference between:

(a) Spending an hour with a hotel van—waiting for it to arrive, watching your luggage being loaded, counting off the terminals on the van's seemingly endless passenger loading, peering out into the darkness wondering how many more miles before your hotel will appear and finally elbowing your way out of the van in an attempt to beat your fellow passengers to reception; and

(b) Simply walking out of the terminal concourse into your hotel.

Modern Airport Hotel Check-In Rituals

You begin by filling out the reception form with your name, address, date of departure, method of payment and employer. When you finish the form, you give it to the deskclerk.

As the deskclerk reads it closely, he will punch selected keys on his countertop computer terminal. Then, he will stand there, staring at the information on the screen for some time—longer, in fact, than would be necessary were he merely memorizing it backwards.

After a while, apparently getting lonely, he will call another clerk over to stare at the screen with him. They both then stand there, eyes riveted on the display, as the world passes them by, until one or two minutes minutes later when the second clerk, acting, I am certain, on direct instructions from the terminal, abruptly leans down and presses a button. I usually take this to be a good sign, indicating that only one or two minutes more of blank staring remain.

I don't know much about computers but I suspect that one or two minutes is the length of time it takes a terminal to input data into a deskclerk.

In any case, like clockwork, one or two minutes later one of the clerks will suddenly snap to and, smiling at you in perfect imitation of a living human being, say, "Sorry, sir, we do not have a reservation for you. However, since the hotel is half empty, we hopefully will be able to find you a room."

Then, for the next few minutes the deskclerk performs a subtle pantomime that involves pulling invoices out of file boxes and looking askance at them, moving pieces of paper aimlessly from one end of the counter to the other and sticking his fingers in one after another empty cubbyhole while dubiously shaking his head. At the end, as if by magic, he produces a key from a drawer somewhere underneath and hands it to you.

"This room may not be made up yet," he says. "If not, please give us a call and we will get housekeeping to come up as soon as possible."

What he really means, of course, is that the room is a mess and housekeeping doesn't come back on duty until eight in the morning, but hopefully, once you get into your room, you'll discover you're too tired to do anything about it.

And, you know what? He's right.

How to Choose a Quiet Room in an Airport Hotel

To the extent you have a choice of rooms, you will want to choose a hotel room which is quiet. Some of the major sources of noise in airport hotels are:

(a) airplanes taking off and landing,

(b) road traffic,

(c) music from discotheques and ballrooms,

(d) the slamming of entryway doors,

(e) the dropping of ice machine covers,

(f) the crash of soft drink cans from the dispenser,

(g) the pinging of elevator bells and the whirring of elevator shaft mechanisms, and

(h) people talking as they walk down the corridors.

In asking the hotel staff for a quiet room, be sure to insure specifically that your room is as far as reasonably possible from each of these potential sources of noise.

Of course, there may not be one single room which will avoid all the potential noises. For instance, to avoid aircraft noise, you would want a room facing onto a courtyard as close as possible to the ground; on the other hand, to avoid the cacophony of an outdoor dance being held in the courtyard, you would want a room facing the outside as high up as possible.

In deciding which of two such rooms will be quieter, don't rely on unspoken assumptions; instead, find out everything you can from the staff about the duration and loudness of each of the conflicting sources of noise. Don't assume, for example, that if you get a room on the outside, you will necessarily be disturbed by aircraft noise. To placate nearby residents, some airports do not allow planes to take off and land late at night; therefore, there may be no aircraft noise during the times you want to sleep.

If you have to choose blind, probably the room which is most likely to avoid most of the noises listed above will be one:

(a) near the top,

(b) on the courtyard or nonrunway side of the hotel, and

(c) at the far end of a corridor, or, if the corridor has a main entrance at either end, then in the middle of the corridor.

Being near the top will help avoid the road traffic noises and loud music; being on the courtyard or nonrunway side will help avoid the airplane noises; and being in the far end or middle of the corridor will help avoid the balance of the noises since they tend to be congregated around the entrance to the corridor.

After a day of battling the airlines and their running dogs, you deserve a good night's sleep.

CHAPTER TWELVE

HOW TO DEAL WITH SPECIAL PROBLEMS OF AIR TRAVEL

What Causes Air Crashes

On average roughly three-quarters of commercial airline accidents are due to errors by the cockpit crew—especially on takeoff and landing. (Seventy-five percent of accidents occur within a thousand yards of the runway; ninety-five percent in the vicinity of the airport.) Once away from the runway, the main cockpit-crew error causing accidents is running into mountains and other aircraft which shouldn't be there.

How can cockpit crews cause such a high percentage of crashes? All you have to do is listen to the flight recorders retrieved from the little black (actually orange) box after the crashes. Were the pilot and copilot talking about how best to fly the plane? No. They were chattering away about sex, politics, sports and how to fix their home lawn-mower.

Following the cockpit crew, the next major causes are mechanical. This is not surprising, considering the number of things which could go wrong. The average 747, for instance, has 4.5 million parts and over 135 miles of electrical wiring. Each engine alone has over 5,000 moving parts. The breakdown of mechanical causes of crashes in order of most common occurrence: engine problems, in-flight fires, airframe failure (doors blowing out, tail sections breaking off, engines deciding to go off on their own with part of the wing in tow) and instrument faults.

After mechanical causes comes weather: hail, ice, lightning, cargo breaking loose in rough air, bird strikes, clear-air turbulence, mountain waves, wind shear and low density air— although often these weather problems are tied in with pilot error.

Finally come the miscellaneous causes, such as ground staff putting in X *liters* of fuel when it should have been X *gallons,* hijackings (approximately 500 in the last 15 years, although few resulting in accidents), bombs (approximately 25 in the last 15 years) and being shot down by Russians or Americans.

Are Flights as Safe as They Could Be?

Answer: No.
And why not?
Two reasons:

1.   **The airlines' cost/benefit approach to safety.** Of course, no airline wants a crash. There are the costs of replacing the plane, the costs of claims for dead or injured passengers and the loss of future business due to the bad publicity. (One of the first things an airline will do after an accident is get a crew out to the scene to cover the tail logo with a

tarpaulin or paint, so it doesn't feature on the nightly news.) But in deciding how much it should do to avoid a potential crash, the airline necessarily has to apply a cost-benefit analysis.

In principle, I don't have a problem with employing a cost-benefit analysis to safety. There has to be a financial limit somewhere. The problem I have is that in practice the cost/benefit calculation employed by the airline is not necessarily the same one I would employ. The benefit to the airline of my living is a lot less than the benefit to me of my living. At the same time, unless the safety requirements are government-mandated for all airlines, the costs to the airline of additional safety will be much greater for the airline since it will be unable to pass much of the costs on to me and its other passengers.

Even the benefits to the airline of avoiding a crash are not always that clear. Do you remember when that former prominent regional airline crashed a narrow-body in the southeast a few years ago? Well apparently the airline booked a $1.5 million *profit*. The insurance proceeds, which covered the plane's fair market value, exceeded by $1.5 million the depreciated value of the plane on the airline's books.

I'm sure in the long run the crash cost the airline money—in damages to passengers and future lost business from nervous customers. It's just that thereafter when the airline weighed all the costs and benefits of some marginal safety requirement, the costs of losing the plane would not have been as great as it otherwise would have been.

Because of this cost/benefit problem, one has look primarily to the government to make flights as safe as they possibly can be. And here, in the US, we encounter the second problem.

2. The government's "nightly news" approach to improvements in safety regulation. Under this approach, safety problems only become critical when they appear on the nightly news accompanied by harsh comments about the failure of the government to act—at which time the government immediately makes the least amount of improvement in the safety regulations necessary to take the matter out of the nightly news.

A few blatant examples:

(a) Safety inspectors. From 1981 to 1987, air traffic went up substantially. Airlines, however, did not increase their maintenance staff to keep pace. The government's response during this period: Reduce the number of FAA air-carrier safety inspectors by 20 percent and reduce the number of inspections. That is, until Ralph Nader's Aviation Consumer Action Project brought the issue onto the nightly news and the FAA suddenly whacked its forehead, announced plans to increase the number of inspectors and began levying large fines on a few of the airlines which were violating the maintenance rules. (Even now, a few years later, the number of inspectors per aircraft flight is still significantly less than it was before 1981.)

(b) Aircraft age. During the same period air traffic increased, the average age of aircraft in service increased by over 25 percent, making airframe failure more likely. The government response: Nothing, until an aged Aloha Airlines plane was shown on the nightly news coming in for a landing without its roof. Then the FAA bravely began ordering stepped-up inspections of airframes and indicated that sometime in the 1990s it would begin to put an upper limit on the age of aircraft in service (by which time the 737s and other aircraft which are currently the problem would probably have already fallen apart).

Box 12-1.	Average Age of US Airline Fleets

Airline	15 Yrs Or Older
Pan Am	65.67%[1]
TWA	64.19%
Northwest	58.68%
Eastern	52.59%
United	51.94%
Continental	43.73%
American	35.58%
USAir	30.57%[2]
Delta	22.19%

1. The average age of aircraft for Singapore Airlines is four years; for Lufthansa, seven.
2. Includes data for Piedmont Airlines, which was acquired by USAir.
(Source: AVMARK, Inc.)

(c) Employee security screening. Consumer groups warned the FAA that there was inadequate security screening at the airport for airline employees. The government response: Nothing, until the nightly news showed the remains of a PSA plane which crashed after a disgruntled ex-airline employee boarded the plane with a gun and shot the pilots during the flight; then the FAA quickly instituted security screening for all airline employees.

(d) Interior smoke and fire. For years the FAA had continually been warned by consumer groups of the dangers to passengers of smoke and fire in the cabin in the event of a crash. The government's response: Very little, until the nightly news reported:

(1) A fire caused by a cigarette butt in the lavatory litter bin which killed all the passengers in the plane; then the government ordered smoke detectors put in all lavatories and eventually automatic fire extinguishers in the lavatory litter bin.

(2) Passengers dying of smoke inhalation in another aircraft fire because they couldn't find their way out. Then the government ordered the airlines to install lighting in the floor to show passengers the way to the exits.

(3) A crash in which all the passengers survived initial impact only to die from poisonous gases and smoke from the smoldering walls, carpets and seating. Then the government ordered all existing planes to have fire-blocking seat covers and the interiors of all new planes to meet more stringent flammability standards.

Needless to say, this "nightly news" approach does not lead to the most comprehensive approach to safety. Cabin walls are still not insulated from outside fire. Windows can still melt and fall out. Interiors, in existing planes, are still made of flammable and/or poisonous-smoke-producing plastics. Automatic fire extinguishers are still not required in sealed cargo holds. Sprinkler systems have still not been installed in the cabin. Smoke hoods have still not been required. Smoke sucking fans in the cabin ceiling have still not been installed. Airline seats are still designed to withstand fewer G-forces than an automobile seat. There are still no upper-body seat belts (although most passenger deaths during crashes are from head injuries) or, for that matter, rear facing seats (which are the norm on military flights). The life vests are still of World-War-II vintage, non-standardized and difficult to put on. The aircraft's floatable seat cushions are still rated by the US Coast Guard as unsuitable for nonswimmers and children. (If you hold them to your chest as advised, they'll turn you upside down and drown you.) The flight attendants' safety instruction still fails to tell you how to open the aircraft's emergency doors. Fuel tanks are still not crash-resistant. Fuel lines are still not self-sealing (as they are on military aircraft). The jet fuel used is still the type which will catch fire upon impact. (A recent test crash of a jet loaded with fuel designed to retard burning had to be terminated when the firemen were unable to put out the flames.)

Flights are still nowhere near as safe as they could be.

So Should You Be Afraid of Flying?

No.

Despite all the problems mentioned in the section above, statistically airline travel is still very safe. One study of the risks of various activities came up with the following rough estimates of deaths per million participant hours:

Climbing 40.000
Motorcycle Racing 35.000
Private Flying 30.000
Canoeing 10.000
Skiing 0.700
Amateur Boxing 0.500
Scheduled Airline Passenger 0.004

According to the Federal Highway Safety Administration, the rate of US automobile deaths per hundred million miles driven is roughly 2.41. According to the National Transportation Safety Board, the rate of scheduled commercial airline passenger deaths per hundred million aircraft miles for the last ten years has varied between zero and 0.2. In other words, looking at the worst year for aircraft, the risk of death in an automobile on a per-mile basis was still twelve times larger than in a plane.

Unfortunately, the Federal Highway Safety Administration does not keep records of automobile deaths per trip. However, for scheduled airline passengers, the National Transportation Safety Board reports that the deaths per million departures over each of the last ten years has varied from zero to a high of one. In other words, even in the worst year in the last ten years, the chances of you having a fatal accident on a given flight were one in a million.

What's one in a million mean? Well, according to the National Safety Council, each year on average more people are killed by lightning than in commercial air crashes.

So getting hyped up about the possibility of your flight crashing just ain't logical.

How Some People Try to Get Rid of an Irrational Fear of Flying

Polls have shown that about two out of five US passengers experience some level of fear while flying. About one-third to one half of these can be said to have a real fear of flying. And a large number of this latter group will not be calmed by the safety statistics recited in the previous section. Instead of becoming less afraid of flying, they will merely become more afraid of lightning.

Most people with an irrational fear of flying who have to fly try to handle their fear by attempting to concentrate on something else—reading a sexy magazine, engaging in conversation, getting blind drunk.

(Note, the latter route seldom works. Many alcoholic drinks contain congenors which after a few hours break down in your body and produce amphetamine-like substances which can increase your anxiety. If you're going to drink on a long flight, you've got to keep drinking more and more as you go along to counter the congenors.)

Some people try concentrating on what they will do in case of an accident. Determining how to brace their body. Picking the best emergency door, their route to it and the number of seats between them and it (in case they have to find it in the dark or smoke). Studying how the emergency door handle works. Rehearsing how their plans would differ if there were fire. *Etc.*

Although this approach is more likely not only to occupy their mind but also to make them feel much more confident about surviving a crash, it does require a special effort to overlook the fact that when the plane hits the ground at 650 miles an hour, nothing that they're doing inside is going to make a damn bit of difference.

The problem is that no matter how you try to block the fear of flying from your mind, you can't really block out the truth that you're crammed with several hundred people inside an aluminum can zooming through the air at close to the speed of sound with absolutely no control over your destiny.

The Only Sure Way to Fight an Irrational Fear of Flying

The only sure way to fight the fear of flying is not to try to avoid it but instead to confront it head on. Admit that your fear of flying is irrational and that the only way you'll lose it is to attack the fear itself.

There are three major techniques for doing this:

1.   Force yourself to take a lot of flights. If you reward your phobia by avoiding flying, you'll only increase its power. So first and foremost you've got to get in an airplane and keep flying. If your fear of flying is minor, then by constant air travel you hopefully will tend to become blasé about zooming through the air in an aluminum can, in the same way as by constant car travel you've become blasé about zooming down a two-lane highway with nothing but a white line and a few feet of air separating you from the cars coming the other way.

If you are a real aviophobic, however, taking a lot of flights is seldom sufficient by itself. Unless you are a member of airline staff, it's difficult to fly enough to overcome a fear of flying based on claustrophobia or acrophobia. Where the fear of flying is based on a fear of crashing, flying a lot may actually make real aviophobics begin to feel that the law of averages are starting to work against them. Although, as with dice, the odds on the next throw are exactly what they were at the beginning, emotionally the aviophobic begins to question whether the result can possibly come up "safe journey" for the ten-thousandth time in a row.

For that reason, forcing yourself to take a lot of flights usually has to be combined with the second technique.

2.   Judo your fear. Use the fear's greatest strength against the fear itself. Go it one better.

If your fear of flying is primarily one of claustrophobia, think of yourself trapped inside a coffin under the ground. If your fear of flying is primarily one of acrophobia, force yourself to look out the window and imagine yourself falling thirty-thousand feet. If your fear of flying is primarily a fear of an aircraft accident, try to imagine the effect on your body of being ejected into the freezing, near-vacuum of the upper atmosphere, of hitting the ground at the speed of sound, of being consumed alive in a ball of fire. Imagine your life ending or, worse, continuing, with your skin melted, your eyelids burned off, your internal organs exploded, your bones smashed to smithereens.

The more you do this, several things happen.

(a) First, by your imagining the most horrible occurrences, you make the more likely occurrences, *e.g.*, simple instant death, seem more attractive.

(b) Second, as there is nothing more fearful than an undefined fear, by describing explicitly what is likely to happen, you will tend to dissipate your fear.

(c) Third, by bringing your fears down to the most concrete level, you actually help to distance yourself emotionally from the disaster; you begin to look at yourself as an object and find yourself taking a morbid curiosity in how the disaster would affect you.

(d) Fourth, as with TV violence, by constantly repeating to yourself the horrors of a disaster, you tend to deaden the emotional impact of those horrors; after a while your mind just refuses to respond.

3. Practice relaxation techniques. By controlling the behavior of your body you can control your emotions. All the while you are judoing your fear, breathe slowly and deeply. As you find your mind wandering from the horrors you're describing (even phobias eventually get boring if you force yourself to continually confront them), begin consciously relaxing each part of your body from your toes up to your head. By the time you get to your head, don't be surprised if your fear of flying has been completely absorbed.

Fear of Flying Courses

For a longer, more detailed and undoubtedly less brutal method of confronting your fear of flying, consider enrolling in the perhaps oldest and best known fear of flying course, that given by Captain T.W. Cummings, (305)261-7042. His seminar of three three-hour evening meetings costs $300. In addition, he has an audio cassette with booklet for $25 and a book available in most airport book shops called, *Freedom From Fear Of Flying*, published by Pocket Books, ISBN 0-671-62863-1, for $3.95. If the difference between $300 and $3.95 means something to you, you might try the book first.

How to Survive a Crash

According to the statistics, two-thirds of the people involved in air crashes survive. Approximately one-third of the third who do die could have survived if they had known what to do and almost all of these died from smoke or fire.

If it seems certain the plane is going to crash, here's what to do while the plane is going down.

(a) Put your seat belt on and fasten it as tightly as possible.

(b) Check where all the emergency exits are, put them in order of priority and plan your route to each one. Interviews with survivors of air crashes confirm that the common element among the overwhelming majority was that they had a specific plan of action and followed through with it on their own. If you have time, study the emergency safety card; studies have shown that you are three times more likely to be injured during a crash if you haven't read the emergency safety card.

(c) Take sharp pencils, pens out of your clothes and remove dentures, high-heeled shoes and eyeglasses.

(d) Empty your bladder to reduce the chance of internal injury. (I bet you didn't think of that one, did you?)

(e) If you don't have a personal smoke hood (see below), moisten a handkerchief, headrest cover or shirttail, so if there's smoke after impact, you can hold it over your mouth. If no other liquids are handy, use your urine.

(f) If you've got time, pack for outside the plane, such as a sweater or coat to keep you warm and any medicines you will need.

(g) Cover your head, preferably with a pillow. Then either cross your arms over your calves and grab your ankles or put your palms-forward, crossed wrists between your head and the seat in front of you. In the latter position, it's best to slide your feet forward until they touch the seat leg or under-seat baggage in front, so your legs are less likely to snap forward on impact.

If you're still alive after the plane comes to a stop, that's when you should do the one thing which will most likely save your life, and that is, very simply, get the hell out of there as fast as you can.

In crash after crash in which the passengers survive impact, they just sit there, stunned, waiting to be told what to do. Often, the flight attendants, themselves stunned, fail to give directions right away. When the flight attendants finally do start talking, many of the passengers will still sit there as though in a trance. (Sometimes, on overseas flights, this is because the flight attendants in the pressure of the moment forget to speak in other than their own native tongue.) By the time the passengers finally get moving, the plane has filled with smoke, with flames and/or with panic-stricken fellow passengers trampling each other to get out.

So, as soon as the plane comes to a stop, undo your seat belt, leap out of your seat and move quickly to the exit. Don't take anything with you; you'll need your hands free to keep your balance in the aisle as you step over bodies and luggage or find yourself being pushed from behind by panic-stricken passengers. If the aisle is blocked, walk over the backs of the seats. Don't waste your time crawling on the floor to avoid any smoke; you'll only end up being trampled by and/or buried under all the other passengers who are suffocating. But if there is smoke, do keep your head down. You'll know you've arrived at the doors when the floor lights are red rather than white.

Do not, I repeat, do not push the passengers in front of you. You won't get through any faster and will only increase the chance of your being punched in the face, trapped by squirming bodies in the aisle or, most seriously, stuck behind a blocked door (see below).

When you finally arrive at an exit door, if it's not open, take a quick look out the window to see if there's fire there. If there is, run to the other side of the plane and open the door there.

The Trick to Opening an Airline Door

After you rotate the handle, the trick for most airline doors is to be sure you first pull the door *inwards*. For the major doors, you then slide the door *sideways out* through the door hole. For the emergency window doors, you simply keep pulling inwards and remove the door like a plug.

The doors operate this way to make it difficult for them to explode outward in case of a defect in or accidental opening of the latch. Unfortunately, this design also increases substantially the risks of panic-stricken passengers blocking up a door so that it can't be opened.

For that reason, if possible, in a post-crash situation, you should always try to avoid doors which have a lot of people around them. The more people pushing against the door, the less likely it is the door will be opened.

Where to Get a Smoke Hood

The FAA and its British counterpart, the CAA, have considered making smoke hoods compulsory but have decided that passengers stand a greater risk of injuring themselves by not knowing how to use them. I don't know what kind of dummies they conducted their tests on but the one smoke hood I'm familiar with is exceedingly simple. Known as the Survivaid smoke escape hood, it is basically a plastic bag which fits over the head. If you can pull a plastic bag over your head, you can use a Survivaid hood.

The Survivaid hood is made of a flame-retardant, nonmelting (up to 720 degrees Fahrenheit), clear polyimide and has a built-in filter capable of straining out smoke and neutralizing many of the fast-acting killer gases produced by the burning of synthetic materials, such as those in the interior of a plane. It can provide clean air for up to 30 minutes. In addition, during that time it will protect your skin, your hair and, most importantly for finding your way out, your eyes. The only major thing it won't protect against is carbon monoxide but in many fires, carbon monoxide apparently does not reach toxic levels during the first 30 minutes anyway.

Survivaid comes wrapped in a package eight-inches long, five-inches wide and a third-of-an-inch high and weighs less than two-and-a-half ounces. You should be able to find it in the airport shops—except in Britain where the CAA, so afraid that the average passenger would not know how to pull a plastic bag over his or her head, has banned the sale of any smokehoods at Heathrow and Gatwick. (Those British must be a pretty uncoordinated lot.) If you can't find a smoke hood in the shops, call Survival Products, Inc., at (817)923-0300. Cost: about $35.

Three Hints in Case Your Cabin Suddenly Loses Pressure During Flight

1. **Keep your mouth open.** You've got to equalize the pressure between inside and outside as quickly as possible. Trying to hold your breath will lead only to your lungs, your ears and various other parts of your body exploding.

2. **Pull the oxygen mask towards you until the string opens the valve.** No open valve, no oxygen.

3. **If you're a tobacco junkie, be sure to forget to take your cigarette out of your mouth when you put the oxygen mask on.** The explosive combination of oxygen and the smoldering weed should cure you rather quickly of your addiction—as well as cause you, after landing, to embark on a fairly extensive program of plastic lip surgery.

The Miracle Anti-Jet-Lag Drug

You know what jet lag is. That's when you fly from Los Angeles to Hong Kong for a conference and, while listening to the dinner speaker, distinguish yourself by falling asleep face-first into your mo-shu pork; or from San Francisco to London where, after a night watching *I Love Lucy* reruns on your hotel's closed circuit TV, you finally fall asleep at seven in the morning, are awakened at eight by the buzzer alarm and spend the next 45 minutes crawling around the bed trying to locate the off-button.

Well, there now exists a miracle drug which may immediately allow you to adjust to the change in time zones. It's called melatonin, a hormone secreted by the pineal gland, which helps regulate the sleep-wake cycle. Double-blind tests at the University of Surrey in England involving melatonin and placebos have shown that the substance can significantly reduce jet lag in over half the people taking it. And a great number of those experience virtually no jet lag at all.

So far all experiments have been conducted with just one dosage; the head of research on the project, Dr. Josephine Arendt, believes she may be able to increase the proportion experiencing no jet lag even higher once she begins varying the dosages to reflect differences in individual body chemistry.

The main problem with the drug for those who find it wipes out their jet lag is that it is not yet available on the market. The only way to get it is to be a guinea pig in the University's experiments—which I have been. And even that source is restricted since the project, as most University projects in England, is grossly underfunded. (Any drug companies out there reading this?)

If the project was properly funded, melatonin could be on the market in two years. As it is, it may take up to ten years before we can buy it at our local drugstore. Until then, we'll have to beat jet lag in the more traditional, labor intensive ways.

How to Adjust to Jet Lag Without Melatonin

Generally, traveling westward, if the average person doesn't do anything to combat jet lag, his body will adjust to the new time zone at roughly an hour a day. Traveling eastward the adjustment can take up to 50 percent longer. This is due to the simple fact that most people find it easier to fall asleep when they go to bed later than earlier and, likewise, most people find it easier to lie around in bed in the morning for a few extra hours than to bounce out of bed a few hours early.

Certain personality types find jet lag bothers them less: the young, the extroverted, the stable, the regimented (the latter because they are accustomed to living by the clock) and, depending in which direction they are going, morning people or night people.

To increase the speed at which you adjust to jet lag, you can do several things:

1. **Schedule an appropriate flight.** You want to choose a flight in which you:

   (a) **Have not been deprived of sleep.** Lack of sleep only compounds the problem of jet lag. This means not having to get up too early or stay up too late to catch your flight and, if possible, avoiding having to sleep on the plane.

   (b) **Arrive during the nonsleeping time on the destination clock,** so the strenuous activities involved in arrival are in sync with the destination clock.

   (c) **Arrive just a few hours before destination bedtime,** so one of the first things you do is go to bed, allowing the healing process of sleep to take over.

   Of course, it will be difficult, if not impossible, to find a flight which fits these three requirements, especially if it also has to fit the requirements of your business schedule. But at least you can take them into account.

2. **Follow the anti-jet-lag diet.** The anti-jet-lag diet is based on the following discoveries:

   (a) If the body's energy reserves are low, the body's internal clock is more easily adjusted by chemical and environmental stimulants.

   (b) Alternate days eating heavily and eating lightly prior to the change heightens this effect.

(**c**) High-protein meals give you five hours of long-lasting energy.

(**d**) High-carbohydrate meals give you a surge of energy for an hour and then make you want to sleep.

(**e**) A certain class of stimulants, of which caffeine is the major one, when administered in the morning, sets the body's clock back and when administered in the evening, sets the body's clock forward (despite the stimulative effect of the caffeine).

(**f**) These stimulants also deplete the body's energy reserves.

(**g**) In order for the stimulants to work most powerfully you have to go without them for a few days beforehand.

From these discoveries, the basic dietary rules which have been deduced are as follows:

Box 12-2.   The Four Anti-jet-lag Diet Rules

1. For one to three days before the change, alternate a day of heavy eating with a day of light eating (800 calories), scheduling the breakfast after you arrive to fall on a heavy-eating day.

2. Eat high-protein breakfasts and lunches and high-carbohydrate dinners both before and after you arrive.

3. Drink no caffeine or similar stimulants for one to three days before the day you want to initiate the change (depending how big a change it is). If you absolutely have to have a fix of caffeine, drink it between three and five o'clock in the afternoon.

4. When you want to initiate the change (usually the day of your flight):

(**a**) On westbound flights, drink caffeine (two or three cups of black coffee or strong tea) when it's morning time on your body clock.

(**b**) On eastbound flights, drink the caffeine between six and eleven in the evening body-clock time.

After that lay off the caffeine for at least a day.

From these four rules you should be able to construct a diet to fit into the practicalities of your own particular flight. However, if you need step-by-step instructions for each type of flight, I suggest you read *Overcoming Jet Lag*, by Dr Charles F. Ehret (the inventor of the diet) and

Lynne Waller Scanlon, published by Berkley Publishing Company, ISBN 0-425-08905-3. Cost: $5.95.

Note, if you are trying to adjust to a new time zone, you should probably avoid alcohol. Although the evidence is not clear, it appears that alcohol slows down the body's ability to adjust. Likewise avoid smoking; it brings on fatigue and carbon monoxide poisoning.

3.   Control your light. Light, particularly sunlight, is possibly as powerful as any chemical stimulant in adjusting your body's clock.

If you are at your destination, try to get outside into the sunlight as much as possible. Don't wear sunglasses. In the evening, keep your room brightly lit. Then when you go to bed, turn out all the lights, pull the curtains and put on eyeshades.

If you're in the plane and trying to adjust to a new time zone before you get there, alter your light in the plane in much the same way.

4.   Exaggerate your activities. The body adjusts to meet the requirements of its environment. The stronger the signals you give it, the faster it will adjust.

If on local time you should be active, then go out and do active things. Walk around. Exercise. Play a game of some sort. Be gregarious. Concentrate. Scheduling your flight to arrive at an active time can be a major assistance.

Do not, I repeat, do not take a nap; you'll find it hard to get up and you'll slow down your body's adjustment.

If on local time you should be inactive, then deprive yourself of all stimuli, including music, breath slowly and deeply and go to sleep. If you wake up in the middle of the night, try meditating, saying the word "OM" over and over again.

If you've started to change your time on the flight (as you normally would with the anti-jet-lag diet), then do the same sorts of things on the plane. On flights which arrive in the early morning local time, always try to get a few hours of rest immediately before arrival—even if your body clock is at afternoon. The quiet time not only helps reset your clock but refreshes you for the long day ahead.

5.   Reset your mind. Don't keep asking yourself what time it is where you came from. Don't try to adjust your schedule to fit your body's clock, such as eating a meal other than at the locally-proper time. Instead, throw your mind into the present as though you had no jet lag at all.

6.   Take a sleeping potion. If you can't get to sleep, you can turn to pills. Two of the better ones:

(a) **Halcion (generic: Triazolam).** A short-acting hypnotic your doctor can prescribe for you. Different from other sleeping pills, it is almost entirely metabolized in eight hours. There have been some cases of short-term memory loss and other side effects with the drug, so be sure to follow your doctor's advice precisely.

(b) **Tryptophan.** A relaxant extracted from turkeys available from health stores. (Now you know why you're so sleepy after Thanksgiving dinner.) Two 500 milligram tablets will make you sleepy and apparently, unlike sedatives, there's no lingering effect in the bloodstream. If you don't have any tablets, try drinking a glass of milk before bedtime; it's got tryptophan in it as well. (Note, tryptophan use has recently been linked to a rare blood disorder, eosinophilia; however, as of this writing, it is unclear whether the culprit is tryptophan or capsule contamination. To be safe, please consult your doctor first.)

How to Make Jet Lag Work for You

Whether or not you can easily adjust to jet lag, you should always consider trying to make jet lag work for you.

I have one investment banking friend in New York, who always schedules his negotiating sessions in London to start after lunch. He takes a red-eye over from New York, arriving about six in the morning. He gets to his hotel by seven, sleeps until one in the afternoon, has a "breakfast" and starts his negotiating at 2:30 P.M. (which would be 8:30 A.M. New York time). The negotiation goes on straight through into the evening, with dinner being sandwiches brought in about seven. After dinner when his London opponents begin to flag, he's still going strong. He keeps the negotiating going until two in the morning, by which time the Londoners are totally worn out.

The next day he sleeps again until one in the afternoon (while his opponents have to go into their offices in the morning to do other work) and starts the negotiations again at 2:30 P.M.

By forcing his opponents to conform to his own time zone, he effectively inflicts the jet lag on them rather than himself.

It's a neat trick but I don't think it would work against an American. It requires a polite opponent.

Remember to Synchronize Your Medicines

If you are taking periodic medication which depends on the body's rhythms, such as insulin or oral contraceptives, you may have to adjust the periodicity as your body adjusts to a new time zone.

Be sure to consult your doctor before you leave.

The Rights of the Disabled Air Passenger

Throughout the history of air travel, the disabled air passenger has faced a myriad of conflicting and often discriminatory airline rules. Many airlines had quotas. Some refused point blank to carry certain types of disabled. Each had its own definitions, notice provisions, charges, permitted mobility-aid devices, and so on.

Then, in 1986 Congress enacted the Air Carrier Access Act. Under this short, three-sentence Act, the Secretary of Transportation was instructed to:

> *promulgate regulations to ensure nondiscriminatory treatment of qualified handicapped individuals consistent with safe carriage of all passengers on air carriers.*

In mid-1988 the DOT promulgated a set of proposed regulations. Comments on the proposed regulations have been submitted by interested parties and the DOT will probably issue final regulations in mid-1989.

If you have a disability, when the final regulations come out you should go to your local law library and obtain a copy. They'll be under Title 14 of the Code of Federal Regulations, Part 382. They're likely to be less than ten pages long.

What's in the Currently Proposed Air Carrier Access Regulations

No one yet knows what will be in the final regulations; however, they're likely to contain much of what is in the proposed regulations. Basically those regulations prohibit the airlines from imposing any requirements or restrictions on you as a handicapped passenger unless such requirements or restrictions are necessary for the safe carriage of all passengers. There can be no other reason for imposing such requirements and restrictions. Following this basic idea, the proposed regulations then lay out a series of specific rules. Some of the more interesting ones:

1. **An airline cannot refuse to transport you solely because your handicap results in appearance or involuntary behavior that may offend, annoy or inconvenience crew members or other passengers.** Thus, for example, if you suffer from Tourette's Syndrome, which causes you to swear and make other loud noises, you can't be kept off the plane.

2. **You can't be prohibited from boarding because of any quotas for disabled passengers.**

3. **You can't be required to travel with an attendant, unless the you:**

(a) **Have a mental disability,** and either (i) are unable to comprehend or respond to safety instructions, or (ii) are brought to the airport under the supervision of the agent of a custodial institution and have not been discharged from the institution; or

(b) **Are on a stretcher;** or

(c) **Are (i) a quadriplegic who, in the opinion of the airline, cannot travel alone; or a blind and deaf person who, in the opinion of the airline, cannot receive and respond to safety-related instructions; and (ii) are not the first such quadriplegic or first such blind and deaf person on the flight.** If you're the first, you don't have to travel with an attendant, provided you accept the seat assigned by the airline.

4. **The airlines cannot require advance notice from you, unless you wish to use a respirator hookup, a stretcher, an onboard wheelchair or special packaging for a battery for a wheelchair or other assistive device.** In that case, the airline can require up to 48-hours notice, provided that if the airline can make the equipment or service available with a reasonable effort without delaying the flight, it must do so even if you fail to give the proper notice.

5. **The airlines can't require you to have a medical certificate as a condition to travel, unless you are on a stretcher, need oxygen, are in an incubator or have a communicable disease.**

6. **The airlines can't exclude you from a seat in an exit row or other location, or require you to sit in a particular seat on the basis of your handicap, except in order to comply with the requirements of an FAA safety regulation.** As of this writing the FAA is trying to decide whether there really is a safety reason to prohibit disabled passengers from certain rows—especially since the FAA doesn't prohibit the drunk, the elderly and the obese from sitting there. For discussion purposes, the FAA has proposed rules prohibiting such seating for anyone who is unable to open the exit door and has included automatically under that definition the deaf and the blind.

7. Subject to certain transition rules, all facilities provided by the airline on the ground or in the air must be accessible to you. On the ground, this includes things such as each terminal having at least one Telecommunication Device For The Deaf (see below) and each airline providing at least one TDD reservation line at the same cost to the passengers as other reservation lines. In the air, the regulations require most aircraft to have aisle seats with removable armrests, storage space for at least one folding wheelchair and specially-designed airline-provided onboard wheelchairs.

8. Upon request, the airlines have to provide the following to you:

(a) On the ground. Assistance in enplaning and deplaning, including, to the extent under the control of the airline, assistance in making flight connections, transfers between gate and aircraft and transportation between gates.

(b) In the air. Assistance in:

(1) Preparation for eating, such as opening packages and identifying food (but not in the actual eating itself).

(2) Moving to and from the rest-room with the aid of an onboard wheelchair if you need it (but not within the rest-room).

(3) Loading or retrieving carry-on baggage, including any mobility aids stowed on board.

Airline personnel do not have to provide medical services to you. Nor do they have to lift you personally onto the plane if the plane has under 19 seats.

9. Subject to FAA safety rules, the airlines have to permit you to bring on board (i) a personal ventilator/respirator with FAA-approved nonspillable batteries, (ii) a cane or other mobility aid and the equipment to carry these, and (iii) a folding wheelchair, and store them or their components in overhead compartments, under seats or in a first-come-first-serve special wheelchair storage compartment.

10. If your wheelchair cannot be stowed onboard, then each aircraft will have a dedicated wheelchair storage area in the cargo hold. Your wheelchair will have priority over all other baggage except baggage brought by passengers who made their reservation before you did—

which means you should make your reservation as early as possible. The airline must check the wheelchair and return it to you as close as possible to the door of the aircraft. The wheelchair must be among the first items retrieved from the baggage compartment.

11. Electric wheelchairs must be transported in an upright position, if possible, so that batteries do not have to be removed. If the battery has to be detached, the airline will provide special safety packaging. If the wheelchair has been disassembled in any way, including removal of the batteries, the airline has to put it back together before returning it. The airline cannot not drain the batteries. You have right to assist with the disassembly and reassembly.

12. The airline liability limit for damage to mobility aids on domestic flights is twice the normal limit. That is, $2,500 rather than $1,250. For international flights, the airline limit is the same as for other baggage. That is, the Warsaw Convention limit of approximately $640. (See above at page 298.) The regulations provide that the airlines cannot require you to sign waivers of liability for damage to your mobility aids.

13. You are allowed to take any required service animal to your seat. Service animals includes not only seeing and hearing guide dogs but animals such as trained monkeys used to provide manual assistance to the paralyzed. The airline can require you to produce proper documentation that your animal in fact is a service animal. As long as there is no safety problems, the animal can be in any row you can sit in. Of course, it sits on the floor, not on the seat.

14. Airlines cannot restrict your movement in the terminals, require you to remain in a holding area or other location or otherwise impose separate treatment for you, such as requiring you to preboard if you don't want to.

15. Upon request the airline has to tell you what limitations there are on disabled persons seating, mobility aids storage and lavatory accessibility, so you can decide whether another flight would be better for you. The airline also has to make sure you get the same information as all the other passengers.

16. You can't be required to accept an individual safety briefing, unless, in the airline's judgment, you'll need assistance to get to an exit in the event of an emergency, or unless you request special assistance in boarding or respond to an invitation to preboard due to disability. In addition, even if you have to accept the individual briefing, you can't be required to demonstrate that you have listened to, read or understood it, unless the airline imposes that requirement on all of its passengers.

17. You can't be subject to special security screening. Basically this means you get a chance like everyone else to go through the security system with your mobility aid without setting off the alarm, and, if you get through, the security personnel can't search your mobility aid unless they feel it might conceal a weapon or other prohibited item. You can't be forced to have a private screening to a greater extent or for a different reason than nondisabled passengers. On the other hand, if you request a private screening in a timely manner, the airline must provide it in time for you to enplane, unless the airline employs technology which obviates the necessity of a physical search. Note the DOT defines a "timely manner" as arriving at the screening area 30 minutes earlier than normal.

18. The airlines cannot charge you for any of the above special services they are required to provide. However, this does not mean that they can't charge you for other services, such as providing oxygen.

19. Complaints resolution procedure. To ensure airline compliance, the regulations provide for the following:

(a) **A complaints resolution officer.** Each airline has to have an immediately-available, specially-trained complaints resolution officer who will have the power to resolve complaints on the spot.

(b) **An officer's written explanation.** If the officer does not resolve the issue to your satisfaction, he or she must provide you with a written explanation at the airport if possible, otherwise forwarded to you within five days.

(c) **Written complaint.** Whether or not you complain at the airport, you can, within 30 days, complain in writing to the airline. Within 30 days of receipt, the airline must make a written disposition of the claim.

(d) **DOT appeal.** A written explanation of the adverse decision of the complaints resolution officer or the airline must state that you have ten days from receipt to appeal to the DOT. If you do appeal, the DOT will give the airline 30 days to respond and then make a final administrative determination.

20. Compensation for a denial of your rights. Similar to the denied boarding compensation rules, if your rights are violated, the airline must pay you the following compensation:

(a)   Unnecessary attendant. If the airline has illegally required you bring along an attendant, it will pay you all the costs of bringing along the attendant up to twice the cost of the attendant's ticket.

(b)   Denied boarding. If the airline has prevented you, your service animal or essential mobility aid from going on board and the airline cannot arrange alternate transportation which will arrive within two hours of your original flight (four hours on international flights), the compensation is the lesser of (i) twice the one-way value of your ticket and (ii) $400. The airline can offer you flight vouchers of equal or greater value, but must inform you that you can demand the cash if you want.

(c)   Other violations. For other violations, the compensation is halved to the lesser of (i) the one-way value of your ticket (or if you didn't get a ticket because of the violation, then the value of the ticket you would have purchased) and (ii) $200.

(d)   DOT appeal. If the airline loses on appeal to the DOT, an additional $150 is added to the award.

(e)   Other rights. You, of course, still have your rights to sue for damages, including, possibly, a private right of action under the Air Carrier Access Act itself.

21. **Who must comply.** The requirements of the Act apply to:

(a)   All US airlines. This includes charter airlines but does not include any foreign airlines, even when they are flying within the US.

(b)   All persons under contract to US airlines. To the extent the airline contracts out any of its services, the contract must contain a requirement that the contractor obey the regulations. In addition, the airline will remain liable for any discriminatory actions of the contractor. This includes not only airport personnel but also travel agents.

How much of these proposed regulations will survive the current intensive airline industry lobbying against them is open to question. To the extent that any of the provisions do not survive (or you are flying a foreign airline, to which the regulations do not apply), you will have to fall back on the various airlines' conditions of carriage to determine your rights.

(For an idea of what foreign airlines require, there's a good pamphlet put out by IATA entitled, *Incapacitated Passengers Air Travel Guide*, available from Publications Agent, International Air Transport Association, 2000 Peel Street, Montreal Quebec, Canada H3A 2R4, for US$3.)

Which Flight a Disabled Passenger Should Choose

Before choosing a flight, you should have your travel agent compare the handicapped passenger sections of the conditions of carriage of the possible airlines in order to determine which gives you the greatest rights. After that, you should try to choose a flight which:

(a) **Is nonstop or direct,** so you don't have to change planes.

(b) **Is uncrowded,** so you (and your service animal, if you have one) can spread out. (See *How to Choose the Less Crowded Flight* above at page 30.)

(c) **Departs and arrives from gates close to the entrance to the terminal.** (See *The Most Important Speed Factor* above at page 21.)

(d) **Boards via a skyway rather than stairs or, if all flights board via stairs,** has either a lifting device for raising you (and your chair, if you have one) onto the plane, or a special wheelchair which can climb the stairs with you in it.

(e) **Allows you to take your wheelchair into the cabin,** or, if the wheelchair is stored in the baggage hold during flight, allows you take the wheelchair to the aircraft door on departure and pick it up there after arrival.

(f) **Provides a bicycle container to protect your wheelchair** while it is in the hold.

(g) **Has a wide aisle.** (Ask your travel agent or check the *Airline Seating Guide* mentioned above at page 42.)

(h) **Provides you with an aisle seat near both the exit door and the rest-room.** Many airlines reserve specific seats for handicapped passengers. (See the *Airline Seating Guide*.) Others also prohibit handicapped passengers sitting in certain seats, such as at emergency exits or on opposing aisles.

(i) Can get you from the door of the plane to your seat with a minimum loss of dignity. The better airlines have armless, narrow wheelchairs which can take you down the aisle.

(j) Uses an aircraft specially configured for handicapped passengers in onboard wheelchairs, such as certain of the new 767s which have movable aisle-seat armrests, oversize lavatory doors, low-entry thresholds, built-in assist devices, a lowered door latch, lever handles for toilets and doors, increased floor space and a ten-foot-square screened area next to the toilet to accommodate an attendant or extra maneuvering room.

Three Tips for the Disabled Passenger

1. Medical certificates. If you are a frequent flyer, ask the medical department of any IATA airline to issue you a Frequent Travellers Medical Card. This prevents you from having to get airline-physician approval every time you fly (especially on international flights) as well as avoiding the hassle, as sometimes happens, of having to get such approval on each leg of an interline connecting flight.

2. Accompaniment. If you feel you will need someone to accompany you but don't know anyone or don't want to pay the full extra fare, try Travel Buddies at (612)881-5364, a membership exchange which assists in finding traveling companions. You may find someone going your way who will accompany you for a cut price.

3. Route planning. Before you leave home, obtain the free booklet, *Access Travel: A Guide To Accessibility of Airport Terminals*, published by the Airport Operators Council International, Inc. You can get it from the Consumer Information Center, Pueblo, CO 81009. The booklet covers over seventy factors for over 500 terminals in 62 countries, including handicapped parking, hand-controlled rental cars, medical services, escort services, slope of ramps, placement of handrails, door threshold heights, handles versus knobs, height of elevator controls, height of mirrors in the toilets and raised lettering on the phone buttons.

A copy of the above information is also available in your travel agent's *OAG Travel Planner* (mentioned above at page 27) under the section on airport facilities for the handicapped and the elderly. In addition, the *Planner* also has lists of which buses, limousines, car rental companies and tour operators provide handicapped services.

Using this information in conjunction with the *Airport Pocket Guide* or similar source, you can plan your route from ground transportation to the gate at the departure airport and from the gate through baggage claim and out to ground transportation at the arrival airport.

Note, in the newer US airports you shouldn't have much problem moving around, since federal law requires any airports built with government funds to have barrier-free facilities.

The Rights of a Disabled Passenger in Case of Emergency

Airline safety procedures generally require nonambulatory passengers to be exited last in order not to block the aisle for ambulatory passengers. So if your plane has crashed and is being evacuated, don't start demanding your rights. You haven't got any.

If You are Hard of Hearing, Three Devices You Can Use in Connection with Airline Travel

1. **Phone amplifiers.** Some banks of public phones at airports have at least one amplifying handset. You may also purchase a pocket amplifier from your hearing-aid supplier.

2. **Induction devices.** Most hearing aids have "T" switches which allow them to pick up radio signals by induction. All US public telephones at airports should have a "blue grommet" at the base of the handset indicating that the phone has an induction coil which will broadcast the electronic sound signal to a hearing aid with the "T" switch. The advantage of this is that the hearing aid will then pick up only the sound from the phone, cutting out all background noise.

3. **Telecommunication Devices For The Deaf.** TDDs are Teletype systems which operate over any phone line, allowing the deaf person to communicate by sight rather than hearing. Many major airlines, rental car agencies, hotel chains and airport Travelers Aid stations now have them. There are also portable models which you can take with you when you travel and hook up to a phone.

For more detailed information on available hearing assistance devices, write to Self Help for Hard of Hearing People, Inc., 7800 Wisconsin Avenue, Bethesda, MD 20814.

Box 12-3.	TDD Phone Numbers	
Transportation Company	**800 Number**	
Alaska	.686-2221	
American Airlines	.543-1586	
	582-1573	OH
Braniff	.356-3889	
Continental	Use Eastern's	
Delta Airlines	.831-4488	
Eastern Airlines	.325-3553	
Midway	No 800 #	
	(312)582-9152	
Northwest Airlines	.328-2298	
	692-2105	MN
Pan American Airways	.722-3323	
Trans World Airlines	.421-8480	
	252-0622	CA
United Airlines	.426-1122	
USAir	.245-2966	
	242-1713	PA
Avis Car Rental	.331-2323;	
	942-8819	IL
Hertz Car Rental	.654-2280	
	(405)751-6122	OK
National Car Rental	.328-6323;	
	(612)830-2134	MN
Directory Assistance/		
Operator	.855-1155	

When You are Too Sick to Fly

The Commission On Emergency Medical Services of the American Medical Association has published a list of several medical conditions which may make it dangerous for you to fly. Most of the dangers arise because of (i) the reduced cabin air pressure, (ii) the lowered oxygen content of the air in the cabin, (iii) the motion of the plane, (iv) the stress of traveling or (v) the unavailability of adequate medical treatment if something should go wrong. Among the more prominent items on the list:

1. Severe high blood pressure or heart disease, particularly if you've had a heart attack within 30 days or a stroke within 14 days. [What the reason is for the 16-day difference, I haven't a clue.]

2. Pneumothorax (air outside the lung).

3. Cysts of the lung or severe lung disease.

4. Acute sinusitis or middle ear infections.

5. Abdominal surgery within 14 days, acute diverticulitis or ulcerative colitis, acute esophageal virices or acute gastroenteritis.

6. Severe anemia, sickle cell disease (above 22,500 feet) or hemophilia with active bleeding. [Good God.]

7. Recent eye surgery.

8. Wired jaws. [At first I thought this was because you wouldn't be able to yell for help. Later I learned the real reason: You might become airsick and choke on your own vomit.]

9. Pregnancy beyond 240 days (or less if threatened miscarriage).

10. Epilepsy (unless medically controlled and cabin air pressure is below 8,000 feet).

11. Recent skull fracture.

12. Brain tumors.

13. Violent and unpredictable behavior. [Hear, hear.]

14. Scuba divers if within 24 hours of last dive (because of danger of the bends).

If you think you may be one of these people or have some other similar affliction, consult your doctor and then be sure to book a flight other than mine.

There's nothing I can imagine worse than being stuck on a flight full of epileptic, wire-jawed, one-eyed pregnant scuba divers engaging in violent and unpredictable behavior brought about by the air outside their lungs blowing up their chests to twice normal size and popping the stitches in their abdominal surgery.

I mean, let's have a little consideration for others, huh?

Pacemakers

If you have a pacemaker, do not get near the magnetic metal detector in airport security.

Some of these metal detectors can interfere with a pacemaker's rhythms.

How to Get Your Pet into the Cabin with You

Very simple. Before you choose your flight, have your travel agent get out the good old conditions of carriage for each prospective airline and read what their detailed policies are. Then, choose the one which:

(a) Allows pets in the cabin. Some of them, such as Delta, don't.

(b) Allows your type of pet into the cabin. Most allow dogs, cats and household birds. Others also allow rabbits and similar animals.

(c) Has the largest quota of pets in the cabin. Many which do allow pets in the cabin, allow only one per cabin; others, one per section. The larger the plane, usually the larger the quota.

(d) Does not charge you for taking your pet into the cabin. Some of them, like Eastern, do.

(e) Allows you to make a reservation ahead of time for a pet in the cabin. Some board pets only on a first-check-in, first-serve basis.

(f) Has the largest under-seat space, since in most cases you will be able to take the animal into the cabin only if you can keep it in a cage which fits under the seat.

A friend of mine claims he got his pet dog on once by using a square-handled halter and pretending to be blind. Guide dogs, as mentioned above, are not only accepted in the cabin on most flights without quota but they also don't need to be caged.

My friend points out that this trick is unlikely to work if your dog is a Chihuahua. In that case, with sufficient chutzpah, you might consider trying to qualify under the exception in most conditions of carriage for (i) dogs trained to sniff out explosives ("I tell you, these here little buggers have got amazing noses. Here, boy! Smell! Smell!"), or (ii) dogs on an official search-and-rescue mission. ("You ever seen one of these little babies pull an ox out of quicksand? It's downright unbelievable!")

Don't be surprised, though, if the airline asks you to produce an official photo-identification card which describes you as a dog-handler or as someone who is blind, deaf or totally insane.

How to Ship Your Pet as Excess Baggage—General Rules

"What?" I hear you saying. "Ship my pet as excess baggage? What kind of pet owner do you think I am?"

Well, I imagine, like most pet owners, you are a person with an emotional void which can be filled only by a creature with sub-human intelligence. However, that has nothing to do with the issue at hand.

"Excess baggage", you see, is the way most airlines classify pets shipped in the cargo-hold when their owners are in the cabin. The airlines classify them that way so they can charge you for the shipment. (Usually $25 to $50.) Otherwise you might be able to include it in your free baggage allowance.

Of course, there are a few airlines which allow you to ship the animal for free if the container fits within the free-baggage-allowance dimensions. On the other hand, there are also a few (primarily the smaller) airlines which won't allow you to ship animals as baggage, no matter how little the containers are or how much you pay.

Of the majority of airlines which allow animals to be shipped as baggage, many will not allow it (i) on some of their (often smaller) aircraft, (ii) on certain routes (often those involving interline connecting flights if you're not going to claim the animal between flights), and (iii) at certain times of year (usually excessively hot or cold periods). Also, several of these airlines have quotas for checked animals which might be filled by the time you show up.

Moral: Always check ahead of time with the airline you are flying to see what is allowed.

How to Ship Your Pet as Excess Baggage—Special Rules

If your animal is being shipped as baggage (excess or free), the airlines and the US Department of Agriculture normally have several rules you must follow. Among the major ones:

(a) Notice. You have to give advance notice (usually 24 to 48 hours) to the airline. This is particularly important for the airlines which have a quota on the number of pets they will carry.

(b) Age. If traveling alone, the pet must be at least 8 weeks old and fully weaned.

(c) Health certificate. The pet must have a health certificate from a veterinarian issued not more than, usually, seven to ten days before the flight. (You'll want to check with a veterinarian anyway to make sure your pet will survive the flight. Certain animals, such as pug-nosed dogs, have difficulty breathing.)

(d) Temperature certificate. If it's winter, the airline may also require a veterinarian's certificate (issued ten days before) stating that your pet is acclimated to temperatures lower than 45 degrees Fahrenheit.

(e) USDA-approved container. You can purchase these from pet stores and most airlines. Among other things, they should:

(1) Be large enough so that the animal can freely stand, turn around and lie down.

(2) Contain no more than one adult dog or cat; or no more than two puppies or kittens younger than six months or under twenty pounds.

(3) Include a water dish (empty) which is accessible from the outside.

(4) Contain absorbent material or litter.

(5) Display feeding instructions (even if your pet is to receive neither food nor water); if any food is necessary, it should be in a bag attached to the outside of the container.

(6) Display a "LIVE ANIMALS" label with letters at least one-inch high and arrows or other indications of which end should be up.

Not all the above requirements are observed by all the airlines. In addition, several of the airlines have additional restrictions they can impose. So be certain to consult your airline before booking your flight.

How to Ensure that Your Pet Has a Comfortable Trip

1. Book an uncrowded nonstop or direct flight. If you have to book a connecting flight, go for the on-line connection. On interline connections, the container will often have to go to baggage claim first for you to claim it and then be rechecked onto the other airline, repeating again all the approval procedures you went through on the first leg.

2. Choose a time of day when the temperatures are unlikely to be either too hot or too cold. The USDA sets allowable temperature limits for animal holding-areas but it's best not to push your luck. If the airline thinks the USDA limits can't be maintained, they won't ship your pet.

3. Get the pet used to the container. Leave it around the house for a few weeks before the trip with familiar objects inside.

4. Limit eating and drinking. Keep your pet from eating anything within six hours before departure and drinking anything within two hours before departure (except in hot weather).

5. Don't try to sedate your pet with drugs unless your veterinarian recommends it. The effect at lower air pressure could be fatal.

6. Mark the container with your pet's name, your name and the telephone number at your destination. If the container gets lost, your pet will want to be found as soon as possible.

Shipping Your Pet as Unaccompanied Cargo

If you fail to meet the excess baggage requirements for some reason or you aren't going to be traveling on the same plane (so your pet can't qualify as baggage), you can ship your pet as unaccompanied cargo. The rules and techniques are generally the same as for excess baggage, except (i) you deal with the airline's cargo staff rather than passenger staff, (ii) you'll pay the (probably higher) cargo rates, (iii) on interline connections, the container will go straight from one plane to the other without having to be claimed at baggage claim in between, and (iv) at your destination it will probably take longer to get your pet.

Picking Up Your Pet at the End of the Trip

Some of the airlines have set deadlines for your picking up your animal after the flight. For those that do, the deadline is usually four to six hours, although a few, such as Midway, give you only an hour. If you don't show up in time, the airlines send the animal off to a shelter and send the bill to you.

Taking Your Animal Abroad

If you are taking your animal (including a guide dog) to another country, be sure to check what the vaccination and quarantine requirements are in the foreign country. Many of the "island" countries, such as Britain, Ireland, New Zealand and Australia require a quarantine of four to six months, no matter how vaccinated your animal has been.

Shipping Cheaply by Air

The cheapest and often quickest way to ship an article by air is to find a passenger who is intending to fly to the appropriate destination and ask him or her to take your article with them. If the package is large and/or difficult to inspect, the only free couriers you will be able to find will be friends. To encourage them, offer them some payment. You'll be able to afford it, as the savings will be considerable—particularly if the item is too large to mail.

On international flights back to the US, you not only save the air freight charges but also the customs handling-charges. For instance, if you wanted to ship door-to-door from London to New York a $400, 70-pound item, the various charges would be as follows:

Box 12-4. Comparative Shipping Costs			
	Shipping	**Handling**[1]	**Total**
Vessel[2]	$75	$50	$125
Airline's Freight[3]	$165	$37	$202
Air Freight Forwarder[3]	$66	$66	$132
Friend Excess Baggage[3]	$63	-	$63
Friend Within Baggage Limit[3]	-	-	$0

1. Includes customs handling. Duty would have to be paid in all four methods. Since the item was not owned by your friend, it would not qualify for the $400 duty exemption for returning residents. You might save the duty by having your friend claim the item was his, but you would be encouraging him to commit a crime for which he could be fined and possibly jailed.

2. Takes six weeks rather than overnight.

3. Assumes that the packages handled by freight forwarder, air freight company and friend are all sent on the same flight on same airline, just under a different procedure.

Now you know why DHL, the international air package express company, was built primarily on their perfection of the transporting of packages as the luggage of couriers on commercial flights.

If your package is small, it's probably easier to use the various express small-package services. Most of them have offices at the airport as well.

If (i) you're at the airport, (ii) there's no small package express service easily available and (iii) what you want to ship are unbomblike-appearing documents, you could look up in your pocket flight guide the next flight home, go to the check-in desk for that flight and approach respectable-looking people in the line to take them for you. If someone agrees, you could then have them met by a home-office employee outside flight arrivals with the appropriate sign. I used this a few times on flights from London to San Francisco, choosing young Englishwomen who looked like they were going on vacation. I told them that they'd be met by a young single man from the firm who would show them around San Francisco. It worked every time and was great for employee morale at the San Francisco office.

How to Air-Hike

Air-hiking, or hitching by air, takes place at the "general aviation" or private air terminal at the airport. It requires a lot of time and patience.

Different from normal hitchhiking there will be a lot fewer people going your way so the wait can be quite long. But like normal hitchhiking your chances of getting picked up when people are going your way depends on you (i) having little luggage, (ii) appearing nonthreatening, and/or (iii) being sexually attractive to the person in charge.

Females, as you might imagine, find air-hiking much easier than males. If you are a male, you are most likely to be picked up if you can appear as an overawed student or marine recruit ready to be impressed by a flight in a private plane. If you're too old for that, then your best chance is to create a sense of urgency.

"There aren't any more commercial flights out of Bismarck to Minneapolis today. You're my only hope."

Air-hiking, as I indicated, is used primarily as a method of traveling free. Occasionally, however, you might be in a situation where, in fact, air-hiking is your only hope of reaching your destination in time. In that case, you can increase your chances of getting a flight by offering to pay the pilot what your commercial airfare would have cost. Since he's flying to your destination anyway, everything you're willing to pay him is pure gravy.

How to Travel with Children

Robert Benchley once said there are two classes of travel: first class and with children.

If you are unfortunate enough to be traveling with small children, then most of the advice I've given you in this handbook will be irrelevant. Most of that advice, you see, is based on your ability to travel light, travel fast and travel free—none of which you'll be able to do with small children.

You'll be weighed down with an extra case—twice as large as one would expect for the average four-hundred-pound adult—and half a ton of extra carry-on—a stroller, a fleece, two or three life-sized stuffed toys, several spare layers of fireproof clothes and the ubiquitous big bag of disposable diapers. Try to sneak your two normal carry-on bags onto the plane as well and the gate staff will fall about laughing.

In addition, you'll be covering the distance between two points with all the pace and linearity that someone with fifteen-inch legs and the attention span of a hamster can muster. "Daddy, come back here, look, a gum wrapper on the floor! Oh, can I have a Coke from this machine? What's that wire coming out of the wall over there? Look at this thing in the window! Can I have it? Oh, no, did you see that funny lady who just passed us? Stop, no, the one down there. Wait, an airplane's taking off, can I watch it, please. Oh, no, Daddy, I've got to go wee-wee, quick!"

So much for traveling swiftly and inconspicuously from one flight to another.

With children, you will also have a much more inflexible schedule. Your family-plan tickets will probably be cancelable only with a substantial penalty. If there is no penalty, you will find it next to impossible to make suitable new arrangements on the spot for your spouse and children (rather than just you). And if you can make such an arrangement, you're unlikely to be able to move your children and their luggage (much of it no doubt already checked) to the correct places in time to take advantage of such arrangements. Just as in most other areas of your life, children will have severely limited your freedom.

The worst thing about traveling with children, of course, is the disturbances they create on the plane—fighting, crying, yelling, running up and down the aisle, spilling food all over the floor, kicking the seat in front of them, cornering some neighboring passenger in an interminable, mindless conversation, or standing on the seat and leaning over to smile with a variety of missing teeth at the people behind. (This is the real reason D.B. Cooper bailed out of that TWA night-flight over the Cascade mountains in 1971.)

The primary goal in traveling with children, you see, is not to travel lightly, quickly or flexibly, but merely to get through the experience without committing pedocide.

Some parents try to deal with the problem logically by drugging the little cretins before departure. Most, though, like me, forgo chemical assistance and reduce themselves to either bickering with the kid on the same childish level or, in the alternative, desperately catering to its every whim.

One mother I know, however, a reader of pop psychology books, has come up with what she describes as the perfect approach.

"Take the case of your toddler heading off by himself down the aisle," she says. "What concerns you is not really his safety. He's unlikely to get run over or trampled, and, wherever he goes, he'll still be on the plane when it lands. Nor are you concerned that the noise he may make as he stumbles along will disturb your concentration on your airport novel. With any luck, by the time he gets really noisy, he'll be out of earshot.

"No, what concerns you is that your child's activities might disturb the other passengers and thereby cause you embarrassment."

According to this woman, if that is the real problem, then the solution, from the briefest reading of any self-help psychology book, is obvious.

"Forget about what other people think. As long as the kid isn't bothering you, why should you worry whether he's bothering anyone else? I mean, if you've got to put up with him for a lifetime, they can damn well stand him for a few hours."

No, the woman is not my wife.

When a Child Under Two Can't Travel for Free and How to Avoid the Situation Arising

On most domestic flights, you can take a child under two years of age with you for free (ten percent on most international flights). However, for most airlines, this exception applies only to *one* child per adult. If you have a second child under two, that child must pay the fare for a child over two, usually 80 percent of the adult fare (60 percent, on international flights).

Fortunately, since there is no requirement that the child be related to the adult, with a little planning you can fly your second child for free by finding another passenger on the plane who will officially "accompany" your second child. Note, normally, to qualify as an "adult" that other passenger need only be 12 years of age.

US Airline Policy on Unaccompanied Minors

Each airline's conditions of carriage set out its policies on minors flying unaccompanied. Generally, however, most US airlines conform to some version of the following policy:

(a) **Definition of child.** A child is defined as someone under 12 years of age and is treated as unaccompanied if he or she is not accompanied by someone 12 years or older.

(b) Under five. If under age five, the child will not be accepted unaccompanied under any circumstance.

(c) Five through seven. If aged five, six or seven, the child may be accepted on a nonstop or direct flight, and must be accompanied by a responsible adult until boarded and met by a responsible adult after deplaning.

(d) Eight through eleven. If aged eight through eleven, the child may be accepted on connecting flights as well if reservations are confirmed through to his or her destination. Again, the child must be accompanied by a responsible adult until boarded and met by a responsible adult after deplaning. The airline will assist children to make connections.

(e) Twelve through fifteen. If aged twelve through fifteen, assistance may be requested from the airline in making connections.

(f) Unaccompanied-minor form. Before the flight an unaccompanied-minor form or travel card must be filled out for the child giving all relevant information, including name and phone number of the responsible adult meeting the child. Proper identification and signature are required before the child's release.

(g) Fare. The fare for the child will be the *adult* fare plus a charge of $20 to $30 if the flight involves escort assistance in making a connection. The latter charge is per group rather than per child.

Of course, as with everything else, different airlines have different versions of the above rules. Some allow only on-line connections. Others don't allow connections if it's the last flight of the day. Some don't allow any bus travel if the flight is diverted. So, again, check with the various airlines to determine the details.

Note, if you can't meet any of the above conditions, so your child would otherwise have to fly accompanied, there are child escort services which will accompany your child. Check with your airline to see what they recommend or try Travel Buddies mentioned above at page 360.

Note, also, for most airlines, unaccompanied children cannot ship pets as checked baggage.

For additional information, write for the free pamphlet, *Kids and Teens In Flight*, available from the Office of Consumer Affairs, Room 10405, US Department of Transportation, 400 Seventh Street, S.W., Washington, DC 20590.

How to Get the Most Assistance When Traveling with Children

I don't want to leave you with the impression that if you travel with children, you will find everything stacked against you. Far from it. There are many sources of assistance for parents traveling with children. You need only be aware and ask.

1. Special supervised play areas at some airports. Contrary to what some parents would hope, these are usually not in the middle of the runway. And not all airports have them. But the better ones, such as Heathrow and La Guardia, do. They're not well signposted, so you need to ask airport information or call on the courtesy phone to locate them.

2. Elevators and alternate ramps for strollers. Although many escalators say that no strollers are allowed, I have never seen an airport authority enforce this prohibition.

3. Nursing mother rooms. These are designed both to give the mothers privacy and to protect fastidious passersby who find suckling babies offensive. The rooms usually also have facilities for changing a baby's diapers.

4. Special baby-changing toilets. The better airlines provide at least one on the airplane which is larger and has a fold-down table on which to change the baby. Again, these are both to give the mothers privacy and to protect fastidious passers-by—this time from the horrors of baby poo.

5. Free spare diapers available on the plane. See the "horrors of baby poo" above.

6. Stroller to the plane. Although the airlines tell you to check your stroller, if you take it to the gate, they will often store it in the cabin for you. If not, they will almost always check it at the gate into the baggage hold. In that case, you not only will have been able to use the stroller on the walk to the gate, but also, since the stroller is one of the last things placed in the baggage hold, it will be one of the first things out on arrival.

7. Preboarding. Most airlines allow invalids, such as people with children, to board the flight before the rest of the passengers. Be sure to ask for preboarding when you get to the gate; sometimes the staff get so rushed they forget.

8. Reserved bulkhead space. When booking your flight, you can ask the airline to reserve the bulkhead seats for your family. These seats have the advantage of providing more floor space for the children to play on with no passengers in front to be disturbed. The best arrangement is for the parents to sit at either end and box the children in the middle as a sort of playpen.

9.   Blocked baby seats. As mentioned earlier, babies who fly free (or at 10 percent for international flights) do not have reserved seats. Nonetheless, when you arrange for your seating you can ask for the seat next to you to be blocked. The blocking means that that seat will be one of the last to be filled, so that if the flight is not full, you are likely to have a free seat on which to lay the baby.

10. Infant's luggage allowance. Though an infant is traveling free in the US (or at ten percent on international flights on which the weight method is used), the parent can usually bring on board for him a small carry cot, changes of baby clothes and diapers, blankets and a supply of baby food. (See page 105 above.) You can also check usually a stroller and, on international piece-method flights, one bag with total dimensions of 45 inches. (See page 111 above.)

11. Bassinets. If you don't have your own carry cot, many airlines will provide you with one if you order it in advance. The cot can be placed on your lowered tray table or, in some planes, hooked onto the bulkhead wall. Your kid probably won't stay in it longer than a few minutes and you'll then have a great place to store all those extra diapers and bloated soft toys you had to bring along.

12. Special baby seat restraints. A few American airlines stock small loop-belts which fit onto the front of the parents' seat belts; ask if your airline has them. Most airlines will also allow you to install a government-approved baby seat. Qualifying seats manufactured after February 26, 1985, bear the two labels:

> This child restraint system conforms to all applicable Federal Motor Vehicle Safety Standards.

> THIS RESTRAINT IS CERTIFIED FOR USE IN MOTOR VEHICLES AND AIRCRAFT. *[In red letters.]*

Qualifying ones manufactured between January 1, 1981, and February 26, 1985, bear the first label and are of the vest and harness-type. No seats manufactured before January 1, 1981, qualify.

Of course, to use such a seat, you've got to lug the thing around with you. Some of the airlines stock them but only for you to buy, not to rent. In addition, you may have to pay a child's fare for your infant, because several airlines don't allow the seats to be used on a space-available basis.

Note, if you are not using a special baby seat restraint device, then during takeoff and landing it is safer for the baby to be held in your arms than strapped into a vacant seat. Your arms will give its body more support and instinct will keep you from letting go on impact—unless, of course, you lose consciousness. Don't try putting the baby inside your own seat belt; on impact, the weight of your body will cut it in two.

13. Entertainment kits. Most airlines will give kids on the plane free booklets of games, puzzles and magic tricks and occasionally aviator's wings. Generally, these things are only given out upon request, so be sure to ask. If you are depending on the kits to give you some time free from your children, though, forget it. The sole function of the kits seems to be to generate a continuous stream of "What's this mean?", "How does this work?", "I can't fit this together," and "I don't get it," intended by the airlines, as far as I can tell, to effect some perverted idea about bringing families together.

14. Special children's meals. If your children are finicky eaters, you can reserve in advance special children's meals for them, such as hamburgers and french fries. (See discussion of special meals beginning above at page 245.) Some airlines also provide strained meat and vegetables for babies. Check with your airline what is available.

15. Snacks and drinks upon request. If your children get hungry or thirsty other than at the normally-scheduled time, just ask the flight attendant. Unless very busy, he or she will be happy to get them what they want. The flight attendant will also warm your baby's formula if you wish.

16. Flight attendants trained to fawn over babies and small children. If you want assurances that your baby is cute, bright and looks like you, then just put him or her within the line of sight of a flight attendant. The attendants are trained in airline school to seek out babies and small children on the flight and gush over them. It doesn't matter if your kid looks like a toad with an IQ of minus ten; the flight attendants don't seem to be able to discriminate.

How to Get What You Want from an Airline

The more you fly, the more you run up against situations where you need something from the airline—for instance, when you've been bumped or your flight has been canceled or delayed.

In these situations, remember rule number one: Don't complain.

Nobody likes a complainer. If you just want to let off steam, run up and down the concourse for awhile.

Instead, take the following steps:

1.   Before you do anything, decide what it is you want. Reduce what you want to its most specific and concrete form. Not, "I want to be booked on another flight." But, "I want a reservation on the Spring Air flight leaving at 10:45 A.M. with my ticket for the current canceled flight endorsed over to it."

2.   Decide what you can do by yourself without the airline. In the above example, make the reservation on Spring Air yourself over the phone.

3.   Find the person in charge. Most airlines have a troubleshooter at the airport (usually called the "Customer Service Representative"). Ask to speak to him or her.

4.   Decide what the airline employee you're speaking to can reasonably give you. Customer Service Representatives can usually settle claims for up to $100, give free travel vouchers and endorse tickets over to other airlines. (To help to determine what's reasonable, ask to see a copy of the airline's conditions of carriage; you may find they, in fact, require the airline to give you what you want.)

5.   Modify your demands to fit what the airline employee can reasonably give you. If you still want more, save the excess for the airline's home office.

6.   Rephrase "I" to "you". Before you speak, sit down and try to determine how everything that's in your interest can be phrased as being in the interest of the airline employee or the airline. Try deleting all the "I's" in your statements and rewriting the statements to use "you". Make the employee and his needs the focus of the appeal. Don't say "I want my ticket endorsed over to Spring Air." Instead, say, "You'll have one very satisfied passenger on your hands if you endorse this ticket over to Spring Air." To get the employee to identify with you, ask him what he would do if he were you.

7.   Make your case appear unique. If the employee feels whatever he does for you he's going to have to do for all the other passengers on the plane, he may not do it. Show him how your case differs from the other passengers'. In the above example, point out you're probably one of the few passengers who has a reservation on the other airline. When you talk to him, do it privately, out of hearing of the other passengers.

8.   If the employee refuses, then threaten him. Do it, however, in a way that changes the focus from you to him and that allows him to do what you want without appearing to back down. Don't say, "I'm going to call WNBC-TV about you unless you change your mind and endorse this ticket over to Spring Air." Instead, say: "All I ask is for you to think about it for a minute before you make a final decision. You don't want you and your airline pictured on WNBC-TV as having canceled a flight and then not been willing to endorse a passenger's ticket over to another airline. That's not good for the airline. That's not good for you. You want to appear fair. Endorsing this ticket over is fair. How about it?"

9.   If you don't get what you want, write the home office consumer relations department. Go through the same process as in paragraphs 1 through 6 again, only this time in writing. Be brief. One page is enough. Include flight numbers, dates, places, times and names. If you're complaining about staff behavior, be sure to include the name and phone number of any witnesses (which ideally you will have collected before you left the scene of the crime). Send copies of all documentation, including tickets, baggage checks and expense receipts. Type it neatly, preferably on letterhead. Give your daytime phone number so they can call you.

One hint: If your damages are hard to measure, trying drawing an analogy between your situation and that where damages are specified in the conditions of carriage. In the example of my sister kept off a flight by an airline employee who had forgotten he'd already taken her ticket (mentioned above at page 155) , my sister, by drawing an analogy between her situation and that of a passenger denied boarding because of overbooking, was able to collect equivalent compensation—in this case over $400 plus, since the carrier was United (see page 214 above), two free first class tickets anywhere in the continental US.

10.   Once again, this time with threats. If you're not satisfied with the airline's reply (usually sweet words and a free travel voucher), write them one more time suggesting that they certainly don't want to see this matter resolved in small claims court. Note in your letter that you are sending copies to your travel agent, your local TV consumer affairs reporter and the following two organizations:

Consumer Affairs Division, Room 10405
Office of Community and Consumer Affairs
U.S. Department of Transportation
400 7th Street, S.W.
Washington, D.C. 20590
(202)366-2220

Aviation Consumer Action Project
P.O. Box 19029
Washington, DC 20036

If you don't know who your local consumer affairs reporter is, try the referral agency:

Call For Action
575 Lexington Avenue, 7th Floor
New York, NY 10022
(212)355-5965

If the complaint involves air travel safety, mark a copy to:

Community and Consumer Liaison
APO-400, FAA
800 Independence Avenue, S.W.
Washington, DC 20591
(800)FAA-SURE

11. Contact others for help. If you're not satisfied with the airline's further reply, contact the organizations you sent copies to and ask them what they recommend. Usually the Consumer Affairs Division will call or write the airline on your behalf.

12. Go to small claims court. When everything else is exhausted, why not? It'll be fun. If the case has gotten this far, the airline's conditions of carriage are probably against you, but don't worry. If your claim is just, a small claims court may ignore the conditions of carriage and allow you to collect anyway.

More important than the money, you'll have won yet another skirmish against the airlines and struck a blow for the freedom and dignity of airline passengers everywhere.

The Airline's Liability in Case of Your Death or Injury

1.   Domestic journeys. If your death or injury occurs on a domestic airplane journey and the airline is negligent, you or your estate can hold the airline liable for proven damages without limit. (Note, a domestic flight which is part of a direct or connecting international journey is considered an international journey rather than a domestic journey.)

2. International journeys. If your death or injury occurs on an international journey (including the definition in the preceding parenthetical), the amount for which you can hold the airline liable is limited—as long as your death or injury is not caused by the airline's gross negligence or willful misconduct. There are two separate limits:

(a) **US international journeys.** The limit for international journeys with a point of origin, point of destination or agreed stopping place in the United States is the lesser of $75,000 or your proven damages, inclusive of legal fees and costs. If the state you sue in happens to allow you to collect legal fees as part of your judgment, then the limit is the sum of $58,000 plus those legal fees and costs. (Note: The US Congress currently has legislation before it to remove all limits on US international journeys.)

(b) **Foreign international journeys.** If the international journey does not include a US point, most airlines follow one or another version of the Warsaw Convention of 1929, often depending on which route a given international flight takes.

(1) If the Convention as originally written is followed, the limit is 125,000 Poincare gold francs (now an obsolete currency), which at the fixed rate of 12.5 francs per dollar, works out to $10,000.

(2) If the Convention as updated by the Hague Protocol of 1955 is followed, the limit is 250,000 Poincare gold francs, which at the fixed rate of 12.5 francs per dollar works out to $20,000. (This is the rule US airlines currently follow for non-US international journeys.)

(3) If the Convention as updated by the as-of-yet unratified Montreal Protocol of 1975 is followed, the limit is 100,000 International Monetary Fund Special Drawing Rights (SDRs), currently about $135,000. (This is the rule the US airlines will follow for non-US international journeys when the Senate finally ratifies the Protocol.)

Under a 1985 US Supreme Court decision, the gold francs are valued not at the market price of gold but at an "official" price of $42.22 per ounce set by act of Congress, which produced the exchange rate of 12.5 francs per dollar. SDRs, on the other hand, are set daily by the IMF to reflect the relative market rate of a basket of currencies.

Which version the airline follows should be printed on the back of your airline ticket in large type.

According to a Rand Corporation study, the average compensation per death in all air crashes over the period 1970 to 1984 was $363,000. As recovery under most international crashes was limited by the Warsaw Convention to somewhere between $25,000 to roughly $135,000, average compensation for domestic air crashes must have been significantly in excess of $363,000.

How You or Your Estate Can Collect Big Bucks Through the Loopholes in the Airline's Limitations on Liability

If you've got a major air travel claim, don't be put off by the fact that Warsaw Convention, conditions of carriage or other similar pro-airline legal device appears to limit your rights. A good lawyer may be able to find some loopholes to let you sue. Some of the better possibilities:

(a) **The airline failed to show you the conditions of carriage** before you "entered into the contract" when you bought your ticket. In fact, poor, little, innocent you weren't even aware that when you bought your ticket, you were entering into a contract.

(b) **The conditions of carriage are a "contract of adhesion"**, *i.e.*, a form contract which the consumer has no power to negotiate, and hence unenforceable where it violates public policy.

(c) **The Warsaw Convention can be enforced only through the contract** which is supposed to come into effect upon ticket purchase; so if that contract is invalid, *e.g.*, for the reasons in (a) or (b) above, the terms of the Convention are unenforceable.

(d) **The warnings about legal limitations were not printed in the large type required** by the Convention or similar law. The plaintiffs in the Korean Air Lines 007 shoot-down attempted to use this argument to try to invalidate the Warsaw Convention limitations, but recently lost in the US Supreme Court.

(e) **Poincare gold francs should be valued at their current gold content,** not in terms of the theoretical international exchange rates. That would raise the limit ten times or more. As mentioned above, a few years ago this argument lost in the US Supreme Court; but it still may be available in other countries.

(f) **The airline injured you or your baggage through gross negligence or willful misconduct,** in which case the Warsaw Convention or similar limits would not protect the airline. In practice, what gross negligence or willful misconduct means is often what a jury wants it to mean.

(g) The Warsaw Convention or other similar compensation limits apply only to claims against the airlines. They do not apply to claims against the manufacturers for design defects, against the government agency which issued an airworthiness certificate for the aircraft or against other government agencies for improper air traffic control or other regulation.

(h) The Warsaw Convention is unconstitutional. Frankly, I don't understand how a properly ratified treaty can be unconstitutional, but apparently a county district court in Maryland in 1980 found just that and awarded a couple $2,000 for lost luggage rather than the $200 they were entitled to under the Convention.

So, if you feel your claim is just, don't give up without first consulting a good lawyer. There may be a loophole in the law which will allow justice to be done.

How to Increase Your Future Rights

Support those organizations which are fighting for the airline passenger's rights. Three of the major ones are:

1. The International Foundation Of Airline Passengers Associations (IFAPA). This is a Swiss-based foundation funded by research grants, donations and the 100,000-plus members of the International Airline Passengers Association mentioned above at page 68. The sole purpose of IFAPA is to promote, research and represent the interests of airline passengers worldwide. One of its recent surveys of 30,000 frequent flyers from over 100 countries was used as the basis of some schedules in this book. It has also conducted a detailed study of CRSs at McGill University and a study of the effect of airline mergers for the Dutch government. It is also currently conducting at the University of Aberdeen a study of aviation security. Much of IFAPA's time is spent lobbying on behalf of the airline passenger—for tighter security measures, for improvements in safety, for liberalization of air transport, for lower excess baggage charges, for better overbooking compensation, for limitations on smoking, and so on.

Why not mail a check to them or, even better, if you're affiliated with a major company, contact IFAPA to see how your company might become an official sponsor. They're at:

International Foundation of Airline Passengers Associations
Box 462
1215 Geneva 15
Switzerland
Tel: 011-41-22-985255

2. The Airline Passengers Of America (AP/USA). This nonprofit consumer organization, founded in 1987, currently has a membership of 3,000. The organization provides many services to its members, such as (i) lost baggage retrieval, (ii) life and baggage insurance, (iii) publications on air travel consumer discounts and issues, and (iv) various toll free numbers to get up-to-date emergency information on flight schedules, weather conditions, airport delays and consumer rights. More importantly, the AP/USA lobbies the government on behalf of the airline passenger. The AP/USA was active in pushing for the Airline Passenger Protection Act, the release of impounded Aviation Trust Fund moneys and, recently, the protection of passengers holding tickets on bankrupted airlines.

If you are frequent flyer, you ought to join them. Their annual fee: only $24. Their address is:

Airline Passengers of America
4212 King Street
Alexandria, VA 22302
Tel: 1-800-222-9477

3. Aviation Consumer Action Project (ACAP). This nonprofit consumer group was founded by Ralph Nader in 1971 to promote airline safety and the rights of the traveling public before federal agencies, the executive branch and Congress and, when necessary, by litigation. Wherever there is a battle in the US on behalf of the airline passenger, ACAP always appears in the front lines.

Among its many victories:

(a) After a lawsuit and several years of lobbying, ACAP got the CAB to raise the liability limit for lost or damaged luggage from $500 to $1250 and to close loopholes allowing airlines to avoid paying legitimate claims.

(b) After a Ralph Nader lawsuit against Allegheny Airlines and extensive lobbying, ACAP spurred the CAB to institute the overbooking compensation rules.

(c) After four years of petitions and legal efforts, ACAP got the CAB to require nonsmoking seats for all passengers requesting them.

(d) After using the Freedom of Information Act, ACAP uncovered that the FAA had been seriously undercounting the number of midair near-collisions taking place.

(e) After a lawsuit, ACAP forced the FAA to require US airlines to carry emergency medical kits for passengers.

(f) After taking the lead in a major lobbying effort, ACAP persuaded the DOT to reverse the decrease in safety inspectors.

Needless to say, ACAP needs money as much as IFAPA. And if you make a contribution to ACAP, they will send you a copy of their excellent booklet, *Facts & Advice For Airline Passengers*. Mail your check to:

Aviation Consumer Action Project
P. O. Box 19029
Washington, DC 20036

For let's face it. When all is said and done, the best way to beat the system is to change it.

Any Suggestions?

It is likely the *Airline Passenger's Guerrilla Handbook* will be updated periodically. If you have some general air passenger tactics and strategies you would like to share with others or if you have any suggestions on how the *Handbook* can be improved, please write:

George Albert Brown
c/o The Blakes Publishing Group
320 Metropolitan Square
655 Fifteenth Street, N.W.
Washington, DC 20005

Together we shall overcome.

APPENDIX ONE

SELECTED US AIRPORT THREE-LETTER CODES AND PHONE NUMBERS

Airport	Code	Phone
Akron/Canton Regional	CAK	(216)499-4221
Albuquerque International	ABQ	(505)842-4366
Allentown-Bethlehem-Easton Int'l	ABE	(215)264-2831
Anchorage International	ANC	(907)266-1400
Asheville (NC) Regional	AVL	(704)684-2226
Atlanta William B. Hartsfield International	ATL	(404)530-6600
Atlantic City International	AIY	(609)645-7895
Austin Robert Mueller Municipal	AUS	(512)472-5439
Baltimore-Washington Internat'l	BWI	(301)859-7079
Bangor International	BGR	(207)947-0384
Baton Rouge	BTR	(504)355-0333
Billings Logan International	BIL	(406)657-8495
Birmingham Municipal	BHM	(204)595-0533
Bismarck Municipal	BIS	(701)222-6502
Boise Air Terminal/Gowen Field	BOI	(208)383-3110
Boston Logan International	BOS	(617)561-1600
Buffalo International	BUF	(716)632-3115
Burbank/Glendale/Pasadena	BUR	(818)840-8840
Burlington International	BTV	(802)863-2874
Casper/Natrone County Internat'l	CPR	(307)472-6688
Charleston (WV) Yeager	CRM	(304)344-8033
Charleston (SC) International	CHS	(803)767-1100
Charlotte/Douglas Internat'l	CLT	(704)359-4000
Cheyenne	CYS	(307)634-7071
Chicago Midway	MDW	(312)767-0500
Chicago-O'Hare International	ORD	(312)686-2200
Chicago Merrill C. Meigs Field	CGX	(312)744-6892
Cincinnati International	CVG	(606)283-3151
Cleveland-Hopkins Internat'l	CLE	(216)265-6000
Cleveland Lakefront	BKL	(216)781-6411

Airport	Code	Phone
Columbia (SC) Metropolitan	CAE	(803)822-5000
Columbus (OH) International	CMH	(614)239-4000
Corpus Christi International	CRP	(512)289-0226
Dallas-Ft.Worth Internat'l	DFW	(214)574-6720
Dallas Love Field	DAL	(214)352-2663
Dayton James M. Cox International	DAY	(513)898-4631
Denver Stapleton International	DEN	(303)270-1200
Des Moines International	DSM	(515)283-4255
Detroit City	DET	(313)267-6400
Detroit Metropolitan/Wayne County	DTW	(313)942-3550
El Paso International	ELP	(915)772-4271
Fairbanks International	FAI	(907)451-2500
Fargo Hector International	FAR	(701)241-1501
Ft. Lauderdale-Hollywood Intern'l	FLL	(305)357-6100
Ft. Meyers So'west Florida Reg'l	RSW	(813)768-1000
Ft. Wayne Allen County	FWA	(219)747-4146
Fresno Air Terminal	FAT	(209)251-6051
Grand Rapids/Kent County Int'l	GRR	(616)949-4500
Greensboro-High Pt-Winston S'm Reg	GSO	(919)665-5600
Harrisburg International	MDT	(717)948-5015
Hartford/Springfield		
Bradley International	BDL	(203)627-3000
Hilo General Lyman Field	ITO	(808)935-0809
Honolulu International	HNL	(808)836-6411
Hot Springs Memorial Field	HOT	(501)624-3306
Houston Intercontinental	IAH	(713)230-3100
Houston William P. Hobby	HOU	(713)643-4597
Indianapolis International	IND	(317)248-7234
Ithaca Tompkins County	ITH	(607)257-0456
Jackson Municipal/Thompson Field	JAN	(601)939-5631
Jacksonville (FL) International	JAX	(904)741-2000
Jacksonville (NC) Albert J. Ellis	OAJ	(919)324-3001
Juneau International	JNU	(907)789-7821
Kahului (HI)	OGG	(808)877-0078
Kailua-Kona Keahole (HI)	KOA	(808)329-2484
Kansas City International	MCI	(816)243-5200
Kansas City Downtown	MKC	(816)471-4946
Key West International	EYW	(305)296-5439
Knoxville McGhee Tyson	TYS	(615)970-2773
Lansing Capital City	LAN	(517)321-6121
Las Vegas McCarran Internat'l	LAS	(702)739-5211
Lihue (HI)	LIH	(808)246-1460

Airport	Code	Phone
Little Rock Regional	LIT	(501)372-3439
Lincoln Municipal	LNK	(402)474-2770
Long Beach Daugherty Field	LGB	(213)421-8293
Los Angeles International	LAX	(213)646-4265
Louisville Standiford Field	SDF	(502)368-6524
Madison (WI) Dane County Reg'l	MSN	(608)246-3380
Manchester	MHT	(603)624-6539
Memphis International	MEM	(901)922-8000
Miami International	MIA	(305)871-7000
Milwaukee General Mitchell International	MKE	(414)747-5300
Minneapolis-St.Paul Internat'l	MSP	(612)726-1717
Missoula County	MSO	(406)728-4381
Mobile Municipal/Bates Field	MOB	(205)633-4510
Moline Quad City	MLI	(309)764-9621
Montgomery Muni'pal/Dannelly Field	MGM	(205)281-5040
Nashville Metro	BNA	(615)275-1600
Newark International	EWR	(201)961-2000
New Haven Tweed	HVN	(203)787-8285
New Orleans International	MSY	(504)464-0831
Newport News Patrick Henry Int'l	PHF	(804)877-0221
New York John F. Kennedy International	JFK	(718)656-4300
New York La Guardia	LGA	(718)476-5001
Norfolk International	ORF	(804)857-3351
Oakland International	OAK	(415)577-4000
Oklahoma City Will Rogers World	OKC	(405)681-5311
Olympia (WA)	OLM	(206)586-6164
Omaha Eppley Airfield	OMA	(402)422-6800
Ontario (CA) International	ONT	(714)983-8282
Orlando International	MCO	(407)826-2001
Palm Beach Internat'l	PBI	(407)471-7400
Palm Springs Municipal	PSP	(619)323-8163
Philadelphia International	PHL	(215)492-3000
Phoenix Sky Harbor Internat'l	PHX	(602)273-3300
Pittsburgh/Allegheny County	AGC	(412)461-4300
Pittsburgh Internat'l	PIT	(412)778-2500
Portland (ME) Internat'l Jetport	PWM	(207)772-0690
Portland (OR) International	PDX	(503)231-5000
Providence Theodore Francis Green State	PVD	(401)737-4000
Raleigh-Durham	RDU	(919)840-2100

Airport	Code	Phone
Reno Cannon International	RNO	(702)328-6400
Richmond International/Byrd Field	RIC	(804)226-3052
Rochester International	ROC	(716)464-6000
Sacramento Metro	SMF	(916)929-5411
Saginaw Tri-City	MBS	(517)695-5555
St. Louis/Lambert Internat'l	STL	(314)426-8000
St. Petersburg/Clearwater	PIE	(813)531-1451
Salt Lake City Internat'l	SLC	(801)575-2400
San Antonio International	SAT	(512)821-3444
San Diego International/ Lindbergh Field	SAN	(619)291-3900
San Francisco International	SFO	(415)761-0800
San Jose (CA) International	SJC	(408)277-5366
Santa Ana/Orange County/ John Wayne	SNA	(714)755-6526
Santa Barbara Municipal	SBA	(805)967-7111
Savannah International	SAV	(912)964-0514
Seattle Kings County Int'l/ Boeing Field	BFI	(206)344-7380
Seattle-Tacoma Internat'l	SEA	(206)433-5388
Sioux City International	SUX	(712)279-6165
Sioux Falls Regional	FSD	(605)336-0762
Spokane International	GEG	(509)623-3218
Springfield (MO) Regional	SGF	(417)869-7231
Syracuse Hancock Internat'l	SYR	(315)454-3263
Tampa International	TPA	(813)276-3400
Terre Haute Hulman Regional	HUF	(812)877-2524
Toledo Express	TOL	(419)865-2351
Topeka Forbes Field	FOE	(913)862-2362
Tulsa International	TUL	(918)838-5000
Tucson International	TUS	(602)573-8100
Utica/Oneida County	UCA	(315)736-4171
Washington National	DCA	(703)685-8003
Washington Dulles	IAD	(703)471-7596
White Plains/Westchester County	HPN	(914)946-9000
Witchita Falls	SPS	(817)855-3621
Wichita Mid-Continent	ICT	(316)946-4700
Wilmington/New Castle County	ILG	(302)323-2680
Winston-Salem Smith Reynolds	INT	(919)767-6361

APPENDIX TWO

SELECTED AIRLINE TWO-LETTER CODES AND TOLLFREE PHONE NUMBERS

Domestic Airline	Code	800 Number	
Allegheny Commuter	US[1]	428-4253	
Aloha Airlines	AQ	367-5250	
Alaska Airlines	AS	426-0333	
America West Airlines	HP	247-5692	
American Airlines	AA	433-7300	
Braniff	BN	272-6422	
ComAir	OH	354-9822	
Continental Airlines	CO	525-0280	
		231-0855	AK,HI
Delta Air Lines	DL	221-1212	
Eastern Airlines	EA	327-8376	
Empire Airlines	EM	392-9233	
		548-5411	ID
Florida Express	ZO	FAST-JET	
Hawaiian	HA	367-5320	
Jet America	SI	421-7574	
		255-0565	No.CA
		826-1164	So.CA
Midway Airlines	ML	621-5700	
Midwest Express	YX	452-2022	
New England Airlines	EJ	243-2460	
Northwest	NW	225-2525	
Pan Am	PA	221-1111	
Southwest	WN	531-5601	
		442-1616	TX
TWA	TW	221-2000	domestic;
		892-4141	int'l
United Airlines	UA	241-6522	
USAir	US	428-4322	

1. Shares code with its parent, USAir.

Foreign Airline	Code	800 Number	
Aer Lingus	EI	223-6537	
Aeromexico	AM	AEROMEX	
Air Canada	AC	4-CANADA	
Air France	AF	237-2747	
Air India	AI	223-7776	
Air Jamaica	JM	523-5585	
Alitalia	AZ	223-5730	
		442-5360	NY
Avianca	AV	327-9899	
British Airways	BA	AIRWAYS	
BWIA	BW	327-7401	
		432-5621	FL
Canadian Airlines	CP	426-7000	
		552-7576	WA
Cathay Pacific	CX	663-8833	
		663-8838	So.CA
Cayman Airways	KX	422-9626	
El Al	LY	223-6700	
Finnair	AY	323-5700	
		223-5700	
Iberia	IB	221-9741	
Icelandair	FI	223-5500	
Japan Air Lines	JL	525-3663	
		232-2517	HI
KLM	KL	556-7777	
Korean	KE	421-8200	
Lan Chile	LA	225-5526	
Lufthansa	LH	645-3880	
Mexicana	MX	531-7921	
Olympic Airways	OA	223-1226	
Qantas	QF	227-4500	
Pakistani Airlines	PK	221-2552	
Philippine Airlines	PR	I-FLY-PAL	
Royal Jordanian	RJ	223-0470	
SAS	SK	221-2350	
Singapore Airlines	SQ	742-3333	
Swissair	SR	221-4750	
TAP	TP	221-7370	
Thai Airways	TG	426-5204	
UTA	UT	282-4484	
Varig Brazilian	RG	GO-VARIG	
Virgin Air	ZP	522-3084	

INDEX